A
FORCE
SO SWIFT

★

A
FORCE
SO SWIFT

Mao, Truman, and the Birth
of Modern China,

1949

KEVIN PERAINO

CROWN
NEW YORK

Copyright © 2017 by Kevin Peraino

All rights reserved.
Published in the United States by Crown,
an imprint of the Crown Publishing Group,
a division of Penguin Random House LLC, New York.
crownpublishing.com

CROWN is a registered trademark and Crown colophon is a trademark of
Penguin Random House LLC.

Photo insert credits can be found on page 363.

Library of Congress Cataloging-in-Publication Data
Names: Peraino, Kevin, author.
Title: A force so swift / Kevin Peraino.
Description: First edition. | New York : Crown, [2017] | Includes bibliographical
references and index.
Identifiers: LCCN 2017000979 | ISBN 9780307887238 (hbk.)
Subjects: LCSH: United States—Foreign relations—China. | United
States—Politics and government—1945–1953. | China—Politics and
government—1937–1949. | Taiwan—Politics and government—1945–1975. |
China—Foreign relations—United States. | United States—Foreign relations—
Taiwan. | Taiwan—Foreign relations—United States.
Classification: LCC E183.8.C5 P525 2017 | DDC 327.73051—dc23
LC record available at https://lccn.loc.gov/2017000979

ISBN 978-0-307-88723-8
Ebook ISBN 978-0-307-88725-2

PRINTED IN THE UNITED STATES OF AMERICA

Book design by Anna Thompson
Maps by Mapping Specialists, Ltd.
Jacket design by Oliver Munday
Jacket photograph by Henri Cartier-Bresson/Magnum Photos

10   9   8   7   6   5   4   3   2   1

First Edition

★

In a very short time,
several hundred million peasants
in China's central, southern,
and northern provinces
will rise like a fierce wind or tempest,
a force so swift and violent that
no power, however great,
will be able to suppress it.

—MAO ZEDONG

★

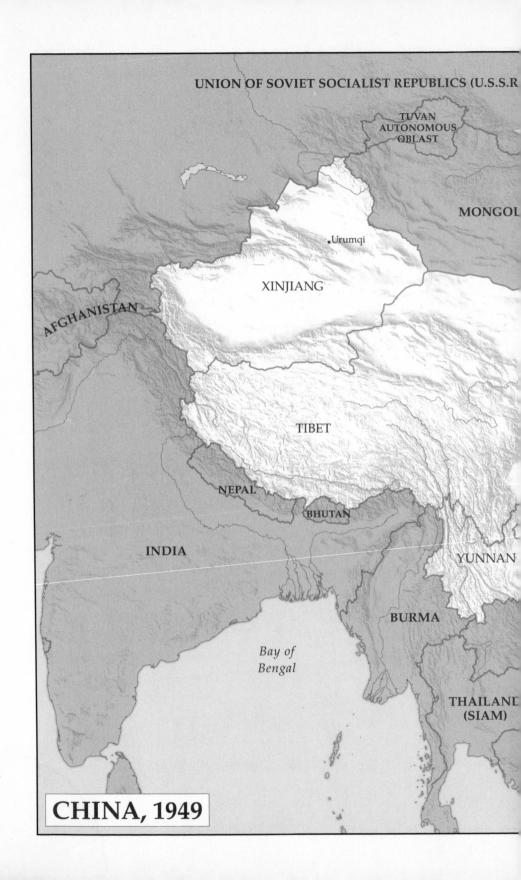

UNION OF SOVIET SOCIALIST REPUBLICS (U.S.S.R

TUVAN
AUTONOMOUS
OBLAST

MONGOL

.Urumqi

XINJIANG

AFGHANISTAN

TIBET

NEPAL

BHUTAN

INDIA

YUNNAN

BURMA

Bay of
Bengal

THAILAND
(SIAM)

CHINA, 1949

MANCHURIA

Shenyang

NORTH
KOREA

Sea of
Japan

Beijing

JAPAN

Xibaipo

SOUTH
KOREA

Yan'an

Yellow River

Qingdao

Yellow
Sea

CHINA

Xuzhou

Nanjing

East
China
Sea

Shanghai

Yangtze River

Xikou

ongqing

Shaoshan

Taipei

Guilin

TAIWAN

UANGXI

Guangzhou

Philippine
Sea

N

W   E

S

South
China
Sea

ENCH
DOCHINA

0	200	400 miles
0	200	400 kilometers

CONTENTS

PROLOGUE

Bodies jostled, elbow to elbow, angling all morning for a spot in the square. Soldiers clomped in the cold—tanned, singing as they marched, steel helmets and bayonets under the October sun. Tanks moved in columns two by two; then howitzers, teams of ponies, gunners shouldering mortars and bazookas. On the flagstones, in front of the imperial gate, men and women craned their necks toward a platform above a portrait of Mao Zedong, painted in hues of blue, hanging beside tubes of blue neon. Underneath, a sprinkling of yellow streamers rippled in the crowd. Nearly everything else in the frenzied square was red.

Shortly after three p.m., a tall figure in a dark woolen suit stepped up to a bank of microphones atop the gate. He lifted a sheet of folded paper, pursed his lips, and glanced down at a column of Chinese characters. A double chin rested against his collar; heavy jowls had long since submerged his cheekbones. Although Mao was still only in his mid-fifties, he was not in good health. He rarely went to bed before dawn. For years he had punished his body with a masochistic regimen of stewed pork, tobacco, and barbiturates. Occasionally, overcome by a spell of dizziness, he would suddenly stagger—one symptom of the circulatory condition that his doctors called angioneurosis. Still, he had retained into middle age what one acquaintance described as "a kind of solid elemental vitality"—a kinetic magnetism that photographs could never quite manage to convey.

On this day, Mao's speech, delivered in his piping Hunanese, was nothing particularly memorable: a few lines praising the heroes of the revolution and damning the British and American imperialists and their stooges. But the celebration that followed, marking the birth of the People's Republic of China, was a cathartic spectacle. Mao pressed a button, the signal to raise the flag—yellow stars against a field of crimson—and a band broke into "March of the Volunteers," the new national anthem, with its surging chorus of "Arise, arise, arise!" An artillery battery erupted in salute; a formation of fighter jets slashed across the sky.

The sun set, and the party went on: fireworks raced toward their peaks, rockets of white flame—then fell, smoldering but harmless, into crowds of giddy children. Red gossamer banners billowed in the evening breeze, undulating like enormous jellyfish; to one witness, the British poet William Empson, they possessed a kind of "weird intimate emotive effect." Lines of paraders hoisted torches topped with flaming rags; others carried lanterns crafted from red paper—some shaped like stars, some like cubes, lit from within by candles or bicycle lamps. Slowly, singing, the glowing procession bled out into the city.

Among the marchers was a boy of sixteen, Chen Yong. He held a small red flickering cube. He had been twelve years old when he joined Mao's army, though he had looked even younger—a year or two, at least. He had studied Morse code, one of the few jobs for a boy his age, then joined a unit that fought its way through Manchuria. As the long civil war was coming to a close, Chen's father had thrown his boy back in school. But on this night no one was studying. The war was over; Mao had won. Chen carried his lantern into the dark.

★

Nearly seven decades after this celebratory light show, I visited Chen Yong at his home in Beijing, an unfussy apartment block in one of the city's western neighborhoods. Chen was now in his early eighties; his hair had gone white, and a gauzy beard descended from his chin. In his hand, trembling slightly, he clutched a pair of eyeglasses. One inflamed eyelid was nearly closed; a furtive intensity had replaced the calm flat gaze of his teenage years.

One of my favorite parts of researching this book—a yearlong chronicle of the Truman Administration's response to Mao's victory in 1949—was the opportunity to spend time with some of the remaining eyewitnesses to the events of those dramatic twelve months. There are fewer and fewer survivors left; some of the key figures have been dead for four decades and more. The rest are elderly, their memories fading fast. In telling this story I have generally clung to the contemporary documents—the diaries, memoranda, letters, and newspaper reports that yield the most accurate portrait of that year. Still, I never passed up the opportunity to talk with those who were actually there. There was something magical about these encounters—a living connection to a bygone China.

In the summer humidity of his apartment, Chen shuffled slowly across the concrete floor, opened a drawer in his bedside table, and pulled out a black and white photo. In the picture, his younger self wore the padded gray tunic of a Chinese Communist soldier—cinched hopefully at the waist, a size or two too big for his teenage frame. As we talked, the emotion of that year seemed as present as it might have been seventy years ago; at one point he quietly began to sing one of his old marching songs. Yet when I pressed him on the granular details of his experiences, he was often at a loss. He would narrow his eyes, looking straight at me, and say with frustration, "It's hard to remember." Still, when I asked him how often he thought back to the events of that year, he said, "Pretty much all the time." And that, of course, is the great paradox of growing old: the less we can remember, the more time we spend remembering.

★

As with people, so with nations: even as the survivors of the revolution are disappearing, Chinese leaders are spending more time trying to recall that era. China's current president, Xi Jinping, said shortly after he took power that he considered revolutionary history the "best nutrient" for a nation making its ascent as a great power. After years of de-Maoification in the 1980s, China's leadership now consciously seeks to reprise some of Mao's best-known political themes. When modern Chinese statesmen look to the past, they gravitate not to the lunacy of the Great Leap Forward, Mao's reckless attempt to transform China's agricultural economy, nor to the depredations of the Cultural Revolution, the fevered campaign to solidify Mao's rule in the late 1960s and early 1970s by mobilizing China's disaffected youth. Rather, today's Chinese leaders celebrate the triumphs of 1949, with all their emotional reverberations. Among other tributes, Xi's government recently inaugurated a new holiday, called Martyrs' Day, to be held each September 30—the date in 1949 that Chinese leaders broke ground on a major national monument in Beijing.

The China of today remains filled with mementos of 1949. On a recent spring morning, I took a day trip from Beijing to Xibaipo, one of the rural base camps that Mao had occupied at the beginning of the year, as his armies prepared to complete their conquest of the mainland. Once a bone-jarring voyage across pitted roads, today it is a painless four-hour drive along superhighways flanked by thick hanging trees. Although the weather in Beijing had been unusually sunny and smog-free, the sky grew hazier as we traveled southwest, into China's industrial heartland. Out the windows, flashes of the new China whizzed by: sand pits, smokestacks, solar panels, power lines, chewed hills that looked as if they had been eaten by a cosmic-scale monster. And yet in other ways, an older China was with us still. On the dashboard of his Ford sedan, my taxi driver had placed a slick white bust of Mao that said, on its pedestal, SAFE AND SOUND.

In Xibaipo, now a stark but bustling tourist town, we passed a restaurant called Red Memory and an information center selling trinkets emblazoned with portraits of Mao and Xi Jinping. Farther in, we arrived at a complex of low-slung, dun-colored bungalows marked with placards written in Chinese and Russian. Wandering beside the pear and locust trees, visitors paid five yuan to sit in a replica of Mao's canvas folding chair; for a little more, twenty yuan, they could pose for a photo behind an embankment of sandbags, wearing an old army uniform and hoisting a rifle. The site, according to a member of the staff, had actually been moved slightly from its original location, to make way for a reservoir. But nobody seemed to mind. On this morning the museum was crowded with tourists filing past glass cases filled with relics of the revolution.

Yet there is another, darker side to this sort of remembrance. Mao's victory in 1949 provoked a reaction across the Pacific; by the end of the year, the United States had extended its policy of containing Communism, once limited primarily to Europe, to Asia as well. The Truman Administration crafted an ambitious plan—including a series of covert operations—to bolster the nations along China's periphery. Even as Mao consolidated his control over the mainland, American operators quietly slipped cash and weapons to his enemies. These historical events, too, inform Chinese views about the present, as the nation continues its fitful rise. Anxious Chinese officials see today's American policy as a sequel to the containment strategy hatched in 1949. They fret over American troop deployments and training missions to East Asia, and they suspiciously eye flashpoints like Tibet, Xinjiang, and Taiwan for evidence of modern American perfidy.

That narrative of 1949—a combination of triumph mixed with grievance—overlooks a great deal. In reality, American policy makers battled fiercely with one another as they struggled to shape a response to Mao's victory. Some wanted to engage him; others wanted to confront him; still others wanted to ignore him completely. In between existed a thousand shades of nuance. These disputes were not simply tactical differences of opinion; they reflected profound disagreements about the nature of the American relationship with China and revealed fault lines in the American character itself. They destroyed careers, reduced a cabinet member to tears, and in the decades that followed gave rise to some of America's most divisive foreign wars, in Korea and Vietnam. The most disconcerting thing is that these fissures—though now largely hidden—still exist. Each approach is fueled by its own self-deceptions, its own brand of remembering and forgetting.

There is no obvious antidote to all this historical make-believe. It is not a matter of simply setting out the facts; the stories we tell ourselves about China are too freighted with emotion to be chased away so easily. Still, by slipping into the participants' skins and looking at the dilemmas of 1949 through their eyes, we can begin to share some of their fears and thrills—and ultimately purge some of our own anxieties and misconceptions. In other words, the only cure for a runaway story is another story.

This one begins aboard an airplane, with a glamorous woman preparing for a fight.

★

PART I

★

I

MISSIMO

Four propellers whirled on their engines as the silver Skymaster taxied to a stop. Though President Truman had once used the modified C-54 as his personal plane, it was not a particularly majestic craft: ten tons of aluminum and steel riveted into the shape of a porpoise. Near the runway, several dozen well-wishers huddled in the cold—a respectful reception, but small. Workers pushed a ramp across the tarmac; a cluster of reporters hustled toward the stairs. Just after ten a.m., the plane's hatch swiveled open and a petite Chinese woman ducked out. As she descended the steps, in the December chill of the Washington morning, she pulled her lips into a smile.

Flashbulbs flickered; newsreel photographers cranked their cameras. Madame Chiang Kai-shek had made herself up for the occasion, plucking her eyebrows down to razor lines and slipping gold studs through her ears. She wore her black hair swept high above her forehead, dark and curving, like a waterfall at night. She had wrapped herself so tightly in her beaver coat, with its tuxedo collar, that she gave the impression of trying to disappear inside it; only her chin, cheeks, and broad forehead exposed themselves to the late-autumn air. As a final flourish, she had knotted a rust-red scarf and tied it high across her throat.

She was tired, and she looked it. Black shadows hung beneath her eyes. She felt dizzy, unsteady. As she stepped down the staircase, two powerful men reached toward her in greeting at the same time: on one side the Chinese ambassador to the United States, and on the other her brother-in-law, a former Chinese finance minister. Sensitive to tender egos and perceived slights, she grasped both of their hands at once. Behind them, camera bulbs still flaring, a small girl swept forward and handed Madame Chiang a bouquet of two dozen roses. Finally, an elderly woman in mink edged through the scrum, took China's first lady by the arm, and pulled her toward a waiting black limousine. "Do you want to say anything?" the woman asked. Madame Chiang said, "I do not."

The departure from the airfield was chaotic: The photographers crowded the women as they climbed into the car, then propped open the door to steal a few last shots. Madame Chiang squinted into the glare, her eyes vacant, her expression blank. Finally, the newsmen scattered and the procession sped toward Virginia's horse country. Though Madame Chiang was accustomed to a large entourage, she had forgone it on this trip. Her mission was too precarious, too likely already to generate unwanted attention. Today she was carrying only a few small bags; into one of them she had tucked a book of secret codes.

After a forty-mile drive, they arrived at their destination, the Leesburg home of George Marshall, the U.S. secretary of state. The paparazzi, who had followed in chase cars, convinced Madame Chiang to pose one more time on the lawn in her furs. After gamely obliging, she begged for a respite. "I have been flying continuously since Sunday morning," she said. "I know you will understand and give me a little time to recover my equilibrium."

★

More than seven thousand miles away, her husband, Chiang Kai-shek, the president of the Republic of China, was about to lose a war, his home, and possibly his life. At his headquarters in his capital of Nanjing, behind gates guarded by sentinels in steel helmets and carrying American carbines, Chiang restlessly scoured military maps as Mao's Communist troops destroyed one division after another of his rival Nationalist forces. In his study, a spacious room heated inadequately by a tiny electric burner, Chiang dispatched hopeless requests from his generals by scratching a laconic reply in the margin of each document: "Can't do."

Chiang and Mao had been battling each other, in one form or another, for more than two decades. At one time, they had considered themselves uneasy allies in a common struggle to modernize China. The enemy then had been the empire's ancient past, its ossified rituals and corrupt bureaucracy. After the collapse of the Qing dynasty, they had both fought the republican government in Beijing and the warlords in the provinces. Over the years, however, the revolution had splintered. Chiang had taken command of the Nationalist wing, the Guomindang, ruthlessly purging his political enemies. Mao, after a series of his own bitter power struggles, had solidified his control of the Chinese Communists.

For decades Chiang had eclipsed Mao in the struggle for international legitimacy. In 1928 Chiang had ascended to the leadership of China's Nationalist government; Mao and his guerrillas, meanwhile, had been forced to flee to the mountains. After Japan invaded China in the 1930s, American leaders had hoped that Chiang's Nationalist armies might serve as a bulwark against Hirohito's forces in the Pacific. Chiang had charmed the American public, winning sympathy and support as he sought to hold the line. American magazines had printed glossy full-page portraits of the man they referred to as the Generalissimo: taut caramel skin, black eyes staring straight into the camera, hair cropped to a military stubble, wool uniform with stars and bandolier. After Pearl Harbor, the attachment grew even more intense, as the U.S. Congress approved enormous shipments of weapons and economic aid to the Nationalists.

Ultimately, however, the Second World War had left Chiang's armies crippled and the Chinese economy in ruins. In its aftermath,

Mao's Communists began slowly retaking territory. American leaders, at first, had sought to reconcile the warring factions, dispatching various missions to the Middle Kingdom in an effort to broker a peace. But when those efforts failed, U.S. statesmen grew gradually more disillusioned with Chiang. Increasingly, against a growing and emboldened Communist opposition, the Generalissimo was on his own.

Now in his early sixties, Chiang was no longer the sleek, youthful hero of the Chinese resistance. Time and stress had turned his bristling mustache nearly white, and a bulging vein protruded from his temple. As the civil war intensified, he had boldly—and foolishly—gambled by going on the offensive against Mao in Manchuria. There alone he had lost twenty-nine infantry divisions and four hundred thousand men. Over a period of four months, the Communists had seized seventy-five percent of his weapons and neutralized half of his fighting forces. In some northern cities, his freezing, starving troops had been reduced to eating horse meat and tree bark. Now, as the winter of 1948 approached, Mao took the offensive again, ordering hundreds of thousands of his soldiers to attack the key Nationalist-controlled cities.

Chiang had hoped to halt Mao's advance by making a stand at Xuzhou, a ravaged, muddy town of rolling hills and lakes a couple of hundred miles north of Nanjing. A vital military prize for centuries, Xuzhou was now a major railroad hub; more important, it acted as a firewall protecting the Nationalist capital from Mao's forces in the north. The Generalissimo had ordered hundreds of thousands of troops to protect the grim village, with its swarms of refugees wandering beside neglected buildings and fields of winter wheat. Wearing yellow padded uniforms and fur hats with ear flaps, Chiang's soldiers had busily fortified the town. Now, with Mao's columns pushing toward the village, Chiang had to decide how critical this redoubt really was. In the end, he chose to retreat—planning instead to regroup farther south on the plain above Nanjing.

On December 1, 1948—the same day Madame Chiang arrived in Washington—the Generalissimo's troops completed their flight from

Xuzhou. In the subzero cold, more than two hundred thousand Nationalist soldiers crept out of the northern village, leaving it in flames behind them. The fleeing troops destroyed fuel and ammunition depots as they went, propelling a column of black smoke eight thousand feet into the air. Looters stripped former government buildings of even the window frames and floorboards. Some Nationalist planes took off carrying freezing, wounded soldiers; other aircraft simply burned on the tarmac. By ten p.m. Mao's troops had taken the city. The rout set off a panic in Nanjing; diplomats and their families packed every departing train for Shanghai, to the southeast. In his private diary, Chiang wrote that his own aides seemed suspicious that he would surrender the Nationalist capital.

In public, however, Chiang tried to remain sanguine in the face of these defeats. On the day Xuzhou fell, the American ambassador in Nanjing wrote to the State Department noting a strange "self-assurance and a serendipity" in Chiang's demeanor; the ambassador found this determination both "magnificent" and somehow "disturbing." At other times, though, Chiang appeared depressed and fatalistic, cursing the heavens for his predicament. If Mao succeeded in taking Nanjing, the ambassador speculated, the Generalissimo might kill himself.

As the Xuzhou pocket collapsed, Chiang drafted a telegram to his wife. He told her he missed her and asked whether she had arrived in the United States. He had not wanted her to make this trip, but now he needed her help. Later the same day he sent along a longer missive with precise instructions for her talks with the Truman Administration. He told her she should ask for emergency aid—money and men: $1 billion for each of the next three years, plus U.S. military advisers. The Americans, he knew, were already skeptical of such military rescue operations. It would be a near-impossible assignment, even for his exceptionally charming spouse. Still, his options were narrowing; this could be their last chance.

★

On the day Madame Chiang arrived, she visited briefly with Marshall in a Virginia hospital, where the secretary of state was being treated for kidney disease. The two had known each other since late 1945, when Marshall—the revered American general who had led the mobilization of U.S. forces during the Second World War—had traveled to China in an attempt to broker a deal between Chiang and Mao. A stolid figure with dull blue eyes and enormous ears, Marshall prided himself on his cool rationality; he liked to boast that he had no emotions at all except those he reserved for Mrs. Marshall. He confided to underlings that he found Madame Chiang meddlesome and often irritating. Still, he also trusted her, and her spirited interventions sometimes managed to sway him. Once, during their negotiations in China, after Marshall had wondered aloud whether they could "get together" on an issue, Madame Chiang had looked him in the eye, put a hand on his knee, and said flirtatiously, "General, you and I can get together anytime."

Now, after a first meeting confined largely to small talk and catching up, Madame Chiang visited Marshall again at the hospital a couple of days after her arrival in Washington. This time she quickly came to the point, asking explicitly and forcefully for the aid her husband had outlined in his telegram. She argued that China needed a "spark plug" in the form of a senior American general to take control of the fight with Mao. She also pushed Marshall to make a public statement in support of her husband's government. Marshall listened patiently from his sickbed but ultimately discouraged her. The Nationalists had done nothing, in Marshall's view, to show that they could successfully defeat Mao's rebels. If the Truman Administration could not say anything positive about Chiang's government, he believed, then it should say nothing at all. Nonetheless, Marshall told Madame Chiang that she should come to see him again once she had met with President Truman.

Madame Chiang sent a report of her conversations with Marshall back to her husband in Nanjing, acknowledging that her efforts had yielded little so far. She complained that she had been sick since she arrived, and that the actions of the Nationalist-controlled Chinese embassy—leaking information to the press and throwing other obstacles in her way—had made her task more difficult. Still, she claimed that she had resolved a number of key "misunderstandings" with Marshall. She advised Chiang to be patient and stay calm. She told him enigmatically that she was doing a "complicated job" and that they should not discuss the details by telegram. Privately, she urged him to say a prayer for the success of their mission.

In the meantime, she herself sought spiritual solace. On a Sunday morning shortly after arriving in Washington, she slipped into a pew at the city's Foundry Methodist Church, a venerable old sanctuary that often hosted visiting dignitaries. A Chinese flag hung in the chancel; from the pulpit, the pastor, Frederick Brown Harris, alerted his congregation to Madame Chiang's presence. Harris praised the Chinese for standing by the United States during the Second World War—and for fighting the Communists now—and then pointed to a female figure depicted in one of the church's stained-glass windows. The pastor explained that the artist had taken Madame Chiang as his model—a tribute to her good works. Harris lauded Madame Chiang as "one of the most distinguished Methodists in the world." The service, he said, was intended to celebrate the "enduring bond between her country and ours."

★

The ties Madame Chiang had nurtured with the United States over the years were tactical—but also personal. Her father, Charles Jones Soong, had come to the United States from China as a twelve-year-old boy, in 1878, working in a small Boston shop run by his uncle. Bored by the job, Charlie stowed away on a ship that made its way to Wilmington, North Carolina. The cutter's captain introduced the precocious boy to some of Wilmington's leading citizens, who began bringing Charlie to a Methodist church and nearby revival meetings. By his mid-teens, Charlie was lecturing family members back in China about his new faith. In one letter, he reminded his father of a trip the two had made to a Buddhist temple in China, where they had prayed to a wooden statue. "Oh, Father," Charlie now scolded, "that is no help from wooden Gods." Eventually Charlie enrolled in Trinity College in North Carolina, a predecessor of Duke University, and later transferred to Vanderbilt, where he studied theology. The young man intrigued fellow students—though not all the faculty. The dean recalled him as "a harum-scarum little fellow, full of life and fun, but not a very good student."

Eventually trained as a Methodist missionary, Soong returned to China in 1886, where he started a business printing Bibles and religious tracts. He also began to involve himself in Chinese politics. By the late nineteenth century, China's ruling Qing dynasty had grown precariously weak, the result of a complex set of demographic, economic, and military factors. China's population had been growing rapidly for more than a century, putting pressure on the regime and its bureaucrats to do more for its subjects. At the same time, the Chinese economy was becoming increasingly integrated into the larger world market. Rural livelihoods were becoming less secure, as traditional methods of spinning thread were being supplanted by new technologies. Meanwhile, sporadic rebellions had erupted throughout the country, with the insurrectionists blaming the Qing elites for corruption and mismanagement.

Foreign powers had also done their part to undermine the stability of the Qing. For years British traders had flooded China with opium produced in their Indian colonies, a practice that had pernicious effects on Chinese society. Millions of Chinese ultimately grew addicted to the powerful narcotic, while the trade had drained the country of silver. After the Qing had tried to abolish the trade, in 1838, Britain had gone to war, crushing the Chinese and imposing a punitive treaty that had granted London full control over Hong Kong and access to five strategic ports on the mainland. A second war with the European powers, in the 1850s, had ended in a similarly harsh settlement. Chinese leaders railed against the "unequal treaties" imposed by their European foes. In one of the most galling provisions, the accords introduced a practice known as extraterritorial jurisdiction, or extrality, making it illegal to prosecute foreigners under local law.

The Qing rulers had never really recovered from these humiliations. As the defeats mounted, some Chinese intellectuals began to question the values underpinning traditional Confucian culture. Influenced by Western scholars like Herbert Spencer, with his notion that only the most capable survive the evolutionary struggle, these reformers called for a large-scale modernization of Chinese society, including improvements to the political and educational systems. In the early 1890s, Charlie Soong befriended Sun Yat-sen, one of the principal antagonists of the Qing. A fellow Christian convert who had spent part of his boyhood in Hawaii, Sun shared Soong's respect for Western political ideals. The two men soon began collaborating in their secret revolutionary project to reform—or topple—the existing dynasty.

Soong, meanwhile, had married Ni Guizhen, a young woman from a prominent Shanghai clan whose parents had considered her unmarriageable because of her large unbound feet. (Foot binding, which Chinese men believed made female feet more dainty and attractive, was still a common practice in rural China at the turn of the century; Charlie, who had spent his teenage years in a different world, saw no appeal in deformed toes.) Over the next several years, Guizhen gave birth to three daughters and three sons. Although most of the Soong children would come to take some role in Chinese politics, it was the couple's youngest daughter, whom they named Mayling, who would one day play the largest part, as the first lady of the Republic of China.

An inquisitive, high-spirited girl, Mayling was nicknamed Little Lantern by her family, for her chubby figure. They enrolled her in an exclusive private school in Shanghai and later sent her to Macon, Georgia, where her sister was already studying. Mayling's American instructors found her vivacious and occasionally exasperating. One friend recalled the girl defiantly tossing some sheet music on top of a piano and declaring, "I do not wish to play this piece!" Mayling acquired a Georgia drawl and joked to other students that the only thing Chinese about her was her face. She considered herself a cultural Confederate. When a summer school teacher asked her to write an essay about General Sherman's March to the Sea during the Civil War, Mayling replied, "Pardon me, I am a Southerner, and that subject is very painful to me. May I omit it?" For college she decided to go north—to Wellesley in Massachusetts, where she was known for sometimes being moody and withdrawn. But as one acquaintance recalled, there was "a fire about her and a genuineness, and always a possibility of interior force."

After college Mayling returned to Shanghai, now something of an alien land to her. While she had been away at school, Sun Yat-sen's revolutionaries had finally succeeded in overthrowing the Qing and had formed their own republican government. Yet the revolutionaries remained rancorously divided; local warlords battled for turf. After so many years in the United States, Mayling felt strangely adrift in this new China. One night, on her way to an appointment in Shanghai, she found herself lost and cold in the city's maze of alleyways; it was only when she heard a man speaking English that she felt safe and at home again. She had grown accustomed to first-world comforts, urging her father—now one of Shanghai's wealthiest men—to update their home with modern amenities. "Don't send your children abroad," Charlie joked to one of his friends after his daughters had returned to China. "Nothing's good enough for them when they come back. They want to turn everything upside down. . . . 'Father, why can't we have a bigger house? Father, why don't we have a modern bathroom?' Take my advice; keep your children at home!"

Charlie Soong's death, in 1918, threw Mayling into a depression. She spent hours on her balcony in Shanghai's French Concession, smoking menthol cigarettes and casting about for purpose in her life. As a girl, she had found her parents' Christianity tiresome; she had scoffed when her mother, having to decide some difficult question, would say, "I must ask God first." Even now Mayling considered herself too willful to be a true Christian. "I am *not* a religious person," she wrote to a friend in 1921. "I am too darned independent and pert to be meek or humble or submissive." Still, slowly, she began reading the

Bible and studying its lessons with the help of her older sister. In time, she would evolve into one of China's most prominent evangelists.

Mayling also began a quest of another sort—for a husband. At Wellesley she had been a bit plain and plump to attract hordes of admirers. Still, her exotic southern accent, worldliness, and bold self-possession now caught the attention of several Shanghai bachelors. She would sometimes meet them for unchaperoned teas, which she considered racy. Though she was not infatuated with any of the men, she enjoyed the attention. "I think if one does not love, the next best thing is to be loved, don't you?" she wrote to one college friend. Mayling was conscious of her growing charisma. After taking a position raising money for Shanghai's Y.W.C.A., she noted with delight how easy it was to convince powerful men to part with their funds. "I go to the managers of the banks personally and look them in the eye, and literally the money rolls in!" she told a friend. "I never say the same thing to two men; I first size them up to see which of my arguments would most likely appeal to him, and then I strike while the iron is hot!"

Mayling attracted one particularly intriguing suitor: Chiang Kai-shek, a promising young military officer. Some members of her family disapproved of the match; Chiang had spent a dissipated youth in Shanghai's brothels and was well known for associating with some of the city's most notorious gangsters. Furthermore he was not a Christian, and he had been married previously. "Don't marry that Blue-beard!" Mayling's sister begged her. Yet Mayling was taken with the rising officer—if not for his looks or character, then for his growing influence in China's politics. As a former commandant of a prominent military academy, Chiang had built strong support among the Chinese officer corps. After Sun Yat-sen's death in 1925, he had launched an ambitious military campaign in an effort to crush the warlords and oust the Beijing government. Now Mayling persuaded her fiancé to travel to Japan, where her mother was then living, to ask for her blessing of their marriage. Chiang promised to make a good-faith effort to study the tenets of Christianity, and the Soong matriarch ultimately approved the match.

By Mayling's wedding day, December 1, 1927, she had morphed into a true beauty. At twenty-nine, her face had shed its childish roundness, accentuating her exquisite features: firm dark eyes, low sloping nose, tightly controlled smile that suggested both mischief and restraint. After a small Christian ceremony at home, the newlyweds hosted a spectacular reception for thirteen hundred guests at Shanghai's Majestic Hotel. A Russian orchestra played Mendelssohn's wedding march as the couple entered the ballroom. Mayling wore a delicate dress of silver and white georgette with orange blossom accents; she gripped a bouquet of pale pink carnations. Near the Chinese-style altar, next to a shield made of red geraniums that spelled out the Chinese character for "long life and happiness," the couple bowed three times to an enormous portrait of Sun Yat-sen flanked by Nationalist flags. While the guests applauded and sipped from their teacups, detectives quietly swept the ballroom for any sign of a security threat.

Dangers to the Nationalist leader were indeed multiplying. Chiang, rising rapidly within the republican establishment, had begun cracking down on internal political enemies; in one particularly bold operation, he had declared war on Shanghai's labor unions, which he accused of taking orders from Moscow. He enlisted hundreds of agents belonging to the Green Gang—a powerful fixture in Shanghai's underworld—to attack picketing unionists. Teams of assassins wearing blue uniforms and white armbands fanned out across the city, assailing the picketers with lethal efficiency. "Heads rolled in the gutters of the narrow lanes like ripe plums and the weary executioners wielded their swords with the monotonous rhythm of *punka wallahs*," one witness reported. The next day, during a massive demonstration protesting the killings, forces loyal to Chiang opened fire with machine guns, killing sixty-six and wounding more than three hundred. Chiang's thugs gored some survivors with bayonets and used rifle butts to fracture the skulls of others. The Shanghai massacres dramatically intensified the enmity between Chiang and Chinese leftists. Soon after the assaults, Mao Zedong—now thirty-three years old and a political rival—fled to the mountains of southern China, fearing he could be the next target.

Yet even as Chiang subdued his domestic adversaries, new foreign threats emerged, temporarily overshadowing the civil strife. As the 1930s unfolded, a rising Japanese empire sought increasingly to dominate its western neighbor. In 1931, Japanese troops invaded Manchuria, compelling Chiang to mobilize his compatriots. Chiang created a paramilitary force known as the Blue Shirts to enforce strict domestic discipline. Unapologetic about his ultranationalism, he explained that the goal was "to thoroughly militarize the lives of the citizens of the entire nation." Partly at the urging of his wife, Chiang also launched a cultural reform program he called the New Life Movement. His allies hung banners urging citizens to "avoid wine, women, and gambling." The movement, with its emphasis on self-improvement, included unmistakably evangelical overtones. ("There's Methodism in this madness," his detractors quipped.) Critics accused Chiang of fascism, although in his mind, the project was simply an attempt to reprise traditional Chinese values and unite a dangerously divided populace.

For Mayling, her new married life combined both hardship and adventure. In 1937, Japanese troops began marching deep into the Chinese heartland. Madame Chiang later recalled traveling the country with her husband, living in tents, train cars, and mud huts along the front (although, considering her well-known taste for luxurious accommodation, some scholars have questioned whether these memories might be self-serving propaganda). The Generalissimo was generally a benign companion—a wiry presence with rigid posture and a demeanor so placid that he "looked embalmed," according to one observer. The couple read morning devotions together, and his soft-spoken mumbling—"*hao, hao;* good, good"—had a soothing quality. Yet he could also be a capricious spouse, especially under the stress of war. His self-control could devolve rapidly into a spasm of anger in which he "yelled, threw teacups or plates about, tore up papers and raged out of control," as one journalist recalled. The tantrums did not unduly trouble his wife. "A bad temper in a man is preferable to a man without a temper," Madame Chiang had once explained to her sisters.

From the Nationalist stronghold of Chongqing, Chiang and his wife took charge of the war effort, coordinating defense and relief missions. The couple won acclaim for their personal bravery; in 1937, *Time* magazine named them Man and Wife of the Year. The physical hazards were genuine. By the end of the year, the Japanese armies had conquered some of China's largest cities, terrorizing the residents who had stayed behind. In Nanjing alone, Japanese soldiers killed twelve thousand Chinese civilians and raped twenty thousand women—a horrific episode that came to be known as the Rape of Nanjing. Chiang, hoping to slow the Japanese assault, destroyed several dikes along the Yellow River. But the resulting floods only compounded the suffering. The deluge killed half a million Chinese and obliterated four thousand villages. As the war ground on, some of the most desperate victims were forced to sell their children or eat other human beings to survive.

In early May 1939, Japanese planes firebombed Chongqing, igniting the wooden dwellings perched on the city's steep hills. Strong winds fanned the phosphorous flames, burning residents alive in their homes. From the edge of the blaze, Madame Chiang watched walls crumble amid bursts of spark and fire and listened to the screams of their citizens. "The bombs," Madame Chiang wrote to a friend, "have reduced rich and poor, wise and stupid, to one common level—pieces of burnt flesh which are extracted from the smoldering piles with tongs." Across the Pacific, the U.S. media published photographs of these horrors, stoking the outrage of Americans. Missionaries, in particular, condemned the amorality of the Japanese invaders and lauded the Chinese resistance, which they viewed as the best hope for the continued Christianization of East Asia.

After Pearl Harbor, with the United States itself now battling Japan in the Pacific, the Chiangs' fight took on a more strategic dimension. But American commanders disagreed about exactly what that strategy should be. In early 1942 the Japanese military succeeded in choking off the Burma Road, an important Nationalist supply route that stretched more than seven hundred miles from Burma to the Chinese city of Kunming. Some American officers—notably Joseph Stilwell, the U.S. officer who had been assigned as a liaison to Chiang—wanted to train and equip the Generalissimo's ground forces until they could push into Burma and reopen this key artery. Stilwell, at least at first, thought Madame Chiang could be an "important ally" in this quest, capable of exerting a positive influence on her husband. The American had recorded a trenchant character sketch of the Chinese first lady in his diary: "Direct, forceful, energetic, loves power."

Other American officers, however, were giving the Chiangs conflicting advice. For years the couple had consulted with Claire Chennault, an American airman who had helped the Nationalists construct airfields and a successful early-warning system in the early days of the Japanese onslaught. Now Chennault pressed the Generalissimo and his wife to replenish their forces by flying in supplies from India over the eastern Himalayas—known as the Hump—rather than relying on the Burma Road. He also wanted to launch bombing raids against the Japanese from air bases in Nationalist-controlled territory. The Chiangs, convinced of the wisdom of this strategy, considered Chennault something of a savior—and the admiration was mutual. In his diary, a besotted Chennault had gushed about Madame Chiang, "She will always be a princess to me." Chennault's aides, on the other hand, did not all share his enthusiasm. The journalist Joseph Alsop, who served with Chennault in China, found Madame Chiang off-putting and phony, hiding behind a "mask of makeup with the consistency of enamel." Alsop complained that Madame Chiang gave him the feeling of "being purposely charmed, the purpose being to make later use of me."

Determined to make the most of her personal magnetism, in late 1942 Madame Chiang flew to the United States to make a direct appeal for aid and sympathy. Americans received China's first lady like a celebrity; newspapers filled hundreds of columns with coverage of her speaking tour stops. (Columnists referred to the powerful first lady as the Missimo.) During one stop, at the U.S. Capitol, legislators marveled at their exotic guest, who wore bright red nail polish, elegant jade jewelry, and a form-fitting black *qipao*, slit at the leg. "There was something about the small, well-proportioned, birdlike woman that left every Senator and the galleries with an overpowering sense that here they were in the presence of one of the world's great personalities," one reporter gushed. Speaking in the Senate chamber, Madame Chiang affirmed the ties of friendship between the United States and China and argued that both nations were "fighting for the same cause." She told the senators that she felt as if she were "coming home."

Madame Chiang stayed at F.D.R.'s White House, where she petitioned in person for aid. The president promised her that the United States would send supplies "as fast as the Lord will let us." Madame Chiang retorted that the Lord helps those who help themselves. F.D.R. privately joked that he was not going to let himself be "vamped" by Madame Chiang, who by the mid-1940s had acquired a reputation as a political seductress. (The cunning Dragon Lady—a central character in the popular comic strip *Terry and the Pirates*—had been styled partly on Madame Chiang and had helped to solidify that image.) Madame Chiang's glamour, the president and first lady observed, came with a hard edge. She clapped haughtily at the White House staff, demanding service, and ordered them to change her bedsheets frequently. She shocked some of F.D.R.'s aides by displaying what Eleanor Roosevelt described as a "casualness about cruelty." One evening, as the Roosevelts sat with Madame Chiang at a dinner party, the conversation came around to union politics. F.D.R. asked the Chinese first lady what she would do about a troublesome labor leader. Madame Chiang "never said a word," Eleanor later recalled, "but the beautiful, small hand came up and slid across her throat."

The American media reinforced the portrait of Madame Chiang as an uncompromising crusader; more than one newspaper cast her as a Joan of Arc figure. Yet the press coverage simultaneously conveyed a subtler message, presenting her as a frail, feminine presence in need of rescue—a storyline that appealed to American notions of paternalism. The *Rochester Times-Union* described Madame Chiang as "fragile as an ivory figurine." By the time she arrived on the West Coast leg of her tour, the damsel-in-distress trope had been well established. In Los Angeles she mingled with movie stars like Gary Cooper and Rita Hayworth and delivered a speech before thirty thousand at California's Hollywood Bowl, a huge outdoor amphitheater dwarfed by dramatic, scrub-covered hills. Her grace and refinement enchanted Tinseltown. Bob Hope joked, "She is the only woman in the world for whom I would shave twice in one day."

The public adulation, however, masked increasing frustration with the Chiangs on the part of many U.S. officials. Stilwell had come to see the Generalissimo as a "grasping, bigoted, ungrateful little rattlesnake." He grumbled that Chiang was not doing enough to help fight the war and was instead merely "milking the United States for money and munitions," stalling in a desperate attempt to preserve his troops. Chiang, for his part, believed that Stilwell and his allies were acting selfishly; the Generalissimo had long complained that the United States treated China like a "decorative object," to be manipulated at will. When F.D.R. finally sent Chiang a personal letter demanding that he put Stilwell in charge of all Chinese forces, the Generalissimo refused—and responded by insisting on Stilwell's recall. Although Stilwell ultimately agreed to leave China, the incident marked a significant deterioration in the U.S.-China relationship.

By this time, however, the Japanese threat was gradually receding. The U.S. Navy had developed a clever strategy of leapfrogging from island to island in the Pacific—an approach that rendered mainland China less critical. In late 1944, General Douglas MacArthur and his forces began sweeping across the Philippine islands, gradually driving out the Japanese military. Truman delivered the final blow in the summer of 1945, dropping atomic bombs on Hiroshima and Nagasaki. Within weeks after the attacks, the war in East Asia was over.

Yet the end of the Second World War reignited Chiang's conflict with Mao's Communists. On the surface, Chiang appeared well positioned for this confrontation; within a year after the armistice, his forces controlled some eighty percent of China's territory. In reality, however, the war with Japan had severely depleted Chiang's Nationalists, militarily and economically. By the end of the war, the fighting had killed more than fifteen million Chinese and created between eighty and one hundred million refugees. Chiang was left with the near-impossible task of healing his nation's physical and psychic wounds.

Diplomatic politics only made matters more difficult for the Generalissimo. In the final months of the war, F.D.R. had secretly granted Stalin concessions in Manchuria and elsewhere in northern China in exchange for Russian support in East Asia. The Soviets then permitted Mao's forces to construct a secret weapons factory along the Manchurian coast. Stalin, eventually, would also turn over a massive stockpile of captured Japanese tanks and artillery pieces to Mao's troops, who increasingly found themselves skirmishing with Chiang's Nationalists. Newly supplied and invigorated, Mao's army now posed a mortal threat to Chiang's weary, spent regime.

THE GREATEST FORCE

Mao had once compared his battles with Chiang to a kind of ferocious sibling rivalry. The two factions, he explained, were "twins born of China's old (feudal) society, at once linked to each other and antagonistic to each other." Both Mao and Chiang had looked to the West for inspiration as they sought to modernize their country. Yet while Chiang and his wife eagerly sought to cultivate close ties to America's political and business elites, Mao, in fits and starts, had come to find Marxist critiques of Western capitalism more appealing.

Mao viewed the dramatic events transforming China through the prism of his own experience—beginning with his grim early life. He was born in 1893 in Shaoshan, a remote village in China's southern Hunan province—a region filled with rice paddies and bamboo groves that was known for its spicy cuisine. Tigers and leopards prowled the lush hills around the village, lending the place a precarious charm. Still, landlocked and remote, Shaoshan felt far from everything—especially for an ambitious young man. News was slow to reach the village. Mao later claimed that when the Qing empress Cixi died in 1908, the village did not get the bulletin until two years later.

Mao blamed his family for reconciling themselves to this backward-ness. His mother, a pious Buddhist, was "a kind woman, generous and sympathetic," he recalled. But he recognized that she was not a modern woman. Like most Chinese of her time—an era when girls were some-times sold by their families to brothels—she could not read at all. Mao loathed his father, a brutal martinet, coming to dread his beatings. Mao once suggested that his father deserved to be "jet-planed"—a tor-ture tactic in which the victim's arms are pulled backward as his face is thrust into the dirt. In a Confucian society that prized filial piety as one of its chief virtues, it was a heretical suggestion.

Mao's reading fueled his rebellious streak. In his home, with its mud floors and earthen walls, he would drape a bedsheet over his window and attempt to read by lamplight. When his father complained that he was lazy, the boy would flee the house. Eventually, Mao chose to enroll at schools outside his village; even when he did not attend, he contin-ued to read on his own at the local library. Mao later recalled how he would buy a couple of rice cakes for lunch, then read straight through until closing time. He avoided the Confucian classics, with their em-phasis on right behavior and personal morality. Instead, he preferred adventure stories like *The Water Margin*, a tale of revolt set during the Song dynasty. He studied Western lives and philosophy, reading biographical sketches of Rousseau and Montesquieu and liberal clas-sics like the works of Adam Smith and Charles Darwin. By his teenage years, Mao later recalled, he had become the "family 'scholar.'"

One of Mao's favorite Chinese writers, Liang Qichao—who coined the term "Sick Man of Asia" to describe his nation—complained that while Chinese society constantly looked to the past for inspiration, Western nations were looking to the future. Liang urged his country-men to spend less time trying to perfect their personal virtue and more effort working to cultivate national strength. "In the world there is only power—there is no other force," Liang had written as the twenti-eth century dawned. "That the strong always rule the weak is in truth the first great universal rule of nature. Hence, if we wish to attain lib-erty, there is no other road: we can only seek first to be strong." Mao later recalled that as a young man he had "worshipped" Liang and his cold-eyed approach to international politics.

Inspired, Mao began to get involved in local politics himself. As the Qing empire crumbled and the reformers gained stature, Mao organized fellow students and wrote muscular political tracts. He echoed and expanded on Liang's ideas—rejecting Confucian culture and urging a wholesale reimagining of Chinese values. Mao derided the "white and slender hands" of effete traditional scholars and instead pressed Chinese activists to strengthen their bodies and wills. He emphasized the possibility of self-transformation. "The weak can become strong," he wrote in one early political tract. "This is not a question of destiny, but depends entirely on human effort." He pushed his readers to exercise vigorously and embrace martial values—to "charge on horseback amidst the clash of arms, and to be ever victorious; to shake the mountains by one's cries, and the colors of the sky by one's roars of anger."

The indispensable element, in Mao's view, was *force:* China would succeed in shaking off the indignities of the past only by relentlessly cultivating the sources of its own power. In Mao's view, that meant galvanizing China's populace. "The greatest force," he argued, "is that of the union of the popular masses." He believed that the rapid population growth that had put so much pressure on the Qing regime could work in China's favor. He had long urged his adherents to strengthen their individual wills. Now he began stressing the imperative of bolstering a collective will.

These efforts intensified during the early 1920s, after agents from the Comintern—the body tasked with spreading Communism internationally in the aftermath of the Russian Revolution—began filtering into China. In 1921, Mao attended the First Congress of the Chinese Communist Party and soon began organizing study groups and holding literacy drives as part of his recruiting efforts. He found eager converts among China's tradespeople—the carpenters, electricians, and railroad workers who were suffering under the existing system—and helped to form unions and encouraged strikes. Other recruits had no jobs at all, possessing little more than their resentments. By Mao's early thirties, he was becoming a skilled organizer and a committed leftist. "I believe in Communism and advocate the social revolution of the proletariat," he wrote in late 1925.

While Soviet Communism placed urban workers at the center of its system, Mao also saw potential in China's rural peasants. He retreated more and more frequently to the countryside, preparing detailed reports on the conditions in these regions. In 1927, he completed a study of the peasant movement in his native Hunan province, predicting that they would soon overthrow China's feudal landlords. "The present upsurge of the peasant movement is a colossal event," he wrote. "In a very short time, several hundred million peasants in China's central, southern, and northern provinces will rise like a fierce wind or tempest, a force so swift and violent that no power, however great, will be able to suppress it."

At first, Mao had agreed to cooperate with China's urban bourgeoisie en route to this goal. He acquiesced in the Comintern position that any successful revolution would need to combine the Chinese business classes and working classes into a united front. For a time, therefore, Mao was technically a member of both the Communists and Sun Yatsen's Nationalist party. It was this arrangement, in fact, that allowed him to build the nucleus of his future guerrilla army. Mao and his allies readily accepted military training from the Nationalist officer corps. As Chiang and the Nationalists prepared to launch a major offensive in the mid-1920s, Mao raised troops from the country's rural villages to assist in the campaign.

Nevertheless, points of conflict between the Communists and the Nationalists were proliferating. After Chiang's brutal purge of leftists in Shanghai in the spring of 1927, Mao retreated with his allies to a base camp high in China's Jinggang Mountains. Mao had long anticipated the possibility of setbacks. "A revolution," he had written, "is not like inviting people to dinner, or writing an essay, or painting a picture, or doing embroidery." It was, he warned, "an act of violence"—with all its untidy consequences. Shifting political tacks, Mao now applied all he had learned about recruiting, propaganda, and military training to strengthening his own small but passionate band of reformers.

From his base in Jinggang, a picturesque setting of misty mountains and forests populated by monkeys and wild boar, Mao embraced a new tactic: guerrilla warfare. He and his men survived by raiding the property of neighboring landowners, often redistributing it to local peasants. In larger engagements, the rebels shrewdly husbanded their military resources, striking only when they could concentrate their forces. Mao explained: "The enemy advances, we retreat; the enemy camps, we harass; the enemy tires, we attack; the enemy retreats, we pursue." In reality, however, it was Chiang's Nationalists who did most of the pursuing. Mao's Communists fled from one hiding spot to another until, in 1934, they attempted to break out toward northern China—a flight that would come to be remembered as the Long March.

Mao and his Communists spent a year trekking northward, enduring Nationalist air raids and grimly austere conditions, before finally settling in Yan'an, a dusty warren of caves that had been carved out of the yellow loess hills of northern China. Mao's acolytes, at this stage, were a young and ragged bunch. Edgar Snow, an American journalist who spent time with Mao in Yan'an, compared the experience to being "in the midst of a host of schoolboys, engaged in a life of violence because some strange design of history had made this seem infinitely more important to them than football games, textbooks, love, or the main concerns of youth in other countries."

Although Mao was now in his forties, he, too, retained a boyish charm, an easy laugh, and an appreciation for sophomoric antics. Snow recalled how Mao once casually pulled down his pants in a hot cave as he studied a military map. He had not yet morphed into the tumid, self-serious personage of his postrevolutionary years. Snow described him in the mid-1930s as "a gaunt, rather Lincolnesque figure," with sharp cheekbones and a quick wit. The humor was partly a mask: Mao had endured some devastating personal tragedies as his armies battled the Nationalists. As he retreated deeper into the Chinese heartland, his rivals had captured his wife and executed her by firing squad. On the Long March, after marrying again, he was forced to leave an infant daughter behind on the trail.

In Yan'an, however, Mao finally had reason for optimism. As China's conflict with Japan intensified during the late 1930s and early 1940s, Chiang's Nationalists were increasingly forced to occupy themselves with their foreign foe—leaving Mao's Communists unmolested. Mao had chosen Yan'an partly for its proximity to the Soviet Union, which he hoped might aid the Chinese Communists. Yet as the Second World War erupted and escalated, Stalin repeatedly urged Mao to leave the safety of his rural base and join the battle against the Japanese. Mao, for the most part, refused. "We are certainly not fighting for an emancipated China in order to turn the country over to Moscow!" Mao had once explained to Snow. "Only where the interests of the Chinese masses coincide with the interests of the Russian masses can it be said to be 'obeying the will' of Moscow."

Mao was a committed Marxist who had come to see class struggle as the mainspring of history. Still, he increasingly sought to adapt Communist ideology to local Chinese conditions. To some extent, this shift was shaped by domestic politics: his most formidable rivals in the Chinese Communist Party had styled themselves as pro-Soviet Marxist-Leninist intellectuals. Mao, instead, positioned himself as a homegrown, populist alternative, calling for the "sinification" of Marxism and advocating mass participation in the political system. He argued that Chinese society should not count on the Soviet Union for support; instead, it would need to regenerate itself. He and his allies, meanwhile, ruthlessly purged their organization of disloyal elements. The Chinese Communist Party increasingly came to orbit around Mao—the first inklings of the cult of personality that would emerge full force in later decades.

As Mao carved out a measure of autonomy from Soviet influence, he also reconsidered his relationship with the United States. Although he abhorred capitalism, he admired Americans in some respects. He had been a supporter of the McKinley Administration's Open Door policy, which sought to keep the European powers from establishing spheres of influence in East Asia. He respected Theodore Roosevelt for his willful self-discipline, and F.D.R. for his antifascism. Still, as the postwar antagonism between the United States and the Soviet Union deepened, Mao feared that he would soon find himself a pawn in the Cold War. During a 1946 interview with the American journalist Anna Louise Strong, he set up teacups and liquor glasses on a table like game pieces to illustrate his view of the conflict. Before attempting to confront the Soviets directly, Mao predicted, the United States would first seek to subdue a "vast zone" on the Russian periphery—a sector that included China.

Mao's distrust of the United States grew, later the same year, when President Truman tried to heal the rift between Mao and Chiang by asking Secretary Marshall to mediate. At one time, during similar negotiations, Mao had tried to signal his goodwill with over-the-top bursts of bonhomie. ("Long live Generalissimo Chiang!" he would exclaim at the negotiations.) Now, however, Truman and Marshall quickly lost Mao's sympathy by playing a kind of double game— presenting the United States as an honest broker while continuing to support Chiang's Nationalists militarily. "It was the first time for us to deal with the U.S. imperialists," Mao later remembered. "We didn't have much experience. As a result we were taken in. With this experience, we won't be cheated again."

The failure of Marshall's mission left American policy makers with little choice but to continue to back Chiang—or retreat altogether. And Congress, enchanted as it remained with the Generalissimo and his wife, was happy to keep the aid flowing. Truman, however, was gradually losing his enthusiasm for the project. The president complained to his advisers that any American assistance program would be like pouring "sand in a rat hole."

★

These remained the prevailing attitudes in Washington in the winter of 1948, as Madame Chiang pleaded with the capital's wire-pullers and prayed for one last miracle. Not all Americans had turned on her, but even some of her admirers seemed to condescend. One U.S.

diplomat recalled how, at a tea for journalists back in China, the assembled men had stared lustfully at her legs as a fan blew her pale-blue skirt in rhythmic waves above her calves. ("That is the best looking pair of legs I have seen in a long, long time," the *New York Times* man reported.) On another occasion, as Madame Chiang sat in a darkened theater box watching an opera, she had caught a young American serviceman gawking at her. The first lady of China slowly turned her head toward him, looked him in the eye—and winked.

Harry Truman would be a harder conquest. Chiang, by telegram, cautioned his wife not to push for too much. Marshall had already expressed his hesitation, and the Generalissimo—who explained that he was "feeling very bad both in health and in spirit"—could not abide another defeat, even a diplomatic one. He now urged her, if she could get an appointment with Truman, to simply brief the president on the military situation. She should not address Congress, as she had in 1943; better to retain the "respect and love" that that visit had won her rather than invite uncomfortable questions about the Nationalists' recent failures. Madame Chiang replied by admonishing her husband to relax and ignore the chattering in the newspapers. On December 9, she cabled him to report that she had secured an appointment with Truman. Chiang would have to trust her.

At five p.m. the following evening, December 10, 1948, a State Department limousine glided to a stop at 1651 Pennsylvania Avenue, in front of Blair House, Truman's temporary residence while the White House was being remodeled. Madame Chiang stepped out of the car and climbed the front steps into the foyer. For a half hour, she chatted with Truman and his wife, Bess. The president's daughter, Margaret, poured tea. After greetings and pleasantries, Truman and Madame Chiang adjourned to his study, where they continued the conversation in private. By the time Madame Chiang left the meeting, the sun had set; as she exited the front door, she stood silhouetted against the light of the vestibule. Photographers blinded her with their flashbulbs as they crowded closer. "Please! I can't see the steps!" Madame Chiang said. "Were you successful?" a reporter asked. "Sorry, no comment," she said. "The president is the one to say." The White House issued a statement shortly afterward announcing that Madame Chiang had "stated her case" and that Truman had "listened sympathetically." Nevertheless, at least one witness to Madame Chiang's departure from Blair House made note of her "grim smile."

Few Americans, aside from a small clique of China watchers, paid any attention to this diplomatic maneuvering. The newspapers that winter favored happier fare. Reuters breathlessly informed royal watchers that a one-month-old infant, Britain's Prince Charles, had "behaved beautifully" at his Buckingham Palace christening, where he was dressed in a delicate gown of silk and Honiton lace. As Christmas approached, Bergdorf Goodman hawked its holiday wares—gold-plated combs, silk chiffon handkerchiefs, cuff links sparkling with ruby cabochons. Even the China news was delivered with a blithe yuletide humor. The *Pittsburgh Post-Gazette* printed a cartoon depicting Madame Chiang sitting beside a stocking hanging on Uncle Sam's doorstep. The caption read: WAITING FOR SANTA.

Actually, far from waiting passively, the Chiangs were actively plotting. As the holidays approached, the Generalissimo weighed a drastic new stratagem. On Christmas Eve, he spoke with his wife by long-distance telephone; although no official record exists of their conversation, a Nationalist newspaper reported that Madame Chiang had changed her plans and decided to remain in the United States. Chiang himself made an even more fateful choice about his future—though he tried, for the time being, to conceal it. As midnight approached, he stepped into his black Cadillac and drove to the Song of Victory chapel, on Nanjing's Purple Mountain, to attend a Christmas Eve service. Inside, worshippers intoned their prayers; carolers rehearsed their hymns. In his high-pitched Zhejiang accent, the Generalissimo sang along.

3

THE OLD DEVILS

Carolers stood in crescents on the lawn, bundled in their overcoats and scarves. Floodlights illuminated the white Victorian frame house in front of them, on the corner of North Delaware Street in Independence, Missouri. Through the window, bordered by neat panes of rectangular stained glass, Christmas lights winked on a ten-foot spruce. Inside, as evening fell, a prim figure sat before a silver microphone atop a small bridge table in his piano room. He had slicked his gray hair tidily to one side, slipped on a dark suit with peaked lapels, and tucked a three-pointed handkerchief into his breast pocket. He peered through the rounded frames of his eyeglasses at a loose-leaf binder on the table. Shortly after six p.m., he reached down and pushed a button.

President Harry S. Truman repeated this ritual every Christmas Eve, addressing the nation from his old midwestern home while he remotely lit the White House tree back in Washington. Although these short holiday talks tended to be crafted from bromides and cant, this one—on December 24, 1948—was revealing. Truman began by praising his countrymen, still fresh from their military and technological triumphs in the Second World War, for displaying "the strength of

giants" and demonstrating the "heroic courage to bring nature and the
elements under control." But even as he celebrated American power,
he warned of the nation's moral responsibility to the rest of the world.
The "very essence of Christmas," he reminded his listeners, was that
"all men are brothers"—including men in distant lands. He concluded
by quoting from Acts of the Apostles: "God that made the world and
all things therein . . . hath made of one blood all nations of men."

As Truman spoke, a light snow fell over the Missouri hills. By
Christmas morning, the sidewalks outside his house had been sealed
in a brittle white crust. Truman came downstairs early, while the rest
of the family slept, stopping in the parlor by the tree. He peeked at his
presents. He grabbed a beige wooden cane, donned a navy blue overcoat, and laced up a pair of army combat boots. Then he stepped out
into the cold for his regular morning walk. In the twenty-degree air,
the president seemed unusually buoyant as he crunched through the
snow—"cheerful as all get out," as the *Chicago Tribune* correspondent
put it. When a reporter asked whether Santa had been good to him,
Truman replied, "Too good."

In one sense, Truman had reason to be upbeat. Like all presidents,
he had endured his share of first-term fillips, but in general his presidency had been a success. When he had ascended to the office after
F.D.R.'s death, in April 1945, he had said that he felt as if he had been
struck by lightning. Even his mother had admitted that she was not
overjoyed at the prospect. ("Harry will get along all right," she had
said.) Yet within a few short years, Truman had managed both to end
the wars in Europe and Asia and to begin the process of mobilizing
wary Americans to help rebuild. In the autumn of 1948, Truman had
surprised the world by defeating Thomas Dewey for the presidency.
Now, a month away from his second inauguration, he seemed confident, even cocksure. As 1949 began, his approval rating stood at fifty-
seven percent.

Nonetheless, the news from China was not good. The newspapers
on Christmas morning described a Nationalist government in the final
stages of collapse. Mao's forces, according to a report in the *New York*

Times, had "completely wiped out" seven divisions of Chiang's men on Christmas Eve—halving the number of troops left available to defend Beijing. Above the Nationalist capital of Nanjing, the Communists had encircled Chiang's frozen and starving recruits; the heavy snow and overcast skies had made food drops impossible. The following day the increasingly self-assured rebels broadcast a list of forty-five "war criminals" on Communist radio; Chiang and his wife appeared at the top. If captured, the announcement warned, the couple would be subjected to the "just penalty," leaving the details to the imagination.

Mao's victories that winter placed Truman in a quandary. Since the end of the Second World War, the United States had maintained a large garrison of Marines at Qingdao, a charming seaside town of piers and cathedral spires on the Yellow Sea. F.D.R. and Truman had once hoped that China would play a major role in postwar Asian security, acting as one of the world's "Four Policemen," along with the United States, Britain, and the Soviet Union. The base at Qingdao, which now housed thirty-six hundred Marines, was designed to bolster Chinese security and help train Chiang's Nationalist navy. Yet by late 1948, with Mao's men pushing rapidly through Manchuria toward the coast, Chiang had given the order to withdraw his troops to safer ports in Taiwan and Xiamen. From his holiday break in Independence, Truman had to make a decision about what to do with the remaining American servicemen, who faced the prospect of potential direct combat with the Communists. As the snow fell in Independence, the president gave the order to retreat.

Truman had another problem that was slowly becoming public: his cabinet was disintegrating. The Sunday paper that Christmas weekend was full of speculation that George Marshall, who remained in the hospital nearly three weeks after a kidney operation, would resign as secretary of state. Marshall had been an inspired choice for the position—a man so popular after the war that Truman had chosen to name his European economic recovery program after him. Marshall, at times, had seemed like the only glue that held Republicans and Democrats together behind the president's foreign policies. Still, Truman recognized that Marshall, at nearly sixty-eight, could not return to a vigorous full-time schedule. An official at Walter Reed Hospital, where the secretary was recovering, warned that it would be "some time" before the ailing general would feel like himself again.

Truman's defense chief, too, was unwell—though, in James Forrestal's case, the problems were psychological. A slender, taciturn figure with stern eyebrows in the shape of a chevron, Forrestal was gradually coming apart under the strain of high office. A series of policy disputes with the president had gnawed at his nerves. Forrestal objected when Truman had tried to pare his defense budget. He was particularly galled by the president's decision to withdraw from Qingdao, which Forrestal considered a significant foreign policy defeat. Increasingly, however, it was clear that Forrestal's troubles were more than political. In conversation, the defense secretary would lapse into weird silences, and he ranted to friends that he felt as if he were being followed. He manically called Truman dozens of times each week, pestering the president with petty queries that he should have been able to resolve himself. Frustrated and overwhelmed, Truman complained that he could not serve simultaneously as president and secretary of defense.

It was to these unhappy circumstances that Truman returned on December 29, when he boarded his DC-6 in Kansas City for the flight back to Washington. Outside, a snowstorm blew against the aircraft as it took off, shortly after eleven a.m. On the plane, Truman took a nap: tonic for an early riser. He needed the rest; he had not been well, despite his cheery glad-handing in Independence. He had never worked so much as he had in the past month, he told his aides; he had been going so hard that his stomach had begun to hurt. The president's landing at Washington National did nothing to salve this edginess. Thick fog and rain obscured the airport as the plane made its approach, compelling the pilots to circle for forty minutes. As Truman finally descended from the plane, in leather gloves, dark chalk-stripe tie, and gray fedora, a reporter asked, "Were you worried?" The president protested. "No, oh, my, no," he said.

★

Early on the morning of January 7, 1949, Truman left Blair House and crossed the street to his office, on the other side of Pennsylvania Avenue. Inside, the president asked a telephone operator to connect him, one by one, to the senior leaders of the U.S. Congress. When he reached Charles Eaton, an eighty-year-old legislator on the House Foreign Affairs Committee, Truman offered a perfunctory New Year's greeting, before saying, "I want to tell you that I'm appointing Dean Acheson secretary of state. I thought you'd like to know it before you read it in the newspapers." Although Acheson's name had been mentioned as one of Marshall's possible replacements, he had been thought an unlikely choice. *Newsweek*, reporting on the appointment, described it as "a stunner."

Actually, Truman had been considering Acheson for some time. On the surface, the two men seemed like an odd match. Truman was folksy, Acheson a snob. The president had been raised on a midwestern farm; his new secretary of state was the Connecticut-bred son of an Episcopal bishop. Truman spoke in a down-home patois; Acheson, in his own aristocratic accent, said *ahfter* and *pahst*. Yet the two men also shared interests: they liked some of the same authors, and both were conspicuous dandies. Truman had come to respect Acheson's mastery of foreign affairs, which Acheson had honed as a State Department bureaucrat during the Second World War and its aftermath. Perhaps most important, Acheson, despite his affectations, was courteous and loyal to the president. After Truman's Democrats had been drubbed in the 1946 midterm elections, Acheson had been one of the few government officials who bothered to meet the deflated president at Union Station upon his return to Washington. Truman always remembered the gesture.

That January, Truman also moved to oust the erratic Forrestal—a more delicate maneuver. As the year began, Forrestal's mental health deteriorated visibly. He had developed a tic in which he nervously scratched the crown of his head; in one spot he had worn his scalp bare. Truman, in need of a functioning defense secretary, summoned Forrestal and apparently tried to fire him. But Forrestal protested and made his dismissal as agonizing as possible. Truman later complained that the "son of a bitch" tried to take "advantage of me and put me on the spot." The president agreed to let Forrestal stay on for a few months and in public remained tactfully mute. It was Forrestal who ultimately, and perhaps unconsciously, gave the first indication of an impending change. After a reporter asked him in early January whether he would remain for Truman's second term, the defense secretary replied, "Yes, I am a victim of the Washington scene."

Truman would eventually select an old political ally, Louis Johnson, to replace Forrestal as his defense chief. A gruff, six-foot-two and two-hundred-and-fifty-pound former collegiate boxer and wrestler, Johnson had worked as a major fund-raiser during Truman's 1948 election push. But he was essentially a hack. A man who aspired to be president himself, Johnson all winter had waged a whispering campaign against Forrestal in the Washington press corps and privately warned Truman that Forrestal had acted disloyally during the last election season. ("I just want to tell you sometime how Forrestal tried to cut your throat," Johnson said.) Johnson surrounded himself with cronies— "vultures," as one Truman acquaintance put it, who "have the overfed, cigar-chewing, red-faced glum look that you see hanging around the courthouse and the city hall all over the country." Although Johnson would not officially take office until the spring, after Forrestal could be eased out, Truman's new cabinet was taking shape.

Any such shuffle had the potential to upset Washington's equipoise. Cabinet appointments, the columnist Stewart Alsop observed, are "like the introduction of a new and powerful chemical into a complicated and delicately balanced formula." Others, however, viewed the refashioning of the nation's foreign affairs leadership as a kind of natural progression: the accidental and once-untutored Truman coming into his own as a statesman. Acheson held nowhere near the stature of a war hero like Marshall. Nor had Johnson distinguished himself beyond the realm of campaigns and elections. As January unfolded, newspapers speculated that Truman's moves were actually a bid to take control of U.S. foreign affairs—a long-overdue development. "For the first time," a writer in the *Washington Star* reflected, "he is his own undisputed policymaker." The paper's headline read: TRUMAN TIGHTENS GRIP.

★

Truman's sense of America's place in the world had developed only haltingly. As a boy in Independence, where his father raised and traded livestock, Truman had little opportunity to see the world beyond Missouri. He liked to read adventure stories set in Europe and the Middle East, but he never came close to visiting. His outlook in his youth remained essentially provincial. Like others of his time and place, he salted his speech with slurs like *chink* and *dago*. He betrayed no hint of cosmopolitanism. "I think one man is just as good as another so long as he's honest and decent and not a nigger or a Chinaman," he wrote Bess, his future wife, when he was twenty-seven. "Uncle Wills says that the Lord made a white man from dust, a nigger from mud, and then threw what was left and it came down a Chinaman. He does hate Chinese and Japs. So do I." Truman, who had been raised in a Baptist family, combined this xenophobia with a self-righteous strain of Christian piety. The passages he memorized and liked to repeat from the family Bible had a proselytizing flavor: "Let your light so shine before men, that they may see your good works."

Truman did not travel overseas until 1918, when he was thirty-three. After the First World War broke out, he volunteered to join the fighting. He took a romantic view of his role in the conflict. "I felt that I was a Galahad after the Grail," he later recalled. "I was stirred in heart and soul by the war messages of Woodrow Wilson." He said he believed the United States owed France a debt for Lafayette's aid during the American Revolution. "I wouldn't be left out of the greatest history-making epoch the world has ever seen for all there is to live for," he wrote Bess from his training site.

Truman took command of an artillery battery of Irish Catholic troops—an unusual assignment for a Protestant from Missouri. But he made it work. The unit fought its climactic engagement near the Argonne Forest on the Western front. On the long march toward the battlefield, Truman and his men hauled their equipment through the rain and mud; mangled bodies lay amid copses of leafless trees and soil pitted with shell craters. German planes dove overhead, dropping bombs and large grenades. Truman conducted himself admirably in his command, though he professed that the experience left him with no taste for further combat—or even interest in the wider world. "Most of us," he wrote to a cousin just after the cease-fire, "don't give a whoop (to put it mildly) whether Russia has a Red Government or no Government, and if the King of the Lollypops wants to slaughter his subjects or his Prime Minister it's all the same to us." On another occasion, he explained that if the Statue of Liberty was going to see him again, "she'd have to turn around." He spent the next decade and a half at home, dabbling in local Missouri business and politics.

As time passed, however, Truman developed a nostalgia for Wilson and his brand of liberal internationalism. Truman had seen firsthand how American foreign policy could shape opinion overseas; he later recalled how French troops had marched past his tent, shortly after the cease-fire, shouting, *"Vive Président Wilson!"* More important, Truman had come to recognize, as Wilson had, that modern innovations in communications and travel had collapsed distances. The planet, as Wilson had once argued, had been transformed into "a single vicinage; each part had become neighbor to all the rest." Truman thoroughly absorbed this worldview, accepting the fact that small, previously local threats now held the danger of igniting worldwide conflicts. American commerce, too, depended on U.S. leadership to protect trade routes, especially now that British power was waning.

As Truman's political profile rose, he began to apply these Wilsonian tenets. In 1934, at age fifty, he won a seat in the U.S. Senate. At this point, he could boast no real foreign policy experience, aside from his war service. Nevertheless, with Germany once again threatening Europe and Japan penetrating China's defenses, Truman swiftly cast himself as an advocate for military preparedness. At one important speech, in March 1938, he fulminated against Americans who refused to accept the burdens of world power after Versailles. The United States would need to abandon its posture of neutrality in Europe's burgeoning conflicts. "My friends, we are living in a world of realities," he said. "We are the richest nation in the world. . . . No man can keep his property or guard his wealth without defending it." After Pearl Harbor, Truman's visibility only increased as he continued to speak out on preparedness and chaired a prominent Senate committee that acted as a watchdog over the war effort.

Truman's political fortunes improved dramatically in the summer of 1944, at the expense of another influential Democrat, Henry Wallace. A bookish Iowan, Wallace had been serving as F.D.R.'s vice president since 1941. Like Truman, Wallace was a globalist who understood that the newly interconnected world was changing in profound ways. Unlike Truman, however, Wallace was far less convinced that American power was always a force for good. Wallace warned that "international cartels that serve American greed" threatened to oppress ordinary men and women throughout the world. Conservatives in Wallace's own party feared that the vice president's leftist politics could harm F.D.R.'s chances for reelection and moved to oust him from the ticket. Roosevelt, aware of the disquiet, sent Wallace on a fifty-one-day mission to China, partly to remove him from the domestic political scene. But by the summer of 1944, Wallace could no longer calm his critics. After F.D.R. told allies that he wanted Truman to replace Wallace on the ticket, Truman exclaimed, "Oh, shit!" At a boisterous Democratic convention in Chicago in July, the fractious party selected Truman to replace Wallace by an overwhelming margin.

Truman stumped loyally for F.D.R., continuing to press his Wilsonian argument that the times demanded America's moral guidance. Only the United States, with its unique political virtues, could save Western civilization from destruction, he believed. "I think Almighty

God intends for this nation to assume leadership in world affairs to preserve the peace," he declared at one campaign stop. He feared that without continued American engagement, Europe and Asia would degenerate into conflict again. On the evening of Roosevelt's election to a fourth term, Truman sent the president a pithy telegram of congratulations that ended, "Isolationism is dead. Hope to see you soon."

In reality, however, Truman rarely saw Roosevelt. The ailing president met privately with Truman on only two occasions before F.D.R. died, on April 12, 1945. Truman, during his first days in office, seemed overwhelmed by his new responsibilities. To those accustomed to Roosevelt's commanding presence, the new president appeared tentative and unfit. "In the long cabinet room," reported one aide, "he looked to me like a very little man as he sat waiting in a huge leather chair." Substantively, huge gaps remained in Truman's understanding of important national security issues—including the details of the secret U.S. efforts to build a nuclear weapon. Nearly two weeks elapsed after F.D.R.'s death before Truman's secretary of war, Henry Stimson, briefed him on the full scope of the Manhattan Project.

In other respects, however, Truman was a good fit for the role. He had thought deeply about the requirements of the postwar world and had long advocated the creation of a "new machine of peace"—an institution backed by the major powers that would provide for worldwide collective security to guard against the outbreak of another world war. Truman blamed realpolitik for extinguishing his hero Wilson's hopes for an international accord a quarter century earlier. Now, as Truman saw it, the solution was to try to eliminate power politics altogether. Despite Roosevelt's death, the new president vowed to go ahead with an international conference in San Francisco that would attempt to create a successor to Wilson's League of Nations—the United Nations. "Let us not fail to grasp this supreme chance to establish a world-wide rule of reason—to create an enduring peace under the guidance of God," Truman had told the closing session of the conference, in June 1945. For Truman, these were old dreams. For decades he had carried around a copy of the Tennyson poem "Locksley Hall," which foretold the creation of a "federation of the world" governed by a "parliament of man" that would maintain global order.

Truman believed that American technological innovations made this goal more attainable than ever. In August 1945, with little hesitation, the new president gave the fateful order to drop atomic bombs on Hiroshima and Nagasaki, swiftly ending the war in the Pacific. The devastating explosions killed well over a hundred thousand Japanese civilians and reduced the cities to ash. Yet in Truman's mind, they also validated the view of America as a central player in a millennial drama; he mused about whether the new technology might represent "the fire destruction prophesied in the Euphrates Valley Era, after Noah and his fabulous Ark." In the aftermath of these horrors, Truman sought to cast himself as a redeemer figure, seeking to rebuild what the war had destroyed.

With Japan in ruins, Truman believed that East Asian security demanded a stable and friendly China. And the United States—the only nation to emerge from the Second World War stronger than it had been at the outset—would have to take the lead role in that reconstruction effort. Winston Churchill observed that it was now the United States—not its former motherland—that stood "at the summit of the world." Shortly after the fighting ended, the *U.S.S. Rocky Mount*, the flagship of the American Seventh Fleet, steamed into port at Shanghai, replacing its British counterpart at the Number One buoy. As Truman began to take a larger stake in China's future, he daydreamed about using atomic power to transform the Middle Kingdom, restoring it to prosperity. For the moment, at least, such ambitious reclamation projects seemed possible—and necessary. Truman's bold vision of the postwar world depended on the success of the China enterprise.

★

And yet a powerful cultural undertow threatened to slow the tide of Truman's ambitious internationalism. Americans were tired; they craved the rhythms of normal life. Most of them, as one diplomat put

it, just wanted to "go to the movies and drink Coke." Truman understood this quietist impulse; he had felt it himself after his own service
in the First World War. Even now, conscious as he was of the vital
necessity of aiding distant trouble spots, he was slowly coming to understand that he could not do it all at once. This tension—between the
things Truman wanted to do and the things he felt he must do—would
eventually define much of his early presidency.

The dire situation in Europe, in particular, had a way of eclipsing
the crises in Asia. This was partly because the Americans making policy in the late 1940s were almost exclusively the products of European
backgrounds; they tended to prioritize European affairs. But Soviet
behavior, too, demanded that Truman focus closely on Europe, which
sometimes took his attention away from East Asia. Almost as soon as
the war ended, Stalin had begun to maneuver for control of Europe's
eastern reaches—fair recompense, the Soviet dictator believed, for his
nation's disproportionate contribution to the war effort. Truman had
once considered Stalin to be the kind of man he could work with, a
calculating deal maker. But by early 1946, the Soviet leader's rhetoric was growing increasingly combative. In February, Stalin gave a
major speech in which he derided the capitalist system for being inher-
ently violent—remarks that alarmed many prominent Americans. The
U.S. Supreme Court justice William O. Douglas insisted that Stalin's
speech amounted to a "declaration of World War Three."

Within days, more Americans and Britons began warning that past
hopes of cooperation with Stalin had been misplaced. In late February 1946, George Kennan, a foreign service officer based in Moscow,
sent a lengthy and influential telegram back to Washington cautioning
that the Soviet leadership had no interest in a "*modus vivendi*" with the
United States and would respond only to the "logic of force." Days
later, with Truman looking on, Winston Churchill reinforced those
warnings, standing before an audience in Fulton, Missouri, and grimly
proclaiming that an "iron curtain" had fallen across Europe.

Fears about Soviet aggression posed a growing political threat to
Truman. In early 1946, Canadian authorities arrested twenty-two

people suspected of involvement in a Russian atomic spy ring. Republican red-baiters used the issue as a cudgel to attack the president and his Democratic allies, accusing them of not doing enough to prevent Soviet spying in the United States. Ultimately the strategy worked. In the midterm elections that fall, Republicans won both the House and the Senate, delivering Truman a humiliating defeat and portending worse to come. The incoming class of legislators included two young Republican firebrands, Richard Nixon and Joseph McCarthy, both still in their thirties.

Nixon and McCarthy had resorted to demagoguery to stoke fears during the campaign. But Truman also had genuine worries about rising Soviet influence—especially as the British Empire continued to crumble. Insolvent in the aftermath of the war, London was rapidly liquidating its overseas holdings. In late February, British diplomats notified the State Department that the United Kingdom could no longer uphold its long-standing commitments in Greece and Turkey. Truman, concerned that the British retreat would leave those critical regions vulnerable to Soviet influence, made an audacious pitch to the U.S. Congress to take over the job. Although the problem was a specific one, Truman painted it in general terms. On March 12, 1947, he gave a speech pledging that it was "the policy of the United States to support free peoples who are resisting attempted subjugation by armed minorities or by outside pressures"—a statement that would come to be known as the Truman Doctrine. By persistently courting powerful Republicans like Arthur Vandenberg, a former isolationist who now chaired the Senate Foreign Relations Committee, Truman and his advisers convinced Congress to approve $400 million in aid.

Northern Europe, too, desperately needed American assistance. Churchill declared that the Continent, in the aftermath of the war, remained "a rubble-heap, a charnel house, a breeding ground of pestilence and hate." Again relying on the support of Vandenberg and other Republican legislators, Truman and his aides devised a program to send billions of dollars in reconstruction funding to Europe over the next several years. The Marshall Plan, as the project became known, revived the Continent's economy—and gave Truman a welcome boost in prestige.

Yet these ambitious schemes also raised some difficult questions. If the United States was really committed to supporting free peoples everywhere, some Republicans asked, why limit the aid programs to Europe? China, too, had been an ally and a victim in the Second World War—but it received far less aid than the Marshall Plan countries. Truman was somewhat sympathetic to this argument, but he was also overwhelmed by the sheer number of foreign emergencies demanding his attention. In addition to the crises in Europe and Asia, he had to make some difficult decisions about the conflict in Palestine, where Zionist settlers were seeking to establish a Jewish homeland. Senior figures in Truman's cabinet and State Department had warned that support for a Jewish state could alienate Arab oil producers. But Truman, both from personal conviction and for domestic political reasons, ultimately decided to recognize the new nation of Israel.

It was against this backdrop of global unrest that Truman found himself campaigning for reelection in 1948. On the one hand, the president's European recovery program continued to earn praise for being bold and visionary, retaining bipartisan support in Congress. Still, Republican lawmakers increasingly pressed Truman to do more for Asia and attacked the president for doing too little to unearth Communist moles at home. Meanwhile, the divisions in Truman's own Democratic Party were widening. Onetime Democratic liberals rallied to Henry Wallace's Progressive Party candidacy, while conservative southern former Democrats backed their own party, the Dixiecrats, led by Strom Thurmond. Surveying the Democratic political chaos, Republican Clare Boothe Luce gleefully predicted that Truman would be a "gone goose" come November.

Undaunted, Truman threw himself into the campaign, often making more than a half-dozen speeches each day. (In between, for sustenance, he sometimes downed a shot of bourbon.) His Republican opponent, New York governor Thomas Dewey, did his best to appeal to those who felt that Truman should be doing more to aid Chiang's regime. Some government documents suggest that the Chiangs and their allies might have actually helped fund Dewey's effort, funneling $2 million to his campaign. In the end, however, whatever they might have spent, it was not enough. Despite the predictions of several major newspapers, Truman surprised the prognosticators by defeating Dewey. Just as impressive, the Democrats recaptured both houses of Congress. When Truman returned to the capital a few days after the election, the staff of the *Washington Post*—one of the papers that had guessed wrong—had hung a large sign on the front of its offices to greet Truman. It read: WELCOME HOME FROM CROW-EATERS.

★

At 6:44 a.m. on January 20, 1949—the morning of Truman's second inauguration—the president walked out the door of Blair House and climbed into a waiting car. It was still dark outside; a bright moon shimmered in the cloudless night. The limousine drove toward the Mayflower Hotel, on Connecticut Avenue, where Truman would host the first inaugural event of the day: a reunion breakfast for Battery D, the artillery unit he had led during the First World War. Inside the hotel, he and his men devoured a heavy breakfast—ham, grits, and fried eggs. The president, in a double-breasted gray suit and striped tie, slipped easily back into the role of jovial commanding officer; his former subordinates called him "Captain Harry." Truman ordered them to stay sober until after his inaugural address. ("Thereafter," he added, "I don't give a damn what you do.") He flattered his guests by speculating that they could still keep their old marching pace—one hundred and twenty steps per minute—despite the "rubber tire" that many of them now carried around their waists.

At sixty-four, Truman now displayed a formidable spare tire of his own. He had put on a great deal of weight, especially compared to the previous summer, when the stresses of the campaign had slimmed him down and added dark grooves to his face. Now an adipose bulge padded his neck and jowls, giving him the air of a mild mumps case. His hair, too, had lost its color, turning from its once-peppery hue to a current bright white. Still, the president's broad smile dispelled any hint of infirmity. He joked and laughed with his war buddies—flashing, now and then, a couple of discolored front teeth. His new bulk lent him a kind of bouncing force, a nimbus of authority that he lacked in his first term.

After breakfast, Truman changed into formal attire: black coat and white dress shirt with winged collar, dark speckled cravat, tall silk top hat. He went to St. John's Church on Lafayette Square, where he attended a short service with Bess and Margaret. The congregation sang the hymn "Oh God, Our Help in Ages Past" and prayed for "Thy servant, Harry, the President of the United States." Just before noon, Truman proceeded to the Capitol, where tens of thousands of spectators had gathered on the Mall. For January, the weather was nearly perfect: crisp, but so bright and clear that the sun threatened to burn bare skin. At 12:29 p.m.—a half hour late—Truman rose before the crowd, lifted his right hand, and pledged, for the second time, to "faithfully execute the office of President of the United States."

Hatless under the January sun, Truman strode to a bank of microphones in front of the white Capitol balustrade, just above a shield adorned with a bald eagle, a field of stars, and the numerals 1949. He began his address by invoking the times, predicting that it "may be our lot to experience, and in a large measure to bring about, a major turning point in the long history of the human race." This metamorphosis, the president said, would require an unwavering faith in democratic principles. He contrasted American values—which he defined as the belief that "all men are created equal because they are created in the image of God"—with the "false philosophy" of Communism. As concrete examples of American-led beneficence, he extolled the major political and economic achievements of the previous four years: the creation of the United Nations and the implementation of the Marshall Plan. These ambitious projects, he said, had succeeded in bringing "new hope to all mankind."

Actually, these efforts had chiefly benefited Continental Europe.

Now Truman suggested broadening them. He proposed a "bold new program" for the developing world—which would come to be known colloquially as Point Four—that would share promising American technologies and encourage foreign investment. On an interconnected planet, Truman argued, the travails of "underdeveloped areas" were becoming "a handicap and a threat" to the entire globe. Although he did not mention East Asia—or any other region—explicitly in the address, his remarks were partly a response to the tumult in China. The collapse of the Nationalist government, Truman believed, provided just one more piece of evidence that policy makers could not afford to ignore the world beyond the Pacific. The inaugural presented an unmistakably Wilsonian solution to this new challenge.

The crowd outside loved the speech, stomping their feet so hard on the wood-plank flooring below their seats, one journalist reported, that "the rumble from the raw lumber" drowned out all other sounds. Although Truman had described a world filled with potential threats, this was an overwhelmingly hopeful keynote. In important ways, it echoed and expanded on his short Christmas Eve remarks a few weeks before. Above all, it was a profession of faith. It revealed not only Truman's views on policy but also his optimistic conception of human nature. He had made the case that change, for the better, was possible. Furthermore, he had argued, the United States now held the tremendous power necessary to bring about these improvements.

The inaugural blowout after the speech unsubtly restated this theme. Truman climbed into a black convertible and took his position at the head of the parade—a three-hour extravaganza along a flag-bedecked Pennsylvania Avenue that included brass bands, drum majorettes, West Point cadets in flowing gray capes, and a horse-drawn circus calliope playing "I'm Just Wild About Harry." Truman beamed in his top hat and frock coat, reveling in the affection. Once he reached the White House, the president took his place in the reviewing stand to watch the rest of the procession, sipping coffee and rocking on the balls of his feet to stay warm as the sun set. The movie star Tallulah Bankhead successfully pushed her way into the box to be closer to the president; it must have thrilled Truman, who once dismissed himself as "a guy with spectacles and a girl mouth." At the climax of the inaugural festivities, an air armada of nearly seven hundred planes—including five of the Air Force's massive B-36 bombers—rumbled across the cloudless sky. "Never," the columnist Drew Pearson wrote in his diary, "have I seen such a show of military might."

And yet not all Americans welcomed the sentiments in Truman's speech or the martial spectacle that followed. Walter Lippmann complained that the president's rhetoric was far too ambitious and unrealistic. "Never before on so solemn an occasion," he wrote, "has an American president promised so much to so many." More than that, Lippmann took issue with Truman's entire approach to human affairs. Yes, individuals possessed the unique capability to reinvent their environments, to change and reshape the world according to their desires—a power limited only by force of will. Yet that same willful nature also guaranteed friction and backbiting, even among allies. If human imagination was universal, so was human concupiscence. Lippmann warned of "the old devils within ourselves and all other men."

★

As Truman prepared his ambitious agenda, he continued to track developments across the Pacific. The C.I.A. had been warning the president for weeks that Chiang Kai-shek was likely to attempt a desperate gambit, abandoning Nanjing and trying to regroup farther south. Truman's intelligence agency was spying aggressively on its erstwhile Nationalist allies, sending memos to the president detailing the private communications between Madame Chiang and her husband. The intel coming out of China reinforced the impression that Chiang was preparing to flee. The U.S. embassy in Nanjing reported that Chinese foreign ministry officials had been spotted boxing up their files, and warned that Chiang was moving "large quantities [of] gold, silver, [and] other mobile assets to Taiwan"—an effort to establish an "island fortress."

As the Generalissimo made these preparations, Madame Chiang had begged her husband not to quit the fight. Although she had known for weeks that he had been considering this move, she had hoped he would not go through with it. Her identity was tied up with the Nationalist project; both her role as China's first lady and her status as an American ally were now in jeopardy. She told Chiang that she had been busily lobbying Americans from "all walks of life" for support. It would be foolish, she argued, to quit the movement at this "critical moment"—just when Truman had shuffled his cabinet and was reevaluating his China policy. Yet the Generalissimo had grown increasingly despondent, complaining in his diary that his wife was "getting nowhere." Resigning the presidency, he reasoned, might allow him to "shake up the inept party, military, and government machine; break up the stalemate in politics, and be ready to regroup for a new start from zero." Visitors in Nanjing found Chiang taciturn and inscrutable. The Generalissimo did not "express any definite view," one guest reported in late January, but he "remained quiet for a long while."

On the morning of January 21, Chiang called a meeting of his top advisers and other allies at his home in the Defense Ministry compound. The large crowd of men strained to hear his barely discernible voice as he announced his plans to depart. Some of his aides sobbed— perhaps contemplating their own fates once Mao's forces captured and executed them as war criminals. Others, however, recognized that Chiang was hedging his bets. The Generalissimo had a history of using this kind of retreat as a political tactic; he had made similar announcements in 1927 and 1931, then returned to power after a period of months. Attentive listeners noted that he used the Chinese word *yintui* ("withdrawal"), rather than the more definitive *cizhi* ("resignation")—a semantic device that left some daylight if he wished to return.

Nonetheless, later that afternoon Chiang left his home in Nanjing, entered a waiting limousine, and drove to the city's airfield, from which he would retreat to his ancestral village of Xikou. On the tarmac, he strode toward his C-47 transport plane, the *Mayling*, named after his wife. He blinked in the winter air and flashed a perfunctory wave at the spectators who had come to see him off. Then he climbed into the plane, and the door closed behind him. Shortly after four p.m., a pilot started the *Mayling*'s twin engines. The aircraft ran along the runway, gaining speed, until it finally separated itself from the earth, supported by the air alone.

4

BEDBUGS

A Dodge jeep bounced along a ragged road, heading toward the mountains. A lanky, unctuous figure with dark eyes and a thick black mustache rode inside. Although the vehicle was American, the passenger was Russian; he was traveling under the name Andreev—though that, too, was misleading. His companions on this trip included experts in time-delay bombs and specialists in electronic eavesdropping; in their baggage they carried tins of Russian food and bottles of exotic liquors. Dust rose from the road as the Dodge wound its way closer to the Chinese village of Xibaipo, a remote settlement in a river basin under the shadow of the Taihang range's jagged peaks—a desolate moonscape in which peasants smoked long-stemmed pipes and carried water on shoulder poles past fields of winter wheat. The pungent odor of the local fertilizer—night soil mixed with ash—perfumed the air. Around one p.m., the convoy arrived at a collection of earth-colored bungalows near the Hutuo River: the rural base camp of Mao Zedong.

Mao met the visitors at the door of his bungalow. As a gift, the arriving delegation presented its Chinese hosts with a bolt of Russian wool. Andreev's real name was Anastas Mikoyan, and he had been sent to Mao on Stalin's orders. Mikoyan was a few years younger than Mao but nearly as powerful. An Old Bolshevik, he had become a trusted fixture of Stalin's inner circle, even something of a friend. He sometimes watched movies with Stalin, and their children often played together. Although Stalin could be mercurial and was not an easy man to get to know, Mikoyan had succeeded at this better than most. He was considered one of the few advisers who could disagree (gently) with the boss without (much) fear of bodily harm. Mikoyan called Stalin by the nickname Soso. With affection, but not without condescension, Stalin referred to Mikoyan as a "duckling."

Mikoyan had traveled to northern China to consult and coordinate with Mao on the final stages of the revolution. For months, as Mao approached victory in the civil war, the Chinese Communist leader had been lobbying Stalin to allow him to visit Moscow. The previous summer Mao had gone so far as to have a coat tailored for the voyage; but Stalin canceled Mao's trip at the last minute. The Soviet dictator believed Mao should remain at home to see the war through to its end, and he argued that a visit to Moscow now would only make him look like a Soviet puppet. Stalin had dispatched Mikoyan to China as a kind of consolation prize: a high-level channel directly to the Kremlin, just when Mao needed it most—as his troops prepared to march into China's largest cities.

At their first meeting, on January 30, 1949, Mao did most of the talking. Mikoyan simply listened—then sent detailed reports of the conversations back to Stalin, whom he addressed by the code name Filippov. Mao told Mikoyan that the military phase of the war was largely over, estimating that he now commanded more than two million men. His own armies dwarfed those of Chiang, whose best units— those equipped with American weapons and supplies—Mao's forces had annihilated in the battles of the last several months. A large portion of the Communist People's Liberation Army (P.L.A.), about nine hundred thousand men, now stood on the outskirts of Beijing. Mao told Mikoyan that he expected some of those troops to move easily into the metropolis over the next day or two, completing the conquest of the ancient imperial city.

Mao had been looping a snare around Beijing all winter. After taking control of Manchuria the previous autumn, he sent columns of his best troops across the Great Wall to encircle the city. Inside its walls, Beijingers under their gray-tiled roofs had waited out the siege, relying on the miserly light of oil lamps and making do with little or no running water. For weeks, Chiang's general in charge of Beijing, Fu Zuoyi, had ordered his men to remain at their posts; in the meantime, Fu himself slowly unraveled. As the siege intensified, Chiang wrote in his diary that Fu appeared "deeply depressed" and "seems to be going insane." Another witness reported that Fu had been spotted slapping his own face. Fu's daughter worried that her father might commit suicide; secretly, however, she had joined the Communists and hoped that he would surrender to Mao's forces. Finally, on the same day Chiang removed himself from power and fled Nanjing, Fu surrendered himself to the Communists—along with the city he controlled.

As these successes mounted, a sense of euphoria suffused Mao's headquarters in Xibaipo. Mao would begin his days with an "almost ecstatic ritual," according to one account, gathering his lieutenants in his map-strewn bungalow to review the most recent conquests. As his armies swept across northern China, one of his bodyguards recalled, Mao would listen to his favorite operas on an old phonograph that his wife had brought from Shanghai. Undoubtedly full of confidence and optimism, Mao would sometimes sing along with the arias.

Now, with China's old northern capital of Beijing open to him as well, Mao told Mikoyan that he was just waiting for the remaining Nationalist troops to evacuate before sending in four divisions of his P.L.A. He did not expect them to encounter much resistance; in fact, Mao said, he anticipated that he would be able to take Nanjing and Shanghai, too, with little or no fighting. Still, integrating the remaining units of the Nationalist army into the P.L.A. would be a complex chore. Chiang would have left behind spies and subversives. Mikoyan reported back to Stalin that Mao wanted to take a "short breather" before launching into the next phase of the revolution. Although Mao remained buoyant, Mikoyan explained, the Chinese Communist leader was still "expecting the worst."

Nevertheless, on the following day, Mao ordered his armies to march into Beijing and complete the takeover. A tremendous convoy pushed into the city on January 31, as an announcer in a sound truck repeatedly proclaimed, "Welcome to the Liberation Army on its arrival in [Beijing]!" Soldiers, red-cheeked in the January cold, advanced alongside long lines of trucks and bands playing martial anthems. As the columns arrived, Beijingers cheered and parading students triumphantly hoisted a large portrait of Mao: the city's new sovereign.

★

In Xibaipo, in those early days of 1949, Mikoyan and his Russian delegation met almost daily with Mao. In their spare time, they shared meals and took sightseeing walks up into the surrounding hills. Mikoyan, a famously heavy drinker, imbibed freely—"as if it were water," according to one of Mao's bodyguards. The Russian flattered his hosts by telling them that he wanted to learn how to prepare Chinese cuisine. More substantially, Mao and Mikoyan bonded over their mutual distrust of the United States.

Mao had two major fears when it came to the United States. First, he worried that Truman might intervene directly in the civil war, ordering the American military to occupy key Chinese coastal cities in an effort to block the P.L.A.'s advance. Although the Truman Administration had publicly announced its decision to withdraw the Marines from Qingdao, the troops lingered on ships just off the coast; there always existed the prospect of a ruse. Mao considered American intervention increasingly unlikely, especially as the P.L.A. continued to demonstrate its dominance on the battlefield. Still, Mao urged his men not to be "caught unprepared."

A second, more realistic, worry was that the United States would attempt to undermine Mao's authority covertly. Mao warned that the Americans were conspiring to "sabotage the revolution from within" and cautioned that they were already meddling along China's periphery. The United States might well choose to recognize the Chinese Communist government diplomatically, Mao reasoned. But he considered such a maneuver little more than a ploy to keep spies on the mainland. He told Mikoyan that he planned to make life difficult for foreign diplomats in China. He would protect their safety but would also ban their use of radio transmitters—unless it was possible to intercept their communications. China had been "tramped through by the imperialists," he said, and was now infested with "dust, fleas, bedbugs, and lice," His first priority, before entertaining additional ties with foreigners, would be to cleanse China of these dangerous pests.

Mikoyan and the Russians, of course, were also foreigners, with their own history of tensions with the Chinese Communists. Mao was particularly uneasy about Soviet aims in Xinjiang, a vast province in China's northwest that included a significant Muslim population. Mao feared that Stalin would encourage Xinjiang's independence from China: a bid for regional influence. Mao told Mikoyan that he had heard rumors that the Soviets, at one time, had sent arms and equipment into the province, and he asked if the stories were true. Mikoyan promised Mao that they were not; Moscow wanted to trade with Xinjiang, the Russian explained, but did not support independence.

Reassured, at least outwardly, Mao went out of his way to demonstrate his own solidarity with Moscow, telling Mikoyan that he considered himself thoroughly anti-imperialist. He had little choice: Mao desperately needed Soviet help. Taking control of China's major cities, as he expected to do all year, would mean accepting potentially crushing economic responsibilities. Nearly all China's potential engines of economic growth had been severely damaged by the conflict with Japan. China's farms were producing more than one-fifth less grain than they had a decade earlier; the country's industrial output had fallen by half since 1936. Mao asked Mikoyan for a loan of $300 million in silver, plus ten thousand tons of banknote paper on which to print a new Communist currency. The issue of paper money was no idle concern. When Chiang had attempted a currency reform just the year before—instructing all Chinese to exchange their gold supplies for paper notes—the inflation that followed had seriously undermined the Generalissimo's support. Ordinary Chinese had begun referring to the worthless Nationalist currency as "wet firewood." Chiang's son had been forced to take the humiliating step of ordering Chinese film-makers not to make fun of the swiftly depreciating banknotes.

When it came to weapons, Mao felt he had enough; his troops were now capturing Chiang's American-made matériel every day. Never-theless, he asked the Soviets for three thousand nonmilitary vehicles and for supplies of gasoline—both of which would help as his forces fanned out across larger swaths of Chinese territory. All Mao could promise Mikoyan in return was his loyalty to the Soviet Union. "We do not have a middle way," Mao assured the Russian.

★

As Mao and Mikoyan were secretly reinforcing the bonds between Communists in China and Russia, a document printed in mauve ink and marked TOP SECRET: DAILY STAFF SUMMARY was delivered to the desks of important diplomats at the U.S. State Department in Wash-ington. Uninformed about the clandestine negotiations taking place in Xibaipo, the bureaucrats at State had come to a rosier appraisal of the Sino-Soviet relationship—a misunderstanding that would have far-reaching consequences as the year progressed. The Soviets, the State Department analysts simplistically surmised, were "distrustful of all Chinese" and were showing little "enthusiasm for the success of the Chinese Communists." While Mao and Mikoyan cheerfully exchanged petitions and promises, the State Department functionar-ies blindly reported that the Sino-Soviet friendship was "running into snags."

5

THE DEAN

Dean Acheson's new office was on the fifth floor of the State Department building in Foggy Bottom—a bland beige structure described by one newspaper columnist as having "about as much character as a chewing gum factory in Los Angeles." Still, the secretary of state's suite, approached through an antechamber adorned with blue leather chairs and mahogany tables, was an impressive space. Oil paintings—one of former defense secretary Henry Stimson, another depicting the signing of the Treaty of Ghent—hung on the walls. An illuminated globe tilted on Acheson's dark wooden desk, near an unabridged dictionary. His red leather chair looked across the room toward a formidable grandfather clock. The chamber was so grand and imposing that Acheson, when he entered, felt as if he were walking into the cavernous dining room of a transatlantic ocean liner.

Each morning, upon arriving at the office, Acheson would consult a leather-bound binder, emblazoned with the words TOP SECRET, that contained the most recent dispatches from his diplomats in the field. Before his morning staff meeting, he would make notes in longhand on a yellow pad. At fifty-six years old, the secretary of state was, as his son David put it, "a thorough, unreconstructed dude, a fashion plate." He obsessed over the tailoring of his suits, commanding his clothiers with gusto and precision. On most days, David recalled, Acheson smelled like a barbershop, having massaged a dab of Pinaud's wax into his mustache and a quantity of Frances Fox lotion into his hair. He let his eyebrows grow long and bushy, like tufts of muhly grass, but his mustache he pulled into aggressive points. (The journalist James Reston described Acheson's facial hair as "a triumph of policy planning.") Still, by middle age, according to David, Acheson had also acquired "a degree of hardness of character." His eyes had dimmed to leaden disks. A whiff of tobacco smoke leavened the spice of the hair oil. Red meat, martinis, and a few choice insults for his foes were, for Acheson, the indispensable staples of a good day.

Good days were rare during Acheson's first weeks in office. The new secretary of state found himself chasing the headlines: never an enviable position for a geopolitical strategist. Although Acheson was full of ideas for Europe—not least a historic security alliance of the North Atlantic nations—Congress and the newspapers were obsessed with Asia. On Acheson's first day at Foggy Bottom, Chiang Kai-shek fled Nanjing. The three-column front-page headline in the *New York Times* the next day howled CHIANG RELINQUISHES POST. Inside, the paper ran a photo of Acheson, right hand raised, taking his oath of office at the White House. Acheson later recalled those chaotic first hours in office. "Chiang was in the last stages of collapse," he wrote in his memoir. "I arrived just in time to have him collapse on me."

Acheson's advisers at State disagreed about how to handle the crisis across the Pacific. Some old China hands, such as the American ambassador in Nanjing, John Leighton Stuart, believed that the United States had a deep and enduring interest in the Middle Kingdom. This, in fact, had been the mainstream American position since at least the Open Door notes of the late nineteenth century. A friendly, independent China, the thinking went, would provide a vast market for American wares and fertile ground for missionaries seeking to spread

American values. Stuart liked to joke that there were three main constituencies with an interest in China—oil companies, tobacco firms, and evangelists—and the motto of all three was "Let there be light."

A former missionary himself, Stuart had once run Yanjing University, a Christian school in Beijing, and had spent an entire career nurturing bonds between Americans and Chinese. He believed the cultural similarities were more than superficial. He argued that the Confucian idea of *ren* was similar to the Christian notion of love, and contended that Chinese scholars like Mencius had frequently espoused democratic principles. American values "reinforce the teachings of their revered sages as to human relationships and social justice," the ambassador wrote Acheson, by way of primer, shortly after the secretary of state took office. Chiang might be gone and the war lost for the Nationalists, but Stuart urged Acheson not to give up on China altogether.

Even if Mao's forces took control of the mainland, Stuart told Acheson, the United States had powerful weapons with which to oppose the Chinese Communists over the long term. "There is an immense reservoir of goodwill for us among the Chinese people," Stuart wrote in one dispatch. The work of American missionaries over the decades had produced a lasting affection for the United States among ordinary Chinese. Stuart predicted that the Communists would soon alienate large swaths of the populace, who would reject the "intolerant regimentation" of the new political system. In time, Stuart wrote, "a spirit of revolt" would arise in China and throw off the Communist yoke. In the meantime, he maintained, the United States could do a great deal to hasten the counterrevolution. Truman's sweeping inaugural address had been a good start. The president's speech, Stuart believed, would "have a profound effect as a declaration of the high-principled, dynamic foreign policy of the present administration."

Other Acheson deputies took a far darker view. On Wednesday afternoons, Acheson would often slip through a door from his office into the adjoining work space of the Policy Planning Staff, a spartan room adorned with little more than a long table and some green leather chairs. Kicking the door shut, Acheson would probe the brain of George Kennan, the director of policy planning, whose brief it was to transcend the daily headlines and think more strategically about the most difficult policy problems. (When Marshall created the position for Kennan back in 1947, the secretary of state's only laconic instruction had been "Avoid trivia.") Kennan, like Acheson, was focused primarily on Europe, and he had gained prominence in diplomatic circles after writing his long memo analyzing Soviet behavior and warning of Stalin's expansionist aims. A conservative realist, Acheson's policy planning director rejected the view, once embraced by F.D.R. and Truman, that China was destined to play a key role in a universalistic postwar order.

China was a backwater, Kennan argued. Although its population was enormous and growing, it posed little threat to the United States. Even the Soviet Union likely considered it a "vast poor house"—a "weak ally" and an "inconsequential enemy," according to a report prepared by Kennan's staff. China's markets had never been as critical to American economic growth as its advocates had claimed. The United States held only $100 or $200 million worth of assets in China, and in the years following the Second World War, American exports to the Middle Kingdom had never reached more than five percent of the United States' total. Democracy was not about to break out on the mainland; the more realistic possibility was either "chaos or authoritarianism." Most important, Kennan and his staff believed, the United States simply did not possess the influence to decisively affect the outcome of the Chinese civil war. Mao's impending victory was the product of "tremendous, deep-flowing indigenous forces which are beyond our power to control."

★

Acheson, by nature and experience, was far more receptive to Kennan's pragmatic approach than to Stuart's grandiose proposals. An Anglophile, Acheson shared the traditional British appreciation for cautious balance-of-power politics. The missionary impulse, on the other hand, frustrated him. Although Acheson's father had been an Episcopal bishop, the secretary of state had never considered himself a particularly devout Christian. He preferred to spend his Sundays playing tennis or clearing brush at his country place in Maryland. He later explained that he was "baffled by the mysticism of most religious teaching" and was far more receptive to the philosophical approach of China's Confucian tradition, which, he felt, emphasized ethics and right behavior over supernatural phenomena.

In most other respects, however, Acheson had little time for Asia. His career had done virtually nothing to prepare him for a crisis in the Middle Kingdom. He had visited China only once, briefly, as a young man, in 1915. The vast majority of his prior experience in the State Department had been spent working on Europe, implementing the war-era Lend-Lease program and helping to design the postwar economic architecture. Some of Acheson's colleagues complained that his interests were too parochial. Dean Rusk, who worked on Acheson's staff at State, described his boss as an "Atlantic man" who "overlooked the brown, black, and yellow peoples of the world." Acheson could sometimes be crass—he liked, for example, to imitate one old Chinese acquaintance using a cartoonish falsetto. But his Eurocentrism owed more to prudence than to intolerance. Acheson believed that the United States simply did not possess the resources to meliorate every postwar problem: a messy world demanded triage.

Acheson's awareness of the limits of his own power began in his youth—courtesy of his imperious father. A Scots-Irish immigrant with a "wild Ulster streak," as his son described it, Edward Acheson on Sundays could be a histrionic presence in the pulpit. At the church in Middletown, Connecticut, where he preached, the older man had been known to cry, "I believe in one God!" as a drumroll trilled. At home, however, the clergyman did not leave justice to a distant deity. Acheson later described his father's discipline as a "force of nature" to be avoided. "The penalty for falling out of a tree was to get hurt,"

Acheson recalled. "The penalty for falling out with my father was apt to be the same thing."

The family lived in the church's rectory, a sepulchral building with opaque stained-glass windows, whose chief architectural idea, Acheson later said, seemed to have been to "exclude light." But it was not a wholly dreary childhood. Although his father's brand of parenting sometimes appeared harsh, it did not leave a "spiritual wound," Acheson recalled. In fact, such matter-of-fact discipline might have helped him to cultivate a useful spiritual resource: the stoicism to persevere on a planet ruled by powerful, often unfathomable, forces. His father, Acheson later recalled, believed that a great deal in life "could not be affected or mitigated, and, hence, must be borne. Borne without complaint, because complaints were a bore and nuisance to others and undermined the serenity essential to endurance."

Perseverance also demanded opportunism and a sense of adventure. Situated on a hilltop overlooking the Connecticut River, Middletown had been built by outward-looking fortune hunters. The elm-lined High Street displayed the mansions of ambitious traders who had acquired their riches exporting tea and silk on clipper ships from China. Although by Acheson's boyhood the town's economy had diversified, the ocean still enthralled him. He would run down to the wharf after dinner and watch as the vessels departed for more glamorous ports. "I imagined myself plowing across the open sea," Acheson later recalled, "some nights to Europe, some nights to China, some nights to darkest Africa."

For high school, Acheson's father sent him to Groton—another stark environment that seemed designed to stifle independence. As an educational philosophy, the Massachusetts boarding school, run by the domineering Reverend Endicott Peabody, emphasized obedience over autonomy. A brutal discipline reinforced its culture of conformity. New students were sometimes subjected to a procedure called "pumping"—a kind of primitive waterboarding. Vulnerability, for an outsider like Acheson, was a dangerous vice. Groton was full of the wealthy scions of American industry; although Acheson had not grown up poor, the son of a clergyman did not rank high on Groton's social scale.

Perhaps as a defense, Acheson adopted an inflated air. "He was the typical son of an Episcopal bishop—gay, graceful, gallant," recalled one of Acheson's classmates at Yale, where he enrolled after graduating from Groton. Yet Acheson "was also socially snobby with qualities of arrogance and superciliousness." Acheson's university studies, meanwhile, introduced the future secretary of state to what he called the "love portion of the love-hate complex that was to infuse so much emotion into our later China policy." Acheson observed how campus organizations like Yale-in-China raised money to help strengthen the cultural ties between the United States and the Middle Kingdom. Although he appreciated the goodwill these exchanges cultivated, he also found something patronizing about the enterprise. "We made pets of them," he later said. "We are emotional about this thing." Acheson, never a romantic soul, preferred less impassioned pursuits. After graduation from Yale, Acheson excelled at Harvard Law School, which exposed him to some of the country's finest legal thinkers and first made him aware of what he later described as "this wonderful mechanism, the brain."

Acheson moved to Washington after law school, in 1919, taking a position as a clerk to Supreme Court justice Louis Brandeis. As Truman was reveling in the pro-Wilson sentiment in France, Acheson occupied a far different vantage point, watching Wilson's ambitious settlement at Versailles—and his dreams for a League of Nations—slowly unravel under the pressures of domestic politics. Acheson later recalled the gloom that settled over the capital during those months, as "wolves tore at the carcass of the Covenant and howled for the blood of the administration. . . . A sack of the city by victorious barbarians appeared a certainty." Wilson, Acheson lamented, had fallen "like Lucifer, never to hope again." The tragic specter of the failure of Versailles would never fully leave Acheson.

In Washington, however, Acheson also spent time in the company of some brilliant statesmen determined to reinterpret American values for this treacherous new world. Still in his twenties, he sometimes stopped in at the Washington home of Oliver Wendell Holmes, Jr., the septuagenarian Supreme Court justice and Civil War veteran, known for his pragmatic reinterpretations of American case law. Holmes, with his thick wave of white hair and walrus mustache, was known around the capital for his "chins"—the instructional talks he gave younger lawyers. Holmes's flair alone made a lasting impression on Acheson: "His presence entered a room with him as a pervading force; and left with him, too, like a strong light put out."

More important, Holmes imparted a choate worldview—a sense that survival in the modern world simultaneously demanded both force of will and humility. Holmes emphasized the indispensability of human effort; nothing, he argued, should be left to fate. On the other hand, Holmes's approach also stressed the limits of human agency: "At the outset of our philosophy we take the step of supreme faith—we admit that we are not God. When I admit you, I announce that I am not dreaming the universe but am existing in it as less than it." This paradox informed every major decision Acheson made as secretary of state—including, significantly, his approach to China.

Well connected in Washington, Acheson in 1921 joined a prestigious capital law firm, Covington and Burling. He found the practice of law to be as much of an education in pragmatism as Holmes's "chins." Working in the legal profession, Acheson explained, meant being "continually made aware of the complex, subtle, and varied nature of human life and of human institutions. The simple blacks and whites, goods and bads, rights and wrongs of the village blacksmith under his spreading chestnut tree have to undergo considerable complicating elaboration to become useful aids to judgment in dealing with the inherent ambiguities of modern life."

In the early 1930s, as the settlement at Versailles continued to fall apart, Acheson joined the Treasury Department, thrusting himself toward the center of the vituperative debates over whether and how to oppose a rearming Germany and an equally bellicose Japan.

Acheson sided with the interventionists, convinced that only the United States could successfully prop up the existing world order, which for decades had been underpinned by the financial system created by the now-foundering British Empire. Acheson considered such a forward posture a matter of security. "I think it is clear," he said, "that with a nation, as with a boxer, one of the greatest assurances of safety is to add reach to our power." Ultimately, Acheson was forced to resign from his position at Treasury, after opposing F.D.R.'s attempt to devalue the dollar. In 1941, however, he rejoined the government as an assistant secretary at the State Department. In his new role, he supported freezing Japanese assets in the United States and restricting oil exports—a fateful position that ultimately contributed to Japan's decision to attack Pearl Harbor.

News of the bombing caught State by surprise. The department, Acheson recalled, "stood breathless and bewildered like an old lady at a busy intersection during rush hour." Acheson thrived in that kind of turbulent environment. By the 1940s, he had earned a reputation as a skilled bureaucratic warrior—"a throat-slitter of a very vicious kind," as one victim put it. Acheson, in later years, liked to quote from Shakespeare's portrayal of the forsaken Cardinal Wolsey, Henry VIII's embattled onetime confederate. Actually, Acheson bore a greater resemblance to Thomas Cromwell—Henry's cunning, ruthlessly efficient hatchet man. Acheson excelled at working the system. One senator joked that if he were to call Acheson at ten a.m. and ask him to deliver the Washington Monument to his office the same day, Acheson would get the job done—and consider it a "proper request." Acheson's admirers began referring to the canny organizational fixer simply as the Dean.

F.D.R.'s death left Acheson—and the rest of Washington—disoriented. Acheson felt as if "the city had vanished, leaving its inhabitants to wander about bewildered, looking for a familiar landmark. The dominant emotion was not sorrow so much as apprehension on discovering oneself alone and lost." Truthfully, however, Acheson did not really care for F.D.R.'s style of leadership. He thought the president's decisions too snap, his quotes too glib. F.D.R.'s successor, on the other hand, felt like someone he could work with. Truman, Acheson wrote to his son shortly after the new president's ascension to the Oval Office, seemed "straight-forward, decisive, simple, entirely honest."

Truman and Acheson were not compatible in all respects. Truman liked to deride the "striped-pants boys" at State; Acheson was the ultimate striped-pants man. Nor, more significantly, did Acheson share Truman's undiluted confidence in ambitious universalistic projects like the United Nations; Acheson complained that even if the world longed to be united, it was still full of brawling nations. He derided the sentiments encapsulated in Truman's favorite poem, Tennyson's "Locksley Hall," rejecting the supposition that violence could somehow be "superseded by reason," as Acheson put it in his memoirs. The world was, and would remain, a Babel of competing worldviews. He considered it futile—and dangerous—to assume that humans might completely eliminate "force and violence."

Nevertheless, when it came to China, Acheson and Truman shared a common strategy—at least at first. Both men had supported Marshall's mission, hoping the legendary general and secretary of state might win the concessions necessary to forge a peace between the Nationalists and Communists. In hindsight, however, Acheson acknowledged that he misjudged the depth of resentment on both sides. The American goals of simultaneously facilitating talks and propping up Chiang were "admirable" but also "mutually exclusive and separately unachievable." Acheson later admitted that he—and nearly everyone else in Washington—misread this dynamic.

In spite of this setback, Truman and Acheson developed a deep mutual respect. On election night in 1948, Acheson found himself getting drunker and drunker as the returns came in and it looked like Governor Thomas Dewey would win—until the final count revealed a surprise Truman victory. Exultant, Acheson downed a highball for breakfast. Later that month, as Marshall continued to struggle with his health, Truman invited Acheson to a secret meeting at Blair House. Truman, grinning, told Acheson to sit down, then offered him the secretary of state job. Acheson protested that there were more qualified candidates. Truman agreed: "You know, twenty guys would make a better secretary of state than you, but I don't know them. I know you."

Despite his demurrals, Acheson was thrilled. High office, he later wrote, provided him with a profound kind of self-fulfillment; he craved it like an addict. He explained by quoting a favorite classical Greek definition of happiness: "the exercise of vital powers along lines of excellence, in a life affording them scope." Public service, he wrote, provided an antidote to the "flatness of life." In this one incongruous respect, Acheson shared a certain worldly sensibility with Mao, who had once admiringly quoted a philosopher who defined the meaning of life as "developing all the human bodily and mental powers without exception to their highest, with no apologies for doing so." Although Acheson was the humbler man, both, in their ways, viewed the cultivation of a forceful will as a prerequisite for survival in a dangerous world.

★

On February 3, 1949, with the P.L.A. now firmly in control of Beijing, Mao's armies staged a massive rally in the city: a message to any remaining doubters. Amid the ripping wind of the season's first dust storm, Beijing, one witness reported, took on a "carnival air." Musicians pounded drums and gongs, and dancers swayed as they performed the *yangge*, a traditional planting dance. The gusting winter air shredded the crimson banners and portraits of Mao, but the overall import was clear: the power shift was complete. In one Beijing neighborhood, the Communists hung woodcut posters depicting Chiang with a pile of skulls at his feet; in the Generalissimo's hand, he carried a sword marked with the initials *U.S.* The accompanying military parade, flaunting a vast arsenal of captured American machinery, reinforced this second, though no less subtle, theme: the Truman Administration had wasted its military aid to the Nationalists.

Later the same day, in Washington, Truman's National Security

Council gathered at the White House to consider this new reality. The N.S.C. in 1949 was still only an infant, created less than two years earlier in an attempt to coordinate the nation's growing national security apparatus. Now, in the cabinet room, with its prominent oil portrait of Woodrow Wilson on the wall, Acheson took Kennan's side, announcing that China should be considered "an area of lower priority" in the postwar world. Acheson told the group that the Nationalist "house appeared to be falling down" and added that there was "not much to be done until it had come down." He cautioned against taking any "hasty positive action" that might commit the United States to a policy it could not sustain for the long term. The only good news, he pointed out, was that Mao now owned the place: putting China back together after so many years of war would be an economic and administrative ordeal for the Communists. Acheson claimed that China's national identity was largely a "fiction"; if Mao wanted to sustain this illusion, he would first need to "create something" from the rubble.

With this dismissive posture as his starting point, Acheson pressed the N.S.C. for decisions on two specific issues: the future of Taiwan, which continued to resist the Communist advance, and the ongoing military and economic aid programs to the Nationalist government. On Taiwan, Acheson favored quietly bolstering a third force, led by "local autonomous groups" that were beholden neither to Mao nor to Chiang. Admiral Roscoe Hillenkoetter, the director of the C.I.A., liked the idea, adding that "we could have a revolution there in a week if we wanted it," according to the meeting notes. But Acheson also urged the men to think through the problem: What if neither Chiang's forces nor the local resistance movement managed to prevent Mao from taking the island? Was Taiwan important enough to warrant American military intervention? Acheson doubted it. The group decided to ask the Joint Chiefs of Staff for their views on the island's strategic value and to present the council with some military options.

The N.S.C. also considered how to handle the flow of American military equipment to the Nationalists. Acheson wanted to cut it off. As the Beijing parade demonstrated all too vividly, American machinery was passing rapidly through Nationalist hands and directly to Mao's forces. Acheson acknowledged that there was no good solution to the aid question; the administration's critics would attack them no matter what decision they took. Ultimately, however, the secretary of state's viewpoint prevailed, and the N.S.C. advised Truman to halt the vast majority of arms shipments—a decision that, if implemented, would end years of American military aid to China.

At his cabinet meeting the next day, Truman said that he supported the N.S.C.'s proposals. But he wanted to talk through the political ramifications. A decision to halt most arms deliveries was certain to antagonize Congress, which funded the aid programs. During his first term, Truman had made great efforts to build consensus among Democrats and Republicans on foreign policies like the Truman Doctrine and Marshall Plan. Now, treading carefully, the president considered whether to invite the key committees to the White House for pro forma consultations on China. His new vice president, Alben Barkley, thought it would be best to keep the group small—perhaps just the committee chairs and a few others. The president agreed and scheduled the conference for the following morning at the White House. In the meantime, Acheson ordered his staff to collect the research he would need to make his case, including lists of all the American weaponry and equipment that had been shipped to China—and then lost to Mao.

Truman and Acheson had been prepared to disappoint Congress, but the vehemence of the legislators at the off-the-record Saturday morning meeting surprised them. Arthur Vandenberg and Tom Connally, two powerful members of the Senate Foreign Relations Committee, told the president that the congressional leadership was unanimously opposed to formally halting shipments. The resistance forced Truman to get creative. The president told Acheson after the meeting that it would be politically smarter to change course and leave the aid program in place—at least publicly. If they wanted to slow the shipments, Truman said, they would need to do it quietly, informally.

The backlash in Congress had been building for weeks. Even some of Truman's onetime allies were beginning to turn against him. A gaunt, thirty-one-year-old congressman from Massachusetts, John F. Kennedy, had taken to attacking the administration's China policy from the hustings. At one strident speech in his home district, Kennedy blamed Truman for withholding aid from the Nationalists. He castigated the White House for the "indifference, if not the contempt," with which it had treated Madame Chiang and her requests. The United States had fought Japan to maintain China's integrity, Kennedy said; now Truman had squandered that victory. "Our policy in China has reaped the whirlwind," Kennedy said. "What our young men had saved our diplomats and our president have frittered away." Although the newspapers largely ignored Kennedy's speech, it did catch the attention of at least one man—a dynamic and determined Republican congressman from Minnesota named Walter Judd.

ALL THE ACES

Night had long since fallen, but the congressman sat awake, writing. He used these hours, when most of Washington slept, to respond to his mail: an endless chore. Sometimes, as he got to thinking, his mind would run on—and so would his letters. Tonight he was haranguing a newspaperman, from the *Minneapolis Tribune and Star*, on his favorite topic: China. He tucked a clipping of young John Kennedy's remarks into the envelope and told his correspondent that he thought it "extraordinarily courageous" of Kennedy to confront his fellow Democrats. He found it tedious to have to listen to "travelers to China" complain about the current bleak conditions in that country. Kennedy's bold speech, on the other hand, was "a genuine case of man-bites-dog," he wrote. He could not understand why so many news outlets had overlooked it.

Walter Judd, the congressman from the Fifth District in Minnesota, had made a career out of these kinds of China policy jeremiads—though he did not, at first glance, project a forceful presence. Physically, everything about Judd appeared somehow attenuated: slim lips, narrow eyes, fine hair. Thin striations crisscrossed his face—scars from a botched acne treatment as a child. Nevertheless, at fifty, Judd had matured into a poised leader and a gifted orator. He spoke with passion and conviction; if he possessed any self-doubt, he kept it well hidden. At the podium, he would work himself slowly into a heat, and then, at the climax, throw both of his arms above his head. One acquaintance compared the congressman's fervent self-confidence to that of a Hebrew prophet.

Truman's attempt to extricate the United States from China kindled Judd's zeal. While the president met with the congressional leadership, Judd circulated a strident letter of protest to his colleagues on the Hill. Signed by fifty-one legislators, the missive announced that Congress was "deeply disturbed" by events on the mainland. "Today," the letter continued, "the Communist armies in China appear to be on the verge of complete victory over our war-time ally and are demanding the heads of the Chinese leaders who supported us and opposed them." The congressmen argued that a free and united China was critical to American security; without one, they insisted, the United States risked another war. The letter urged Truman to appoint a special commission to revamp America's China policy.

For Truman, part of the problem was that he remained personally conflicted. Like Judd, he still wanted, in some deep way, to fix China, to heal it. A week later, on February 14, he met in the Oval Office with David Lilienthal, the head of the Atomic Energy Commission. As Truman waved a hand at a large globe that stood at the far end of his office, he told Lilienthal that he daydreamed about establishing an organization similar to the Tennessee Valley Authority—a New Deal–era government agency—in China's Yangtze Valley. "These things can be done, and don't let anyone tell you different," Truman said. "When they happen, when millions and millions of people are no longer hungry and pushed and harassed, then the causes of wars will be less by that much." The president, Lilienthal told his diary several hours later, "said these things with great self-assurance and an enthusiasm that I have not recovered from since."

Yet even as Truman was fantasizing about making China bloom, his advisers at State were honing the counterpoint. "We are not yet really ready to lead the world to salvation," Kennan said in a speech at Dartmouth College, on the same day Truman met with Lilienthal. "We have got to save ourselves first." Acheson, too, approached the China issue, including the Judd-inspired letter from Congress, with more circumspection. At his own meeting with Truman, shortly after noon, Acheson presented the president with three potential options for dealing with the congressional backlash.

One possibility was what Acheson called a "non-committal reply" to the letter of protest. That would give Truman some flexibility—but it was also sure to intensify the criticism, pushing the congressmen to go public with their complaints. As a second option, Truman could choose to "make a vigorous reply setting forth the facts." The danger there, however, was that by publicly outlining his qualms about the Nationalist government, Truman would ensure its total collapse—an outcome that was likely but not yet certain. Acheson suggested one final alternative: he could try to reach out to the authors of the letter directly, to schedule a meeting and talk through their concerns privately. Truman told Acheson that he thought option three was worth trying—the best of bad choices. Still, the decision virtually guaranteed a face-to-face clash between the supercilious Acheson and the fiery Judd.

★

Even back in grade school, as a boy on the plains of Nebraska, Judd had never excelled in what his report cards had called "deportment." He was too antsy, too spry, to please his weary instructors. One of seven children of a lumberman and a Congregationalist Sunday school teacher, he seemed to be constantly in motion. His youthful preoccupations reflected his wanderlust. He read enviously about the Scottish explorer and medical missionary David Livingstone. In Sunday school, he liked to stare at a map hanging on the wall that depicted the routes that Saint Paul had once traveled. "The first journey was in red, the second was in yellow, the third in blue, and the last one, to Rome, was some other color; I think it was purple," Judd later recalled. "I suppose that had an impact on me—a little boy in a country town dreaming of places that he might someday go to, where the need was great."

Judd enrolled as a freshman at the University of Nebraska in 1916. But when the First World War broke out, he enlisted in the military—serving, like Truman, as an artilleryman. After returning home and restarting his studies, he increasingly involved himself in the Student Volunteer Movement (S.V.M.), a training ground for future Christian missionaries. By 1923, the year he graduated from medical school, he had risen to a position of influence within the organization. Addressing an S.V.M. convention that December, Judd exhorted his audience to take an interest in world affairs and to apply Christian remedies to the planet's problems. He urged the would-be evangelists to "make the world see Jesus's way out of the world troubles of today."

Judd took his own advice, moving to Shaowu, a remote village in China's southeastern Fujian province. There the Nebraskan worked as a medical missionary, traveling the region's winding dirt roads and treating patients with malaria and leprosy. The following year a band of militants captured him and frog-marched him down to a nearby riverbank to be executed. Judd, in later years, liked to say that his captors were Communists; other evidence, however, suggests that they might have been common bandits. Whoever they were, Judd managed to disarm the group with his nascent powers of persuasion. He pleaded with the men that he was an American—not a British imperialist—and they ultimately set him free.

Judd had come to China just as the rift between Mao and Chiang was widening. The young missionary mixed with both Communists and Nationalists during his time in Fujian. It entertained him to hear the leftists complain about "you capitalists"; Judd earned a paltry five hundred dollars per year. The Nationalists, on the other hand, impressed him. Judd considered Chiang "a giant," comparing him to Abraham Lincoln and other transformational figures. "No other political leader in the history of the human race," Judd wrote, "has ever tackled anything even remotely approaching in magnitude and difficulty and complexity this task." He also viewed Chiang as a kind of modern-day Moses, "making a *nation* out of a people."

Judd returned to the United States in 1931, after contracting a case of malaria. But within a few years, he was back on the Chinese mainland—this time in Fenyang, in northern China. He arrived just as Japan's military was boring deeper into the country. The ruthlessness of the Japanese forces appalled him. Judd treated women and girls who had been raped by Japanese soldiers, and he treated the soldiers for venereal disease. He removed shrapnel from the bodies of Chinese women and children who had been caught in the cannonades. It incensed him that many of the munitions the Japanese were using to inflict this suffering were produced using American scrap iron. Judd—a man who believed deeply in America's civilizing mission—found in this detail a repugnant hypocrisy.

After Japanese troops conquered Beijing in the summer of 1937, Judd came home to the United States again. He crossed the Pacific determined to educate Americans about the crisis in China. He used his family savings to pay for a speaking tour, traveling the country and talking about his experiences. "I have been bombed myself over and over again, with American airplanes, and it never helps to know where they came from," he told a congressional hearing in 1939. "One-third of all the stuff that the planes drop down to kill and destroy is still coming from the scrap iron yards and steel mills of our country. . . . I never could go to sleep without wondering if my people back in America knew what they were doing."

Judd's stature continued to rise as he toured—especially after November 1941, when he seemed to predict the attack on Pearl Harbor. He spoke at the Mayflower Congregational Church in Minneapolis on the morning of the raid, warning his audience that Japan might soon launch an attack against the United States. The news of the devastation in Hawaii arrived soon after. Judd's prescience, along with his growing skill as a public speaker, caught the attention of Minnesota's power brokers. He ran for Congress in the following autumn's election and won, taking his seat in January 1943.

Judd got to know Truman in the summer of that year, when the two men traveled together through the Midwest, trying to rally support for the institution that would eventually become the United Nations. Truman, at this point, was still only a U.S. senator, although in less than two years, he would be leading the entire nation. Judd shared Truman's conviction that the United States would need to play a vigorous role in the postwar world. The United States was quickly becoming the world's banker and would need to police its debtors, Judd believed. Furthermore, advances in transportation and communication had collapsed distances. At their whistle-stops, Judd—the better orator—would talk first, making his case first for the future international organization. Truman would then follow with a barrage of facts. Truman, Judd recalled, "wasn't very much of a speaker." Still, the two men liked each other. As they traveled through the country's heartland, they sometimes slept side by side, in twin beds, in the same hotel room. Judd never forgot the sweet, devoted way that Truman spoke to Bess when he called her from their room each night.

Yet when Truman finally took F.D.R.'s place in the Oval Office, he disappointed Judd. Judd admired the Marshall Plan and the Truman Doctrine, with its bold pledge to support free governments around the world. But he could not understand why Truman seemed to apply these ideas only in Europe—in Judd's mind, Asia was just as critical. Why had the United States bothered to defeat the Japanese in the Pacific, he wondered, if it was only going to surrender wide swaths of East Asia to the Soviets? He believed the United States needed to "keep China in the ring" to distract Stalin on his eastern periphery. If the United States lost East Asia, Judd said, "we will lose ultimately in Europe, also."

Judd shrewdly couched these objections in strategic terms. "If China is taken by Communists," he asked, "how long can India, Malaysia, the East Indies, even the Philippines, resist the pressure?" Fundamentally, however, he was motivated not primarily by geopolitics but by a moral impulse—a deep conviction that the United States had an obligation to spread its values, which he defined as "Christian democracy." American power, in Judd's view, was a means to an end. He could not understand why the strongest nation on the planet—with a president who held "all the aces," as Judd put it—would shrink from this responsibility.

Judd believed that Truman, in his heart, shared his global ambitions. But he blamed the State Department for leading the president astray. He considered both Marshall and Acheson selfish and small-minded; he thought racism partly to blame for the administration's Eurocentrism. Acheson, with his haughty demeanor, particularly galled Judd. At one hearing of the House Foreign Affairs Committee, in 1947, Judd had interrogated Acheson over the contradictions he perceived in Truman's China policy. Acheson, unruffled, had responded with thinly veiled condescension: "You know far better than I because you are an expert on that matter." Still, in Judd's mind, Acheson's egotism and hauteur alone could not explain why he seemed determined to abandon Chiang and the Nationalists. By 1949, Judd had begun blaming "hidden sinister forces" in the State Department for abetting Mao's rise.

★

Acheson scheduled the meeting he had suggested to Truman, with Judd and the other congressional leaders, for February 24. Eager to grill the secretary of state on China, thirty Republican congressmen gathered in the House's Ways and Means Committee Room, with its elaborate friezes of shields and eagles. Acheson later wondered what had possessed him to suggest this encounter to the president at all: the first rule of the foreign service, he groused, was never volunteer. He knew that whatever he said in this room, with these jackals, would follow him afterward. Furthermore, Acheson was sick; he had contracted a winter cold so severe that he had gone to the doctor, who had diagnosed the malady only as "virus x." One month into his new job, Acheson already felt weary, broken-down.

Acheson typically managed to stay cool during these conclaves on the Hill. His nerves rarely bothered him. He astounded magazine photographers by remaining eerily motionless in front of the camera as their shutters whirred. Under intense questioning, he took his time formulating his answers, pausing gingerly before responding in his "solemn, slow, careful way," as one acquaintance put it. Still, Judd knew from experience how to ruffle the new secretary of state. "If you prick him a little sometimes," he later explained, "his face gets red."

Acheson had scrawled some notes for the meeting in his plumb, jagged cursive. America's long-standing China policy, he wrote, remained unchanged: the United States would continue to support a united, independent China, as it had since the turn of the century. The administration would do nothing, at least for now, to publicly embarrass Chiang. Still, the Nationalists' struggle had been a "story of gross incompetence," as the secretary of state put it. Acheson enumerated all the ways in which the United States had aided Chiang's government in the aftermath of the Second World War—followed by the ways in which Chiang's government had squandered that assistance.

Acheson concluded that nothing could now be done to help the Generalissimo, who the United States believed was still quietly "pulling wires" for the Nationalists. "No amount of monetary aid, with or without military advice, can help so discredited and inefficient an outfit," he reasoned. Acheson considered Mao's victories a "serious reverse" for American policy. But he also pointed out, as Kennan had, that China was a relatively weak actor on the global stage. Mao would not transform the nation into a "springboard for attack." Truthfully, Acheson had little clear idea of what might emerge on the Chinese mainland: "We cannot tell what the next step is until some of the dust and smoke of the disaster clears away and we can see where there is a foundation on which to build."

Acheson's presentation angered Judd and many of the other men in the room. Chiang and the Nationalists were not the problem, they argued; the real culprit was American incompetence. Judd objected to Acheson's suggestion that Chiang's aides were lining their own pockets and complained that the administration's own strategy was incoherent.

"U.S. policy could almost be expressed in four words," Judd said. "First, aid to China was 'unnecessary,' then 'undesirable,' and then 'too late.' Just what is being done? What are we going to do?"

Acheson lost his composure. According to an account of the meeting that reached the Chinese ambassador, the secretary of state's face turned red—and then white—as the angry congressmen accosted him. Acheson finally grumbled, "We are not getting anywhere." He hastily gathered up his papers, grabbed his overcoat and hat, and stalked out of the room.

In the long run, however, it was Acheson's "dust and smoke" comment that caused him the most trouble. Opponents of the Truman Administration's policy began referring to it as a passive "wait until the dust settles" approach. There was some truth to this caricature; Acheson had long appreciated strategic restraint. ("Don't just do something; stand there!" he liked to scold overeager subordinates.) In this case, however, he felt as if his words had been twisted simply to discredit the administration. "Any stick is good enough to beat a dog," he later wrote, "but this was an example of my unhappy ability—if I may mix a metaphor—to coin a stick."

The newspapers reported on Acheson's Capitol Hill confrontation, but most details of the China policy debate remained hidden from public view. American readers, instead, distracted themselves with trivial gossip (the movie stars Robert Mitchum and Lila Leeds sentenced to sixty days for marijuana possession) or grand ambitions. (Government scientists, according to a front-page story in the *New York Times*, were secretly developing a "space-ship" that "might someday be the key to world military domination.") And yet even amid this sense of the nation's burgeoning strength, doubts lingered about the repercussions. The writer Arthur Miller captured some of this angst in his play *Death of a Salesman*, which debuted on Broadway in early February and wrestled with the darker—even fatal—consequences of American ambition.

The theater remained a popular diversion in the America of 1949. But a new technology—the television set—was beginning to compete for audiences. Although television programming offered viewers new ways to distract and entertain themselves, it also made willful ignorance of troubling events on the other side of the globe far more difficult. With each day that passed, workers strung more coaxial cable—slender wires the width of a lead pencil—that connected city to city, country to country. Electronics manufacturers breathlessly advertised their newest television sets—although in 1949, a "big screen" model still measured only twelve and a half inches.

In this globalizing world, Americans began to challenge some old assumptions about the nation's approach to foreign relations. Since the founding of the republic, U.S. statesmen had done their best to keep their distance from European affairs. Thomas Jefferson had once derided Continental-style diplomacy as "the pest of the peace of the world." Yet with Europe in ruins after the Second World War, and with British influence receding, Acheson and his team sought to take an unprecedented step in an effort to help stabilize Europe. Acheson's plan—for a formal military alliance between the United States and eleven European nations—had plenty of detractors, traditionalists who believed the United States should leave the Europeans to fight their own battles. But Truman and Acheson argued that the North Atlantic Treaty Organization, or NATO, as the new body would be known, would provide much-needed stability in this precarious postwar world. As the early months of Truman's second term unfolded, a censorious debate over the treaty played out in the newspapers and on television.

Amid these transformative events, the China crisis burned on. Although the papers published daily stories about the civil war, it remained somehow hidden in public view, overshadowed by European affairs and the consuming rhythms of daily life. According to one Gallup poll in early 1949, nearly a fifth of Americans said they were indifferent about the events in China, and a full fifteen percent said they had never heard of the conflict.

For Madame Chiang, who remained in the United States as she considered her next steps, this indifference presented both a challenge and an opportunity. She would certainly need to do a better job of rousing ordinary Americans if she had any hope of putting pressure on Truman and Acheson to take dramatic action. Yet the unsettled numbers were also a gift; a shapeless public opinion left Madame Chiang the latitude to help define it. Furthermore, a distracted populace allowed her to operate quietly, methodically—a task she took up from an imposing stone house on a hill beside the Hudson River.

7

RIVERDALE

S now fell in big, wet flakes, piling precariously on power lines and tree limbs. Although February had been the mildest in nearly six decades, on the first day of March the temperature dropped below freezing, sealing New York City in ice. Madame Chiang had moved to this frigid slope in the stately Riverdale section of the Bronx shortly after deciding that she would remain in the United States. Although the house—a gothic structure with a slate roof, crenellated walls, and a large stained-glass window above the door—belonged to her sister, Madame Chiang quickly established it as her own command post. When Chinese embassy officials referenced Madame Chiang in their notes, they referred to the former first lady and her increasingly robust American operation, crisply, as Riverdale.

From this lofty redoubt, near the gray rock bluffs flanking the river, Madame Chiang did her best to organize the pro-Chiang forces in the United States. She hosted regular strategy sessions at the mansion, gathering her closest allies and attempting to unify the fractured Nationalist sympathizers. She invited prominent like-minded journalists and publishing executives for dinner, trying to project a sense of confidence and equanimity. At one such function, the Chinese matriarch impressed her guests with her "combination of Christian fortitude and Oriental fatalism," as one of them later put it. Although she had made no headway with Truman in Washington, she seemed hopeful that the president might still change his mind. As Americans gradually came to apprehend the scope of Mao's victories, she believed, Truman would have little choice but to reengage with her husband.

Acheson, however, presented a problem. She had known Secretary of State Marshall well—even if she disagreed with his policy. But Truman's new secretary of state was an unfamiliar animal. The Generalissimo had cabled his wife shortly after Acheson's appointment, asking her for a précis on Marshall's replacement. Madame Chiang reported back that Acheson had made few "vivid expressions" about China, although there was some evidence that he had been "close to the leftists in the past." As the winter wore on, however, and Acheson began to clash with Judd and other legislators, her appraisal hardened. Increasingly, the Riverdale sessions focused on attempting to hobble—or oust—Truman's chief diplomat.

Madame Chiang first tried to restrict Acheson's freedom of maneuver by tilting American public opinion in her own direction. She cabled the Generalissimo and asked him to allocate $200,000 to help fund a public relations organization that would lobby important journalists and legislators. She sought to model her project after the influential British operation in Washington. Already the Nationalists employed a public relations specialist who set up small dinners between Chinese diplomats and American politicians at locations like the exclusive Metropolitan Club. Now Madame Chiang wanted to expand those efforts, helping to bankroll the efforts of religious figures like the Roman Catholic archbishop Paul Yu Pin. Chiang approved some of these expenditures; still, he cautioned his wife to avoid discussing the details by telegram.

Madame Chiang also attempted to thwart Acheson more directly, taking advantage of the conflicts built in to the American bureaucracy. In those first days of March, as Riverdale froze, Truman had finally pushed out Forrestal and announced that Louis Johnson would replace him as defense secretary. This change encouraged Madame Chiang, who considered Johnson a "very good friend," as she told her husband. A combative anti-Communist, Johnson shared Madame Chiang's disdain for Acheson and her determination to bolster the remaining Nationalist forces. As the year unfolded, the American defense secretary and the former Chinese first lady increasingly aligned their strategies.

There was one man, however, who still needed persuading of the virtues of her cause: the Generalissimo himself. Chiang, after fleeing Nanjing, had retreated to Xikou, the picturesque village of cliffs, caves, and waterfalls just south of Shanghai, where he had grown up. Despairing over his army's failures, he told his wife that he needed to rest—perhaps for as long as a few years. He urged her not to agitate yet in the press for his return to power; he needed more time, he said, to think and recuperate. Chiang believed that China was in a "transitional period," as he put it in his diary: "the old system has been abolished but the new system is yet to be built." He pleaded with his wife to return to China and join him in Xikou, where they could discuss the future in person.

Madame Chiang refused. Her telegrams were sympathetic—she told him that she was glad that he could get some rest, and she complained that she missed him—but she resisted his pleas to return. Only now, she felt, were Americans beginning to comprehend the scale of the Communist threat. Perhaps to bolster her case, she told her husband that she had been ill and that her treatment was continuing. Although this illness might have been genuine—she had often been sick in the past—some evidence suggests that it could have been a ruse to avoid coming home. One doctor, who treated her at Columbia Presbyterian Hospital, later recalled that he believed there had been "a lot of feigning of discomfort" by Madame Chiang during her stay.

With her husband mired in self-pity, Madame Chiang relied instead on blood relatives. The Riverdale house belonged to her sister Ailing and her brother-in-law H. H. Kung, a portly former finance minister and governor of China's central bank, whose close friends called him Daddy. Kung, who claimed to be a seventy-fifth-generation descendant of Confucius, had once worked for Standard Oil and later built a fortune, American officials believed, partly through currency manipulation and inside information. As a government official, however, he had failed badly, allowing the currency to appreciate dangerously. Although he looked, at first glance, like a benign presence—Joe Alsop had once described him as a "large, smooth, fat man with the exterior of a Y.M.C.A. secretary"—his excesses lurked close to the surface. The journalist Martha Gellhorn recalled how Kung once gave her a box of chocolates—but first plucked out all his favorites.

Kung's wife, Madame Chiang's sister, shared her husband's sophistication—though she had a harder edge. Gellhorn wrote that Madame Kung reminded her of the "stout rich vulgar matrons in Miami Beach hotels"; she was "good at clothes," favoring elegant dresses encrusted with diamonds, rubies, and emerald buttons. Alsop thought Madame Kung, who reminded him of a "plainer but tougher-looking Madame Chiang," dominated the household in Riverdale—including her husband. Her brother once remarked that if Madame Kung had been born a man, "the Generalissimo would have been dead, and she would have been ruling China fifteen years ago."

Madame Chiang also enlisted the help of the Kungs' energetic twenty-seven-year-old son, Louis. A graduate of Sandhurst, the British military academy, Louis acted as the "paymaster" of the family, according to one well-sourced magazine report. Although U.S. government investigators were never able to prove conclusively that Louis or other members of the family had distributed bribes to congressmen or diplomats, Washington was replete with stories of the Kungs offering funds to Americans over the years, including, on at least one occasion, money proffered courtesy of "the Generalissimo and Madame." Furthermore, telegrams from Madame Chiang to her husband in early 1949 show that she was actively—and "secretly," as she put it—recruiting sympathetic congressmen and military officials to make statements of support. She pleaded with the Generalissimo to send tens of thousands of dollars "urgently" so that she could finish the job.

No evidence exists to suggest that Walter Judd was one of the men on the payroll of Madame Chiang and her family—although they kept in close touch. "I wish I were an American citizen so that I could campaign for you," H. H. Kung once wrote to Judd on his elegant Bank of China stationery. There was probably no need to bribe Judd; his years in China had convinced him of the righteousness of the Nationalist cause. Nevertheless, Madame Chiang and her allies made every effort to coordinate their salvos with the Minnesota congressman. In early March, according to the notes of the Chinese ambassador, Kung made a "sudden visit" to Judd in Washington to plan their newest offensive.

★

Even as the congressional push to roll back Mao's victories quickened, Acheson worked to cement his own, more patient, approach. On March 3 the N.S.C. gathered in Washington to hash through the options. The Truman Administration, Acheson argued, would need to accept the reality of Mao's dominance. "Preponderant power," he concluded in a policy paper discussed at the meeting, "has now clearly passed to the Communists." In the face of this grim truth, continuing to arm Chiang's "shattered" Nationalists would only drive the Chinese populace closer to Moscow.

Instead, Acheson argued, the United States should try to drive a wedge between Stalin and Mao, exploiting the natural rifts between the two. Stalin's tussle the year before with Josip Broz Tito, the Communist premier of Yugoslavia, offered a useful precedent: After Tito had defied Stalin's attempt to seize greater control of the Yugoslav government, Stalin had responded by expelling Yugoslavia from the Cominform, a Communist umbrella group. Given Mao's history of tensions with Stalin, Acheson was certain that similar fissures would develop with China.

As a first step, Acheson sought to beat back proposals from the Pentagon to reinforce Chiang's remnant on Taiwan—a move he felt would only arouse Chinese nationalism on the mainland. Why, Acheson asked, would the United States want to distract the Chinese Communists from their existing border disputes with the Soviets in the northern provinces? "We are most anxious," he told the group, "to avoid raising the specter of an American-created irredentist issue just at the time we will be seeking to exploit the genuinely Soviet-created irredentist issue in Manchuria and [Xinjiang]." Nevertheless, Acheson once again asked the Joint Chiefs to work up some military options to defend the island—a clever bureaucratic tactic to keep them turning their wheels.

Second, Acheson sought to use American trade to incite jealousies between Mao and Stalin. Rather than sever economic ties with Communist China, as some of Chiang's supporters would have liked, Acheson proposed that the United States continue to permit American exports of nonstrategic goods—a financial incentive for the Chinese Communists to draw closer to the West. As an added benefit, the policy would allow American-occupied Japan to import Chinese raw materials as it continued to recover from the devastation of the Second World War. The United States could live without China as a political ally, Acheson believed, but it could not let Japan succumb to economic collapse or, worse, a Communist uprising.

For Truman, Acheson's restrained approach to China was acrid medicine. The president still harbored fantasies of reversing Mao's advance. He could not believe that the Chinese, the beneficiaries of so many years of American goodwill, would idly accept Communist rule. He continued to dream of using American funds to finance economic development in the Middle Kingdom: a kind of New Deal for East Asia. Only then, he believed, with China prosperous and secure, could he fulfill the grand vision of the Tennyson poem he kept in his wallet, with its idyllic image of a peacefully slumbering planet, "lapt in universal law." For now, though, there was no realistic path to this utopia. At the March 3 meeting, Truman approved his secretary of state's pragmatic blueprint.

Truman continued to hope that, in time, the Chinese would overthrow Mao and replace him with a more amenable ruler. But the president also recognized that temporizing carried its own risks. Mao's successes already seemed to be buoying like-minded revolutionaries throughout Asia—notably in French-controlled Indochina, the territory that includes modern-day Vietnam, Cambodia, and Laos.

The French, for the previous century, had steadily increased their influence in Southeast Asia. This process had begun slowly, with the arrival of merchants and missionaries. In the mid-1880s, however, French colonial armies had taken full control of Indochina. The French had then reengineered the local economy, creating a plantation system that made some local figures immensely rich while simultaneously leaving many others destitute. Homegrown nationalist resistance movements swiftly sprang up to challenge French rule. Among the most prominent rebels was a Vietnamese nationalist and Communist named Ho Chi Minh. Espousing ideas about self-determination that had originated with Western philosophers and American statesmen like Woodrow Wilson and F.D.R., Ho had gradually risen in stature.

Ho viewed the chaos unleashed by the Second World War as an opportunity to press his advantage. Although French officials had remained in place for much of the conflict, in early 1945 Japanese forces delivered a humiliating blow to the French-controlled government, forcing the Europeans to relinquish control and elevating anti-French local figures to key positions. Japanese domination was short-lived, but it demonstrated to the Vietnamese that the French were not invulnerable. Then, on September 2, 1945, the day Japan formally surrendered in the Second World War, Ho declared Vietnam's independence from French authority. Over the succeeding years, the French did their best to reassert sovereignty. But the guerrilla resistance led by Ho and others only grew, eventually erupting into a full-scale war. By the late 1940s, the Communist-led Viet Minh controlled large swaths of territory and had managed to make its presence felt deep inside French-administered Saigon, launching attacks on cafés and other public places in an effort to sow discord.

The revolution in Vietnam would increasingly weigh on Truman as the year wore on. The U.S. president needed a good working relation-ship with French leaders if he wanted to succeed in his goal of restor-ing stability in Europe; on the other hand, he remained committed to the principle of self-rule, in Indochina as elsewhere. The deepening guerrilla war in Southeast Asia was beginning to expose the paradox in Truman's position. On March 4—the day after the N.S.C. meeting at which Truman and his team had finalized their China strategy—a crowd collected at a busy bus stop in Saigon. As they waited, a deter-mined figure moved steadily toward the throng, lifted a hand grenade, and pulled the pin.

★

PART II

★

8

WAIT, LOOK, SEE

The thunder of an explosion woke Truman at eight a.m. on the morning of March 7. For a man who usually got up at five-thirty, the president had been sleeping late. He blinked groggily in his bed. Deep blue walls surrounded him, punctured by white-curtained windows. A white fan dangled from the ceiling. Outside, heavy rain slapped against the pavement. Truman lay listening, suspended at the edge of slumber. *Boom. Boom, boom.* Seventeen shots total, then the cannon went silent. The rain continued to pour down. Truman rolled over and went back to sleep.

The president was vacationing at his house in Key West, a wicker wonderland where guests wore flowered shirts and the president favored a pith helmet and white shoes. The cannon fire, from the three-inch guns at the nearby naval station, was one of the few drawbacks to this address. Otherwise it was Eden: Truman napped, fished, swam in the Gulf. Only occasionally did he need to attend to business, signing papers and jotting notes. The world crises never seemed to stop, but he was at least closer to managing one of them. After months of flailing as Chiang imploded, Truman had finally approved a China strategy.

Still, the president worried. For years, Americans had been conditioned to expect a more sympathetic approach to the Middle Kingdom.
Habit was on the side of his foes. Although the United States had never
made the same muscular commitments to China's security as it had to
Europe's, a number of vocal Americans had long argued that Washington should be doing more. Already a loose group of U.S. legislators, journalists, and other activists—inspired and organized by Judd,
Madame Chiang, and others—were attempting to sell Americans on a
more interventionist policy. In late February, Senator Pat McCarran,
of Nevada, had introduced a bill in Congress that called for $1.5 billion
in new aid to Chiang's Nationalists—a throwback to the long-standing
program of American subsidies.

While Truman relaxed in Key West, Acheson considered how
to break this stubborn cycle. At nine-thirty a.m. on the morning of
March 8, the secretary of state gathered his deputies in his office for
his daily staff meeting. Acheson, reclining in his red leather chair and
jotting notes on his legal pad, would typically use this conclave to as-
sign tasks and review the most pressing issues of the day. His advisers
called it the Prayer Meeting.

Today Acheson complained that Chiang's American supporters were
refusing to accept the new reality. He wondered aloud whether it made
sense to launch an offensive in the media defending his own position.
He knew that his enemies would press their case in the newspapers.
But Acheson and Truman, until now, had tried to keep their qualms
about Chiang private; they did not wish to be seen as undermining
the Generalissimo as he battled Mao. Acheson told the group that he
was not so sure it was still necessary to shore up Chiang's regime with
statements of public support. Instead, he thought they should consider
the possibility of what one Acheson aide referred to as a "full airing of
the question" in the press.

Before going to the media, however, Acheson decided to test this
approach at a closed-door congressional hearing. The Senate Foreign
Affairs Committee had summoned him to respond to the latest calls
for aid to Chiang. Acheson probably saw the invitation for what it was:

an attempt by the China bloc to embarrass him. But he took it as a challenge. Acheson's friend Felix Frankfurter, the Supreme Court justice, liked to say that a "frustrated schoolteacher" lurked inside the secretary of state. As Acheson arrived in the committee room for the two p.m. session, he prepared to try his hand at educating the legislators.

Acheson, in his testimony, sought to recast the entire narrative of America's relationship with China, reaching back to the earliest roots of the conflict. When asked whether Mao was subservient to Stalin, he tried to administer a dose of context. Although he did believe that Mao and Stalin were likely to cooperate in the short term, Acheson thought viewing the conflict only through this lens vastly distorted it. He countered that the Chinese Communist Party was only the latest product of a revolutionary impulse that stretched back into the nineteenth century. "Almost for one hundred years," Acheson said, "China has been faced with unrest of the sort which is going on now." He attributed this ferment to the pressures of a rapidly growing population on China's largely agricultural economy—an assessment that modern scholars share.

Acheson suggested that the Taiping Rebellion, in the 1850s, foreshadowed Mao's own revolt. During those years, a charismatic revolutionary named Hong Xiuquan, who claimed to be the younger brother of Jesus Christ, had led a massive uprising, defying China's Qing dynasty rulers. In many ways, the Taiping's modernizing agenda and passion for social justice prefigured Mao's own. In the territories the Taiping came to control—including their capital, Nanjing—they banned gambling, slavery, and prostitution and advocated communal property rights and equal treatment for women. At their height, more than a million soldiers fought for the Taiping. By the 1860s, however, the Qing—assisted by forces led by American and British adventurers—managed to roll back the Taiping advances, and Hong committed suicide. Still, even into the twentieth century, the rebellion's legacy endured as an example for future revolutionaries.

Now, at the hearing, Acheson described how, at the turn of the century, Sun Yat-sen and his allies (such as Madame Chiang's father) had eventually picked up the mantle of revolt from the Taiping. Then, after Sun's death, in 1925, Chiang and his Nationalists had placed themselves in the vanguard of the revolutionary forces. In time, however, according to Acheson's version of the story, Nationalist morale dissipated: "That new revolutionary party lost its drive, lost its initiative, became established in office, became attached to the fleshpots, and finally unrest developed against that leadership." Acheson implied that the Communist challenge to Chiang's leadership—far from originating in Moscow—had its provenance in Chinese domestic politics.

Nevertheless, he insisted, the United States had continued to stand by Chiang's Nationalists throughout the Second World War. The American government, he recalled, had provided China with more than $1.5 billion in Lend-Lease aid over the course of the conflict—most of it flown from India over the Hump by U.S. airmen. After V-J Day, this assistance had only grown. Acheson recounted how U.S. Marines had taken over ports at the conclusion of the war, then begun the "colossal job" of expelling some three million Japanese soldiers and civilians from the Chinese mainland. "They had to be rounded up," Acheson said, "brought to rail heads, and brought down to ports, and vessels of every sort were pulled together out of our naval forces in the Pacific—landing craft, transports, everything—and three million Japanese were rounded up and put on ships and taken to Japan and unloaded."

In the years following the war, Acheson said, the U.S. government had funneled another $2 billion to the Nationalist government, and the American military had trained thirty-nine divisions of Chinese troops. But then, he recalled, even as Marshall and his delegation attempted to broker a peace between Chiang and Mao, "extreme elements" in Chiang's party urged him to go on the offensive against Mao, to seek a "solution by force." Acheson continued:

> General Marshall, month after month, pointed out to the Generalissimo that this was suicide, that he did not have the forces, he did not have the technical competence in the army, he did not have the

supplies to carry out an operation which was of great difficulty. The Communist forces were in very difficult country. They were expert at guerrilla tactics. The Nationalist forces had long lines of communication if they were going to attack the Communists. These lines of communication were not only long, but they were studded with tunnels and bridges which were very easily destroyed, so that they could be cut off at all times. . . . The Communists would never meet him except under conditions where they had superiority, and what they would do would be, being very mobile, to keep most of his forces occupied and then pounce on one and then pounce on another.

Nevertheless, Chiang had ignored Marshall's warning and attacked the Communists. "These operations," Acheson recalled, "met very speedily with the complete disaster that General Marshall had predicted. They were conducted by the Chinese Nationalists with incredible incompetence." Since Chiang had launched his full-blown offensive, in mid-1947, the Generalissimo had lost more than a million men, mostly to defections. Acheson estimated that Mao's troops had now seized ninety percent of the matériel that the United States had shipped to China.

The committee's chairman, Tom Connally, broke in and asked, "Some of those supplies were furnished by us?"

"They were all furnished by us," Acheson replied. "The whole works was furnished by us, and the Communists got them. . . . As I say, the disaster is complete."

Acheson's version of the story left the deliberate impression that Chiang's forces had simply squandered this American largesse. Chiang had indeed erred strategically by going on the offensive against Mao in Manchuria, and his Nationalist Party was hobbled by organizational problems. Chiang had derided his own outfit as a "lifeless shell" that had lost its own soul.

Yet the reality was more complex than Acheson's caricature. During the Second World War, American commanders had never viewed China as a war theater critical enough to send large numbers of troops.

Instead, the United States had largely relied on Chiang's forces to fight the land war in the East. On one occasion, F.D.R. had bullied Chiang so forcefully to send reinforcements to Burma that the Generalissimo had wept. All the while, Mao's troops had holed up in the caves of northern China, trying to avoid the conflict. By the end of the war, China had lost any hope of a swift economic recovery. These factors had made it extraordinarily difficult for Chiang to unite his country in the aftermath of the conflict.

Acheson also glossed over the fact that some American China experts had warned, years earlier, that the postwar aid program would not be enough to prevent Mao's victory. In 1947, Albert Wedemeyer, a U.S. general who had served as chief of staff to Chiang during and after the Second World War, wrote a report detailing the chaos in the Generalissimo's ranks. Although Wedemeyer had been frank about the Nationalists' faults, he also urged Truman to do far more to bolster the Generalissimo's regime. Marshall and Truman, however, had no desire to commit more American resources. They blocked the report's publication, stoking the fury of the China bloc.

Now, at the hearing, Acheson tried to massage this inconvenient history. "I do not want to be understood as trying to rationalize myself out of the fact that we have experienced a very serious disaster," he said. "I am not trying to be a Pollyanna about something which is very dead, but I think there is always the tendency to treat a disaster as though it were the end of the world."

He then rehearsed his position—familiar to Truman and the N.S.C. staff—that the situation in China demanded a patient approach. Acheson said that he held no illusions that the Chinese guerrillas would break with Moscow soon: "My own personal belief is that as they gain control of China they are going to go out of their way to show their sympathetic attitude of cooperation with the Russians. I think they are going to show a considerable amount of hostility to us and to the West." Still, Acheson repeated his assertion that China was too weak to be a genuine threat, even if it drew closer to Moscow. The Middle

Kingdom, he said, was more likely to become a "strategic morass" for Stalin.

Senator Arthur Vandenberg, the Michigan Republican who, as former chair of the committee, had supported many of Truman's internationalist positions, asked, "Mr. Secretary, the net of what you say, I take it, means that so far as our policy is concerned, it is to be sort of a wait, look, see policy. Is that correct?"

"That is what we would recommend," Acheson replied.

"In order to justify that to countless zealous friends that China has in the United States, something has to be told to them, and at that point you find yourself on the horns of a dilemma, do you not?"

"That is the difficulty, yes."

Other senators broke in and changed the subject, but Vandenberg quickly took back the floor: "Your conversation got away from my question. I would like to know the answer to my question."

"Yes, it did," Acheson said. "I was happy to see it drift. I think it is true that something has to be said. I think we have to be very frank about what the problem has been."

"Do you mean we have to be frank here, or somewhere else?"

"Frank here always. . . . However, if we had the choice to make between telling the American people what I have told you and never telling them, I think we had better go ahead and do it. I would dislike doing it. I think there are drawbacks to it, but if it has to be done now, I am willing."

9

A NEW WORLD

On the morning of March 23, Mao ate a breakfast of rice and Chinese pickles, then climbed into an American-made jeep for the trip to Beijing. Until now, he had remained at his camp in Xibaipo, under the jutting Taihang range, while his P.L.A. consolidated control of the city Mao had chosen for his new capital. Yet two months after Beijing's fall, Mao and his senior aides finally prepared to move their headquarters to the fringes of the ancient walled metropolis. As his convoy rumbled north over the chewed dirt roads, Mao joked to one of his deputies that it felt as if they were going to the city to take their "examinations"—a reference to the tests aspiring Chinese civil servants once needed to pass if they wanted to serve the emperor. Mao's traveling companion, Zhou Enlai, replied that he hoped they would not fail and be sent home.

Beijing would indeed test Mao. For more than two decades, he had survived in the wastes of China's backcountry, ceding the big cities to Chiang and conserving his strength. Unlike Stalin, who placed great emphasis on the urban working class, Mao had long operated by the motto "First the rural areas, then the cities." Since his youth, Mao had cast himself as a disruptive force, seeking to eliminate the vestiges of imperial rule. Yet now, as the P.L.A. prepared to conquer both Nanjing and Shanghai, Mao understood that he would need to invert his old strategy, reconstructing the big Chinese cities and attempting to re-write an outmoded narrative. "We are not only good at destroying the old world," Mao now explained, "we are also good at building the new."

At two a.m. on March 25, determined to thwart potential assassins, Mao and his party switched from the jeeps to a train for the final leg into Beijing. As the sun rose over the city, it illuminated a landscape still ravaged by the conflict. A wide ring of barren earth, dotted with piles of rubble, hugged the city walls, where the Nationalists had razed buildings to create a defensive perimeter. Inside Beijing, mounds of brick and soil lay on the ground beside Chiang's old trenches. Although the P.L.A. had made progress over the past two months, hauling away garbage and reopening the city walls to pedestrians, Mao must have grasped the daunting scale of the task to come.

Later that evening, as dusk approached, Mao made his way to Xi-yuan airport, near the old Summer Palace, to celebrate his arrival in the city. He wore an oversize winter coat, double-breasted with a fur collar, that somehow evoked the heavy cloaks of the Manchu emper-ors. He stood in his open-topped jeep, gripping a steel bar above the windshield with ungloved hands, as the vehicle rolled past the slender upturned barrels of his artillery batteries. Under the brim of a soft military cap, he smiled boyishly and flashed salutes at his troops. A band played "March of the Volunteers." After sunset, the Communist guns lobbed five hundred starburst shells into the air above the western hills. Mao's propaganda organ printed its report on his visit under the exuberant headline TODAY IS THE HAPPIEST DAY EVER!

Mao moved into a small house in the Fragrant Hills, just northwest of Beijing. Although the complex, which had been labeled "Labor Uni-versity" to throw off curious neighbors, was only a short distance from the city, it was also somehow a world apart. The air was crisper and clearer, and birds sang amid the smoke trees and pines. From his villa, situated in the shadow of an imposing Buddhist temple, Mao spent the spring strategizing about the most effective ways to consolidate and expand his conquests.

As Mao sought to bring order to postwar China, he also dealt with chaos in his personal life. He had met his fourth wife, Jiang Qing, a former Shanghai actress, during his years in the wilderness in Yan'an. Short and exceptionally thin, with nervous flashing eyes, Jiang had married Mao in 1939. At times, she could be charming and vivacious, with a quick wit and a blithe demeanor. But she also made enemies easily, turning on them with the same blunt intelligence. ("I have never met a more cold, graceless person," Richard Nixon would observe when he met her, years later.) Mao recognized his wife's flaws as well as her virtues. He once confided to one of his bodyguards, "A week after I die, people will kill her."

Just as Mao was making the transition from Xibaipo to Fragrant Hills, Jiang Qing traveled to Moscow for medical treatment. Although she seems to have been genuinely ill—one Russian witness recalled seeing her carried off a plane on a stretcher when she arrived—her health might not have been the only reason for the trip. Mao's bodyguard later recalled that the two had been arguing ferociously about their daughter's seventeen-year-old babysitter. According to the bodyguard's account, Jiang Qing had called the girl "stupid," and Mao had retorted that his wife could not get over her own "bourgeois egotism." There might well have been another dynamic at play: Mao was known for his sexual approaches to the young women who populated his inner circle, picking them up at dances or slyly touching feet under the table during mah-jongg games.

Yet even as Mao's wife temporarily vanished from his household, another female presence entered it: his twelve-year-old daughter, Li Min. Li Min had been living in the Soviet Union with her mother, He Zizhen, Mao's third wife, but had returned to China as Mao's armies began to advance across the mainland. Once he was comfortably ensconced at Fragrant Hills, Mao invited his daughter to come live with him. The girl's presence provided him with a much-needed distraction. Although Mao was exceptionally busy that spring—traveling into Beijing most afternoons and returning close to midnight—he carved out time for the daughter he was only now getting to know. Li Min later recalled how the two would take walks through the leafy hills around their villa, her father stomping briskly ahead, hands clasped behind his back, while she playfully raced to catch up.

Despite these pleasant diversions, potential threats preoccupied Mao. Although the Americans had announced that they would be giving up their foothold in Qingdao, U.S. Marines remained on ships just off the coast. Chiang's successor, acting president Li Zongren, had asked the Truman Administration to keep them in the region as he negotiated with the Communists earlier in the year. Mao was concerned that the Marines might represent the vanguard of a future American counterattack. His intelligence services reported to Stalin's representatives that one of their agents had come into possession of a secret American plan to launch a war in East Asia. The strategy, according to the agent, would begin with U.S. nuclear strikes on one hundred targets in Manchuria and elsewhere in the region. The opening salvo would then be followed by a ground invasion of two to three million U.S. troops, reinforced by a reconstructed Nationalist Chinese army.

It remains unclear whether Mao believed this far-fetched scenario, or if he was only using it to frighten Stalin into sending more aid. The Soviet leader later responded by saying that he did not think the United States was prepared to fight another large-scale war. On the other hand, Stalin added, history was full of examples of leaders acting irrationally—just look at Forrestal's erratic personal behavior, he pointed out. Regardless of whether Mao believed the implausible doomsday sequence his men were reporting to Stalin, the Chinese Communist leader certainly fretted over the prospect of American intervention. Mao cautioned his military commanders in areas along the coast to guard against "the possibility that the imperialists and the [Nationalists] might attack or harass our rear areas."

Mao, however, felt more threatened by implosion than by invasion. He urged his army—now more than two million soldiers—to fan out

across the captured territory and help subdue his regime's internal enemies. As a first task, he believed that the P.L.A. would need to root out
counterrevolutionaries among the population, reeducating them when
it was possible and suppressing them when not. "After the enemies with
guns have been wiped out, there will still be enemies without guns," he
had warned at a recent meeting of the Communist leadership.

Just as important, Mao sought to swiftly reconstruct China's political and economic architecture. "The army is not only a fighting force,"
he argued, "it is mainly a working force." He wanted to turn his massive military into a professoriat: a "gigantic school," as he put it. The
Communist leader urged his forces not to rest on their victories but
instead to learn—and then to teach—how to govern China's largest
cities and keep their economies pumping. With roughly ninety percent
of China's economy stuck in "ancient times," he observed, the task of
revitalizing the cities would be far more difficult than simply subsist-
ing in the countryside. He warned his leadership that they would need
to deal with the local bourgeoisie, while at the same time confronting
the "imperialists and their lackeys."

Yet Mao and his senior aides also recognized that "the imperialists" were not a monolithic group. Just as Acheson sought to drive a
wedge between China and the Soviet Union, Zhou Enlai wanted to
encourage rifts between the major Western powers. Tensions existed
between them, Zhou observed—especially between the United States
and Britain. The American interest in China was slightly amorphous,
owing more to spiritual concerns than to material ones. The United
Kingdom's stake, on the other hand, boiled down to money and territory. British investors held roughly $840 million in assets in China,
and the nation's statesmen were determined to prevent Hong Kong
from falling to Mao's armies. As Winston Churchill once declared,
"Hong Kong will be eliminated from the British Empire only over my
dead body."

★

Churchill happened to be touring the United States in late March, giving speeches urging closer bonds between the transatlantic allies. Although he had been turned out of office just after the end of the war, he had remained an operatic presence on the global stage, warning frequently of the Communist threat. He stopped in at Blair House to see Truman, who observed in his diary that he thought the former British prime minister looked old. Then, on March 25, the day Mao traveled to Beijing, Churchill attended a stag dinner at the Ritz-Carlton in New York, hosted by the publisher of *Time* magazine, Henry Luce, one of Chiang's major boosters. Tall white tapers flickered on candelabras beside sprays of white roses and carnations, and cigarette smoke rose from the men in black tie seated around the tables. On the dais, Luce, his chin jutting confidently, introduced Churchill, who waved a long cigar, then donned a pair of round, black-framed glasses to read his remarks.

Churchill began by celebrating the cultural ties between the United States and Britain, which he referred to as "the broad ideals of Anglo-Saxon, British-American, call it what you will, unity, which alone gives an opportunity for the further advance of the human race." The former prime minister had long since rejected utopian visions of a universal world order, arguing instead for a transatlantic alliance designed to balance Soviet power. Now, as he addressed Luce's dinner, he lauded the recent progress toward Anglo-American cooperation. In just a few days, representatives from the United States, Britain, and ten other nations would sign the North Atlantic Treaty establishing NATO. Churchill told his audience at the Ritz that he considered it "one of the most important documents ever signed by large communities of human beings."

But Churchill also alluded to the tensions that still existed between the allies over China. The former prime minister had never quite grasped why Americans were so obsessed with molding the Middle Kingdom in their own image. He believed that China's role during the Second World War had been relatively inconsequential. "I was very much astonished," he said, "when I came over here after Pearl Harbor to find the estimate of values which seemed to prevail in high American quarters—even in the highest—about China. Some of them thought that China would make as great a contribution to victory in the war as the whole British Empire together. Well, that astonished me very much." The audience tittered at Churchill's friendly barb. "Nothing that I picked up afterwards," he continued, "led me to think that my astonishment was ill founded." The crowd dissolved into laughter again.

Although Churchill was alarmed by Mao's victory and thought Americans should be, too, he added that he believed the Truman Administration's wait-and-see policy was "quite right." Provoking Mao by taking aggressive military action would only encourage the Communists to move on Hong Kong. Instead, Churchill counseled quietly bolstering the nations surrounding China. "The Atlantic Pact, in my view, would naturally be followed at no lengthy interval by a Pacific Pact which would deal with that immense, immense portion of the globe," Churchill said. Then he quickly added: "I say Pacific, I didn't mean pacifist. No, no—Pacific. That's the name of the ocean." The audience cackled again.

Although Churchill never shied from the spotlight, he deliberately took a lower profile as sitting British government officials began arriving in the United States for the NATO signing. At five-thirty a.m. on March 30, the angular bulk of the R.M.S. Queen Mary ocean liner steamed into port at New York, and Ernest Bevin, the British foreign secretary, stepped down onto the pier. Portly, with a gut padded by years of whisky sodas, Bevin did not present the elegant figure of a typical British statesman. "His gait," Acheson later recalled, "was the rolling one of a fat man; his clothes gave the impression of being enormous. His best feature was his eyes which, even behind heavy, horn-rimmed spectacles, lit up a face made undistinguished by an unusually broad and flat nose above full lips." At the pier, picketers protesting Bevin's Israel-Palestine policy threw vegetables at his car as he departed for Penn Station, where he quickly boarded a Pullman train for Washington.

Harry Truman did not much care for Bevin, whom he considered a boor, but Acheson liked him. The British foreign secretary could be temperamental and sometimes a little spacey. "He could easily miss a cue," Acheson explained, "and in the resulting confusion not know how to pick it up again." When Bevin was angry, he took on the aspect of a cartoon character, flailing with both arms. Still, Acheson also found Bevin pragmatic, experienced in the craft of wielding power. Though Bevin was sometimes "tough, and often stubborn," Acheson observed, he was "always open to arguments strongly and honestly pushed." Perhaps most endearingly, he knew Bevin to be "defenseless against good humor." The secretary of state eventually came to address Bevin as Ernie; Bevin referred to Acheson as Me Lad.

It helped that the two men largely agreed on China policy. Acheson, already an Anglophile, shared Bevin's (and Churchill's) basically laissez-faire position on Mao's revolution. When they met in Washington at three p.m. on April 2, Bevin acknowledged that Nationalist China appeared to be a lost cause, but did not seem too concerned about it. According to notes of the meeting taken by an American diplomat, Bevin said that he "thought we could get along without" China. "Many of the Chinese would still be on our side," the British foreign secretary pointed out, "and after all, Great Britain had got along by letting the U.S. go its own way in earlier times." When asked by a news reporter whether Britain would support a Pacific Pact, as Churchill was advocating, Bevin replied, "One step at a time."

Bevin first wanted to see whether the U.S. Congress would even ratify NATO, which the foreign ministers signed at a ceremony on April 4. For generations, Americans had prided themselves on avoiding military alliances, and they would likely need some convincing now. The signing ceremony, held in the blue and gold departmental auditorium, provided an inauspicious start to this sales effort. The Marine Band, incongruously, played show tunes from *Porgy and Bess*, and Acheson's staff had failed to invite some key members of the Senate. ("Bad taste . . . poor finesse," Tom Connally grumbled.) Acheson looked "panicky" during the ceremony, one witness reported, and flubbed a number of his cues. After the Belgian prime minister spoke, in French, Acheson introduced the next speaker before waiting for the translation. After a series of boring speeches, Acheson finally introduced Truman—several minutes too early. His microphone still switched off, the president rambled on for a full minute or so, heard neither by the crowd in the auditorium nor by the radio listeners at home, before Acheson's team was able to restore the sound.

The Atlantic pact, as Bevin had foreseen, reignited debate in the United States about America's role in the world. Even as Acheson tangled with critics like Walter Judd over whether to prioritize Europe or Asia, both had to fight off vocal opponents of the treaty like Republican Senator Robert A. Taft. Although the arguments were fierce, they lacked neat fault lines; the treaty also had its left-wing critics. On the same day as the NATO signing, Judd found himself debating fiercely in the House with Vito Marcantonio, a congressman from New York who opposed foreign aid to both Chiang and the European nations. Marcantonio, with his chiseled features and natty three-piece suit, complained that the Marshall Plan and the China-aid programs were rooted in the same imperialism: a plan for "world domination" led by Wall Street barons. Marcantonio warned that these ambitious aid projects would ultimately cripple the American economy. "With empire comes disaster," he said.

Marcantonio's insistence that Mao's revolution was a legitimate liberation movement drew a swift riposte from Judd. Mao's "purpose in China," Judd said from the House floor,

has not been to "liberate" the allegedly oppressed peasants and bring them genuine democracy; their purpose all along has been to unite, first the Chinese and then the billion people in east Asia to work and fight against the United States of America and the other free nations. I am shocked to hear the gentleman from New York urge us to discontinue all assistance to those who, though exhausted, still have the will to resist Communist efforts to mobilize all of Asia against our country. . . . China is at the moment of supreme crisis. Her best friend—the United States—cannot walk out on her, especially at this moment.

Privately, Judd complained that he had never in his life been more depressed over world affairs.

The nuances of these intragovernmental debates did not seem to make an impression on Mao, who considered the Atlantic pact a direct threat. If NATO allies imperiled Moscow, one radio broadcast warned, then Mao's Chinese Communists would "march forward hand in hand" with the Soviets and ultimately "overthrow the entire imperialist system." The Communist-controlled press, according to one American living in Beijing, consistently described the treaty in "sinister" terms. Mao's news agency, Xinhua, seized on the fact that NATO's particularism undermined the universalistic mission of the United Nations—a fair criticism. Still, Mao also recognized that Stalin's post-NATO insecurity could work in his favor. The Atlantic pact made Stalin more conscious of dangers along the Soviet periphery; Mao saw clearly that, after NATO, the shared borders along Xinjiang and Manchuria would make him more useful to Stalin—and lend him more clout.

As April unfolded, the C.I.A. warned that Moscow and Beijing were growing closer. Although the agency shared Acheson's appraisal that Stalin would be able to direct Mao only with "considerable difficulty," its newest report also observed that the Chinese Communist leadership "identifies itself solidly with international Communism as promulgated by Moscow." For Stalin, the geopolitical benefits of an alliance with Mao were clear. The C.I.A. concluded that the Soviet leader was determined to add "the enormous territory and population of China" to his ambit. Mao's domain, meanwhile, was growing by the day, as his armies readied themselves for their final assault on China's coastal cities. "Spring," as Judd pointed out, "is the time when wars begin in China."

HEAVEN AND HELL

The week beginning with Palm Sunday, April 10, brought with it, according to one American diplomat, "a sense of impending crisis." For the superstitious, nature itself seemed full of troubling portents. On the evening of April 11, airline pilots reported seeing a giant ball of blue-white fire, a meteor with a two-mile tail of flame, ripping through the atmosphere over the eastern seaboard of the United States. The following night a "black eclipse"—the first in more than a century—cloaked the moon in the earth's shadow, turning the pale orb a deep reddish hue. A massive earthquake the next morning, the most powerful ever to strike the Pacific Northwest, sent bricks crashing onto parked cars and nervous mothers into panics at the beach, worried that tidal waves would engulf their children. A seismologist at the University of California noted that the temblor had been more powerful than two hundred and fifty atomic bombs.

It was a telling analogy: the power of nature contrasted with the power of man. In the foreign policy battles of 1949, how a person viewed the relationship between those two forces revealed a great deal. Americans, increasingly, were of two minds. On one hand, in overwhelming numbers, they still respected forces that remained outside of

and above human control: the motions of heavenly bodies, the shifting
of tectonic plates, the capriciousness of the gods. The *New York Times*,
after the Pacific earthquake, observed that seismic activity, even in an
age of great technological innovation, continued to defy prediction, remaining "one of nature's mysteries." And yet as the year stretched on,
those attitudes evolved rapidly. Although nature's destructive power
still dwarfed man's own, the fact the people were making the comparison at all seemed to signify that times were changing.

At no time was this juxtaposition, of heavenly versus worldly authority, more vividly on display than during the Easter holiday. Americans in the postwar years had flocked to the established churches; the
Protestant Episcopal church boasted the highest membership figures
in its history, numbers that would continue to rise into the 1960s. On
Easter Sunday, all over the country and the world, worshippers attended sunrise services. Thirty thousand spectators crowded into the
Garden of the Gods, in Colorado Springs, to watch the red ball of
the sun climb above the horizon and illuminate the majestic red-rock
peaks. In Shanghai, too, even as Mao's armies prepared for their final
assault, expats congregated at dawn on the lawn of the elegant British
consulate, just off the Bund at the confluence of the Huangpu River
and Suzhou Creek, for the annual daybreak ritual.

But other, more modern, forces were simultaneously undermining
these ancient traditions. The writer Joseph Campbell, for example, in
1949 published *The Hero with a Thousand Faces*, a book drawing on psy-
choanalytical techniques to argue that the myths of many different
cultures shared similar elements—including a heroic central character
on a quest to redeem his people. Although previous scholars had made
studies of comparative mythology, Campbell's innovation, according
to one reviewer, was to include Christianity as one of the narratives
to be deconstructed. Campbell, like the psychoanalysts who inspired
him, thus inverted the relationship between man and God: The latter became a projection of the former. Taken to its logical conclusion,
Campbell's work cast human beings as active producers of their gods
and myths, not just passive consumers.

This ongoing cultural argument over the promise and limits of human agency provided the backdrop to the China debate and helps explain a great deal. Few of the key players fit neatly into one of these categories; more often they toggled between the two or embodied both at once. Madame Chiang and Walter Judd considered themselves both devout Christians and firm believers in human volition, sharing the millenarian conviction that they could improve the world through their efforts. On the other hand, Acheson—not a particularly devout Christian—nevertheless was convinced that much of the world environment remained resistant to human control. Perhaps alone among the important participants, Mao unapologetically exalted the force of human will. "You are God," he had once written in the margin of one of his philosophy books. "Is there any God other than yourself?"

President Truman was one of those who felt no need, initially, to distinguish between the two worldviews, even as he was being torn by their contradictions. On the morning of Easter Sunday, he went to church twice—first walking down the street from Blair House to St. John's Episcopal Church, where his wife and daughter took communion, and then, immediately after, attending a service at First Baptist Church, his own preferred house of worship. The president, in his gray suit, sat with his family in the eighth row, before an altar decorated with rows of white lilies. He listened as the pastor, Reverend Edward Hughes Pruden, declared that Christian piety offered the only solution to the problems of "our troubled, confused, perilous world." Those upheavals, he said, provided abundant evidence that human beings "do not know how to live intelligently and constructively." Man, he concluded, must look instead to God for redemption.

And yet Truman, in his four years as president, had grown comfortable with temporal power. In the global arena, pondering scripture was no substitute for taking bold action. He had used the atomic bomb with little hesitation when he thought it would end the war. Now he recognized that if he did not act to slow Mao's advance, nobody else would. As the president celebrated Holy Week, long columns of

Communist troops massed in Beijing, preparing for the march south. Outfitted in new olive-drab uniforms, they paraded beside spectators waving red silk banners inscribed with gold Chinese characters. In just days, Mao's armies would descend on the vital center of Chiang Kai-shek's regime.

★

Mao's objective was Nanjing, for centuries one of China's most important cities. The Ming emperors, who ruled for nearly three hundred years, beginning in 1368, had made Nanjing their southern capital. (Beijing, the other key Ming metropolis, means "northern capital.") The emperors enclosed Nanjing in a massive wall that still runs along the shore of the city's glass-calm lakes, which sit in the shadow of Purple Mountain, the capital's most prominent landmark. More than two centuries after the fall of the Ming Empire, the Taiping government, too, had chosen Nanjing for its headquarters. By the time Chiang Kai-shek selected Nanjing as the seat of his own regime, it had been a population center for four thousand years.

The city, however, had lost much of its magnificence by 1949. Chiang had deliberately sought to transform it, carving broad avenues out of the quaint cobblestone *hutongs* and erecting hulking government buildings that reminded one observer of "ships caught by low tide." Diplomats accredited to the Nationalist government considered it a hardship post. Nanjing was, according to the ambassador from the Philippines,

> a third-rate village stretched on a swampy turn of the river with nothing to offer and nothing to show the world except its dull, weedy lakes, the crumbled Ming arch and palace, and the Sun Yat-sen Mausoleum at the peak of the Purple Mountain. Its streets are wide but garbage-strewn and unkempt; its buildings are an ugly conglomeration of unsightly architecture, flat and prosaic; its people are hinterlandish.

The weather, too, was atrocious: bitterly cold in winter and humid all summer. The stagnant air reeked of human feces. As the civil war ground on, the conditions only deteriorated. Starving refugees huddled at the base of the Ming wall, their mouths stained green from eating grass. Others lay by the street under cardboard boxes or make-shift canvas blankets. Visitors to the city frequently noted the contrast between the poverty of most residents and the opulence of Nationalist officials and the foreign diplomatic corps. The American ambassador cringed as the wives of U.S. military officers "in entirely innocent efforts to escape the boredom of their exile unwittingly flaunted their economic superiority" by cruising around the city in fancy cars. Audrey Ronning Topping, the daughter of the Canadian ambassador, remembers attending extravagant National Day receptions, hosted by the Chiangs, at which diplomats mingled beside lavish dinner spreads. "The diplomats were having these grand parties," she recalled. "Then you would go outside in the streets and you were back in hell. Heaven and hell."

By late April, the remaining inhabitants of Nanjing were preparing for a siege. Yellow-clad Nationalist soldiers dug trenches and erected concrete pillbox fortifications in the city and along the south bank of the Yangtze River, which formed a natural barrier between Nanjing and the two million Communist soldiers massing to the north. Americans, at one time, had been optimistic about the city's defense; General Wedemeyer had boasted that the Yangtze could be defended with broomsticks. Now, however, as Mao's gunners began shelling the river's southern bank, panic spread throughout the city. One foreign diplomat described in his diary the "wild yet systematic looting" being carried out by laughing, shouting residents, who ransacked the homes of government bureaucrats for their "plumbing, electric fixtures, doors, windows, floors, and all wood for kindling."

To the north, Mao's troops had been pushing for weeks toward the Yangtze, tramping through muddy paths between rice paddies and camphor trees, pushing wheelbarrows, dragging buffalo, and hoisting artillery pieces on their shoulders. At a lake just north of the river, they assembled a ragged collection of small fishing boats and rafts, then practiced for the crossing. Soldiers balanced unsteadily in their boats, rehearsing how they would lift their weapons aboard. They even tried shooting at their own vessels to see how well they would sustain an assault. When the weather was calm, crossing was easy. But when the wind blew, it took forever. Nevertheless, Mao issued the order to cross. In the villages just north of the Yangtze, soldiers assembled decorative arches and festooned trees with red pennants and posters of Mao to herald the coming advance.

As the Communist attack loomed, the C.I.A. warned President Truman that the Nationalists had altered their war plan. Originally, wrote the agency's director, Admiral Hillenkoetter, the Nationalists had intended to allow Mao's troops to "gain bridgeheads on the south bank, then cut them off by coordinated ground, air, and naval fires, and wipe out the bridgeheads." There were only nine optimal crossing points for the Communists, and these were "easy to defend." If the Nationalists managed to destroy the P.L.A.'s boats, he wrote, it would slow Mao's advance by several months. But Hillenkoetter now warned that Chiang had "completely scuttled" this plan, withdrawing his most important units to Shanghai and Taiwan. Considering the latest intelligence, Hillenkoetter warned the president, "the Government capability to resist is virtually nil."

But before Mao's armies could begin their assault on Nanjing, they nearly started a war with the British, whose ships were still patrolling the Yangtze. On the morning of April 20, the fifteen-hundred-ton British frigate H.M.S. Amethyst moved up the river above Nanjing, on a mission to deliver supplies and protect British nationals. Shortly after eight a.m., Communist gunners on the river's north bank—perhaps fearing a British attempt to scuttle the crossing—fired on the ship, sending artillery shells crashing into the Amethyst's wheelhouse and bridge. More than a dozen British sailors were killed in the barrage; the powerful blasts stripped others of their clothes. Around nine-thirty a.m., unable to escape the Communist salvos, the Amethyst ground to a stop by an island in the middle of the Yangtze, crippled and awaiting a

British rescue mission. The ship radioed a terse message: UNDER HEAVY FIRE. AM AGROUND. LARGE NUMBER OF CASUALTIES. Then another shell slammed into the radio, cutting the vessel off completely.

The British sent a rescue party, led by the *H.M.S. Consort*, but that ship, too, came under Communist fire. Shells exploded around the *Consort*, sending the brown Yangtze water spraying up around the frigate. "They were throwing off three- and four-inch shells at us from about a mile off," one wounded seaman recalled. "We could see the batteries. They were in groups of three and four each." Early on in the battle, a Communist shell struck the *Consort*'s forward wheelhouse and killed the coxswain, sending the ship briefly off course. Ultimately, more than one hundred shells hit the vessel, lacerating its river pilot with steel splinters and nearly blowing off the foot of another seaman. Furiously returning fire, the *Consort* emptied its guns into the paddy fields along the north shore, but the ship never did manage to reach the stranded *Amethyst*. After another couple of rescue attempts, with additional ships, the British gave up—but not before fifty sailors died in gun battles with the P.L.A.

Mao initially approved of the attack, telling his commanders that they should consider any unknown ship in the theater to be a Nationalist vessel, even if it was marked with a foreign flag. Still, although it had been satisfying to challenge the hated British militarily, Mao did not want to risk igniting a wider war. He soon revised his original assessment, ordering his men instead to leave the British ships alone, as long as they posed "no hindrance" to his advance on Nanjing.

Mao's troops finally began to cross the Yangtze in the early-morning hours of April 21. In silence they carried their flotilla of makeshift vessels—sampans, small sailboats, bamboo rafts—down to the shore and dropped them quietly into the water. At first, the soldiers later recalled, the night was so still that they could hear only the buzzing of the mosquitoes and the splash of the oars. But then the P.L.A. artillery erupted, accompanied by the crying of the Communist bugles. Nationalist machine gunners pounded the P.L.A. as it approached the south shore, but Mao's troops jumped out of their boats and splashed their way to the far bank. When the P.L.A. finally took the beachhead, the Communist soldiers launched two green flares—the signal that they had survived the crossing.

The diplomatic corps remaining in Nanjing recognized that the city could fall at any time. As the P.L.A. troops marched on, the Nationalist navy's destroyers "opened up with brilliant flashes of gunfire which rocked the whole city," the Canadian ambassador recorded in his diary. He climbed up to the roof to watch the "spectacular fireworks accompanied by thunderous reverberations." The shooting, he wrote, "continued steadily all night, with occasional explosions that rattled the house. Fires started everywhere across the river, and one could tell the Communists were advancing steadily as the sound of machine gun firing moved forward." The shooting rattled on until nine a.m. the following morning.

Columns of P.L.A. troops finally pushed into Nanjing just before four a.m. on April 24. As the soldiers advanced through the city's northwest gate, the light of burning government buildings illuminated the city. Exhausted but calm, the Communist forces sat on the sidewalk with their weapons and sleeping bags, singing marching tunes. Seymour Topping, an American news correspondent in the city, recalled how the arriving soldiers quickly occupied the "stripped residences of the former Nationalist officials, bringing their small shaggy ponies into the houses or turning them out to graze on the lawns." At the Presidential Palace compound, the future Chinese statesman Deng Xiaoping, then a P.L.A. commissar, planted himself triumphantly in Chiang's chair.

It remained a major question how Mao would choose to treat the foreign diplomats—and the Chinese staff who worked with them— who had stayed behind in the city. Although he had said in the past that he would be willing to establish diplomatic relations with the Western powers, he also had a history of fiery, anti-imperialist rhetoric. Fearful for their families, diplomats and their aides evacuated wives and children to Shanghai—and beyond. Dora Fugh Lee, then the nineteen-year-old daughter of a Chinese staff member at the U.S.

embassy, recalls her father calling her and saying, "Get a small bag—your clothes, your books, and your Bible." Dora had grown up in an aristocratic Manchu family with roots in Beijing stretching back for generations. But Mao's revolution was irrevocably transforming that older China. Dora's father now flew with her to Shanghai, dropping her in the city before returning to Nanjing himself. Shortly thereafter, as the P.L.A. continued its march south, a Nationalist general who was a friend of her father's showed up at her door and told her and her young husband that they would need to leave the country right away. "Do you want to go to Taiwan or Tokyo?" the general asked. Making a spur-of-the-moment decision, the couple chose Tokyo. They would not return to their native China for more than thirty years.

Initially, at least, such drastic escapes seemed justified. Ambassador Stuart's first encounter with arriving P.L.A. troops left him discouraged. Shortly before seven a.m. on April 25, twelve armed Communist soldiers talked their way past a guard at Stuart's residence, then dashed up the stairs into his bedroom. As Stuart dryly put it in his dispatch home to Acheson: "The Ambassador was not quite awake at that hour and their appearance in his bedroom was something of a shock." The soldiers then prowled his room, speaking in "loud and angry tones." At one point, they marched an American economic analyst back into his bedroom at gunpoint. Although the troops did not take anything before they filed back down the stairs, they were heard to remark that "all this would eventually go to people to whom it should belong anyway." In the meantime, the P.L.A. men warned, Stuart should remain inside the embassy complex.

When Mao learned of the incident, it angered him. He told his deputies that he considered the whole thing a "violation of discipline" that should be "quickly investigated." He acknowledged that Nanjing was likely to be full of "the enemy's special agents" and "foreign spies." Still, he ordered his troops to protect Nanjing's foreign communities, prohibiting random searches of their compounds. "No action," Mao wrote, "should be taken without asking for instructions."

Stuart, almost certainly unaware of Mao's genuine views on the incident, decided to carefully test the P.L.A.'s unauthorized order to remain in the compound. Although the Communist soldiers prohibited embassy personnel from taking anything out of the complex—including innocuous items like coats and bicycles—they did, if pressed, occasionally allow some personnel to come and go. That inconsistency led Stuart to believe that his captors were just making rules up as they went along, which he blamed on "capriciousness . . . ignorance, hostility to Americans, and desire to demonstrate authority." Gradually, Stuart began taking short walks around the embassy to see how far he could enlarge his boundaries.

★

Although it had been expected for some time, the fall of Nanjing crystalized the panic in Nationalist China. With Mao's troops charging into the city, Nationalist leaders fought among themselves. From across the Pacific Ocean, in the conference rooms of Washington, D.C., it was easy to view the Nationalists as a monolithic bloc. In reality, the Guomindang leadership was profoundly divided by old rivalries. Li Zongren, who succeeded Chiang as acting president, had long battled the Generalissimo for political influence; Li had been elected vice president the year before only over Chiang's vigorous objections. Li, returning the favor, had then pushed hard to oust Chiang from the presidency. Regional power struggles were at the heart of these disputes. While Chiang was strongest in China's Zhejiang province, just south of Shanghai, Li and and his clique drew much of their support from the Guangxi region, farther south and west.

During the final week of April, Acheson's office received a tip from one of its informants that acting president Li, angered by Chiang's refusal to commit resources to the defense of Nanjing, had threatened to retreat to his old base in Guangxi. That was probably fine with Chiang, who was beginning to second-guess his self-imposed withdrawal from public life. The two Nationalist leaders continued to battle over the best strategy to slow Mao's advance. As the defeated Guomindang forces retreated, Li wanted to use key military units to shore up his southwestern stronghold. Chiang, on the other had, wanted the same troops to instead fortify a "strategic triangle" along China's southeastern coast that would include Fujian, Guangdong, and Taiwan. To this end, the Generalissimo had built an airfield and a harbor off the Zhejiang coast. In the meantime, he drained hundreds of millions of dollars from Shanghai banks to fund this resistance—although during at least one transfer, acting president Li's allies had managed to siphon off millions of silver coins to bankroll their own projects.

As Chiang attempted to reassert leadership of the Nationalist vestiges, he explained to his wife that he had now resolved to leave Xikou. Although he could not yet say where he was going, he gave Madame Chiang a hint, assuring her that "we will defend Shanghai tenaciously." Shortly thereafter Chiang took his son to the family altar in Xikou to pay their respects, and then they made their way down to a dock near Elephant Mountain. As their naval frigate glided out onto the water, Chiang's son asked him where they were going. The Generalissimo replied, "Shanghai!"

It is difficult to believe that Chiang genuinely thought he could defend the city. In the days following the collapse of Nanjing's defenses, Truman's top intelligence officers warned him that the climax of Mao's triumph was rapidly approaching. The C.I.A.'s Hillenkoetter explained to Truman that the "open split" between Chiang and acting president Li was becoming increasingly obvious. Neither of them, meanwhile, had the means to mount a successful stand at Shanghai. "Regardless of real or token defense," Hillenkoetter told Truman, "Shanghai will not hold for more than five days."

11

A VAST AND DELICATE
ENTERPRISE

While Mao consolidated his latest conquest, Beijing celebrated. One resident wrote in his diary of the "impromptu victory parades on the streets—flaring torches,
gongs, drums, a brass band, marching soldiers, cavorting students,
songs, cheers, shouts of 'Take Chiang Kai-shek alive!' and 'On to Formosa!'" A week after the fall of Nanjing, Mao drove from his villa in
Fragrant Hills down into Beijing, where he visited the Summer Palace,
an old imperial complex that had been ravaged by the British military during the Opium Wars. Mao and a well-known poet, Liu Yazi,
climbed into a small boat and pushed off into Kunming Lake. The two
men chatted amiably about Mao's war strategy as the boat passed the
Dragon King Temple and floated under the Seventeen-Arch Bridge.
Mao remained edgy and sleep-deprived, anxious about making a mistake just as victory seemed inevitable. Still, as they drifted in the little
boat, Mao's companion reassured him: "We won."

Mao instructed his military commanders to take their time before
rushing on to Shanghai. Although he had heard that American ships
were evacuating the city, he wanted to confirm those reports before
risking a confrontation—a scenario that had long worried him. He

told his troops to be prepared for anything; if the Nationalist military retreated precipitously, Mao's own forces might need to march into Shanghai to fill the vacuum. For now, though, Mao ordered his columns to keep their distance. He preferred to set his own timetable for the advance.

Mao believed that he could probably take Shanghai without a fight. The city's powerful business class, he told his subordinates, did not really want a battle. Stalin had been coaching Mao to engage with Shanghai's financial elites. That meant, the Soviet leader explained, allowing them to continue to trade with merchants in Hong Kong and "other foreign capitalists." Britain, especially, was "eager to do business with us," Mao agreed. Even the United States, he observed, seemed chastened by Chiang's defeat and now seemed to be moving closer to the possibility of recognizing the Communists diplomatically. Mao told his deputies that they should consider any overtures from the United States, providing the Truman Administration was serious about severing ties with Chiang's regime.

Mao, however, misread American intentions. Truman and Acheson did not want to recognize a Communist-controlled China—at least not yet. On one hand, Acheson, as an experienced diplomat, understood that withholding recognition indefinitely would contravene traditional practice. Except in extreme cases, the United States granted diplomatic recognition to whichever party controlled and administered the territory in question, providing that the ruling power was seen as legitimate by the general populace. Yet Acheson thought it far too early to entertain recognition; his staff pointed out that the Communists had not even officially set up a government yet. The secretary of state feared that offering even de facto recognition would only embolden Mao. In a cable to Stuart in Nanjing, Acheson argued that "we shld strongly oppose hasty recognition Commies either as *de facto* or *de jure* authority by any power." He was determined to convince the British and the other major powers to maintain a "common front" on the question.

Mao also seemed to misunderstand the chaotic nature of American foreign policy making. Even in the age of the imperial presidency,

Truman's secretary of state could not make decisions by diktat. Public opinion ran strongly against recognition; Americans opposed it by a margin of two to one. The bureaucracy, too, was riven by conflicts over the issue. Truman's top officials could not even agree what U.S. national interests were when it came to China. Each of the governmental factions had its own agenda, its own constituency. As 1949 unfolded, these political warriors included diplomats, generals, legislators, columnists—and spies.

★

Although Truman had approved Acheson's largely hands-off China strategy at the N.S.C. meeting back in March, that same policy guidance had also included a final, secret paragraph—a provision that was redacted from the officially published version. Reflecting Truman's belief that the Chinese people would eventually subvert Communist rule, the suppressed passage had instructed U.S. policy makers to rely on "indigenous Chinese elements" in their efforts to undermine Moscow's influence, then added: "Because we bear the incubus of interventionists, our official interest in any support of these elements, a vast and delicate enterprise, should not be apparent and should be implemented through appropriate clandestine channels."

The sentence caught the attention of Frank Wisner, the head of the Office of Policy Coordination (O.P.C.)—the new covert action arm of the postwar American intelligence apparatus. An energetic, patrician Mississippian and former Wall Street lawyer, Wisner had served during the war in the Office of Strategic Services (O.S.S.), the forerunner of the C.I.A., and had taken command of the O.P.C. shortly after the Truman Administration created it in 1948. Now, as Mao threatened to complete his conquest of the mainland, Wisner wanted to know exactly what the N.S.C. had meant by a "vast and delicate enterprise." Did the new strategy merely authorize him to conduct propaganda operations, or did the language empower him to attempt more ambitious covert ops, such as arming renegade generals who were still fighting

Mao? Wisner sent a memo to the State Department, which then over-saw the O.P.C., and asked for clarification.

Acheson's response was vague. For now, the secretary of state's ad-visers told Wisner, the O.P.C. should focus on propaganda alone: leaf-lets, planted newspaper articles, that sort of thing. Still, Acheson's men left open the possibility of a more aggressive effort at some later point. The State Department was not opposed in principle to "large scale clandestine material support," the diplomats explained to Wisner, but for now the conditions were not right: "Both the situation in China and our operations there will have to develop considerably before such possibilities materialize."

In the meantime, Wisner did his best to understand his options, should Truman authorize a more elaborate program of covert aid. On May 9, Wisner stopped by the Hotel Washington to meet with Gen-eral Claire Chennault, the hawkish former commander of the Flying Tigers, the American airmen who had battled Japanese forces in China and Burma during the Second World War. For months, Chennault had been complaining to anyone who would listen that Truman's China policy was too passive. In January the retired general had published a book titled *Way of a Fighter*, which began with the line: "The United States is losing the Pacific War." Walter Judd had loved the book, prais-ing it in the House and wherever else he could find the opportunity.

In Chennault's office at the Washington hotel, the general laid out his plan for Wisner. Chennault did not believe, as some friends of Na-tionalist China did, that it would be possible to easily roll back Mao's existing victories in the coastal cities. On the other hand, he thought that if the United States simply maintained Acheson's wait-and-see policy, Communist revolutions would spread throughout the wider re-gion, setting off a "chain reaction" from Indochina to the Philippines to Japan and exposing the West Coast of the United States to potential attacks from enemy submarines and long-range bombers. Chennault, instead, proposed a middle course: he wanted to freeze Mao in place, halting his advance by arming provincial leaders who could create a "belt of resistance" around the Communist-controlled territories—a "cordon sanitaire" that would separate Mao's China from sympathetic potential allies in Siam, Burma, and other regional governments.

Chennault thought the whole project could be accomplished relatively inexpensively. He had already identified a number of provincial leaders who he thought would make stout allies; many of these were "hardy mountaineers" who commanded mounted cavalry. He was particularly optimistic about the Muslim leaders in China's northwest. Furthermore, the weapons they were asking for were modest—small arms, bazookas, mortars. Chennault pointed out that a great deal of U.S. surplus equipment was still floating around Asia in places like the Philippines and the Pacific Islands. He estimated that the United States could fund the entire operation for between $200 and $350 million per year.

Perhaps the general's biggest hurdle: convincing skeptical American policy makers that the aid would be used wisely. Despite Chiang's growing reputation for mismanagement, Chennault believed that there was no getting around the Generalissimo. As he told one congressional hearing: "There is only one man in China today that can command all of these leaders and that is Chiang Kai-shek." Still, in order to prevent graft, Chennault believed that the aid could be funneled through a network of American advisers. Chennault, undoubtedly, was thinking also of his own bottom line: the retired general now operated a private airline, Civil Air Transport, which would stand to gain from a partnership with the O.P.C. Still, Wisner liked Chennault's plan. He left the meeting determined to pursue it with his superiors.

★

Yet even as Washington's covert operators discussed how to halt Mao's advance, other senior officials wanted to engage the Communist leadership. In Nanjing, U.S. embassy officials reported that the P.L.A. had "greatly relaxed" the restrictions that had been keeping their personnel confined to the compound. Now Stuart wanted to test how pragmatic the city's new administrators would really be. For months he had been lobbying Acheson to allow him to open a line of communication with the Communists—an attempt to establish a "better mutual understanding," as he put it. After so many years building relationships in China, the ambassador thought he was uniquely well positioned for the role: "I should like to approach the Chinese Communists not only as an official representative of the American Government but as one who through long residence here is known to have consistently stood for Chinese national independence and democratic progress as well as for closer American-Chinese relations primarily because of the benefits these would bring to the Chinese people."

Stuart considered it a stroke of good luck when, shortly after the fall of Nanjing, Mao's authorities appointed a young diplomat named Huang Hua as head of the city's new Alien Affairs Bureau. Clever and affable, Huang had once been a student of Stuart's, when the ambassador had run Yanjing University. Stuart and his staff had stayed in touch with Huang over the years. The ambassador, in meetings with Huang during Marshall's mission a few years earlier, had found his former student to be "thoroughly communized" but also "friendly to me personally." Now, with tensions beginning to ease with Nanjing's new rulers, Stuart dispatched his aide Philip Fugh, another former classmate of Huang's at Yanjing, to make contact with Huang, who had established himself in the brick building that once housed the Nationalist foreign ministry.

Huang, at first, responded by saying that it would be "inconvenient" for him to visit Stuart at the ambassador's compound. Still, Huang eventually invited Fugh to visit him at his own office. The two former classmates chatted politely, though cautiously, for an hour. Huang asked about his "old college president" but was obviously wary of referring to Stuart by the more formal title of Ambassador. Fugh raised the issue of the P.L.A.'s treatment of Stuart when the soldiers first arrived in Nanjing, and Huang "obliquely acknowledged it," adding that top Communist officials had been "distressed" by the episode. Stuart reported to Acheson that Huang's attitude toward Fugh had been "most friendly" during their talk. Huang had walked Fugh out to the street after their meeting, Stuart wrote, and had promised that he would call to follow up.

Huang shrewdly kept Mao informed about these early contacts with the Americans and also briefed Soviet diplomats about the talks. Mao responded by authorizing Huang to meet in person with Stuart, but provided Huang with a series of specific guidelines. Mao instructed Huang to refrain from asking for any kind of aid from the Americans. Rather, he explained, his chief goal was to get the United States to cut all ties with Chiang's Nationalists. Mao also saw the meetings as a chance to gather intelligence about American intentions, just as his armies were preparing to close on Shanghai. Huang should "listen more and talk less," taking his cues from the Americans. "If Stuart's attitude is cordial," Mao wrote, "Huang Hua should also be cordial, but not enthusiastic." Still, he should keep his options open. If Stuart wanted to stay in Nanjing as ambassador to negotiate further commercial ties, Mao told Huang that he "should not reject" the proposal.

Stuart and Huang finally met in person on the evening of May 13, at the ambassador's home. Their discussion, which lasted nearly two hours, was "friendly and informal," Stuart later told Acheson. The ambassador had begun by trying to convince Huang of his personal goodwill toward the Chinese people. Stuart told his former pupil that he believed that "much, but not all, present tension [was] due to misunderstandings, fears, [and] suspicions which could be cleared away by mutual frankness." Huang, too, was conciliatory: he told Stuart that the Communists genuinely sought to establish diplomatic relations and commercial ties with the Western powers. The early hiccups, such as the P.L.A.'s entry into Stuart's bedroom, had been unauthorized by Mao. The American ambassador reported home to Acheson that Huang had "promised to do his best in constantly shifting military situation to trace offenders. He explained that first Communist troops in city had not been prepared or properly instructed on treatment of foreigners."

Despite the friendly assurances on both sides, Mao gleaned some useful intelligence from the talks. Stuart revealed to Huang that he had been authorized to remain in Nanjing in the short term but would withdraw to the United States for consultations soon. Stuart also explained that the Marines stationed in Shanghai were there only to protect American citizens, not as an offensive force. (Huang, Stuart told Acheson, had been "obviously impressed" by this remark.) The reason that the United States was withholding recognition, the American ambassador explained, was that Mao had not yet established a formal government. For now, Stuart said, the United States and the other big powers "could do nothing but await developments in China." If Mao was seeking assurances that the United States would not act to stop his conquest of the mainland, Stuart's comments would have given him hope.

★

To court Mao or to confront him? Truman did not really want to do either. David Lilienthal met with the president in early May and found Truman unexpectedly obsessed with the China issue. On one hand, Truman firmly opposed the push from those Republicans in Congress who wanted to arm Chiang's loyalists and attempt to roll back Mao's advances. "Nothing can be done about China until things kind of settle down," Truman told Lilienthal. The president seemed committed to Acheson's wait-and-see approach. "I had a couple tough Republican senators up here the other day and I gave it to them hot and heavy and kind of pulled the rug out from under them," Truman said. "I haven't heard a peep out of them since."

But neither was Truman eager to embrace Mao. The president still considered Mao a usurper and referred to his followers, dismissively, as "so-called Communists." Truman remained convinced that the Chinese people, at some point, would rise up and overthrow the Communist government. "Joe Stalin says that the people of North China will never be Communists, and he's about right," Truman told Lilienthal. "The dragon is going to turn over, and after that, perhaps some advances can be made out of it." The president's dismissive attitude

toward the long-term prospects of the Communists reinforced his caution about recognizing Mao's regime.

Still, Truman felt he had no viable partner in China to lead this
eventual revolt. He complained to Lilienthal that "grafters and crooks"
had siphoned off a great deal of the aid his government had sent to
China. "I'll bet you that a billion dollars of it is in New York banks
today," he said. The president had grown so concerned about the pernicious effects of well-funded lobbyists—like Madame Chiang and
her family—that he had instructed F.B.I. director J. Edgar Hoover
to launch an investigation into Nationalist assets held in the United
States.

Truman was right about one thing: as Mao's forces bore down on
Shanghai, Madame Chiang and her allies had begun intensifying their
efforts to influence the Truman Administration's policy. After a relatively quiet spring, Madame Chiang in May began peppering her husband with telegrams asking for money and guidance. She appeared to
pin her greatest hopes on the intervention of defense secretary Louis
Johnson, who was now beginning to assert himself as a key member of
Truman's cabinet. Madame Chiang told her husband that Johnson was
asking for specific details about exactly which areas Chiang thought he
could prevent from falling into Mao's hands, as well as how much additional weaponry he would need to accomplish that mission. As May
unfolded, she continued to press Chiang for granular detail about the
disposition of the remaining Nationalist forces and their prospects for
success on the battlefield.

At the same time, Madame Chiang urged her husband not to foolishly squander their existing resources. For weeks, she had been urging
Chiang to complete the removal of the Bank of China's assets and staff
from Shanghai. If the Generalissimo did not believe he could successfully defend the city, then he should begin a "safe withdrawal" at an
"early stage." In her telegrams, Madame Chiang did not seem confident that her husband could hold China's coastal center of commerce.
She reminded him that the remaining Nationalists would likely face
crippling food shortages. She also admonished him to avoid letting

Nationalist weapons fall into P.L.A. hands—a development that would sour Americans on future aid shipments.

As the Chiangs struggled to identify the best defensive line, they also scrambled to prevent the Western powers from recognizing the new regime. Madame Chiang passed along the latest rumors about possible contacts between Washington and Beijing. She warned her husband that she had learned of "secret negotiations" being planned by the Truman Administration, which was being spurred on by American and British businessmen. "The situation is tense," she wrote. "Reliable sources" had informed her that the British, especially, were behind the latest push for recognition. She told Chiang that she had made some progress in her efforts to convince friendly members of Congress to resist these overtures. Still, she needed more money and better organization. She urged her husband, once again, to authorize the creation of a "national propaganda institution" to fight back against the doves.

The Generalissimo, meanwhile, continued to battle political rivals at home. With his forces in retreat, Chiang found it extraordinarily difficult to know whom to trust. Every former subordinate officer had the potential to be a coup plotter. During one stop, in the Zhoushan Islands, on May 12, a group of ten Nationalist air force officers showed up at Chiang's door and demanded that he turn over control of Taiwan to the air force. Although Chiang ultimately managed to parry the officers' thrust, he complained to his diary that he felt increasingly vulnerable.

Against the backdrop of such threats, operational security remained of concern to the Chiangs. After dispatching one sensitive telegram that included information about her contacts with members of Congress, Madame Chiang told the Generalissimo that she would destroy their code book. Chiang appeared frustrated by the continuing habit of his wife—whom he referred to in the cables as Younger Sister—of sending sensitive details by telegram. "On the issue of the propaganda work and the names of congressmen," he wrote, "younger sister should not send them via telegram and should know well that the secret codes are very easily stolen and translated."

Nevertheless, the Chiangs and their allies did seem to be having some success pushing China toward the top of Truman's agenda. The issue now dominated the president's cabinet meetings. Vice President Barkley, at one session in mid-May, asked for more details on Chennault's plan. Acheson dismissed the general and his rescue plan as "misguided," adding tartly that he thought Chennault was "a better soldier than politician." The secretary of state complained further that Chennault was too close to the "reigning families" in the Nationalist government. Still, Truman's top advisers increasingly found themselves tangling over the issue.

In fact, the newspaper columnist Joseph Alsop wrote in late May, Truman's approach to China had reached "a great turning point." Alsop credited Johnson with pushing the cabinet toward more aggressive action. "For four long, sorry years," Alsop wrote, "American policy in the Far East has floated, to put it plainly, like a chip of driftwood on a sluggish open sewer." Now, however, the new defense secretary was demanding a "positive definition of our Far Eastern interests and program." Alsop did not think Johnson, Chennault, and the other hawks would ultimately convince Truman to make a stand on mainland China itself. Still, Alsop was hearing from his sources that the president was now determined to fight back against the spread of Communism in East Asia. Somewhere, the columnist wrote, "a line will be drawn."

NEVERLAND

An overseas voyage was still something of an event in 1949, even for the nation's chief diplomat. On May 20, as Dean Acheson prepared to depart for a meeting of the Council of Foreign Ministers in Paris, President Truman and other key dignitaries showed up at National Airport to see him off. Against the backdrop of the airfield's boxy terminal, the British ambassador, Oliver Franks, pressed forward and gallantly handed Mrs. Acheson a bouquet of roses. Truman, in a double-breasted suit with peaked lapels and a pocket handkerchief, hovered nearby, sunlight glinting off his eyeglasses, holding a white fedora in one hand. As Acheson made his way toward the ramp to board the blue and silver aircraft, the president reached out, gripped his hand, and melodramatically intoned for the cameras, "Goodbye, Dean."

The major powers had called this meeting of the foreign ministers primarily to discuss Europe, not Asia. Acheson hoped to make progress toward an accommodation with the Soviets over the future of Germany. For more than a year, Washington and Moscow had been battling over Berlin, which remained divided in the aftermath of the Second World War. After the Allies began consolidating their zones of occupation, the Soviets had blockaded West Berlin, isolating the city. The United States countered by airlifting in food and supplies—a dramatic and successful response. The Soviets had finally lifted the blockade just days before Acheson took off for Paris.

Acheson had gone out of his way to assure his diplomatic counterparts that China and the wider region were not expected to be on this meeting's agenda. Still, he knew that anything could happen at these high-level conclaves. As British foreign secretary Bevin commented as he made his way to Paris: "It's all in the lap of the gods."

Increasingly, however, Acheson was unwilling to leave important decisions to fate. Even before the Paris summit, his China policy had begun to evolve. Although the bones of his position remained the same—he opposed ambitious schemes to reverse Mao's conquests—he worried about his policy's effect on public opinion. Acheson's foes were successfully painting him as a passive weakling. Whatever the virtues of prudence, the American secretary of state could not afford to be seen as a do-nothing. Foreign statesmen were watching, judging him by his action or inaction. In this sense, at least, Acheson agreed with Johnson that the Truman Administration needed to articulate some sort of "positive" policy.

Acheson began by resurrecting an old idea of Kennan's. The State Department's director of policy planning had long complained of what he called the "confusion and bewilderment in the public mind regarding our China policy." For years, both Truman and Acheson had believed that voicing any criticism of Chiang's regime would undermine American interests. Kennan, on the other hand, argued that it was time to publicly denounce Chiang: "It is now less important to cover up the inadequacies of the Chinese government than it is to regain the understanding confidence of the American public." Kennan wanted the State Department to prepare and publicize a dossier laying out the historical background to the current impasse.

Acheson seized on the plan, ordering his deputies to prepare a document that would come to be known as the China White Paper. The secretary of state's staff wrestled for months with what to include and what to omit. Any such report would risk making Acheson new political enemies, since it would necessarily include once-classified diplomatic dispatches and other sensitive materials. Still, the secretary of state saw the compilation of the White Paper as a critical step toward recalibrating American opinion.

One of Acheson's central dilemmas, as his staff crafted the paper, was whether to include General Wedemeyer's 1947 report, the document that Marshall had once suppressed. Although the Wedemeyer report bolstered Acheson's case that Chiang's forces were disorganized and his leadership flawed, it had also urged Truman to commit more resources to China—a recommendation that the president had rejected. Now, over the course of the spring, Truman and Acheson debated once again whether to include Wedemeyer's analysis. Although Truman maintained that he still did not want to pull "the rug out from under" the Nationalist government, the president ultimately agreed to include the document, as long as it was presented in context.

Truman and Acheson nevertheless stopped short of endorsing some of the more radical potential fixes to the China quandary. Ever since the NATO signing, some regional actors had been urging Truman to back a Pacific Pact as a complement to the Atlantic alliance. Although the notion had some support in the West—Churchill, for instance, was for it—Acheson considered the whole idea "quite unsound." Acheson argued that the circumstances in Europe were completely different from those in Asia. In Europe the alliance had grown organically, over years. In East Asia, however, the United States lacked that same "solid foundation" on which to build. Acheson believed that the Asian nations would need to resolve their own "internal conflicts" before the United States might consider a formal alliance.

By the time Acheson touched down in Paris, the newspapers were full of speculation about China. Reporters hashed through the arguments for a Pacific Pact and pondered the wisdom of diplomatic recognition. On May 23, Acheson and the other foreign ministers arrived at the Palais Rose, the pink marble mansion loaned to the envoys for the conference by the Duchesse de Talleyrand. Acheson and Bevin circulated among the delegates, past green-baize-covered tables and beneath crystal chandeliers. Corinthian columns—"the color of an acute sunburn," according the *New York Times*—adorned the palace walls. On the ceiling, frescoes of satyrs chasing nymphs amused the diplomats. Although Acheson was determined to discuss Germany, the Soviet foreign minister, Andrei Vishinsky, almost immediately brought up Asia. "The Far Eastern problem," one newspaper correspondent observed, "is the uninvited guest at the table where the future of Germany is to be discussed."

There were other distractions, too. The day after Acheson arrived in Paris, he learned that former defense secretary James Forrestal had committed suicide by jumping to his death from the window of the Bethesda, Maryland, hospital where he was being treated for mental illness. Forrestal, who had never really recovered after being ousted from his position in favor of Johnson, had copied out a poem from Sophocles, walked out of his room to a small kitchen nearby, and then thrown himself out the window, falling thirteen stories to his death. Truman announced that he was "shocked and grieved" by the news, adding that he considered Forrestal "as truly a casualty of the war as if he had died on the firing line."

Yet it was the fate of Shanghai that really shifted the spotlight at Paris. In the days leading up to the conference, reports arrived daily of P.L.A. units inching closer to China's financial capital. Shells fell in the city's western neighborhoods and threatened the supplies of British and American oil companies along the waterfront. As the Paris forum opened, the Communists still seemed hesitant about forcing a crisis by pushing all the way into the city center. But on May 25, Mao's forces finally began their invasion. The headline splashed across three columns on the front page of the *New York Times* read: RED TROOPS ENTER SHANGHAI.

★

In Chinese, the name Shanghai means "above the sea"—a description only barely true of a city that sits on mud flats just a few feet higher than the waterline. Situated at the mouth of the Yangtze River, along the central coast of China, the city had served as a trade entrepôt for the past century. After the Opium Wars of the mid–nineteenth century, when the European powers demanded major concessions in the city, foreign capital flowed into Shanghai, fueling a building boom. British merchants hired coolies to drive piles into the mud, covering the flats with Western-style architecture. An eclectic array of foreign-owned mansions sprouted in the French Concession, along the city's western fringe. Hulking neoclassical bank buildings with imposing sandstone facades filled the Bund, Shanghai's waterfront promenade.

As in other Chinese cities, the foreigners in Shanghai developed an insular culture. Edgar Snow once described the Westerners living in Beijing as inhabiting "their own little never-never land of whisky-and-soda, polo, tennis, and gossip, happily quite unaware of the pulse of humanity outside the great city's silent, insulating walls." In Shanghai, that neverland slowly spread across wide sections of the city. Well-fed Western businessmen, known as *taipans* ("big managers") to the locals, drank pink gins at the Long Bar of the Shanghai Club on the Bund, and honed their lawn bowls skills at the International Sporting Club. After the Russian Revolution, White Russian refugees filled the city, some of them working in cabarets and bordellos. Gangs and secret societies flourished. Thousands of taxi dancers worked the nightclubs, selling companionship and often sex. By the outbreak of the Chinese civil war, observed one foreign ambassador, Shanghai had become "probably the most un-Christian city in the world."

As the P.L.A. approached, in May 1949, Nationalist soldiers had transformed the freewheeling city into a fortress. Troops in steel helmets and carrying tommy guns built concrete pillboxes, strung barbed wire, and erected cheveaux-de-frise with bamboo spikes at once-busy intersections. Snipers set up machine gun nests on the roofs of strategically located buildings. Commanders ordered the once-popular golf course cleared of trees and turned the space into a rifle range. American-made B-24 and B-25 bombers rumbled overhead, controlling the airspace. Shanghai's leaders declared the city under curfew, emptying the once-thronged neon-lit thoroughfares after dark of their bustling bicycle and pedicab traffic.

In the days leading up to the Communist takeover, the Nationalist government did its best to cleanse the city of internal enemies. Police staged public executions as warnings to would-be subversives. City authorities transformed the courtyard of the Central Police Headquarters into a "Roman arena," as one witness described it. Guards dragged the alleged perpetrators to the center of the enclosure, then brought them a final meal—a bowl of noodles and a glass of wine. A crowd of curious onlookers spilled from the windows and balconies of the adjacent buildings. Police then packed the prisoners into a black van, which sped, sirens wailing, to the killing ground. After ordering the men to kneel, the executioner shot them in the head.

The Nationalist authorities paired this public brutality with public celebration. Local leaders held sham "victory parades," draping Shanghai's buildings with patriotic bunting and drawing tens of thousands of residents into the streets. Flying Fortresses flew in formation overhead, while other planes dropped leaflets urging the defense of the city. Military vehicles rolled down the city's broad boulevards, alongside police cars fitted with loudspeakers. Bands played martial anthems like "Marching Through Georgia" and "Britannia Rules the Waves." By late May, however, the streets had largely emptied. As the *North-China Daily News* described it, the Bund "looked as though a tornado had swept through it, dispersing its human population to the four winds."

Now, for the residents of Shanghai, the nighttime clashes between the P.L.A. and the Nationalists provided their own ominous spectacle. Locals climbed to the roofs of the city's tallest buildings to watch the light show. Tracer bullets streaked in bright arcs through the night, and shells burst overhead, heralding the approaching Communist armies. Fires dotted the landscape across the river in Pudong. "The whole sky glowed," reported one photojournalist, who made his way repeatedly to the roofs of Shanghai's skyscrapers to observe the firefights as the P.L.A. drew nearer. He added:

> Star shells and Verey lights dropped by planes cast shimmering patches of eerie light on the soggy skies. Rain clouds muffled the bark of the big guns, although their shells exploded less than five miles from the heart of the city. Planes droned overhead, followed by the dull whoomp-whoomp of bombs dropped aimlessly in the drizzly darkness. . . . Burning villages ringed the city like the campfires of a besieging horde of Gargantuans. . . . Periodically, bright flames billowed up as a fresh cluster of peasant huts caught fire. The dried straw of their thatched roofs threw off sparks like a display of fireworks.

On May 24, thousands of Nationalist troops began descending on the Bund, preparing to make a last stand—or in some cases, a clean escape. "They proceeded on foot, in trucks, handcarts, pedicabs, rickshaws, carrying their belongings. Some hauled artillery while others led mules and horses," a Shanghai newspaper reported. The defending forces did their best to fortify the enemy's routes of approach. The Nationalists sank four tankers in the Huangpu, hoping to slow the P.L.A.'s advance from Pudong. In the west, the soldiers detonated large explosions that destroyed key bridges. In a hopeless attempt to enforce party discipline, Nationalist propagandists hung banners that read: FOR EVERY HOUSE THAT HIDES ONE COMMUNIST, TEN HOUSES WILL BE PUNISHED. Around sunset, long convoys of Nationalist military vehicles pulled up in front of city hall and at the police headquarters. Mariano Ezpeleta, the Philippine envoy in Shanghai, recalled looking on as the soldiers hoisted hundreds of boxes and steel cabinets into the trucks, before hauling them away.

For weeks, the weather in Shanghai had been damp and gloomy. But on the morning of May 25, the skies cleared. Under the bright sunshine, columns of Communist troops began marching east along

Avenue Joffre, one of the French Concession's main thoroughfares. Wearing their standard olive green uniforms and sneakers, Mao's forces appeared "plainly tired," according to one witness. Still, they were also orderly and well behaved, especially in contrast to the retreating Nationalists. As the Communist soldiers closed on the city center, marching on the sidewalks and sending scouts down the byways, shop boys scrubbed the walls just ahead of them of Nationalist slogans. White flags replaced the Nationalist pennants—until the red banners of the Communists supplanted them both.

To Ezpeleta, the arriving Communist troops seemed to consist primarily of "teenagers in the first blush of youth, slightly built boys still awkward in gait." Their green uniforms were made of the "coarsest cotton, tailored with manifest disdain as to size or length, dangling around their still young and unformed bodies." They seemed poorly equipped—"no helmets . . . no medals, or decorations, or service ribbons"—and appeared almost timid as they gawked at the city's imposing architecture. When Shanghailanders approached the conquering troops and bowed in deference, the soldiers looked "mortified," Ezpeleta recalled. "They returned the bows apologetically, almost obsequiously."

Although the Nationalist military put up little resistance, it did try to delay the P.L.A. at the Bund, stationing troops near the Garden Bridge, which crosses Suzhou Creek, and atop the Broadway Mansions, a large Art Deco–style brick building just across the water—a maneuver designed to give the rest of the fleeing Nationalists time to escape. A remaining few defenders had dug in at a park across the street from the British Consulate. One journalist, Harrison Forman, watched through binoculars as a column of Communist troops marched up Nanjing Road, one of Shanghai's main thoroughfares, then turned the corner onto the Bund, running into a Nationalist ambush. A P.L.A. man shouted, "Come out. Don't be afraid. The People's Liberation Army will not harm you." But then "a blast from a heavy machine gun fired at point blank range sliced him in two," recalled Forman. "His companion stared at the corpse, then at the blood streaming from a wound in his head. He started running back down the Bund. Bullets whipped all around."

The Communist forces slowly pressed toward the Nationalist redoubts, taking the abandoned pillboxes one by one. Still, the defenders were well armed, outgunning the P.L.A. with heavy weapons. "Bullets cracked past the consulate windows, chipped concrete from pavements, and slammed into the low brick wall surrounding the Public Gardens," Forman recalled. Nationalist gunfire sprayed out from a stone ticket booth and from under a bandstand. The Communists lobbed mortars in the direction of the Nationalist guns; the Nationalists responded by using flamethrowers to maintain a buffer between themselves and the advancing columns.

By nightfall, the Nationalist leaders had largely retreated. As they left, they detonated a massive store of aviation fuel at their airfield north of the city. "The whole sky lit up with bright orange flames that leaped hundreds of feet into the air," Forman recalled. "They billowed and blossomed with long tongues shooting off in all directions."

Nevertheless, the following day sporadic fighting continued along the Bund. At the nearby American consulate, John Cabot, the U.S. envoy, tried to protect himself and his staff from the fighting. On May 26, he told his diary: "Firing starts again beneath my window. I have moved my bed into the living room for safety. By breakfast the going is getting a bit rough—a number of grenades explode in front of us. Commies try to bring up mortars but driven back. One member of the staff hit by flying glass when bullet entered kitchen." But the Nationalist resistance was swiftly waning. By the morning of May 27, the fighting was largely over and the conquest of Shanghai complete.

As they spread out across the city, Mao's forces worked to commandeer key symbols of the former regime. At the twenty-room former residence of Madame Chiang's brother, T. V. Soong, Communist organizers hung a red star on the front gate and used the building as the headquarters for their youth league. Inside, volunteers made new armbands to be worn by the traffic police. As the Soong family's former servants hovered nearby, girls arranged bouquets of carnations for the newly arrived soldiers.

Although the P.L.A. continued to enforce the Nationalist curfew, activity quickly returned to Shanghai's streets—albeit with a slightly altered character. Money changers traded silver dollars for worthless gold yuan notes at exorbitant rates. Other merchants sold "canned goods, candies, biscuits, cigarettes, and flowers," according to one newspaper report. The New China Bookstore ordered fresh printings of Mao's most famous tracts. Communist authorities debated whether to change the names of streets that they considered "semi-colonial and feudalistic in nature or which were adopted for pleasing the foreigners." Among the soon-to-be-renamed routes: Wedemeyer Road, which had honored the American general.

For the most part, the American expat community in Shanghai survived unscarred. Cabot announced that none of the seven hundred and fifty U.S. citizens remaining in the city had been harmed. Yet the fall of Shanghai did trigger a readjustment of the American military posture. Although Truman had made the decision back in December to withdraw U.S. forces from their foothold in Qingdao, some troops had remained behind at the request of the Nationalist government. Now, fearing a military confrontation with Mao's advancing armies, American officials decided to pull them out for good. As the P.L.A. marched into Shanghai, the remaining U.S. ships finally steamed away from Qingdao.

As they had done all year, the Americans and the Chinese misunderstood each other's intentions. Mao, determined to consolidate his gains, had no desire to start a war with the Americans. In fact, in the days following the fall of Shanghai—even as the U.S. troops were retreating—Mao remained as concerned as he had ever been about the prospect of Western intervention. On May 28, he cabled his commanders that there were "some signs recently that imperialist countries are preparing for a joint intervention." He cited talks between the United States, Britain, France, and "ten other countries on coordinating their policies toward China" as evidence of American and European collusion. He noted that Britain had recently bolstered its forces in Hong Kong, and he referred to reports that some Nationalist units seemed to be in oddly good spirits. Mao worried that the departure of foreign diplomats from Nanjing might also herald a Western invasion. With these concerns in mind, the Chairman enigmatically ordered his deputies to "make due preparations" to repel an American counterattack.

13

HEAT

On the morning when Mao warned his aides of an impending American attack, President Truman climbed aboard his
personal yacht, the *U.S.S. Williamsburg*, and steamed down
the Potomac River. The *Williamsburg*, with its oval smokestack and
imposing steel hull, was Truman's refuge in Washington. On deck,
he liked to plink at the keys of the upright pianos that were scattered
throughout the vessel, and he spent long hours playing cards with his
aides at a custom-designed poker table. Although the *Williamsburg* was
technically a commissioned ship, aboard which alcohol was forbidden, the commander kept it well stocked with "all kinds of whisky," he
recalled, particularly the president's favorite, Old Grand-Dad. If the
weather was warm, Truman would jump off the side of the boat, still
wearing his glasses, and paddle away in his own peculiar stroke, head
always above the water.

For Truman, the fall of Shanghai, cementing Mao's hold on China's
coast, represented without doubt the worst foreign policy defeat of his
presidency. He could not resist playing the age-old capital blame game,
griping to his aides about the scoundrels in Congress. Still, he tried to
remain upbeat—and largely succeeded. The conversation around the

poker and dinner tables aboard the *Williamsburg* that Memorial Day weekend was as much lighthearted banter as it was weighty politics. The weather, too, was flawless. Sunday, recalled one Truman aide who spent the weekend with the president, was "a perfect day, clear, sunny, and comfortably cool but not chilly." The sun and the whisky must have taken some of the sting out of the nettlesome crisis on the other side of the globe.

Moreover, when Truman returned to his office the following week, he finally got some good news from the Middle Kingdom. According to the U.S. consul in Beijing, one of Mao's top lieutenants, Zhou Enlai, had secretly made contact with the consulate through an assistant military attaché. Zhou's message, if authentic, was stunning: he told the Americans that Mao's deputies were deeply divided by "disagreements of [a] serious nature," primarily over economic and foreign policy. Although the party had not yet actually split, its "liberal" and "radical" factions were increasingly at odds. Some in Mao's inner circle believed that they should ally themselves squarely with Moscow, but others feared that Stalin's government lacked the financial resources to fund the kind of massive reconstruction projects that postwar China would require. Zhou, according to the dispatch, considered himself one of the liberals, and favored establishing "*de facto* working relations" with the United States and Britain. Otherwise, he warned, China faced the prospect of "complete economic and physical collapse." According to the memo, Zhou had appeared "very nervous and worried" as he conveyed his message.

Truman's diplomats took the overture, which came to be known as the Zhou démarche, very seriously. Stuart, in Nanjing, wrote in his diary that the message represented an "extremely hopeful line of effort." The memo's suggestion that the United States and China shared deep mutual interests was the kind of sentiment Stuart might have written himself. Yet if the document's encouraging message contributed to Truman's sanguine outlook, Chinese officials later insisted that it had been designed to—a clever bit of misdirection from Mao's camp, intended to avert an American invasion. Scholars have never been able to corroborate the Zhou démarche with records in the Chinese archives, and they note that such a bold move would have been out of character for the loyal Zhou. More than forty years later, former Chinese officials continued to dismiss the alleged proposition as a fraud. Huang Hua, in his old age, complained to the Stanford historian Gordon H. Chang that any such talk of a rift in the upper echelons of the party was "nonsense."

But it was a story that Truman wanted to believe. His entire hands-off approach to China had been crafted to exploit just this type of rift. For weeks, the president had been telling acquaintances that he thought the Chinese would eventually rise up and drive out the Communists, even if it took decades. His outlook was rooted in a conviction—a strongly held hope, really—that Chinese political values were fundamentally similar to those of his fellow Americans. Even as experience slowly whittled away at this ideal, Truman never gave it up completely.

In the narrative that Truman told himself, it was only the machinations of venal outsiders that corrupted this utopia. If his own conscience was pure and most ordinary Chinese were people of goodwill, as he believed, then the trouble must lie elsewhere—with Mao, to be sure, but also with Mao's opponents in the Chiang family inner circle. On the same day the Zhou démarche arrived in Washington, a staff member from Truman's N.S.C. apprised the president of another memo, this one written in reply to Truman's order that the F.B.I. investigate Nationalist assets in the United States. The bureau reported that the Bank of Canton and the Bank of China, in which the "Soong-Kung group" was thought to hold major stakes, had a net worth of nearly $73 million ($740 million in today's dollars). The F.B.I. could identify only one outside account, with deposits of $30,000, in the name of Madame Chiang. Even so, the investigators speculated that the bulk of her family's wealth rested in Chinese-controlled accounts or difficult-to-track safe-deposit boxes.

Despite the inconclusive F.B.I. file, Truman and his aides could not ignore the sense that something had changed in the Chiang camp. At the very nadir of the Generalissimo's fortunes, his allies seemed to finally vault into action. Loyal columnists pushed back against talk of recognition and began speculating again about a Chiang-led Pacific Pact. Congressmen like Judd openly touted the aid program that Chennault was trying to sell to the C.I.A. The catalyst for all this energetic opposition remained, at the time, somewhat unclear. Still, the open hostility was becoming a problem. As June unfolded, Acheson later recalled, the Truman Administration began to feel "some real signs of heat."

★

On June 6, under the glare of the late-spring sunshine, five hundred picketers paraded in circles around Manhattan's Foley Square, hoisting placards and chanting, "Join the Communist Party. Fight for peace." Inside a nearby courthouse, one of the most sensational spy trials of the twentieth century was unfolding. Although the commotion outside was neither violent nor particularly disruptive, it was the sort of spectacle that inspired outsize fears. Americans, in mid-1949, had grown nearly obsessed with allegations of Communist subversion. According to one analysis of New York newspaper coverage, thirty-two percent of all front-page space in that first week of June was allotted to stories about "the 'spy' theme or matters closely related to it."

America was not yet in the grip of the hysterical McCarthyism of the early 1950s. Still, popular concerns about Communist infiltration had been slowly building for more than a decade. In 1938, Congress had established the House Un-American Activities Committee, or HUAC, to investigate allegations of disloyalty and subversion. By the late 1940s, the committee had launched a series of high-profile inquiries targeting Hollywood screenwriters and other influential cultural figures. Truman, for his part, recognized that apprehensions about Communist spying posed a growing political threat. At one point, he had issued an executive order creating his own loyalty program for federal employees—an effort to outflank his critics. But by the 1948 presidential campaign, he understood that HUAC was out of control. In a speech that was broadcast across the country, he warned that the committee's "wild and false accusations" had "injured the reputations of innocent men."

The particular case that had drawn Truman's attention was that of Alger Hiss, a former State Department aide accused of spying for the Soviet Union. Now, as the protesters marched in Foley Square, Hiss was getting his day in court. In a chamber on the thirteenth floor of the courthouse, the tall, slender Hiss "sat quietly against the back rail of the court, dressed in a tan suit, looking somewhat younger than his forty-four years," as one reporter described the scene. Hiss listened as his lawyer cross-examined Whittaker Chambers, a former *Time* magazine editor, who had told investigators the previous year that he and Hiss had collaborated in the theft of sensitive government documents detailing American weapons systems. Chambers had admitted under oath to passing the documents to a Soviet operative. Hiss, however, had denied Chambers's claim, insisting that he had not seen Chambers since 1937. Although the statute of limitations on espionage had expired, the grand jury had indicted Hiss for perjury.

The Hiss trial presented a serious political problem for Acheson. During the Second World War, Acheson and Hiss had worked together in the State Department, and they were neighbors in Georgetown. The secretary of state's foes quickly linked the two men; Madame Chiang mentioned the Hiss connection in a telegram to her husband. Acheson protested that his acquaintance with Hiss had been overblown. When Acheson's detractors whispered that his law firm had once employed Hiss, the secretary of state was forced to correct them, pointing out that it was Alger's brother, Donald, who had actually worked for the firm. Nevertheless, Acheson acknowledged that he remained friends with Alger, boldly (but perhaps foolishly) professing that "my friendship is not easily given, and it is not easily withdrawn."

Acheson's personal troubles were compounded by a broader social trend: Americans were beginning to fear their own government almost as much as they dreaded Communist infiltration. Just days after the Hiss trial began, a British writer named Eric Blair—better known by his pen name, George Orwell—published his chilling dystopian novel *Nineteen Eighty-Four*, which described a world in which all individuality had been suppressed by an omnipotent government led by a sinister figurehead, Big Brother. Although the book could be read as a critique of Communist or fascist totalitarianism, many readers in the United States saw their own increasingly powerful government reflected in Orwell's futuristic vision. Americans were still uncertain about the implications of new technologies like the atom bomb and the television. Would they lead to government coercion? Brainwashing? Orwell's publisher was confident that the story would resonate with anxious and disoriented postwar readers. "If we can't sell fifteen to twenty thousand copies, we ought to be shot," one publishing executive wrote. The book ultimately sold in the millions.

Jitters about both high-handed government control and stealthy Communist subversion combined to energize Acheson's most determined foes. The secretary of state's enemies insinuated that he and his staff were actually radical leftists determined to undermine American national interests. This conspiratorial attitude is partly what attracted so much interest in the Hiss trial. During the Second World War, Hiss had served as an aide to F.D.R. at the Yalta Conference, which played an outsize role in the imaginations of Chiang's supporters. At Yalta, the ailing Roosevelt had granted the Soviets concessions in Manchuria in exchange for support against the Japanese—a secret deal that had incensed Chiang and the China bloc. In reality, the Generalissimo had brokered his own treaty with the Soviets in which he had made similar compromises. But Chiang knew an opportunity when he saw one. The growing American unease over Communist spying and treasonous plots provided Chiang with a convenient political asset, just as he prepared to reassert himself on the world stage.

★

At five p.m. on Sunday, June 12, a man appeared at the door of the Tudor mansion in Riverdale where Madame Chiang was staying. Although Wellington Koo was a professional diplomat, his jagged grin and slicked hair lent him the air of an obsequious schoolboy. Technically, Madame Chiang and her caller were on the same side in the battles of 1949; Koo served as the Generalissimo's ambassador in Washington. Actually, however, Koo and Madame Chiang were just as often rivals, jockeying passive-aggressively for control of the Nationalist operation. Madame Chiang liked to keep Koo guessing about her contacts with American officials, and Koo, for his part, made a practice of bad-mouthing the former Chinese first lady behind her back.

Today, however, Madame Chiang seemed determined to make amends. She questioned Koo about the field of play in Washington, and he briefed her on his mission's latest efforts. The envoy acknowledged that the Nationalists' past attempts at shaping public opinion had sometimes been clumsy. But he protested that it was not his fault. To make a difference, he told Madame Chiang, the Nationalists needed "an incessant supply of facts and figures as our ammunition," a "centralized organization," and the cash necessary to get the job done. Koo lamented that there was "no coordination, either at home or abroad." He recommended modeling a reinvigorated Nationalist lobbying organization on the effective and efficient British operation.

For once, Madame Chiang agreed with Koo. In fact, she had been urging Chiang to do the same. Until recently, however, the Generalissimo had wanted to maintain a low profile. Chiang's views only really began to evolve after the fall of Shanghai. Now, as mainland China was slipping from his control, he once again sought a leadership role. This time, however, he looked outward, toward greater East Asia. Chiang told his wife that she should go ahead and float the suggestion of a regional pact of the Pacific powers—with himself, of course, atop of the chain of command in China.

To accomplish this, Madame Chiang believed that both she and her husband would need to begin speaking out. After six months of

silence, she hinted to friends that she might make another address before Congress, as she had done in 1943. She told her husband about her
meeting with Koo and arranged for a journalist from a major American newspaper chain to travel to Taipei, where the Generalissimo was
now spending time. She even sent Chiang a list of potential questions
and answers. The Generalissimo, despite his desire to engage anew in
public affairs, protested that he was not yet ready to do a formal interview. But his wife continued to press. She forwarded him a draft of a
speech that she had written for him, admonishing him not to revise the
manuscript too much.

Madame Chiang wanted to go even further. It would not be enough
to simply spin the news; they needed to shape it. She urged her husband
to use his remaining resources to sabotage Mao's efforts at reconstruction, making life as miserable as possible in the Communist-controlled
cities. The Nationalists, she said, should cut the radiophone lines that
linked Shanghai and the United States. She also relayed the suggestion
of one politician who advocated infiltrating agents onto the mainland
to secretly harass the remaining foreigners, an effort to stoke Western
anger toward Mao. The Nationalist air force, she argued, should bomb
the airports, isolating the city. She even proposed that the Nationalists
research how to print and circulate phony banknotes to prevent Mao's
new government from stabilizing its finances.

Koo, meanwhile, returned to Washington, newly determined to
make the Nationalist case. Shortly after noon on June 15, he visited
the Pentagon office of Louis Johnson, the man Madame Chiang considered her "good friend" in the president's cabinet. The Chinese ambassador warned Johnson that "the whole situation remained critical"
on the mainland. But he also argued that hundreds of thousands of
Chinese troops continued to resist Mao's advances in China's western and southern provinces. He ticked off a list of local commanders
who were still determined to fight—largely the same men identified by
Chennault. The Chinese ambassador told Johnson that the Nationalist
leadership was making a serious effort to unite these disparate factions,
forging a "united front" to oppose Mao.

With new leadership in the Pentagon, Koo also revisited some of the policies Madame Chiang had tried—and failed—to win support for earlier in the year. He suggested that the United States send several officers to lead a survey of the Nationalist military's position on the mainland. Johnson, Koo later recorded in his memorandum of their conversation, "appeared to be interested" in this proposal and told his secretary to take notes. On the other hand, when Koo requested a loan of silver, Johnson demurred. The defense secretary replied that "money had run out," according to Koo's notes. Still, Koo did his best to flatter Johnson, praising him for being a "great friend" of China. Johnson assured Koo that he had "not lost interest" in the Middle Kingdom's fate and promised to raise it with Truman.

★

On June 16, dozens of news correspondents carrying pens and reporter's notebooks gathered around Truman's desk at the White House, for the president's weekly press conference. Acheson always feared for Truman at these encounters. He considered the freewheeling sessions a "constant menace" to the president—and the president a menace to himself. Truman's mind, Acheson liked to say, was "not so quick as his tongue." The president sometimes jumped to offer answers before the reporters had finished asking their questions. "Not seeing where he was being led, he fell into traps," Acheson recalled. Now, for twenty minutes, the journalists hounded the president about the scorching political climate inspired by Mao's victories and the domestic spy trials.

"Mr. President," asked one reporter, "an awful lot of fine people are being branded as Communists, Reds, subversives and what not these days at any number of trials, hearings . . . and things of that sort. Do you have any word of counsel you could give on this rash of branding people?"

"Yes, yes," Truman said. "The reporters should read the history of the Alien and Sedition Acts in the 1790s, under almost exactly the same situation. They would be surprised at how parallel the cases are when they had read how they came out."

"Mr. President, regarding the alien and sedition laws, how can we apply their lesson to the problem of today?"

"Just continue to read your history through the Jefferson Administration and you will find out that the hysteria subsided and that the country did not go to hell at all, and it isn't going to now."

For Truman, things might not have been going completely to hell—but they were getting warm. The same day, a C.I.A. report cautioned that "the U.S. cannot reverse or significantly check [the] course of events" in China. Chiang's forces, the agency warned, had now "ceased to be an organized, cohesive, and centrally directed military machine." The Generalissimo's renewed assertiveness was only compounding the problem. "Although Chiang retired as President without resigning," the report continued, "he has continued to control armies, military and financial resources, the secret police, the party agencies, and many leading officials." Chiang was now pouring money and men into Taiwan and continuing to hamstring any rivals.

According to the C.I.A. analysis, what Mao wanted most from the United States was diplomatic recognition—a conclusion that the Zhou démarche seemed to reinforce. Yet Truman, penned in by the domestic red-baiting and fiercely anti-Communist at his core, urged his aides to take things slowly. When a State Department official came by Truman's office that day to ask the president to approve a response to the Zhou démarche, Truman admonished the adviser "to be most careful not to indicate any softening toward the Communists but to insist on judging their intentions by their actions." The department's reply ultimately stressed that the United States sought to "maintain friendly relations with China and continue social, economic, and polit[ical] relations with that country." But it also warned that "friendly sentiments" would need to be "translated into deeds."

On the surface, at least, Mao's deeds continued to baffle—and trouble—Truman. On June 19, the Communist news agency published a broadside announcing that it had uncovered an American spy ring led by the U.S. consul in Shenyang, Angus Ward. Truman had been aware of the simmering crisis for months: after Mao's troops had captured Shenyang, one of Manchuria's major cities, late the previous year, they had quickly confined the U.S. consulate staff there to house arrest, cutting all communications. Still, this was the first time Mao's media had publicly denounced the staff as spies.

The article asserted that the U.S. Army Liaison Group, which had been operating out of Shenyang, was really a cover name for a secret unit known as External Survey Detachment 44. It accused the American unit of hiring Japanese and Mongolian agents to erect a clandestine wireless radio station. According to the report, the conspirators had been caught with "six American-made transmitting and receiving radio sets of fifteen watts, three generators, sixteen code books of American espionage service, ten gold ingots for espionage expenses," and other supplies. The goal of the operation, according to the Chinese-language version of the article, was the "destruction of [the] Chinese people's revolutionary enterprise."

There was almost certainly some truth to the report. The Truman Administration had secretly acknowledged a spying operation back in March: the "vast and delicate enterprise" referred to in the C.I.A. documents. Recently declassified intelligence reports confirm that the United States ran a number of operatives on the mainland over the course of 1949 and indeed would have been guilty of malpractice if it had not maintained listening posts in the major coastal cities. Roy Rowan, an American journalist for *Life* magazine, who visited the Shenyang consulate just before the Communist takeover, recalls watching a soldier hacking a shortwave radio to pieces with an ax in the building's courtyard. Still, recent Chinese scholarship has suggested that Mao's officials might have exaggerated the scope of the spying operation, perhaps under pressure from Moscow, which did not wish to encourage an American-Chinese rapprochement. Whatever the truth, Mao's decision to publicly raise tensions, just as Stuart and others were exploring new diplomatic channels, puzzled Truman's aides.

★

After more than a month in Paris, with little to show for it, Acheson flew home on the evening of June 20. "By midnight," he later recalled, "the lights of Paris and then London disappeared behind us as the *Independence* gained altitude on her northerly course back to Washington." In the cabin above the Atlantic, Acheson worked through the China quandary. Ultimately, he had made little progress at Paris with Vishinsky and the Soviets in resolving the fraught question of Berlin. Furthermore, Vishinsky had tried to press his advantage in East Asia, asking the delegates to consider a formal peace treaty with Japan, which would end the American occupation. Since China had been a party to the original armistice agreement, Vishinsky implied, it should also participate in any new talks. The trouble, as far as Acheson was concerned, was that with Mao now in control of much of the Middle Kingdom, the Soviets would hold far more leverage. "Acheson went to Paris a month ago worried about Germany," observed the journalist James Reston, "and came back today slightly disturbed about China."

With Mao and Vishinsky already making Acheson's life difficult, Chiang now decided to do the same. Perhaps inspired by his wife's suggestion to disrupt daily life in the Communist-controlled territories, the Generalissimo on June 20 ordered a blockade of much of the Chinese coast. Although such an order would be nearly impossible to enforce—and therefore illegal under international law—American and other foreign shipping companies would nevertheless run the risk of striking Nationalist-laid mines. The blockade was also certain to further antagonize Mao, who tended to assume that the United States and the Nationalists were coordinating their strategies.

Nearly simultaneously, Chiang's fleet of Canadian-made Mosquitoes and other fighter planes began intensifying their bombing of the major Communist-held ports. The jets flew at high altitudes, sometimes above the clouds, dropping bombs near the Shanghai wharves and the Huangpu River. One strike ignited storehouses of kerosene, and another disabled a British-flagged freighter, flooding the engine

room with water. The State Department mildly protested these attacks, but Acheson told his aides that he did not want to get in the
middle. In Shanghai, furnace-like temperatures only compounded the
misery. By June 22, thermometers had climbed to ninety-six degrees—
with the "season of the Great Heat," as one Chinese newspaper put it,
still "a month away."

14

KILLING THE TIGER

On the afternoon of June 22, Truman's chief of protocol swept into the president's office, accompanied by Wellington Koo and another Nationalist diplomat, Gan Jiehou. Face time with the American chief executive was always a precious commodity, and the arriving visitors had carefully honed their pitch. They began by striking an optimistic note: the Muslim troops fighting in the country's northwest seemed to be slowing Mao's advance, as were the Nationalist forces near Changsha. The men pulled out several maps and explained to Truman where they thought it possible to hold the line against further conquests.

Truman listened and asked a few questions, but he made no commitments. Although the president told the men that he had "always cherished great sympathy for the Chinese people," he added, pointedly, that the wholesale collapse of Chiang's forces over the past several weeks had been "most disheartening and disturbing." After years of broken promises, Truman would not take any new claims of battlefield victories on faith. "I am from Missouri," he said, referring obliquely to his home state's unofficial motto, "Show me." He wanted to see results. Before the diplomats left, Truman asked his guests one more time whether they knew what he meant by invoking his state slogan. He was determined to leave no doubt about his disgust with Chiang and his allies.

Truman's views on China were undergoing a subtle—but critical—metamorphosis during these first days of summer. The losses of Nanjing and Shanghai, coupled with Chiang's troublesome blockade and bombing raids, had intensified Truman's distaste for the whole venture. He had long viewed the Nationalist government as a failure, a "rat hole" that had served only to swallow American money and supplies. At first, during the early months of 1949, Truman had sought to simply ignore Chiang, neither supporting him nor openly criticizing him. Now, however, the president had begun to view the Generalissimo as one more force to be confronted—a project that would require an audacious change of strategy.

The journalists covering the State Department quickly picked up hints of this new approach. On June 23, Acheson held a news conference, ostensibly to debrief the reporters about the Paris talks. Once again, however, the correspondents brought up China. Acheson, wearing a necktie emblazoned with dice in the lucky combinations of seven and eleven, firmly parried questions about his department's preparation of the White Paper, which had proceeded apace while he was abroad.

"Mr. Secretary," one reporter asked, "there is a report that the department is considering or has decided to publish a good many documents referring to our relations with China, documents which have hitherto been kept classified. Can you say anything about that?"

"The department," Acheson replied, "has under consideration the preparation of a very extensive report on our relations with China and events in China during the past several years. I can not tell you what the decision will be, or when any such paper will be published, but it is under active consideration and a good deal of work is going forward in that connection."

Privately, some Acheson aides worried that publishing the White Paper would risk doing more harm than good. Acheson's deputy James Webb complained that there were just too many ways that the China bloc could distort the document's findings. Webb thought the report's drafters needed to clarify why the administration had not done more to aid Chiang's forces in the past. As it was, he warned, the department's foes would have a "field day" with the report.

Already, Congress was giving Acheson grief for his tepid support of the remaining Nationalist forces battling Mao. On the same day as the press conference, the House Foreign Affairs Committee summoned Acheson to appear before a closed hearing on the Hill. Walter Judd, relishing his role as inquisitor, demanded to know why Acheson refused to back the kind of last-ditch arms deliveries that Chennault and others were advocating. The secretary of state retorted that Truman's own military staff had dismissed such plans as unsound. "I am not in a position," Acheson told Judd, "to come to Congress and ask Congress for money at this time to do something which we do not believe can possibly be effective." Word of Acheson's newly combative posture must have made it to Riverdale—perhaps through Judd, Koo, or both—because Madame Chiang cabled her husband on June 24, warning that the White Paper was likely to be a "hostile attack" on the Generalissimo.

Chiang decided to weather this offensive from a new headquarters on Taiwan, to which he had increasingly been forced to retreat. A mountainous, tropical enclave one hundred miles off the Chinese coast, Taiwan had long existed as a world apart. The population was a cultural mishmash, the product of overlapping waves of immigration. Although Taiwan's original inhabitants had been Austronesian aborigines, starting in the seventeenth century large waves of Han Chinese immigrants from the southern provinces of the mainland began arriving on the island, igniting conflicts with the existing population. Then, after Japan defeated China in the Sino-Japanese War in 1895, Japanese troops took control of Taiwan, ruling the island until Japan's defeat in the Second World War. After V-J Day, as the Chinese civil conflict intensified, waves of mainlanders made their way to the island, seeking refuge—and power.

Taiwan was more secure than most of Chiang's remaining strongholds on the mainland. Still, ruling the island, which was larger than the state of Maryland, would be no easy task. Although Chiang had spent months trying to solidify his control of a strategic base area that included Taiwan, he had succeeded only in part. Indigenous resistance to the mainlanders remained strong, particularly in the aftermath of a brutal Guomindang crackdown on native protesters two years before—known as the February 28 Incident—that had killed thousands of Taiwanese. Nationalist leaders on Taiwan, meanwhile, played Chiang and acting president Li off each other, heightening tensions between the two figureheads. Chiang, continuing to fear his intraparty rivals, remained deeply uncertain of how much support he really had on the island. When he landed in southern Taiwan, according to one recollection, Chiang had anxiously asked the general who met him, "Am I safe here?"

By early summer, however, Chiang had little choice but to try to consolidate his control of this island refuge. On June 25, he flew from southern Taiwan to Taipei, then took a limousine up the graded route to a villa atop Grass Mountain, with its panoramic views of the lush Taiwanese landscape. Understanding the peril of losing his most powerful ally in Washington, Chiang now reversed himself and told his wife that he agreed with her: they would need to raise their public profiles. Go ahead, he told her: she was free to send the American news reporters to Grass Mountain if she thought it would help. Chiang would do the interviews—and whatever else it took to survive the coming assault.

★

Mao, ensconced in his own pleasant redoubt in the hills outside Beijing, was unimpressed by—or oblivious to—these subtle portents of change. Even as Truman and Acheson were preparing to publicly humiliate Chiang, Mao complained to his aides that the Americans remained too close to the Nationalists. The Truman Administration, Mao wrote in one cable to the Shanghai municipal committee, was playing a double game. He grumbled that the United States wanted "legal status" for its diplomatic representatives at the same time that it was still supporting his enemies. Mao urged the committee to prepare for a long struggle, warning of Western agents seeking "to conduct sabotages from within."

As summer unfolded, Mao was forced to think harder about how he would deal with foreign nations—not just the Americans and the British, but also those on China's turbulent periphery. Chinese emperors had long sought to dominate their border regions, cleverly allowing them a degree of autonomy and trade privileges while simultaneously demanding tribute and influence. Experience had shown that if the emperors lost the periphery, China's vital center would also be at risk. Mao recognized that if he wanted to protect his revolution at home, he could not afford to ignore China's coastal islands, its far western provinces, or its Southeast Asian neighbors.

To start, Mao cast an eye toward Taiwan, which Chiang had been busily fortifying. Just weeks after the fall of Shanghai, Mao ordered his P.L.A. commanders to "pay attention to the problem of seizing Taiwan immediately." He asked his officers how long such a mission would take and wanted to know if they could induce large portions of Chiang's military to defect. Mao asked his commanders to send their "preliminary opinions" by telegram. "If we fail to solve the Taiwan problem in a short period," he concluded, "the safety of Shanghai and other coastal ports will be severely threatened."

Mao also gave thought to Southeast Asia—particularly to Indochina, where Ho Chi Minh's Communist-led Viet Minh fighters were swiftly gaining strength and territory. Earlier in the year, in a desperate attempt to stabilize the situation, French and Vietnamese officials had come to an agreement, known as the Élysée Accords, that had laid the groundwork for Vietnam's nominal independence from colonial rule. Although the French retained a large measure of influence, they permitted Bao Dai, a Vietnamese nationalist and former emperor of Annam, to head the new state. Few observers believed that Bao possessed the charisma or resources to prevent Ho's guerrillas from over-running his government. (An American diplomat later described Bao as "a dissolute playboy in the pay of the French whose total loyal following probably comprised some half dozen Hong Kong concubines.") Yet Mao and his top aides viewed Bao's weakness as an opportunity to secure a vital buffer zone. Stalin ultimately pushed the Chinese to take the lead in supporting Ho and his rebels.

Stalin also urged Mao to "pay serious attention" to Xinjiang, the home of China's Muslim Uighur population, which the P.L.A. had not yet subdued. Mao told Stalin that he thought any such operation would need to be postponed until the following year. But the Soviet leader argued that Beijing should move more quickly. Stalin believed that Xinjiang, rich in oil and cotton, could help revitalize the Chinese economy. "It will be difficult for you without your own oil," the Soviet leader reasoned. In just a few years, Stalin thought, Beijing could develop a formidable supply, running pipelines and developing water routes from Xinjiang to the major cities. Stalin urged Mao to speed up the timetable and act more aggressively in Xinjiang. The local commander there, Stalin insisted, was "not that strong."

These wider regional objectives were ambitious, especially for a movement that already had so much work to do at home—and Mao knew it. He would need Soviet help or acquiescence to accomplish any of them. In late June, Mao dispatched a delegation led by the senior Communist official (and future Chinese president) Liu Shaoqi to liaise with Stalin in Moscow. For the Chinese team, it was a stomach-churning trip. As Liu's plane hurtled toward Moscow from northern China, it took frequent evasive maneuvers, climbing so suddenly and steeply in the subzero atmosphere that some of the men got sick. Liu's plane was forced to make several refueling stops along the way. By the time it arrived in Moscow, on June 26, the Chinese delegation felt thoroughly drained.

Stalin threw a reception for the visitors at his summer villa, then summoned them for a more substantive meeting late the next evening. The Soviet dictator was in a jolly mood, joking and gripping hands. He quickly promised Mao's representatives that he would provide a loan of

$300 million to aid the revolution: $60 million for each of the next five years. When Stalin had suggested an interest rate of one percent, Mao had protested fawningly by telegram that the terms were too generous. "Well," Stalin now replied, laughing, "if you insist on a bigger annual interest rate, this is your business. We can accept an increased interest rate."

Stalin recognized that Mao would need to build a navy if the P.L.A. were to protect China's coastline and extend its domain to nearby islands like Taiwan and Hainan. The Soviet leader offered to provide Mao with mine-sweeping equipment, along with specialists to help operate it. He wondered aloud whether the Communists had managed to commandeer any ships from their defeated foes. Either way, he added, he would be willing to provide experts who could help raise previously sunken ships and repair them. He also promised, once Mao officially proclaimed his government, to send a squadron of Soviet sailors to reinforce Qingdao.

Finally, Stalin once again emphasized the need for Mao to swiftly take Xinjiang. If Mao delayed, he warned, foreign powers like the British would try to "activate the Muslims, including the Indian ones, to continue the civil war against the Communists." After subduing the region, Stalin counseled, Mao should populate the province with Han Chinese immigrants, increasing their share of the total population from five percent to thirty percent. He reiterated that such a strategy could also work elsewhere along the periphery. But Xinjiang, where the local strongman's cavalry would be easy targets for the P.L.A. artillery, was a priority. If Mao needed a few dozen fighter planes to finish the job, Stalin was happy to provide them.

★

As Liu's delegation parleyed with the Russians, Stuart sent Secretary of State Acheson an urgent cable, which arrived in Washington at 5:38 a.m. on June 30. The American ambassador reported that Huang Hua, two days earlier, had asked for a meeting, at which he had delivered a startling message from the Communist leadership: Mao and Zhou were inviting Stuart to make a trip to Beijing. Although the message had been somewhat oblique, suggesting only that Stuart might want to "visit [Yanjing] University," the ambassador had no doubt that the overture was a "veiled invitation from Mao and [Zhou] to talk with them while ostensibly visiting [Yanjing]." Stuart told Acheson that he thought such a meeting would go a long way toward strengthening U.S.-Chinese relations at an otherwise tense moment.

Still, Stuart worried that it would be politically risky. The China bloc in Congress would try to sabotage the talks if word got out. The visit might also antagonize the rest of the diplomatic corps in Nanjing, which had been trying to maintain a "united front" as it dealt with Mao's revolution. Lastly, Stuart reasoned, meeting with Mao would legitimize the Communists, appearing to the world like one more step toward diplomatic recognition. Despite these risks, however, Stuart wrote that he was "ready to make [the] journey" if Acheson thought it wise. Stuart had the impression that "Mao, [Zhou], and Huang, are very much hoping that I make this trip, whatever their motives."

But almost as soon as Stuart sent his cable, Mao seemed to contradict himself. To commemorate the twenty-eighth anniversary of the party, Mao published an essay, "On the People's Democratic Dictatorship," in which he declared that Communist China would align itself squarely with the Soviets. "All Chinese without exception must lean either to the side of imperialism or to the side of socialism," Mao wrote. "Sitting on the fence will not do." He derided the "bankrupt" civilization of the Western "imperialists and their running dogs" and urged his countrymen to crush the reactionary forces inside China. "You have to choose between the alternatives," he wrote, "of either killing the tiger or being eaten by it."

Mao's speech ended any talk of accommodation. The next morning's headline in the *New York Times* read: MAO EXPECTS NO HELP FROM WEST; HAILS SOVIET AS CHINA'S TRUE ALLY. On the evening of July 1, Acheson dashed off a curt cable to Stuart in Nanjing: "You are instructed under no, repeat no, circumstances to make visit [Beijing]."

The secretary of state cited Stuart's own rationale for prohibiting the trip, which would have raised hackles from the China bloc, especially after Mao's most recent article. Stuart told Acheson that he thought the United States owed Mao a "vote of thanks" for his essay; at least the Communist leader's true position was now "etched in clean sharp lines."

But Stuart was disappointed. He felt that there was now little left for him to do in China. Out of worldly options, the former clergyman embraced the spiritual. On a Sunday shortly after Mao's essay appeared, Stuart found himself leading a prayer service at the embassy, where he read from the last two chapters of the Apocalypse of John. "And I saw a new heaven and a new earth," the ambassador read, "for the first heaven and the first earth were passed away."

15

THE GREAT CRESCENT

On July 4—Independence Day in the United States—sixteen thousand U.S. and British soldiers paraded in neat columns through central Tokyo, past the Imperial Palace, with its centuries-old stone walls and moat, then on to the hulking modern headquarters of the Supreme Commander for the Allied Powers, known as S.C.A.P. For nearly four years, in the aftermath of the Second World War, Japan's fate had been worked out within these walls by the American occupying forces. Now, at ten a.m., a tall figure in a crisp khaki uniform and ornate gold-embroidered cap strode into the plaza across from the building to examine the troops. As he did, nineteen gunners ceremoniously discharged their weapons—a theatrical tribute to the most powerful man in East Asia, General Douglas MacArthur.

Brilliant but also headstrong, MacArthur did not merely seek to administer postwar Japan; he wanted to completely dominate it. Humility was not one of the general's strong suits; in casual conversation, he liked to compare himself to Julius Caesar. Like Judd, he believed that American security depended as much on control of Asia as on mastery of Europe. He predicted that the "great events of the next thousand years" would play out in East Asia, and he saw his mission, partly, as a long-term struggle for the region's soul. Material reconstruction, he felt, was only the beginning. The occupation forces would also need to "plant the seeds of the appreciation of Christianity and democracy": a wholesale effort to transform the culture of East Asia.

Mao's conquest of China put this ambitious project at risk. Already some evidence existed that Communists in Japan were seeking to subvert MacArthur's rule. A cache of documents seized earlier in the year revealed that Japanese leftists had hoped to turn a recent labor strike into a full-scale revolution. (One captured document urged Japanese Communist women to use "sex tactics" to weaken the enemy's defenses.) MacArthur had long scoffed at the threat of a Communist revolt in Japan and had swiftly suppressed the would-be picketers. Still, the radicals persisted, continuing to hold rallies. Even if Mao's victories in China did not directly imperil America's security, a Communist-controlled Japan certainly would.

The fall of Shanghai, along with Mao's strident declaration that he would lean to the side of the Soviets, forced Truman and Acheson to think harder about the consequences for Japan—and for East Asia as a whole. In early July, Acheson forwarded a paper to the N.S.C. that made the case for a more ambitious, integrated approach to the region. The paper, which had been written by Kennan and his staff, urged the administration to extend its policy of Communist containment to Asia, working quietly to buttress the nations along China's periphery. America's security, the paper's authors had written, depended on the strength of a "great crescent" of friendly nations that surrounded the Middle Kingdom, including India, Australia, the Philippines, and Japan. The United States could not permit Mao's revolution to embolden revolutionaries in those countries as well.

Japan represented, by far, the most critical of the nations along the Great Crescent. Yet it was impossible to separate Japan's fate from the welfare of its Pacific neighbors. Japanese emperors had long sought to cement trade ties with Southeast Asian countries, which provided a steady supply of raw materials to Japan in exchange for finished manufactured goods. In the 1930s, the Japanese emperor depended so heavily on these routes that he risked war to maintain the integrity of a regional bloc designed to strengthen such commercial bonds. Now, as MacArthur and the Truman Administration attempted to rebuild Japan's ravaged economy, they recognized that they would need to fall back on these same reliable avenues of trade.

Economics was important, but so was politics. Kennan worried that the United States would be accused of "imperialist intervention" if it tried to construct a regional political architecture on its own. Instead, Kennan wanted to induce a local leader—such as the president of the Philippines, Elpidio Quirino—to play an "active and constructive role in developing a counter-force to Communism." Given the fraught history between the United States and the Philippines, this would be a delicate task. In the immediate aftermath of the Spanish-American War, the United States had ruled the Philippines as an imperial possession. Although American presidents had gradually permitted the territory increasing autonomy, it was not until 1946, after MacArthur wrested the archipelago back from the Japanese, that the United States granted the Philippines full independence. Nevertheless, Kennan understood that the United States retained a measure of influence with Philippine officials. Quirino, only a year in office, was battling his own Communist insurgency, and he could use U.S. funds. In exchange for economic aid, Kennan hoped, the Philippine president might accept some "confidential and friendly guidance." Still, it would take some finesse to manage the relationship. Another official in Kennan's department recommended inviting the Philippine president to visit the United States, as soon as possible, to begin building the necessary goodwill.

Walter Judd was encouraged by the State Department's new energy. He observed, with apparent schadenfreude, that Kennan seemed "shaken by events." Judd felt that he and his allies were making steady progress in their efforts to convince Washington's decision makers to arm Chinese provincial leaders. These residual Nationalist forces, Judd believed, should now emulate Mao's old guerrilla strategy. "By withdrawing into areas that are relatively easily defensible so that a

minimum of effort has to be spent for military purposes," he explained
to one correspondent in early July, "the government can begin to get
the grass on its side of the fence greener than that which the Communists are likely to be able to develop now that they have taken on
the headaches of feeding the cities, maintaining communications, and
making good on all the fancy promises they and their apologists have
been so generous in making."

Still, these anti-Communist holdouts would need money and weapons. Acheson continued to oppose such deliveries, which he considered
a waste. The secretary of state refused to subsidize Chennault's airline, which the general hoped might be used to facilitate weapons shipments. And yet as Wisner's staff interpreted it, the State Department's
guidance did permit the O.P.C.'s covert operators to quietly begin con-
ducting preliminary intelligence-gathering missions in the Chinese
border regions. Wisner hired Malcolm Rosholt, a former journalist
who had worked in southern China as an intelligence operative during
the Second World War, for one of the first assignments. As the summer unfolded, Rosholt, who was fluent in Chinese, secretly flew to the
Middle Kingdom and began opening lines of communication with the
most important local strongmen.

★

Madame Chiang did not wait passively for the Truman Administration
to fortify its defensive line in the Pacific. To start, there was no guar-
antee that the United States would even choose to include Taiwan—
and by extension, her husband's regime—in its Great Crescent. With
Acheson increasingly hostile toward the Nationalists, she warned Chiang that the White Paper would try to place "all the blame" for Mao's
victory on the Generalissimo. Madame Chiang assured her husband
that she was doing everything she could to try to stop the publication
of the paper. She explained that she had "reached an agreement" with
certain congressmen to make public statements of support. Still, taking on the U.S. State Department was a "very difficult" task, she told

him. If Chiang wanted to maintain a leadership position in East Asia, he would need to rely on his own force of will.

Chiang took his wife's advice. In the first days of July, he finally met with the two American news correspondents, as she had urged him to do. After carefully studying the answers she had written out, he recited them almost verbatim. He tried to project confidence, appearing happy and hale as he sat talking with the journalists in his hilltop villa. Despite his more than five-month sabbatical, Chiang insisted that he would never relinquish the "revolutionary leadership" of his nation, and he vowed to fight on. "If Communism is not checked in China," he told the men, "it will spread over the whole of Asia. Should that occur, another world war would be inevitable."

Chiang shared the Truman Administration's conviction that the region required an integrated approach—yet the Generalissimo wanted to lead it himself. Less than a week after his interview, Chiang flew to the Philippines to discuss the prospect of a regional alliance with Quirino. At Baguio, the site of the Philippine president's picturesque summer residence, Quirino hosted him for two days of talks. In the shadow of the nearby mountain peaks, the two men toured the attractive city, which was bedecked with ceremonial arches that the local Chinese community had erected for Chiang's visit. Back at Quirino's compound, the Asian leaders sat in a thatched pavilion as they discussed their mutual ambitions, including the formation of a Pacific alliance. (According to a report that reached the U.S. embassy in Manila, Chiang also raised the possibility of storing his vast gold stocks in the Philippines for safekeeping.) After issuing a joint statement with Quirino, Chiang boarded his plane and flew home the following day, making a loop in the air around Manila. He stopped briefly in the Philippine capital, then raced north again across the water to Taiwan.

Chiang's freelance diplomacy aggravated Acheson. At the secretary of state's morning meeting on July 14, he groused that the "Quirino-Chiang get-together" was complicating his own strategy. Acheson wondered aloud whether it still made sense to invite Quirino to the United States, as his advisers had been recommending. At a meeting with Truman later the same day, Acheson told the president that he and his aides were reconsidering the prospect. Truman and Acheson, with the White Paper, had been trying to rid themselves of the Nationalist albatross. The last thing they wanted was to see Chiang meddling in the new Pacific network that they were hoping to engineer. To make matters worse, Acheson's representative in Manila reported that Quirino himself was now displaying "considerable resentment against the U.S."

But from the vantage point of mainland China, these jagged fault lines were completely hidden from view. The Chinese newspaper *Dagong bao* speculated that Chiang's visit to the Philippines was part of a secret U.S. conspiracy to shore up his forces. Quirino, whom the article dismissed as a "small stooge of American imperialism," was funneling American money to the Nationalists, the report warned. It went on to complain that the American "super-god" and its "imperialist magicians" were concerned only with "manipulation of the puppets" in Asia. It was true that the State Department was working conscientiously to forge a chain of Pacific partners, and some senior American officials, like Johnson, did want to shore up Chiang and his allies. But many others, like Acheson, were actually working feverishly throughout the summer to undermine the Generalissimo.

★

By mid-July, these bitter debates over China policy were crowding out other important issues. Johnson, now several months into his position as defense secretary, was beginning to feel more comfortable challenging his colleagues in the cabinet. He was not known for his tact, frequently tangling with both underlings and peers. ("General, you're a liar," Johnson once snapped at an officer who was briefing him.) One Truman Administration official, in his private diary, liked to refer to the two-hundred-and-fifty-pound Johnson as "Big Boy" and "Man of Heroic Mould." Acheson complained that Johnson seemed mentally ill—"nuttier than a fruitcake," as he later put it. But on China, Johnson was relentless. "I'll keep asking what our China policy is until I find out," the defense chief liked to say.

Johnson, for all his domestic political chops, did have some experience in Asia. He had worked, during the Second World War, as a U.S. liaison in India, attempting to help facilitate a political compromise between British and Indian leaders. In the intervening years, he had developed tight ties to some of the Chiangs' closest associates. The newspaper columnist Drew Pearson later told President Eisenhower that Johnson had once offered him $10,000 (about $100,000 today) if Pearson would make a "favorable reference" to Madame Chiang's brother-in-law, H. H. Kung, in one of his columns. Pearson considered Johnson's overture a vivid example of how Chiang's allies sought to influence policy.

Now Johnson had the ear of the president. On July 14, Truman called Johnson, Acheson, and other top aides to a late-night meeting at Blair House. The president, according to one attendee, looked terrible—old and fatigued, like a "tired owl." Age or worry had etched deep lines into the skin beside his eyes. He displayed none of his usual swagger and bonhomie. Sitting in a small room with a bright yellow couch beneath a large oil portrait of F.D.R., he listened as his top advisers debated the China quandary. Johnson, for days, had been pushing for more control over the contents of the White Paper. Just that morning Truman had ordered Acheson to let the defense secretary review the draft. Although the Blair House conclave was meant to be confidential, some details leaked out. A Chinese journalist with sources close to Johnson reported that the defense secretary had pushed hard for new aid shipments. Acheson, another witness recalled, appeared "very cool and serene" as he defended his position, doing "a beautiful job of exposition." Ultimately, however, the meeting failed to resolve the most divisive issues.

All summer Acheson had been honing the White Paper, editing the draft on weekends at his country house in Maryland. In Acheson's view, the document was basically finished; he hoped to release it to the public in the next week or two. But Johnson's protests threatened to upset this timetable. At around noon on July 15, the day after the Blair House meeting, Acheson called Johnson, hoping to iron out their remaining disputes. Acheson asked the defense secretary whom he wanted to vet the draft. Johnson replied that the aide whom he wanted to do it was away for the weekend and would not be home until Sunday night—could it wait until then? Acheson insisted that he needed approval by Monday and offered to fly the document out that weekend. Johnson, sounding irritated by the pressure Acheson was putting on him, told the secretary of state that he would have to get back to him about whether this tight timetable was feasible.

On Monday, still without the assent he needed from Johnson, Acheson once again took his complaints to the president. Truman assured his secretary of state that he was still committed to releasing the document, adding that he was hearing from aides that the most recent drafts were excellent. The president stressed that he did not want the paper to be "watered down" as a result of Johnson's meddling. He promised Acheson that he would help him stand up against any objections from the military.

Acheson saw the White Paper as theater—a bold gesture designed to catch the attention of a distracted public and begin to change the conventional wisdom about Chiang. It needed to be dramatic. Alone, however, the paper seemed too negative; Acheson was determined to underscore that the administration was also taking "positive action" in Asia. Although he opposed shipping weapons to Mao's enemies on the mainland, Acheson was now committed to containing the spread of Communism elsewhere in Asia.

At his meeting with Truman, Acheson raised the possibility of a wider regional strategy. Truman liked the idea and told Acheson to pursue it further. The same day, Acheson dashed off a pointed, secret memo to one of his top aides, clarifying the new approach. "You will please take as your assumption that it is a fundamental decision of American policy that the United States does not intend to permit further extension of Communist domination on the continent of Asia or in the Southeast Asia area," Acheson wrote. He added that he wanted to "make absolutely certain that we are neglecting no opportunity that would be within our capabilities to achieve the purpose of halting the spread of totalitarian Communism in Asia."

Nevertheless, Acheson and Johnson continued to tangle over the best ways to do that. Johnson, like Chennault, could not see how it could be accomplished without the leadership of Chiang, whom the White Paper was designed to undermine. "You and the President," Johnson wrote Acheson on July 21, "should carefully consider whether the usefulness of this Paper . . . is greater than the risks inherent in the disclosures which are made." Johnson invited Acheson out to Bohemian Grove, in California, to discuss the paper further. But Acheson, who was growing impatient, declined. Instead, he once again warned the president that Johnson was causing trouble. Truman reassured his secretary of state, ordering Acheson to "proceed with the publication as now planned," despite Johnson's objections.

Amid these sensitive policy discussions, Johnson seems to have found ways to keep Madame Chiang and her allies informed. On July 23, one of Johnson's closest confidants, Paul Griffith, invited Wellington Koo to visit him at his country home along the Potomac River. Griffith briefed Koo on these very private disputes, adding that Johnson had even offered Acheson the use of his private plane, *Dewdrop*, if it would get the secretary of state out to California to further discuss the matter. The very next day Koo traveled to Riverdale to see Madame Chiang and coordinate their responses to the White Paper. Ultimately, Madame Chiang was too ill, with a stomach ailment, to see Koo (or so she said). But Koo nevertheless left behind memos with talking points suggesting how they should respond to the Truman Administration's coming salvo.

By the last days of July, according to the diary of one administration official, Acheson was beginning to look unusually "harried and drawn." Despite Truman's firm support, the secretary of state's new China policy was taking far too long to unfold. Once confident in his choice to let the dust clear before committing himself, Acheson now worried that, when it came to the wider region, the risks of equivocating were increasingly grave. On July 28, Acheson received a classified report stating that French officials in Saigon were now warning that Mao's forces were planning "an early invasion of Southeast Asia starting with Indochina and ending with the oil fields in Indonesia." The U.S. consul added that an "increasing number of French civil and military officials" now considered such an attack to be "imminent."

★

On Friday, July 29, the temperature in Washington soared to almost ninety-eight degrees—the hottest day of 1949. As the capital sweltered, Acheson met with Truman, telling the president that he would be sending over the finished thousand-page manuscript of the White Paper later that day. Truman, undoubtedly desperate to escape the heat, promised Acheson that he would read it over the weekend, which he would be spending at his retreat in the Catoctin Mountains. Later that afternoon, Truman, dressed in a light blue summer suit and white fedora, climbed behind the wheel of a silver convertible and drove himself the seventy miles into the Maryland hills. When he arrived, the president swiftly dove into the swimming pool. He told the reporters who accompanied him that he would spend the next couple of days "getting as much sleep as he could."

Over the weekend, as Truman relaxed and reviewed the State Department's draft, Acheson's policy received a small nudge from an unlikely source—Walter Judd. That Saturday Judd cabled Chiang Kai-shek from a personal Western Union account, urging him to distance himself from the behind-the-scenes maneuvering over the White Paper. Perhaps aware that Truman was nearing a decision, Judd told Chiang that he and his allies would be making a "serious mistake" if they continued to try to quash the publication of the paper. Any such effort, Judd warned, would be "interpreted as [a] confession of guilt by [the] Chinese government." Instead, Judd told the Generalissimo that he thought it would be far more effective to "deal with charges if published than when mere rumors and insinuations as at present."

On Sunday morning, Truman slipped back into his convertible and drove home to Washington, his mind made up. Although he was not a particularly sentimental person, he must have recognized that his presidency had reached a turning point. Truman had never been naïve about the tragic aspects of world affairs; he had lived through two cataclysmic wars in the past thirty-five years, and he had given the fateful order to drop the atomic bomb. And yet for almost his entire life, he had tried to do better—to break this age-old pattern of international conflict. For decades, he had harbored stubborn dreams of Wilsonian concord. A robust and friendly China, despite Truman's occasionally crude prejudices, had long played a central part in this hopeful story.

And so Truman's betrayal of the Chiangs was also a kind of self-betrayal—even if he knew that it was ultimately the right decision. On Monday, August 1, after returning from his weekend retreat, the president met with Acheson and gave him the final go-ahead to release the White Paper, at eleven a.m. on August 5. For four more days, Truman and Acheson waited anxiously, preparing for the inevitable backlash when the news finally broke. When it did, the journalists covering the event seemed to quickly grasp the significance of the president's unforgiving thrust. On August 6, the New York Times displayed the story boldly across four columns on the top of its front page. The headline read: U.S. PUTS SOLE BLAME ON CHIANG REGIME.

★

PART III

★

FIRECRACKER

T he publication of the White Paper threatened to induce a kind of identity crisis in Madame Chiang. For four decades, she had considered herself almost equally at home in both China and America. At times, she had felt even more at ease in the United States, where she had studied and grown up, absorbing Western values and Atlantic idioms. Her roots in the community stretched back to her father's days as an ambitious immigrant, mastering Methodist prayers and hymns, then passing his faith on to his daughter. Yet her parents' Christianity was only one legacy of her family's ties to the United States. Another was her embrace of that secular American creed: untrammeled individual freedom. It was a belief system well suited to a woman who possessed what one of her friends had once described as a powerful "interior force."

And yet here was the American president—the leader of the nation she so admired, and China's ally for years—blaming the region's problems on her own family. For Madame Chiang, avoiding self-doubt required making a difficult decision. She could decide to stay in the United States and fight, convincing herself that Truman and Acheson's approach was actually the anti-American one: a treasonous betrayal of their own country and values. Alternatively, she could attempt to slip out of her American identity altogether, returning to China and joining her embattled husband. But the mainland was nearly lost, and Chiang was on the run. She would be trading one exile for another.

For Madame Chiang, the situation was even more complicated. Her life with the Generalissimo had never been as serene as in the public portrait. They were both strong willed; they argued. Both dodged rumors of affairs. They often disagreed over politics and strategy. Once, after a particularly heated fight, Madame Chiang had run, in tears, to one of the foreign ambassadors in Nanjing. The Generalissimo, she said as she wept, had shot and killed her dog, a pet Alsatian. To the ambassador, she insisted that Chiang's behavior had followed a cruel kind of logic. She explained by quoting a Tang dynasty poet: "To kill the rider, shoot his horse."

If she returned to China, renewed marital squabbles would be the best outcome. The worst case, and perhaps the most likely, would be widowhood or death. As city after city fell to the Communists, she worried that her husband might commit suicide; she begged him to assure her that he would not. Either way, if Mao's troops captured the Generalissimo, they would likely execute him—and probably Madame Chiang, too. Even in more forgiving times, statecraft in the Middle Kingdom could be a merciless business. "Chinese politics is impossible," she had once written a friend. "One never knows when one's head is going to be the next to be chopped off."

These contingencies, understandably, kept Madame Chiang on edge all summer. She would call friends in the middle of the night, waking them up just to talk. She had never been a particularly sound sleeper and for years had been haunted by nightmares, which she considered to be prophetic. The threat of assassination was a common theme. Once, as the Japanese invasion of China loomed, she had dreamed of a room with a sign on the door with her name on it. Inside, she saw a vision of herself, wearing white. A man with a "coarse and brutal face" approached and raised his arms, a revolver in each hand. Madame Chiang screamed herself awake.

Now, by the midsummer of 1949, her waking hours were nearly as grim. As Truman and Acheson unveiled the White Paper, Madame Chiang fled from the Riverdale house to a college friend's modest apartment in Manhattan. There, at least, there were fewer reminders of her predicament. She and an assistant busied themselves by sprucing up the place, cleaning and buying a new bedspread and drapes. For the time being, she tried to simply block out the diplomatic news, distracting herself from the political inferno in Washington. Still, she knew that she could not hide forever. Ultimately, she would have to make a choice.

★

In Nanjing, Stuart, too, had reached a crisis point. With Mao increasingly hostile, and Truman unwilling to authorize further talks, the American ambassador felt useless. For months he had known that he would have to leave China, but now, he decided, it was finally time. He arranged his departure to coincide with the White Paper's release, taking off from Nanjing just ahead of the news. In an overloaded embassy plane, he flew across the East China Sea, stopping first at Okinawa, where he took a swim in the ocean, and then boarding a larger B-27 for the next leg, to Guam. At a third stop, in Honolulu, he was finally given a copy of the White Paper—and was appalled at what he read. The ambassador could not believe that Acheson had published so many once-secret documents, which he knew would destroy his remaining relationships in China. By now, though, Stuart had resigned himself to the tragedy of Chiang's collapse. He stretched himself out on the beach, bathing for a moment in the Oahu sun.

Stuart was particularly dismayed by the document's cover letter, written by Acheson, which was unsparing in its indictment of Chiang's regime. Acheson argued that the Nationalist government's "leaders had proved incapable of meeting the crisis confronting them, its troops had lost the will to fight, and its government had lost popular support." He continued:

> The Communists, on the other hand, through a ruthless discipline and fanatical zeal, attempted to sell themselves as guardians and liberators of the people. The Nationalist armies did not have to be defeated; they disintegrated. History has proved again and again that a regime without faith in itself and an army without morale cannot survive the test of battle.

Acheson explained that the contents of the White Paper would elaborate "in some detail" on these failures of Chiang's government.

Even as he laid the blame on Chiang, Acheson absolved American policy makers. Neither U.S. perfidy nor neglect had led to the current crisis, he insisted. Washington had tried, repeatedly, to shrink the gaps between the Communists and the Nationalists, but such efforts had come to nothing. "The unfortunate but inescapable fact is that the ominous result of the civil war in China was beyond the control of the government of the United States," he argued. "Nothing that this country did or could have done within the reasonable limits of its capabilities could have changed that result; nothing that was left undone by this country has contributed to it. It was the product of internal Chinese forces, forces which this country tried to influence but could not."

Back in Washington, Acheson later recalled, the release of the White Paper was like the detonation of a "giant firecracker." The reverberations were immediate and intense. Walter Judd launched a counterattack from the floor of the House, inverting Acheson's argument. After viewing the document, he said, Nationalist China's record was "not as bad as I expected, while that of the American government is worse." The Minnesota congressman praised Chiang's regime for taking the Communist threat seriously, while his own government dithered. But Judd was most concerned about what to do next. The White Paper, he complained, was "almost wholly negative. The main concern still remains—what do our officials have to offer that is positive? Diagnosis is useless without remedy."

Judd continued to see a remedy in Chennault's plan to arm anti-Communist rebels on the mainland. As the White Paper debate smoldered, Judd and Chennault traded ideas about the practical details of such an approach. Acheson, for his part, remained unenthusiastic about weapons shipments to the mainland, overt or covert. Still, in congressional testimony on August 8, the secretary of state subtly—but significantly—refined his position. Increasingly, Acheson was looking for ways to shore up the governments of Southeast Asia. He conceded that he would not turn away additional congressional aid if the appropriations were structured in the right way. "A comparatively small amount which could be used in the Far East at the discretion of the president would have considerable possibilities of usefulness," he told the legislators.

When he made the remark, Acheson was probably thinking, at least in part, about the Philippines, which his staff continued to view as the linchpin of any regional strategy. Truman had been pressing his advisers to firm up an aid package for the government of President Quirino ahead of the Philippine president's upcoming visit to Washington. Chiang's desperate trip to Baguio had complicated matters, but Truman and his aides saw little choice but to court Quirino. If Truman and Acheson were going to successfully slow Mao's advance, they believed, they would need to renew old friendships in the Pacific.

★

On the afternoon of August 8, a moonfaced man in a baggy summer suit strode across an airstrip under the sun, flanked on one side by an honor guard of white-capped U.S. Marines, and on the other by the president of the United States. Despite the conspicuous pomp, there was something vaguely vaudeville about the scene. The two heads of state, Truman and Quirino, looked as if they had coordinated their costumes: white fedoras, saddle shoes, handkerchiefs flopping from breast pockets. The late-day sun cast long shadows as the men moved toward their cars for the trip downtown. Outside Blair House, the American and the Filipino doffed their hats and smiled theatrically as the camera shutters clicked. Acheson was there, too, but he stood off to the side, eyebrows furrowed, looking as if he were trying to smile but could not.

Truman hosted Quirino that night at a glitzy black-tie stag dinner at the Carlton Hotel. Lavender asters and bronze pompons adorned the tables as the two men traded compliments. For sheer glamor and grandeur, it was difficult to compete with an American state visit. Quirino reveled in the attention. The following day, the Philippine president mounted the dais to address the U.S. Senate, cautioning against inaction in the face of the "advancing tide of Communism." Although he praised the Truman Administration for its recent efforts to tighten the bonds with Europe, he complained that "the task of securing our free world is only half done." The stability of Korea, Vietnam, and other countries in the region was now at risk. Quirino stopped short of asking the United States to join a formal military alliance of Pacific nations. But he did not shrink from requesting money. As a first step to resisting the Communist advances, he said, "Asia must properly feed and clothe and house its millions, and raise their living standards."

Privately, Acheson grumbled about Quirino's prodigal tendencies. Although his initial conversations with the Philippine president had been "vague and haphazard," he now lectured Quirino about the need for better fiscal discipline. If Quirino wanted additional U.S. aid, Acheson said, the Philippine government would need to spend more on postwar reconstruction and less on consumer goods. But the conversation seemed to go nowhere. Acheson's notes reflect his frustration. Quirino, he wrote, "launched into a thirty-minute dissertation which added up to an expression of confidence that all was well in the Philippine Islands; that everything was being done that could be done; and that without the application of any painful measures it would turn out all right in the end."

Chiang's allies in the United States worked the cocktail circuit during Quirino's visit, trying to glean any useful intelligence about the

Philippine president's talks with Truman. At an evening gathering at the Philippine embassy on August 10, Wellington Koo lobbied for a few minutes alone with Quirino, to gauge how the meetings were going. The Philippine ambassador warned that the party was full of Secret Service agents who would report any conversations back to Truman, but he ultimately arranged for the two men to talk. After flattering Quirino with praise for his "statesmanlike" remarks before the Senate, Koo aggressively pressed him for information. Did Quirino discuss the idea of a Pacific union with Truman? No, Quirino replied, he did not want to expose any daylight between himself and the president. Did Truman raise the issue? "No," Quirino said curtly. As Quirino ushered the Chinese ambassador out, he shrugged off his reticence. "We understand each other at heart without speaking much about it," Quirino said.

Judd, too, slipped into a Washington reception for Quirino—but the congressman seemed more interested in defending Chiang than in trying to gather secrets. Judd protested that the Generalissimo was being unfairly accused of manipulating Nationalist politics from be-hind the scenes. The Minnesota congressman groused that an Ameri-can general—presumably George Marshall—was doing exactly the same thing. (Actually, Marshall was not.) Still, Judd was encouraged by Chiang's new diplomatic offensive, including a trip the Generalissimo had made in early August to discuss the potential Pacific union with South Korea's president, Syngman Rhee. From the House floor, Judd praised Chiang, Quirino, and Rhee for moving ahead with their vision for a regional alliance, even if they could not convince Truman to go along. "If we cannot lead," Judd said, "let us at least follow these three wise men from the east."

After issuing an anodyne joint statement with Truman, Quirino left Washington for New York on the morning of August 11. Fifty-six motorcycles roared up Broadway at the head of his motorcade as a hundred thousand spectators fringed the route in the scorching heat, tossing ticker tape from the windows. At Fordham the following day, Quirino stressed the spiritual bonds between the United States and the

Philippines, arguing that the two nations would need to reinforce the "tie of our common religion" if they wanted to work together to halt Mao's advance. "The best hope of conquering Communism lies in the internal renewal of Christianity and democracy," Quirino said, sounding a lot like MacArthur. Quirino's warnings only seemed to grow more strident as he flew west. At his last American stop, in Los Angeles on August 14, Quirino declared that China was now a "nation on fire." The only way to stop the spread of Communism, he cautioned, would be to build a "firewall" in the Pacific.

★

The Truman Administration's assault on Chiang did nothing to win Mao's goodwill. Chinese newspapers sympathetic to the Communists lumped together both the White Paper and Quirino's visit as part of the same imperialist conspiracy. The United States, with its "plans for world enslavement," was "behind every move" of its puppets Chiang and Quirino, according to one left-leaning Shanghai newspaper. Now, however, since Chiang had failed his American overlords, Acheson had been forced to administer a "stark and merciless whipping," Mao's official news agency added, quoting an article in the Soviet newspaper *Pravda*. The goal, according to this logic, was to set an "example" for the "other slaves," encouraging them to "work harder." Truman, the editorialists went on, had selected two "insignificant" Asian leaders—Quirino and Rhee—as Chiang's replacements, showering them with money and weapons in exchange for their obedience. Chiang would continue to play a role in the conspiracy, according to this interpretation, but only as a subordinate—a "slave of the slaves."

Of course, this wildly simplistic propaganda completely glossed over the real rifts among Washington policy makers: internecine battles over diplomatic recognition, covert operations, and a potential Pacific Pact among them. And for all Mao's conspiracy theories, American operatives seemed unable to discover even the most basic intelligence from behind Communist lines—including the state of Mao's health. In mid-July, the C.I.A. had informed Truman of a tip the agency had received indicating that Mao might have died. Although that rumor had turned out to be false, now, in August, another intelligence source was suggesting that the Chinese Communist leader was gravely ill. With no way to reliably corroborate this information, leaders in Washington had every reason to believe that Mao might permanently disappear from the political scene, with potentially dramatic consequences for his revolution. Although Mao was certainly not healthy in 1949—he suffered from lumbago and sleeplessness, among other ailments—he would ultimately live to rule China for another quarter century.

Mao, in fact, was well enough in the summer of 1949 to issue a scathing personal rebuttal to the White Paper. In his cover letter, Acheson had written hopefully that China's history of "democratic individualism" would reassert itself soon on the mainland. Mao now picked up on this phrase as a not-so-veiled threat, a clear indication that U.S. "troublemaking" would continue on the mainland. The Americans, Mao believed, would seek to recruit Chinese business leaders and intellectuals as they quietly worked to overturn his revolution. These Chinese "middle-of-the-roaders" might not like Chiang and his Nationalists, Mao wrote, but neither were they firmly behind his own regime. He worried that they could still be vulnerable to the "honeyed words" of Western leaders.

Partly to win over these moderates, Mao wanted to puncture their perceptions that the United States and its allies remained as a countervailing force just off the Chinese coast. All summer Mao had been pushing his commanders to formulate a plan to crush Chiang's last major stronghold, on Taiwan. Without faster boats, however, the distances involved would be too great. As it was now, it would take twenty-four hours to cross the hundred-mile strait. The Communist military would also need to vastly improve its air force if it were to successfully compete with Chiang's fleet of Mosquitoes and other foreign-made fighter planes. Mao reconciled himself to the fact that it could take a year or more to build and train these new forces.

Still, he wanted to start right away. Stalin had already promised

Mao's liaison in Moscow, Liu Shaoqi, that he would help the Chinese Communists build their navy and air force. Encouraged, Mao's central committee instructed Liu to order one hundred to two hundred Russian-made Yak fighter jets and another forty to eighty bombers from the Soviets, along with the requisite munitions and replacement parts. The Chinese delegation also wanted to send seventeen hundred pilots and ground technicians to the Soviet Union for training. Stalin countered with an even more lavish offer: The Soviet leader would help to establish air force training facilities right in Manchuria, staffing them with Russian experts. Ultimately, Mao had succeeded in wringing the aid he sought from Stalin, but Soviet influence in China was growing. On August 14, when Liu finally returned to Beijing after nearly two months of negotiations in Moscow, he made the trip alongside ninety-six Russian-speaking companions.

NO DEVIL SHALL ESCAPE

O n the morning of August 17, in the free moments before his regular staff meeting, Truman peered down at a number of weather maps that he had unrolled onto his desk. For more than three decades, predicting the weather had been a sort of hobby for the president. He liked to study the data—the positions of the warm and cold fronts, the height and type of the cloud cover—and then make his best guess about what would happen next. As 1949 rolled on, he grew increasingly competitive about his forecasts, sometimes challenging staff members and reporters to petty wagers. Pulling stacks of maps from his alligator-leather briefcase, he would offer eighty-to-one odds that his opponents could not outguess him.

For Truman, it must have been a reassuring parlor game: an affirmation of his power to foresee the essentially unforeseeable. All year he had been struggling with the tension between the things he could control on the world stage, and the things that seemed to control him. With the White Paper, he had acknowledged that Mao's revolution was ultimately beyond his influence. And yet the document, with its merciless indictment of Chiang, was itself an attempt to shape an outcome. Truman, despite his caution, could never bring himself to completely abandon his efforts to bring order to what he viewed as an increasingly disorderly East Asia.

Even if he had wanted to forget about China, Truman's political opponents—men like Walter Judd—would not let him. Judd, after all, shared the president's desire to control the weather—and then some. But their days barnstorming the Midwest together, pushing their ambitious proposals to heal the world, were long past. Now, infuriated over the publication of the White Paper, Judd unloaded on his old friend. On August 17, on the floor of the House, the Minnesota congressman launched into a vicious attack on the administration. He argued that it was still possible—and necessary—for the United States to fight back against Mao. Past American statesmen, he insisted, had long recognized the importance of keeping China "in the hands of friends and not under the control of some nation hostile to us." Truman was standing up to Stalin in Europe, Judd argued; why wasn't he doing the same in Asia? "I have never been able to understand why we cannot get a policy that makes sense in both oceans at the same time," he said. Judd urged his colleagues to reverse the president's approach, shifting the strategy "from appease to oppose."

As Judd pushed publicly for more vigorous action, he met privately with key legislators to try to secure the funding. Judd wanted John Davis Lodge, the Connecticut congressman, to slip an amendment providing aid to China into an existing bill to bankroll military assistance to European nations. Judd thought the program should be modeled after the Greek aid package that Truman had approved two years before. He was not asking for "all-out intervention on a major scale with American troops," Judd said, but rather "limited American military assistance with the equipment and supplies carefully planned for the particular type of operation needed." These programs, Judd added, should be "led, supervised, and almost directed by American officers."

Discussion of the Judd-Lodge proposal dominated Acheson's staff meeting on the morning of August 18, crowding out all other issues. Acheson repeated the assertion he had made at his testimony before the House Foreign Affairs Committee the week before: if Congress felt the need to authorize an aid package for Asia, he would welcome it, so long as it could be used at Truman's discretion. Acheson added, however, that he thought the number they originally proposed—$200 million—was far too high. The secretary of state suggested cutting that figure in half. Later the same day, at a meeting with Truman, the president told Acheson that he approved of this approach.

Although Acheson did not believe that additional aid could reverse the tide on the mainland, he did think it might help along the periphery. As the Judd-Lodge proposal was worded, it lumped China together with Southeast Asia—a region that Acheson actually did want to shore up. Only a few days earlier, the Burmese foreign minister had warned Acheson that his own country was now susceptible to Communist subversion, particularly in the form of infiltrators who might slip across the Indochinese border from the east. Judd, too, warned from the House floor that the region was vulnerable. If Mao's government was permitted to establish diplomatic missions in Burma and the Philippines, their capitals would become hubs of "propaganda, intrigue, espionage, and conspiracy," Judd said. "Every one of them will be a pistol aimed at the United States."

Still, in Judd's view, simply buttressing China's perimeter was not enough. He described East Asia as if it were a kind of wagon wheel, with a hub in the middle and individual spokes leading out from the center. Trying to enact a policy of containment around the edges, he said, was "like letting the hub of a wheel be chopped out and imagining we can save or make anything out of the individual spokes. . . . How are you going to hold the wheel together if the hub is gone?"

For now, though, Judd said that he took Acheson at his word when the secretary of state wrote in the White Paper that his long-term goal was to encourage China to "throw off the foreign yoke." The amendment, Judd believed, would be a start. In the long run, however, it would become far more than that. Although neither Judd nor Acheson could have known it at the time, the initiative had set in motion a series of events that would profoundly alter American life—a first step into the morass of Southeast Asia's wars.

★

Although Judd and Acheson appeared to be moving closer on military aid, when the amendment finally came to a vote, on August 18, the House of Representatives defeated it. Angry about his inability to forge a bipartisan consensus, Judd took his frustration out on Truman and Acheson. Nearly two weeks after the release of the White Paper, the Minnesota congressman took to the floor of the House and began picking the document apart, point by point. Judd complained that the Truman Administration "intends to rest on the 1,000 pages it has dug out of the past to try to justify the colossal defeats its policies have suffered in Asia since the war."

The problem with the White Paper, Judd said, was that Acheson's narrative was too restrictive; the secretary of state had included only those documents that bolstered his own case. If Acheson wanted to revisit the past, Judd added, "then we have a right to all the past, not just selected parts of it." Judd ticked off a list of sixteen documents—many written during the Second World War—that he felt should have been included but were not: telegrams that exposed the tensions between Chiang and the Roosevelt Administration, as well as classified dispatches from State Department aides whom Judd accused of having "pro-Communist" sympathies. A wider selection of the documentary evidence, he implied, would have revealed a tale of betrayal and subversion—not only one of Nationalist incompetence.

Judd hammered away on this theme all weekend, releasing a summary of a secret military report produced during the Second World War, which had warned that Nationalist China might collapse if the Soviet Union were permitted to secure a zone of occupation in the north. The New York Times printed Judd's revelations at the top of the front page of its Sunday editions. The following day, the paper ran an editorial praising Judd as "a person of outstanding integrity" with a "profound knowledge of China." After nearly eight months of frustration, Judd's attacks finally seemed to be gaining some traction in the news media.

Even some cautious realists like the columnist Walter Lippmann, who had excoriated Truman two years earlier for the globalist pretensions of the Truman Doctrine, now groused that the president and his aides were unfairly trying to evade blame. America's China policy, Lippmann wrote, was a "diplomatic disaster, perhaps the greatest that this country has ever suffered." Lippmann could not understand how, "at the zenith of American power and prestige," its nation's policy makers had seemed so impotent. "Mr. Acheson is entitled to argue that the outcome of the Chinese civil war was inevitable and beyond our control," he wrote. "But the secretary of state cannot contend that our own actions and commitments in relation to that civil war were also inevitable and beyond our control." Lippmann complained that Acheson's response was merely political, an effort to "dispose of Congressman Judd."

Lippmann was not far off. By late August, Acheson's morning meetings, once crisp reviews of world events, had devolved into war councils dominated by discussion of how to answer the Minnesota congressman's attacks. At the August 22 meeting, Acheson's top aides—men like Kennan, who were usually determined to avoid trivial political flaps— agreed to convene separately to comb through the charges. Someone suggested that Acheson should eventually hold a press conference to offer a rebuttal. Acheson agreed, indicating at the next morning's session that he thought that he should speak out as soon as possible. He asked his staff to make sure that he was "properly briefed."

By the last days of August, Acheson looked exhausted. The secretary of state had become "a very tired man," one of his aides observed; he seemed incapable of fighting back effectively against the assaults of men like Johnson and Judd. But he was trying. On August 24, Acheson convened the State Department press corps, handing out a mimeographed sixteen-point rebuttal to Judd's accusations. Acheson also told the group that he had recruited a group of consultants to review his department's policy, adding that he was "trying to view the situation in China in its setting in the Far East and not as an isolated situation." The overriding goal, he said, was to determine "what is possible, what is impossible, what are the consequences of some actions, what are the consequences of others."

Failing to quiet his antagonists, Acheson held an off-the-record meeting with a smaller group of journalists on the evening of August 26. The secretary of state, perhaps fortified by a cocktail or two, protested that the White Paper had been "a completely honest baring of the bosom. There wasn't anything suppressed." Acheson bemoaned the fact that China had "dissolved into its primitive and elemental units." Chiang had drained the Nationalist treasury, carrying the country's wealth off to Taiwan, which he used as a home base as he frantically traveled back and forth to the mainland, trying to organize a last-ditch resistance. Under those circumstances, Acheson told the group, any further aid to the Nationalists would be "madness." Petulantly, he continued:

> People come to my office every day asking that I take some money for aid to the Chinese military. I don't propose to be bullied by Congress or public opinion. I won't take a cent in military assistance. If they want another of secretary of state they can have it.

★

And yet even as Acheson was privately disclaiming military aid, Truman appeared to be inching closer to experimenting with covert weapons shipments. On the same day as Acheson's first press conference, a State Department adviser wrote a memo suggesting obliquely that Truman's views on China were beginning to evolve. According to the memo, the State Department's China hands had been "immediately instructed to explore in more concrete terms the possibility of aid" to key figures like acting president Li Zongren and his ally Bai Chongxi, one of the Muslim generals whom Chennault had been pushing to support.

Chennault, meanwhile, continued to quietly discuss his proposals with Wisner's covert operators. And the general's associates in the press—particularly the Alsop brothers—helped to build support for the strategy among senior decision makers. In late August, Stewart Alsop published a column in the *New York Herald Tribune* calling for "an unpublic, realistic, clandestine effort" to aid Mao's remaining Chinese adversaries—essentially a version of the Chennault plan. The columnist seemed oblivious to the contradiction involved in publicly advocating for a covert operation. Still, Alsop warned breathlessly that anything less would "make a third world war inevitable."

Quietly, steadily, all over Washington, momentum was building for a program of secret aid. As the summer wound down, State Department aides asked their counterparts at Defense to analyze the feasibility of the Chennault plan, in order to present military options to the N.S.C. The diplomats, according to the department's secret daily staff summary, wanted to know "whether such assistance could be delivered within sufficient time and in sufficient volume, and could be utilized with sufficient effectiveness by the recipients, as to be likely to deny to the Communist forces those parts of China still free from their control." Even the churchly John Leighton Stuart, newly returned from Nanjing, recorded in his diary in late August that he had met with the C.I.A.—though he did not commit to paper the details of their talks.

Around the same time, Malcolm Rosholt, the agent whom Wisner had chosen to survey conditions in southern and western China, returned to Washington to present his findings. Rosholt, over the course of the summer, had managed to meet with many of the key military figures that Chennault had identified as possible collaborators. Some of them were useless. Rosholt reported that one, Ma Hongkui, was so ill with diabetes that he would be little help. Nevertheless, Rosholt was able to provide Wisner's operators with a far more accurate picture of the vigor and strategic goals of the key resistance fighters.

Finally, on September 1 and 2, Wisner held a series of meetings with Acheson, Kennan, and other key State Department officials to review the possibilities. Acheson's deputies seemed particularly concerned that word of the operations might leak out, undermining their broader strategy. For months, Acheson had been arguing that it would be foolish to provide Mao with an excuse to blame the United States for interfering in Chinese affairs. If the Americans left Mao alone, on the other hand, the Chinese Communists would eventually tangle with their erstwhile Russian allies to the north. Now Acheson's aides wanted to know: How could Wisner's team ensure that their plots would remain secret? And what would they tell the world if they did not? According to a recently declassified internal C.I.A. account of the meeting, Acheson's man grumbled that "he could not understand why the Russians were able to do these things and get away with them," while everyone just assumed that the Americans would get caught.

★

To Mao, the logic of covert American intervention seemed obvious enough. Mao thought the White Paper revealed a great deal about American intentions. "Acheson is a good teacher, giving lessons free of charge," he wrote in one article that was distributed widely on the mainland. "He is telling the whole truth with tireless zeal and great candor." While in Acheson's mind the document was intended as an assault on Chiang, to Mao it only showed how much money and effort the United States had already put into backing the Nationalists. Mao urged his allies to assume that this American strategy would continue—even if the tactics might take a different form.

Mao told his compatriots to expect quiet subversion, which he viewed as the only option left to the Truman Administration. Washington, he reasoned, was clearly worried about "getting hopelessly bogged down in a quagmire"; the American public would reject a full-scale military adventure in East Asia. Still, he fully expected Truman and Acheson to fund a "fifth column" in China through clandestine channels. Mao cautioned his supporters to be wary of such American largesse. "He who swallows food handed out in contempt will get a bellyache," he warned.

Mao's exhortations reinforced a xenophobic mood that had been building all year. As the P.L.A. swept south, Chinese newspapers increasingly highlighted instances of bad behavior by Western expatriates. In a society in which much of the traffic was confined to bicycles and rickshaws, the newspapers seized on reports of Americans recklessly driving their massive sedans. One local paper denounced a "drunken American telephone operator" for plowing her Plymouth into a crowd of pedicabs and pedestrians. In Shanghai, over the summer, Chinese authorities had arrested William Olive, an American consular official, after he had driven his car through a P.L.A. victory demonstration in the city, and then, under questioning, was reported to have adopted an "'overlording' attitude." The *Jiefang ribao* newspaper considered it "absolutely intolerable that an American resident should treat our people and the people's government with the barbarous and shameful attitude of an imperialist." Although American officials complained that Olive was being railroaded, such incidents nevertheless fed Mao's narrative of Western heedlessness and rapacity.

Mao's warnings about a fifth column jibed neatly with this anti-foreign pique. He continued to refuse to release Angus Ward and the other Americans being held incommunicado in Shenyang. Even as Truman and Acheson leaned closer to approving a program of clandestine aid, the *Dagong bao* newspaper urged its readers to be on guard against American schemes to "sabotage the people's New China." The editorialist continued:

> The eyes of the people are similar to the eyes of the Buddha in that no devil shall be able to escape them. Let us eliminate the reactionaries and oppose American imperialism to the end!

DIG UP THE DIRT

One day in early September, a news correspondent for the *New York Journal-American* arrived at the door of 4904 Independence Avenue, the stone Tudor mansion in the Bronx where Madame Chiang was staying. For most of the past year, she had avoided the press, preferring instead to conduct her business quietly, away from the cameras. Now, however, stung by the public betrayal of the White Paper, she decided to make an exception. Dressed elegantly in a high-collared dark jacket and garnet earrings, she welcomed the reporter into the living room, which was adorned with a large framed portrait of her husband. Over tea, she told the journalist that she was now leaning toward returning to China. "I am flying back next month," she said quietly. "I believe the Generalissimo needs me. I will go wherever he goes."

Although Madame Chiang continued to maneuver for advantage, she felt increasingly listless. Her life in the United States now seemed hollow, devoid of meaning. Rejoining Chiang, as he fought to hold the line in southern China, would at least restore some sense of purpose. Although her friends warned her against it, convinced that she and Chiang would ultimately share the same grim fate, Madame Chiang insisted on her choice. "I have complete faith, along with the Generalissimo, that China will eventually defeat Communism," she told the reporter as they sat talking in the living room. "It may take years of sacrifice and unswerving determination, but we will win." Nevertheless, a melancholy smile seemed to betray her ambivalence.

As autumn approached, the Chiang family's gambits to save their government grew increasingly desperate. For months, the Generalissimo and his allies had been lobbying the Truman Administration to appoint an American general to take charge of the fight against Mao. Madame Chiang, in her interview in Riverdale, suggested that they believed MacArthur would be the best choice. Her husband, however, was also quietly considering Albert Wedemeyer, the Nebraskan who had served as Chiang's chief of staff during the last year of the Second World War. Tall and lanky, with a thick sweep of gray hair, Wedemeyer was known for his analytical brilliance, and he had worked well with Chiang during the war. Now the Generalissimo formulated a scheme to bring Wedemeyer back to China as a private contractor.

To make the approach to Wedemeyer, Chiang and his family chose as their intermediary an executive from the Reynolds Tobacco Company, who called on the general at his Pentagon office at ten a.m. on September 9. According to Wedemeyer's memorandum of the conversation, the businessman explained that Chiang and his associates were prepared to offer "any amount of money" if Wedemeyer would take a role advising the Nationalist military. The tobacco executive emphasized that the general "should not hesitate to ask for a large amount."

Still, Wedemeyer was skeptical. If he resigned from the U.S. Army to take the post in China, he would lose his military pension. The general explained that he could not agree to take the job "unless my dependents were economically secure, including my wife, my mother and two boys." With that in mind, Wedemeyer said, the Nationalists might have to pay him as much as $1 million (more than $10 million in today's dollars) for each of the next five years. And even so, Wedemeyer was far from sure that he could make a difference. Although he ultimately agreed to consider the offer, the general explained that he "would make no commitments whatsoever."

Among China hands in Washington, word of the offer quickly spread. Stuart, who dined with Madame Chiang in Riverdale in early September, might have discussed the proposal with her. If not, he was certainly aware of it by September 11, when he wrote a cryptic note in his diary indicating that he had been approached by "several people" who had come to discuss what he called "the 'W' proposal." The following afternoon Stuart himself paid Wedemeyer a visit at the Pentagon, explaining that he had heard that the general had "agreed to accept or had demanded a $5 million salary." Stuart warned Wedemeyer that taking an exorbitant salary would deplete the resources of the Nationalist government; the general would be deluding himself if he thought the money would come only from "rich individual Chinese." Wedemeyer assured Stuart that he would never take the job if that were the case. On the other hand, the general recalled in his memorandum of the meeting, "I did add that I would gladly accept $5 million or even more from rich Chinese."

As these conversations unfolded, Chiang eagerly pressed his wife for news of Wedemeyer's response. He asked her what Wedemeyer's terms were, urging her to close the deal "speedily." The next day he cabled again, demanding to know whether something vague had been "arranged." Although she later replied that, yes, it had been arranged, if they were talking about the Wedemeyer proposal, it appears to have been wishful thinking. Coming far too late in the war to be effective, the overture ultimately went nowhere.

Still, the Chiangs were managing to make steady progress on other fronts. From his perch at the Pentagon, Madame Chiang's ally Louis Johnson continued to needle Acheson and the State Department over Asia. Using an upcoming state visit of Indian prime minister Pandit Nehru as a spur to action, the defense secretary urged the N.S.C. to expedite its review of the administration's Asia policies. In a memo to the N.S.C.'s executive secretary, Johnson argued that finalizing a strategy was now "a matter of great importance." He asked the council to push the deliberations to the top of its autumn agenda.

At the same time, Congress was inching closer to a compromise over the Military Assistance Program, the European aid package that Judd had tried to beef up with an additional $100 million for Asia. While the House of Representatives had voted down Judd's proposal, a Senate committee now resurrected a version of it, voting to give Truman the discretion to spend up to $75 million in the region. The president's opponents complained loudly about giving him so much latitude, demanding to refine the terms of the fund's use. Ultimately, however, the committee agreed that Truman could decide himself how to spend the money, so long as it was deployed in the "general area of China."

Although their long-term prospects remained dire, by mid-September Madame Chiang, Judd, and their associates were finally beginning to build some much-needed momentum. Still, Judd warned that Chiang's foes would lose no opportunity to "crucify" the Generalissimo if they could find a way. The Minnesota congressman urged his confederates to keep fighting, exhorting them to employ all the weapons of political warfare. To survive, he told them, they would need to "dig up all the dirt" on the administration that they could.

★

While Judd and his sympathizers readied themselves for battle, Acheson attempted to recruit allies of his own. One evening in September, he took the British foreign minister, Bevin, who was in town for the upcoming U.N. General Assembly, to a performance of *South Pacific*, the hit Rodgers and Hammerstein musical that had opened earlier that spring. For two statesmen preparing to discuss the fate of Asia, it was a fitting choice. The show, based loosely on a book by James Michener, tells the story of a nurse from Arkansas who is stationed in the South Pacific and falls in love with a French plantation owner. Eventually, however, the woman realizes that her new lover already has two children from an ex-wife, who is Polynesian. The narrative follows the nurse's evolution as she moves from her initial disgust at the revelation—fueled, in part, by her own racism—to her eventual embrace of the children.

This storyline, of an American woman's growing acceptance of her responsibilities in Asia, resonated powerfully with Americans in 1949. Viewed against the backdrop of the China debacle, the musical offered something for everyone. For those, like Judd, who believed that the United States should play a more vigorous role in the region, the show's finale seemed to symbolize and legitimize the creation of "an international community that transcends the potentially divisive boundaries of race, nationalism, and generation," in the words of one modern scholar. Others, who viewed Mao's victory as a fatal blow to that same global community, might well have found a kind of escape in the spectacle. Regardless of politics, the music—catchy tunes like "You've Got to Be Carefully Taught"—enchanted Broadway audiences.

On this night, as Acheson and Bevin sat in the front row of the orchestra at the Majestic Theatre, some of the cast members recognized the British foreign minister and sang right to him. Bevin thrilled at the attention. But when the lights came up and the rotund diplomat rose to leave, he collapsed in the aisle of the theater. Acheson and the others cleared a space for the sweating Bevin, who was splayed out on the floor. Someone swept in with a cold towel and dose of nitroglycerine; Bevin slowly regained his composure. As they finally made their way out of the theater, Acheson announced that he was going home for a nightcap. Coming to, Bevin retorted, "I need a drink more than any of you." The doctors eventually determined that Bevin had suffered a minor heart attack.

In the days that followed, while Bevin recuperated, Acheson and his staff gathered in the secretary of state's cavernous fifth-floor office to game out their strategy. Bevin's health was troubling, but so was the fact that the British and American China policies were beginning to diverge—a development that worried both Acheson and diplomats from several smaller nations, who increasingly did not know whose lead to follow. While Stuart and his top aides had returned to the United States, the British, Australian, and Indian ambassadors had remained in Nanjing, leading some to believe that their governments would soon offer diplomatic recognition to Mao's regime.

Now, in Acheson's office, the secretary of state and his top advisers bounced around ideas about how to sway Bevin. "The over-all British attitude toward China," a State Department aide wrote in his notes of the meeting, "is that the civil war is over, that they must deal with the Chinese Communists, that they will not liquidate their commercial interests, that they will not hurry recognition but will probably recognize sooner or later." For the most part, the Americans—at least those in Acheson's office—shared the basic assumptions that underpinned the British position. They agreed that Mao was "here to stay for some time" and that neither Chiang nor any other military leader was likely to overturn his rule.

Nevertheless, the Americans groused about London's short-sighted greed. Acheson's staff did not want to jump to conciliate Mao, which they thought would just make the administration look desperate. Instead, the State Department officials believed that they might be able to use their trade ties as a diplomatic carrot. Stuart argued that it would be impossible for Mao to wring all the financial aid he was going to need from Stalin alone. Eventually, the ambassador believed, the Communists would have to establish a robust exchange with the United States as well. The men who were gathered in Acheson's office recognized that such a strategy would require tremendous patience and forbearance on their part; they would need to avoid rash provocations. Over time, as they envisioned it, Mao's government would begin to understand these economic realities—but it would have to learn "the hard way."

Acheson told his staff that he would press Bevin to "go slow" on the question of recognition, the biggest point of friction between Washington and London. But there were also smaller rifts that needed to be sealed. The secretary of state's staff urged him to try to convince Bevin to support Bao Dai in Indochina, bringing the United States and Britain closer to a unified Southeast Asia policy. Acheson's team was also skeptical of London's desire to flood the region with development aid; the Americans felt there were still too many political question marks. Still, both sides saw the need to play an active—if clandestine—role in the region. According to one set of meeting notes, dated September 12 and marked TOP SECRET, American and British diplomats concurred that they should continue to attempt to "pull the strings" in the politics of Southeast Asia, even as they sought to "keep out of the limelight."

The staff work complete, Acheson and Bevin met to discuss these issues in person on September 13, not quite a week after the British foreign minister's heart attack. As promised, the American did his best to persuade Bevin that "hasty" diplomatic recognition of Mao's regime would serve little purpose. Mao did not even control the entire mainland yet, Acheson pointed out; they could at least wait until the political situation stabilized before deciding on recognition. Still, Acheson was skeptical that anything would change dramatically in the coming months. He did not even expect that Chiang would be able to hold Taiwan, acknowledging to Bevin that he was "depressed" about the island's prospects for resistance.

Bevin replied that he was in no hurry to recognize the Communists, but he also added, according to Acheson's notes of the conversation, that the British had "big commercial interests in and trade with China and were not in the same position as [the Americans] were relatively or absolutely." Bevin's biggest concern was Hong Kong. He did not expect Mao to attack it, but if the P.L.A. did invade, Bevin believed that Britain could defend the island—a position, he added, that was not up for discussion. Although the door to a negotiated turnover was not "bolted for all time"—some leases, Bevin noted, would expire as early as 1997—conditions for such talks did "not exist at present" and were "unlikely to exist in the foreseeable future."

So what positive steps might the United States and Britain take together with respect to China? Bevin wanted to launch a massive propaganda campaign designed to exacerbate the tensions between Mao and Stalin over Manchuria. The American diplomats agreed, briefing Bevin on some of the operations that were already under way, such as their efforts to use the Voice of America radio network to do just that. Someone also mentioned that distributing pamphlets stamped with the words TOP SECRET seemed to have been particularly effective. Whatever their approach to Mao's victory, Acheson said, the United States and Britain should coordinate their efforts. "The Communists," he concluded, "would be delighted if they could drive a wedge."

★

In recent years, some scholars have raised a tantalizing question about these British-American strategy sessions: What if Stalin knew all about them? Furthermore, what if he shared that information with Mao? Since the end of the Cold War, the U.S. government has declassified thousands of pages of once-secret intelligence intercepts that reveal a great deal of previously unknown detail about Soviet spying operations in the United States, much of it gathered by the U.S. Army's top-secret Venona counterintelligence program. One of Venona's most startling discoveries was that a clique of British Communists had for years been stealing secrets from Washington and London. Known as the Cambridge spy ring, the group included the now-notorious British moles Kim Philby, Anthony Blunt, Donald Maclean, and Guy Burgess.

Burgess, in particular, had access during 1949 to high-level British sources on Asian affairs. Based in London and assigned to the Far East department of the British Foreign Office, he was in a position to review much of the diplomatic correspondence related to Britain's China policy. Thirty-eight and handsome, with blue eyes and a wave of dark hair, Burgess had enjoyed a relatively typical upbringing for a child of British privilege. He had attended Eton, the prestigious English public school (he wore his old school tie into adulthood), and briefly studied at the Royal Naval College in Dartmouth. At Cambridge University, he met Anthony Blunt, who initiated him into the Apostles, a secret society that included many leftists and served as an incubator for future Soviet spies. An acquaintance recalled Burgess during these years as a "menacingly healthy" athlete, although his "rolling, lurching walk gave the impression that he was about to charge into somebody or something, and go overboard."

More than fifteen years later, in 1949, Burgess was still leading a reckless life—drinking heavily, getting into fights, and, more seriously, passing diplomatic secrets to Moscow. He threw boisterous parties at his Bond Street apartment in London; during one, someone threw him down a flight of stairs. "Whenever I saw him he seemed to have some part of his body in bandages," one acquaintance recalled. "At other times his arm would be in a sling." The English diplomat Harold Nicolson remembered that Burgess would say "anything that came into his head, and cared nothing about who heard him. Of course, he was a heavy drinker. He drank anything in any order, and when he had too much his eyes went out of focus." Still, Nicolson added, "he was charming. And his mind was brilliant."

Reading Burgess's internal reports on China now, one finds little about them that suggests subversion—no telltale indications that he was trying to shift British policy in ways that were dramatically out of the mainstream. Burgess observed that Mao's revolutionaries were essentially orthodox Communists, unlikely to break from Moscow. At first, he urged his government to go slowly on the question of recognition, taking care to first see how Washington decided to handle the question. As the year went on, however, he grew more frustrated with the American position, which he viewed as contradictory. By late September, he was complaining of the "muddled thinking" of Americans who opposed recognition.

No concrete evidence has been uncovered to prove that Burgess passed details of the Bevin-Acheson talks to the Soviets. Burgess's own reports on China, although they do favor diplomatic recognition of Mao's government, do not differ substantially in their logic from those of Bevin, who saw a compelling British financial interest in the same policy. Still, it is certainly possible that Burgess would have chosen to keep his Soviet handlers informed of the evolving discussions in the Western chancelleries over China—providing Stalin with valuable intelligence in his intensifying shadow war with Truman.

19

FIRST LIGHTNING

From a fortified observation post high atop the Kazakh steppe, a scientist peered anxiously toward an abandoned town in the distance. Nine miles away, strung out along the horizon, he could see an entire Potemkin village: wooden structures designed to simulate homes, deserted bridges, farm animals in pens. A steel tower pointed toward the heavens, topped by a gray metal capsule in the shape of a teardrop: a compact machine that resembled nothing more than an antique submarine, like something out of Jules Verne's imagination. Viewing this tableau from afar, the scientist understood that, if the next moments went badly, he could end up dead or in prison. It was shortly before seven a.m.

Moments later, a brilliant flash obscured the top of the tower. "For a moment or so it dimmed," the scientist recalled, "and then with new force began to grow quickly." He continued:

The white fireball engulfed the tower and the shop and, expanding rapidly, changing color, it rushed upwards. The blast wave at the base—sweeping in its path structures, stone houses, machines— rolled like a billow from the center, mixing up stones, logs of wood,

pieces of metal, and dust into one chaotic mass. The fireball, rising and revolving, turned orange, red. Then dark streaks appeared.
Streams of dust, fragments of brick and board, were drawn in after
it, as into a funnel.

At another post nearby, a voice cried out, "It works! It works!" Elated
men hugged each other. Although the official name they had given
to the device—the Soviet Union's first atomic bomb—was RDS-1, in
Russian they nicknamed it *Pervaya Molniya:* First Lightning.

★

To outside observers, the first indication that something important
had taken place in eastern Kazakhstan came several days later, when an
American B-29 weather plane picked up indications that a radioactive
explosion had occurred in Asia. Truman could not shake off a sense of
disbelief: his intelligence apparatus had given him no advance warning
that Stalin was so close to building a bomb. For the past four years,
the United States had held a monopoly on atomic power, a knowledge
gap that permitted Truman a measure of confidence in America's military superiority. Now those assumptions had evaporated. "It changed
everything," Acheson later recalled, "and [Truman] realized it ten sec-
onds after it happened."

Still, Truman tried to keep calm, concealing the news until he could
be absolutely sure of what had happened. On the afternoon of September 20, David Lilienthal, the chairman of the U.S. Atomic Energy
Commission, arrived for a meeting to find the president sitting in his
office, reading the *Congressional Record.* Lilienthal later told his diary
that Truman appeared "quiet and composed," with "bright sunlight in
the garden outside, the most unbusy of airs." Truman and Lilienthal
agreed that it was important to project a calm, buoyant persona, even
in the face of bad news. Referring to the Russian bomb reports, the
president added, "Can't be sure, anyway." But Lilienthal, an expert in
the field, told Truman that there was no doubt that Stalin had exploded

a bomb. The president threw a cutting glance in the direction of his guest. "Really?" Truman asked.

Truman finally announced the news on September 23. "We have evidence," the president said carefully, "that within recent weeks an atomic explosion occurred in the U.S.S.R." He tried to downplay his own surprise. "Ever since atomic energy was first released by man," he explained, "the eventual development of this new force by other nations was to be expected. This probability has always been taken into account by us." But the president convinced few. The *New York Times*, on its front page, just under the text of Truman's statement, printed a story headlined SOVIET ACHIEVEMENT AHEAD OF PREDICTIONS BY 3 YEARS. The article went on to project that the Soviets could now produce another bomb every week; in less than a year, it warned, Moscow would possess the capability to attack fifty U.S. cities at once, killing forty million Americans in a single strike.

Considering the new dangers, "people took it calmly," Kennan told his diary the following day. Americans, only four years from V-J Day, were still war weary, eager to avoid new battles abroad. Conversations around the dinner table that autumn tended to revolve around baseball's pennant race; the Brooklyn Dodgers were closing on St. Louis in the National League, and in the American League the Yankees were battling it out with the Red Sox, making a Subway Series a real possibility. "The American public," the newspaper columnist Drew Pearson wrote in his diary, "is basically probably more interested in this race than in the race of atomic energy."

The growing popularity of television made it easier than ever for Americans to follow the games; ten million people would ultimately tune in to the first game of the World Series later that autumn. But the new technology was also beginning to alter some basic human behaviors. The baseball mania was a perfect example. On the one hand, the new medium was turning the players into minor deities. Audiences marveled at every seemingly superhuman feat. One of Ted Williams's teammates referred to him, simply, as God. Even the umpires found themselves reveling in their newfound celebrity. "Conscious of the great unseen audience," one sportswriter observed, "they play every decision out like the balcony scene from *Romeo and Juliet*." Yet television also had a way of exposing every flaw, revealing every secret. Under the glare of the klieg lights, the new gods were in danger of falling as fast as they rose.

As with athletes, so with statesmen. Truman and his advisers recognized that the power of television cut both ways. For a leader with dramatic flair, with some of the instincts of a ham, the new medium provided a potent new means of connecting with constituents. Truman, with his broad grin, crisp suits, and glib self-assurance, was a natural performer. Yet the stage demanded action; passivity bored audiences. Politicians who wanted to cast themselves in the role of the hero needed a dragon to slay. For anti-Communist crusaders, Stalin and Mao might serve as convenient foils. But this type of dramatic conflict also had a way of raising expectations. Leaders who failed to live up to their promises risked the wrath of a disappointed public.

For Truman and Acheson, this was one real danger of the Russian bomb news. Together with Mao's victory, it fed a growing sense of governmental impotence. The administration could not afford to leave the impression that it was unwilling to meet these new threats. Men like Judd, eager to raise new enemies, would use the news to attack the White House. Louis Johnson, too, could leverage the disclosure to increase the pressure on Acheson. Yet there was also a genuine, substantive policy question for Truman and his advisers to decide. The bomb revelation had shifted the global balance of forces—or so, at least, it seemed. After so many years of American dominance, the Soviets and their allies now appeared revitalized and assertive.

This ferment opened opportunities for anyone claiming to have a good solution, however unorthodox. On September 27, Truman's head of covert action, Frank Wisner, sent a memo to Kennan outlining a strategy for more aggressive clandestine operations on the Chinese mainland. Even if nothing could be done to keep Mao from consolidating his conquests, Wisner argued that the U.S. spy agencies needed to buy time to strengthen their "stay-behind networks and underground

As Mao's armies closed in on Beijing, Nationalist recruits gathered
in the shadow of the city's Imperial Palace.

At Truman's inaugural in 1949, the president derided the "false philosophy" of Communism.

Truman chose Dean Acheson as his secretary of state in January 1949. "I arrived just in time to have [Chiang] collapse on me," Acheson later recalled.

Mayling Soong married Chiang Kai-shek in December 1927. "A bad temper in a man is preferable to a man without a temper," she told her sister.

Truman and Walter Judd (second from right) toured the Midwest together in the summer of 1943, trying to rally support for the institution that would become the United Nations. They would later fall out over China policy.

Mao believed that China would succeed in shaking off the indignities of the past only by galvanizing its populace. "The greatest force," he said, "is that of the union of the popular masses."

In the spring of 1949, Mao moved to a small house in the Fragrant Hills, northwest of Beijing. The complex was dubbed "Labor University," to throw off curious neighbors.

Truman named Louis Johnson to be his defense chief in 1949. Another member of Truman's inner circle referred to Johnson as "Big Boy" and "Man of Heroic Mould."

Johnson (front row, far left) and Acheson (front row, second from left)
battled each other all year over China policy.

After Chiang's government attempted a currency reform in 1948,
steep inflation undermined the Generalissimo's support. Here, Shanghai residents
wait in line for a ration of forty grams of gold.

As Communist troops approached Nanjing, Nationalist refugees fled the city. Some left China altogether, and would not return until decades later.

In April 1949, Mao's troops crossed the Yangtze River and entered the Nationalist capital of Nanjing. Mao warned that the city was full of "foreign spies."

On October 1, 1949, Mao proclaimed the birth of the People's Republic of China from atop the Gate of Heavenly Peace in Beijing.

Al Cox, an American intelligence operative, slipped baskets of cash to Mao's enemies on the mainland.

Indian prime minister Pandit Nehru arrived in Washington in October 1949. One American journalist observed that Nehru generated as much excitement as "a motion picture star."

Madame Chiang Kai-shek spoke to U.S. listeners in a farewell address on January 8, 1950. "It is either in your hearts to love us," she said, "or your hearts have turned from us."

channels": vital listening posts as Mao slowly closed off the traditional avenues of communication. This strategy, Wisner implied, would be useful even if it ultimately failed to halt Mao's advance. In the meantime, he suggested, the United States should swiftly dispatch American agents into the field to help bolster the remaining anti-Communist commanders—essentially a version of Chennault's plan.

The C.I.A., simultaneously, began shifting around the assets that it already had in place. On September 27, the same day that Wisner requested additional men in the field, the C.I.A.'s lead operative in Urumqi, the capital of China's northwestern Xinjiang province, prepared to depart the area as Mao's forces closed in. For years, the American, Douglas Mackiernan, had been working out of the Urumqi consulate, under State Department cover. An expert in the equipment that the United States used to detect nuclear explosions, Mackiernan's mission included surveilling Soviet activities in Xinjiang, including any potential efforts to mine uranium in the largely Muslim province.

Now, as the local Chinese security forces began switching their allegiances to Mao, Mackiernan filled a jeep with guns, ammunition, and grenades, along with several hundred small gold bars the size of sugar cubes. Under his clothes, he strapped ten thousand dollars in cash to his body. He also packed a number of "one-time pads"—special notebooks that he could use to send encrypted messages. Although Urumqi was in danger of falling to Mao any day, Mackiernan hoped that he might be able to escape south to Tibet, where the largely autonomous government seemed better capable of resisting the Communists. Still, before he could do so, Mackiernan would have to travel nearly fifteen hundred miles to Lhasa—a trip that would include long stretches on horseback through the desolate Taklamakan desert.

In Washington, meanwhile, Acheson's deputies at State began discussing whether to formalize and coordinate some of these otherwise ad hoc paramilitary operations. In late September, the Senate had finally approved the Military Assistance Program, with its authorization of $75 million to be used at Truman's discretion in the "general area of China." Now, with fears rising in the capital after Stalin's atomic bomb test, the men debated how the State Department should respond. Although Acheson had departed for a much-needed vacation in the Canadian backcountry, his advisers met for their regular daily Prayer Meeting on September 30. According to the minutes, the men deliberated over how to answer critics who thought the news demanded "a major shift in U.S. foreign policy."

★

As October approached, with Mao preparing to announce the formation of the People's Republic of China on the first of the month, the Communists intensified their own covert operations around Beijing. Concerned that an assassin might take a shot at Mao during the ceremony, they ordered additional police patrols and counterintelligence sweeps. Mao had originally wanted to wait until the end of the year before taking this monumental step; he felt that he needed more time to consolidate his victories on the ground before making it official. But Stalin pressed him to do it sooner. The Soviet leader feared that if China went too long without a functioning government, foreign powers would use the vacuum as an excuse to intervene.

On the historic morning of October 1, according to one of Mao's bodyguards, the Chairman overslept. As Mao often did, he had stayed up through the night, falling into bed at close to six a.m. Mao's bodyguard later recalled that he woke Mao up at around one that afternoon, then watched as the Chinese leader wiped his face with a hot towel. Clutching a cup of tea, Mao scanned the day's newspapers. After dressing himself in a woolen tunic, the Chinese leader made his way to the edge of Tiananmen Square for the ceremony, climbing the stone steps to the top of the Gate of Heavenly Peace.

In 1949, Tiananmen Square had not yet evolved into the "vast totalitarian space" that it is today. Although Mao's foot soldiers had made an effort to widen it in advance of the ceremony, chopping down silk trees and planting a massive flagpole in the center, the square was still walled in and filled with small bushes. For centuries, the enclosure had served a singular purpose: providing a majestic footpath for the emperors when they wished to leave the Imperial City. But now the square bustled with revolutionaries. Atop the gate, which was adorned with huge red pompons, the assembled guests included Soong Ching-ling, one of Madame Chiang's sisters, who had decided to support the Communists, in defiance of the rest of her family. Perhaps as a jab at her younger sister, Chingling had declared that she had no desire to "leave my country and retreat to a small white Connecticut farmhouse and prepare my memoir."

For Mao, the show of unity served an important purpose. After so many years of war, it was crucial that he now reconcile with former foes—a task that demanded a peculiar kind of national amnesia. As he surveyed his supporters in the square below, his laconic statement proclaiming the birth of the new China mentioned his enemies only in passing. "Our People's Liberation Army," he said, "backed by the whole nation, has been fighting heroically and selflessly to defend the territorial sovereignty of our homeland, to protect the people's lives and property, to relieve the people of their sufferings, and to struggle for their rights, and it eventually wiped out the reactionary troops and overthrew the reactionary rule of the Nationalist government." He continued:

> Now, the People's War of Liberation has been basically won, and the majority of the people in the country have been liberated. . . . This government is the sole legal government representing all the people of the People's Republic of China. This government is willing to establish diplomatic relations with any foreign government that is willing to observe the principles of equality, mutual benefit, and mutual respect of territorial integrity and sovereignty.

For decades afterward, spectators remembered the elaborate light show in the city that night: the soaring fireworks, the flickering lanterns, the billowing red silk of the banners. Elsewhere in China, however, the weather did not cooperate. In Shanghai, party organizers had planned a massive parade and "water carnival" that was set to roll on for three full days. But instead, torrential rains pounded the coastal city, flooding the streets and dampening spirits. Only a few brave souls ended up joining the celebration, twirling their flaming torches in the sodden murk.

In a week's time, however, the skies finally cleared. Tens of thousands of marchers gathered at Shanghai's race course, where Communist cadres had hung huge, thirty-foot portraits of Mao and Stalin, and then paraded out into the city. Stepping in formation, columns of P.L.A. soldiers hoisted their rifles, red pennants fluttering from the barrels. Singing, smashing gongs, and lighting off firecrackers, Shanghailanders lined the route and crowded the tops of buildings, looking on as a stream of floats, designed to resemble planes and warships, moved past. At times, the celebrations took on a vengeful air. The *North-China Daily News* reported that one group of marchers carried an effigy of "the battered, injured figure of Chiang"; another displayed a picture of the Generalissimo and his wife "walking hand in hand with a 'Japanese warlord.'"

The celebrations culminated on the evening of October 10, as a stately procession of ships glided along the surface of the Huangpu River. "The dark and muddy river flashed with color," the newspaper reported. Fireworks exploded overhead as sirens screamed and whistles shrieked; searchlights looped across the sky. Thirty-two vessels— everything from rowboats to steamships—joined in the festivities. At the head of the line, a ship with electric lights strung up both of its masts displayed a large star, framed by twinkling bulbs. An image of Mao occupied the place of honor at the center, as the flotilla drifted triumphantly across the water.

★

While Mao's supporters celebrated, Truman and his cabinet worried. The C.I.A. was especially concerned about Indochina, which it warned was particularly vulnerable to Mao's growing influence. In early October, the agency cautioned that the territory was in imminent danger of slipping from French control. "In about six months," according to a C.I.A. memorandum, "it is expected that the Chinese Communists, having assumed control of South China, will increase the flow of arms to the Indochinese resistance, either openly or by smuggling. The balance of military power will then begin to shift in favor of the resistance." Barring unforeseen developments, the C.I.A. projected that the French would be pushed out completely in as little as a year or two.

After the humbling China debacle, agency analysts jumped to worst-case predictions. If "a Communist government emerged in Indochina at a time of Communist triumph in China," the memo went on, "then Burma, Thailand, and Malaya would undoubtedly turn to Communism and the U.S.S.R." The French puppet in Saigon, Bao Dai, was "untrustworthy," the C.I.A. believed; his regime "cannot be relied on under any circumstances to gain true popular support." With a "determined, Communist-dominated, nationalist resistance led by the Moscow-trained Ho Chi Minh" in control of some ninety percent of the territory, the C.I.A.'s Asia hands could see few appealing alternatives.

Increasingly, Truman and his advisers looked to regional leaders for answers. One of the most important—and potentially problematic—local figures was Jawaharlal Nehru, the prime minister of India. Nehru led a nation that was still in its infancy, having gained independence from British rule only two years before. Although nationalist resistance to the British Raj had been building for decades, it was not until August 1947 that London finally relinquished effective control, partitioning the territory into predominantly Hindu India and chiefly Muslim Pakistan. This broad division, however, was misleading; in reality, the region was home to a welter of ethnic and religious sects. Partition unleashed a frenzied wave of violence that ultimately left up to one million people dead. It was into this turbulent environment that Nehru stepped when he became the new nation's first prime minister.

Proud and assertive, but also conscious of India's precarious position, Nehru was less eager than his American counterparts to confront

Mao directly. Although some in the Truman Administration hoped that he would help organize a regional bloc to oppose the Communists, he seemed more interested in conciliating Mao. Nehru was a secular politician with an appreciation for Marxist thought; in practice, however, his approach to China was rooted in what he saw as India's own geopolitical interest. Nehru was wary, for instance, of shipping arms and equipment to Tibet; he feared that any such aid would unnecessarily provoke Beijing. As for Indochina, he liked to emphasize that the revolt there was nationalist as well as Communist; he doubted whether a full-blown Communist revolution could ultimately succeed there.

Primed for confrontation, Nehru arrived in Washington on October 11, planning to tour the United States for three weeks. Americans did not know quite what to make of him. To some, the Indian leader—with his intense glower, flowing *kurta*, and white Gandhi cap—seemed a glamorous figure. One Truman aide, who spotted the Indian nationalist on his way into the White House, observed that he generated as much excitement as would "a motion picture star." Stewart Alsop gushed about Nehru's elegant "way of holding a cigarette in a long holder," his "handsome regularity of feature," and his "conscious charm consciously employed as an enormously effective weapon of persuasion." Others were less impressed. The U.S. ambassador to India, Loy Henderson, saw Nehru as "a vain, sensitive, emotional, and complicated person." Acheson, too, later recalled that the Indian prime minister had shown up for his visit in "a prickly mood."

Acheson did his best to diffuse the tension, inviting Nehru back to his own home after one state dinner. In Acheson's red brick Georgetown lair, with its oil paintings and English country decor, the secretary of state tried to loosen Nehru up. Acheson told the prime minister that he was ready to listen; Nehru should feel free to share any complaints with "the greatest freedom." Still, Acheson recalled, Nehru "would not relax." Even amid the warmth of his private home, Acheson complained, Nehru chose to address his host as if he were at "a public meeting."

Nehru quickly made it clear that he was leaning toward recognizing Mao's new regime. Acheson then presented his own case for withholding recognition—at least for the time being. Acheson considered himself a realist, willing to accept that circumstances had changed. Still, he did not want to rush the decision. He tried to convince Nehru to wait until Mao controlled more of the country before taking such a step. In the meantime, he said, the United States could use Voice of America broadcasts and political pamphlets to help persuade ordinary Chinese to reject Mao's rule. Nehru, however, thought spreading agitprop would make no practical difference. "His general attitude," Acheson wrote, "seemed to be that since recognition was doubtless inevitable, there was little purpose in postponing it by diplomatic maneuvers." By one a.m., after talking through some other tricky issues, Acheson recalled, "I found myself becoming confused and suggested that we adjourn the discussion" for the night.

Truman, too, had little success in persuading Nehru to hold off on recognition. The American president had made a poor first impression on the Indian nationalist. At their initial meeting, Nehru complained, Truman had boorishly gone on and on about the virtues of bourbon whisky. (Nehru did not drink.) Now, at a meeting late on the afternoon of October 13, Nehru lectured Truman, pointing out that "India's proximity to China put India in a somewhat different position from that of other countries," according to Acheson's notes of the conversation. Truman, nevertheless, said that he hoped the two nations could continue to "consult and if possible concert their action" on recognition. But Truman and Acheson could not budge Nehru. Ultimately, Acheson later griped, the Indian prime minister "wasn't very consulting."

Louis Johnson also tried his hand at swaying Nehru, inviting the prime minister to White Sulphur Springs, West Virginia, for a dinner at the Greenbrier Hotel, with American business leaders. Johnson bragged about the event; the newspaper columnist Drew Pearson told his diary that Johnson gave him "an ecstatic account" of the dinner. Actually, however, Nehru had been turned off by the gaudy costumes of the waitstaff and the ballroom full of business magnates, many of whom had likely opposed Indian independence. The menu, furthermore, was too "long and exotic," Nehru complained. On the flight back, one witness reported, Nehru appeared "dead tired." The Indian ambassador to the United States (who happened to be Nehru's sister) later observed that this and other such functions "could not have been more wrong" for Nehru "had they been carefully planned to upset him."

Even Walter Judd, a cosmopolitan figure whose own wife had been born and raised in India, seemed wholly unable to comprehend Nehru and his worldview. While Nehru saw Mao's victory as a manageable local headache, Judd viewed it as an imminent global threat. The Minnesota congressman expressed his "grave doubts" that India would be able to survive a leftist revolt. The Communists, Judd insisted, "have frankly announced for a long time that as soon as they have completed their conquests in East Asia, India will be next on the list." Still, even the once-energetic Judd was beginning to doubt how much of an impact he could really make. Success in Asia, as he saw it, would require "faith in God, human sympathy, and charity"—three qualities that were in increasingly short supply as the battles of 1949 raged on.

RISKY BUSINESS

As Nehru was making his rounds in Washington, the Truman Administration finally approved a program of covert aid to Mao's enemies on the mainland. Wisner arranged for Chennault's airline, Civil Air Transport, to provide cover jobs for two American intelligence operatives, who would be based in Hong Kong and travel back and forth to the mainland. Wisner's orders closely resembled the strategy that Chennault had laid out for him at the Hotel Washington back in May. The Americans were to meet secretly with anti-Communist military figures in key cities, then provide them with the cash necessary to bolster their forces. Wisner also instructed his men to establish "adequate standby facilities" in China that would allow U.S. spies to continue to operate in the country—even after a complete Communist takeover.

That day now seemed uncomfortably near. Almost as soon as the American operators arrived in Hong Kong, Mao's army penetrated the Nationalist front north of Guangzhou, sending panicked refugees streaming out of the city. The chaos forced Wisner's men to focus, for several days, on the evacuation of people and equipment, at the expense of their original mission. "The Commies have been advancing without opposition, and never knowing exactly where they were has made quite a bit of nervous tension," one of the American intelligence operatives, Alfred Cox, wrote to his wife on October 14. "We got the last of our personnel out last night, but had to leave a good bit of equipment behind. We believe the Commies moved in last night, but are flying a plane up there to take a look around." Cox worried that the P.L.A. would be likely to be "pretty rough" on any Americans they managed to capture. The whole mission, he told his wife, was a "risky business."

The following day, Cox and Chennault traveled to Taiwan for a meeting with Chiang Kai-shek. Cox was impressed with the grandeur of the setting. He boasted to his wife that a "beautiful limousine" had brought them to the guesthouse, which included elegant Japanese-style gardens and hot sulfur baths. Inside, the Americans were told to remove their shoes and replace them with slippers. Compared to the pandemonium in Guangzhou, the accommodations near Chiang's headquarters in Taipei seemed more like a spa.

That afternoon Chennault briefed Chiang on his plan to deliver aid to individual commanders in the field—but he did not reveal that he was working with U.S. intelligence. Instead, he told the Generalissimo that private American businessmen had put up the funds. Chiang, at first, was wary of Chennault's approach, understanding that the program would only strengthen his intraparty antagonists. All summer Chennault had been publicly urging Americans to aid one of Chiang's chief rivals in Guangxi, Bai Chongxi—a strategy that was certain to weaken Chiang's position within the party. The Generalissimo caviled to Chennault that piecemeal deliveries would incite jealousies among commanders who had not received any American aid. Still, despite his objections, Chiang eventually assured Chennault that he would do nothing to stand in the way of the operation.

One reason Chiang went along—despite the fact that the Americans seemed determined to strengthen his foes in the Guomindang—might have been that after months of focusing on China's southeastern coast and Taiwan, Chiang himself was now seeking to establish a foothold in southwestern China. He understood that his position on Taiwan remained tenuous, threatened by enemies in his own party, an unsettled local political climate, and foreign powers playing favorites. He needed a backup plan if the situation on Taiwan deteriorated. He was particularly eager to broaden his influence in Yunnan, a mountainous area in China's far southwest that shared a border with Indochina. As Mao's forces continued to press south, the Generalissimo had forged a shaky alliance with a local leader in Yunnan, paying him one million silver dollars for his support.

Chennault and his operators, however, chose to focus first on strengthening Guilin, a Nationalist bastion about three hundred miles northwest of Guangzhou. Controlled by Bai Chongxi, Guilin was one of the most spectacularly beautiful settings in China. Dozens of jagged limestone peaks bit into the sky like shark's teeth, towering over manmade lakes that had once served as city moats. Now, however, despite the natural splendor, the whole place had a garrison feel. Guilin was "raw and cold," Cox told his wife, with no running water or electricity. Although he stayed in one of the city's best hotels, the accommodations were grim; he slept on "wooden planks with a very thin covering." With only a small oil lamp for light, he found himself falling into bed by nine p.m.

After a preliminary visit to assess Bai's needs, Cox agreed to return to Guilin in mid-October with stacks of cash. To avoid a money trail leading back to Washington, Cox had arranged to make the payment using Hong Kong dollars instead of American greenbacks. (At first he had wanted to use silver dollars, but he ultimately determined that they would weigh too much.) Now, wary of raising suspicions by exchanging large quantities of U.S. currency on the Hong Kong markets, he enlisted a colleague to help make the trades in small increments. Although the precise sum of the payment to Bai is still classified by the C.I.A., Cox discovered that the formidable piles of cash filled two large wicker baskets.

In Hong Kong, Cox and Malcolm Rosholt boarded a C-46 for the flight to Guilin, where they were met by a "dilapidated but still operable" truck sent by Bai's troops. The Americans then watched in horror as a group of coolies loaded the baskets of money onto the truck—and drove away. "You can imagine the mental state of Cox and Rosholt at that moment," Cox later wrote in his internal report describing the incident. Panicked, the Americans climbed into a second vehicle and raced toward Bai's command post. When they arrived, the men were relieved to find the baskets of cash sitting by the door of Bai's office, unmolested. Together, the Americans and the Chinese counted out the bills, and Bai's men wrote out a receipt.

Even after delivering the money, Cox told his superiors that he was not particularly optimistic about Bai's prospects. His biggest concern, he explained, was that Bai would try to prove himself worthy of the aid, unwisely remaining for too long in Guilin as Mao's troops surged northwest from Guangzhou. In that scenario, Cox warned, Bai's troops could get "pretty badly cut up." Cox did retain some hope that Bai's forces would be able to conduct guerrilla attacks on Mao's advancing columns, assaulting the Communist supply routes. But he recognized that the general's future remained dire. "Things are certainly going badly out here," Cox wrote home in one letter to his wife. "Time is running out."

★

By mid-October, just weeks after the celebrations in Tiananmen Square, Mao had already begun cementing ties with key foreign partners. At five p.m. on October 16, he held a ceremony in one of his new palace halls to receive the credentials of the Soviet ambassador to Beijing, N. V. Roshchin. Mao, in his speech, praised the Soviets for being the first foreign nation to recognize the new People's Republic. The Chairman's remarks were suitably diplomatic: he used the word *esteemed* seven times in his one-hundred-and-eighty-five-word address. Behind the scenes, however, Mao still seemed insecure about his relationship with Stalin. After the official ceremony, he invited the new ambassador for a private chat. Although Mao politely raised a toast to Stalin's health, he also complained bitterly that the Soviet leader had not yet sent him a personal telegram of congratulations after the founding of the state. Roshchin, in his notes from the conversation, observed that Mao appeared "extremely upset" about the snub.

Yet Mao was even more sensitive about the prospect of establishing diplomatic ties with the Western powers. The Chinese leader understood that some factions in the United States—and especially in Britain—were pushing to recognize his new regime. Still, he did not want to appear too eager for Western approval as he was consolidating his revolution at home. On the same day that he met with Roshchin, Mao's state news agency issued a bulletin advising his subordinates to take a "wait-and-see attitude" toward the United States and Britain. Under no circumstances, the instructions read, should the Communists "make any propaganda for establishing diplomatic relations at an early time."

They did not need to. The British, increasingly, were self-motivated by their large commercial interests in the Middle Kingdom, as well as their desire to protect Hong Kong. Shortly after Mao's proclamation, Bevin's government sent the new Communist regime a letter that some American diplomats interpreted as "a strong step toward recognition," as the State Department's internal summary put it. Acheson and Truman, who had been working hard to maintain a common front with the British, were appalled. Acheson dashed off a personal note to Bevin complaining, according to the departmental summary, that unilateral British action would be "exploited by the Communists" and would weaken the resolve of China's neighbors.

Truman, when he met with Acheson on October 17, was still seething about the British betrayal. The president griped that "the British had not played very squarely with us on this matter," according to Acheson's notes of the conversation. Truman worried that the Soviets already regarded the British note as an important step toward recognition. In the days that followed, Bevin attempted to salve the wound, acknowledging that he had violated his previous understanding with Acheson and apologizing for failing to coordinate with the Truman Administration. Nevertheless, although Bevin assured the Americans that he would consult more closely in the future, he made no promises that the two Western powers could ultimately succeed in concerting their strategies.

While U.S. and British statesmen debated the merits of recognition, Americans argued among themselves about where, precisely, they should be making a stand against Mao's military. The collapse of the Nationalist headquarters at Guangzhou had sent Chiang's men streaming toward Taiwan, adding urgency to the Truman Administration's deliberations about how—or whether—to defend the island. By late October, Mao's troops had begun to assault other coastal islands. But Truman's N.S.C. had still not determined which Nationalist-held territories the United States was willing to help safeguard. On October 18, Johnson drafted a memo to the N.S.C., urging the body to clarify its strategy. "The Department of Defense," Johnson wrote, "is actively pursuing its studies of feasible military means to achieve the objective of denying to Chinese Communist forces those parts of China still remaining free from Communist control." Still, those efforts were destined to remain desultory until the N.S.C. provided more concrete guidance.

Although Johnson protested that the Chennault plan was "too vague" to make informed predictions about its success, the defense secretary was determined to prevent a Communist conquest of Taiwan. In late October, Johnson took the extraordinary step of traveling to Riverdale to dine with Madame Chiang, who by this time was leaning strongly toward returning to the island to be with her husband. Although neither Johnson nor Madame Chiang seems to have committed the details of their conversation to paper, there are some clues about what they might have discussed. Months later, Johnson referred to a "promise" that he had once made to Madame Chiang. It is certainly easy to imagine the defense secretary assuring his anxious dinner companion that he would protect the island to which she was now hoping to return.

Acheson, on the other hand, was far less concerned about Taiwan, which he considered both indefensible and immaterial. One State Department staff member complained that the N.S.C.'s early drafts of its new strategy were "unrealistic, impractical, and even starry-eyed." Although Acheson's team remained committed to shoring up a "great crescent" around the Chinese periphery, Taiwan did not necessarily have to be a part of it. Acheson, furthermore, had no personal relationship with Madame Chiang and her allies. Although the secretary of state was disturbed by what he viewed as the Chiang family's undue influence in American politics, his position was rooted more in a general skepticism about American omnipotence. In late October, as the debate over Taiwan was intensifying, Acheson traveled to New York to give a speech at the annual Al Smith dinner at the Waldorf Astoria hotel. "We can greatly help those who are doing their utmost to succeed by their own efforts," he told the audience. Still, he added, "we cannot direct or control; we cannot make a world, as God did, out of chaos."

★

Truman, however, was still trying—despite the setbacks of the past months. Early on the morning of October 24, he boarded a train for New York, to lay the cornerstone for a new U.N. Secretariat building along the banks of the East River. When the president, in his oxford gray suit and matching fedora, arrived at Penn Station around eleven a.m., a band broke into "Hail to the Chief," and a motorcade, led by an escort of one hundred and seven motorcycles, rolled through midtown, under a shower of confetti from the surrounding buildings. At the site of the outdoor ceremony, Truman sat in a wooden folding chair on the dais, before the crowd of sixteen thousand spectators in their colorful "saris, chipaos, [and] ghararas," as one reporter described the scene. Truman looked on as men with trowels fixed the cornerstone—a massive three-and-a-half-ton block of New Hampshire granite—atop a metal box containing copies of the U.N. Charter and the Universal Declaration of Human Rights.

The U.N. had been Truman's pet project, a dream he had been

harboring since his days barnstorming through the Midwest with Walter Judd. Now, at the ceremony, the president did his best to present a magnanimous front, genially pumping the hand of the Soviet foreign minister, Vishinsky. In his address, Truman stressed that the world's problems "must be settled on a basis acceptable to the conscience of mankind," adding that the U.N. was "the dynamic expression of what all the peoples of the world desire, because it sets up a standard of right and justice for all nations." Even so, he acknowledged that the new organization was still an experiment. Ultimately, he said, believing in the universalistic mission of the U.N. demanded an "act of faith."

After his speech, Truman climbed into a convertible for the drive to a luncheon at Gracie Mansion. As his car turned into the parking lot, a formation of three dozen F-84 fighter jets ripped across the Manhattan sky. Inside, while guests dined on turtle soup, whitefish, and pumpkin pie, Truman made his case one more time. "I sincerely hope that as a result of this meeting today we will come closer and closer to that ideal condition which we all visualized," Truman told the group. "I don't want to see another war. I am trying with everything I have to prevent another war. All I am working for is peace in the world." At two minutes before four p.m., as a battery of twenty-one guns rumbled in salute, he drove out of the mansion parking lot, caught his train, and returned to the wars in Washington.

As Truman pleaded for global brotherhood, Mao picked a fight. On the day Truman spoke in New York, Mao's government formally arrested Angus Ward, the American consul general that the Communists had been holding incommunicado for almost a year. During their captivity, Ward and the rest of the staff had been living in miserable conditions, without hot water or electricity. Nationalist planes bombing Communist positions in Shenyang shattered the windows of the consulate, spraying the place with glass; one diplomat recalled picking the shards out of his colleagues' lips with tweezers. "We would bake bread and the cockroaches would practically line the bread pans as it was rising," one of the American captives remembered. "We would bake it with the cockroaches in it and then just slice the sides off." To stay sane, the men played bridge and pinochle by candlelight.

The Ward drama galled Truman—and seriously complicated his China policy. By late October, Acheson's State Department had begun a thorough review of its approach, convening a large group of regional experts to take a broad-picture look at the "area from Japan to Pakistan as a whole," as one memo put it. The consultants were deeply skeptical that paramilitary operations would make any difference. "The burden of showing that such assistance would be effective in the specific case must lie with the proponents of such a program of aid," they concluded. In fact, they went on, attempting to hobble Mao's regime at all was only likely to make things worse, driving it "more firmly into the arms of the Kremlin while failing to shorten its life." The consultants preferred to wait patiently for tensions to develop between Moscow and Beijing. Although the men stopped short of advising Acheson to offer Mao diplomatic recognition, they urged the secretary of state to "be realistic." Asked at an October 26 press conference about his China strategy, Acheson acknowledged that it was "different now than it was some months ago."

Nevertheless, Acheson still needed to convince Truman of this more dovish approach—a task made far more difficult by Ward's arrest. At a meeting with a State Department official on October 31, Truman wanted to know what the department was doing to get the American diplomats released. When the aide lamely responded that the United States was making "the strongest possible representation to the Communist officials," Truman demanded more aggressive action. "The president," the aide wrote in his notes of the conversation, "indicated that, if he thought we could get a plane in to bring these people out, he was prepared to take the strongest possible measures, including some utilization of force if necessary, and if he was sure it would be effective."

In the space of a week, Truman had gone from praying for world peace to pushing for lethal force—a unique kind of whiplash that only the leader of a global superpower could truly experience. On the evening of November 1, as he wrote in his diary, he brooded about the loneliness of the position. "Had dinner by myself tonight," Truman began, then went on:

> Worked in the Lee House office until dinner time. A butler came in very formally and said, "Mr. President, dinner is served." I walk into the dining room in the Blair House. Barnett in tails and white tie pulls out my chair, pushes me up to the table. John in tails and white tie brings me a fruit cup, Barnett takes away the empty cup. John bring[s] me a plate, Barnett brings me a tenderloin, John brings me asparagus, Barnett brings me carrots and beets. I have to eat alone and in silence in candle lit room. I ring—Barnett takes the plate and butter plates. John comes in with a napkin and silver crumb tray— there are no crumbs but John has to brush them off the table anyway. Barnett bring[s] me a plate with a finger bowl and doyle [*sic*] and John puts a glass saucer and a little bowl on the plate. Barnett brings me some chocolate custard. John brings me a demitasse (at home a little cup of coffee—about two good gulps) and my dinner is over. I take a hand bath in the finger bowl and go back to work. What a life!

THE VOICE

B y early November, Truman was beginning to acquire the telltale physical traits of an embattled second-term president. Crow's-feet creased the skin beside his eyes, and ugly stains darkened the surfaces of his teeth. Bulging jowls had overtaken his face, erasing any distinction between neck and chin. There was something about the aging president that evoked Humpty Dumpty—not only the ovoid curve of his head, but also the tired gaze, the increasingly sheepish expression of a man on the verge of falling and breaking.

On one level, Truman was doing more in China than he had in months. His covert operators had finally established a pipeline of secret aid to Mao's foes, who were steadily consolidating their control of the remaining Nationalist forces. The C.I.A.'s Hillenkoetter reported on November 1 that Bai, newly flush with American cash, was now demanding "full control" of the Nationalist military—a positive development, as far as Hillenkoetter was concerned. As Cox shuttled between Hong Kong and the mainland, his bosses sent him a telegram praising his "magnificent accomplishments thus far." Encouraged by the progress, on November 1 the C.I.A. authorized $500,000 in additional funding to Chennault's organization.

But so much could still go wrong—starting with the behavior of the Generalissimo. After decades at the head of the Nationalist forces, the Americans wondered whether he would really cede so much power to a rival. Chiang, with little other choice, had assured Chennault that he would abide by the arrangement. Still, the Americans knew that Chiang was fickle and might later change his mind. "The joker throughout is the Generalissimo," Hillenkoetter wrote. The intelligence coming out of Chiang's inner circle only reinforced that impression. One C.I.A. memo quoted a Chiang loyalist complaining that Bai was "worse than Mao" and boasting that the Americans would ultimately have no choice but to support Chiang's rival clique on Taiwan.

Mao, meanwhile, refused to relent on the Ward case. Privately, Truman's deputies were flummoxed; they wondered whether Mao was retaliating for the recent arrest of several Soviet officials working in the United States. In fact, Mao probably was trying to send a message—but to Moscow, not to Washington. With the mainland largely secure, Mao now wanted to make his long-postponed pilgrimage to the Kremlin. In early November, Mao reached out to Stalin through a Russian intermediary, indicating that he would like to leave in early December. This time, finally, the Soviet dictator agreed. Scholars now suggest that Mao might have been using Ward's arrest to signal his loyalty to Stalin at this crucial moment.

Whatever Mao's motivation, the Ward insult infuriated Truman. At a meeting with a top State Department official on November 14, Truman suggested blockading the Shanghai coast, preventing the Communists from shipping coal from northern China to economic centers like Shanghai. Such a step, Truman insisted, would demonstrate "that we meant business" and would ultimately lead to Ward's release. The president believed that a show of American force would also make it more difficult for the British to recognize Mao's new China. Practically speaking, Truman said that he "felt sure" that the United States had "both the ships and planes available in the neighborhood to accomplish this." The president, furthermore, warned that he would punish blockade runners severely, sinking "any vessels which refused to heed our warning."

One flaw, among many, in Truman's strategy was that it contradicted his own existing policy. The Nationalist navy was already blockading the coast, an approach that the Truman Administration had publicly disparaged. The difficulty of Truman's position became immediately clear the same day, when an American merchant ship, the *S.S. Flying Cloud*, attempted to run the Nationalist blockade off the coast of Shanghai. After pausing briefly when a Nationalist ship fired a warning shot, the *Flying Cloud* raised its anchor and steamed on. Gunners on a nearby Chinese junk then opened fire with rifles and machine guns, peppering the hull with bullet holes. Through the fog at the mouth of the Yangtze, a larger Nationalist vessel launched three-inch shells from its own cannons, ripping a porthole-size cavity in the side of the *Flying Cloud*. Although no American sailors were injured in the attack, the incident took at least some of the pressure off Mao—and put it back on Chiang and the Nationalists.

Truman, by mid-November, was floundering and confused, caught between the desperate, retreating Nationalists and the emboldened, advancing Communists. On the morning of November 17, he met with Acheson, Stuart, and a number of other experts on East Asia, to hear them present the ideas they had been refining over the past several weeks. Truman, at first, seemed to want "radical suggestions, military or otherwise," Stuart wrote in his diary. But the president, over the course of the meeting, gradually relaxed this belligerent posture.

At the meeting, the East Asia experts tried to convince Truman to take a more dovish, patient approach. There were no "quick panaceas," they believed; the entire region was "now being swept by a deep-seated revolutionary movement," they observed in a memo of talking points for their meeting with Truman. While Truman had wanted to blockade the coast and attack the transgressors, the consultants urged him to do precisely the opposite: to cut off all military aid to non-Communist fighters. Ultimately, the men argued, Truman would have to deal with Mao. With exceptions for strategic materials, they thought the United States should maintain trade ties with the mainland and prepare to recognize Mao's regime once it controlled "substantially all the territory of China" and indicated a "willingness to meet its international obligations."

The men were, however, concerned about halting the spread of Communism elsewhere in the region. They advocated extending the U.S. strategy of containment—once limited to European nations—to Asia as well. The region needed "moral and, to a limited extent, material aid" from the United States, they explained. Although they thought military action there could prove counterproductive, provoking an anti-Western backlash, they viewed economic aid and propaganda as potentially effective tools. The key, as they put it in a memo to the president, would be to "demonstrate our understanding and sympathy for the nationalist aspirations of the Asian peoples and to expose the menace to these aspirations created by Soviet imperialism."

Truman, groping for a solution, found these arguments persuasive. At a meeting with Acheson later the same day, the president told his secretary of state that the session with the East Asia experts had been "tremendously helpful." Truman, according to Acheson's notes of the conversation, explained that he "had gotten a new insight into the reasons for the Communist success in China, a better understanding of the whole situation, and found himself thinking about it in quite a new way." Acheson, seeking to reinforce his consultants' message, told Truman that he thought the president had a basic choice: he could choose to "oppose the [Communist] regime, harass it, needle it, and if an opportunity appeared to attempt to overthrow it," or he could "attempt to detach it from subservience to Moscow and over a period of time encourage those vigorous influences which might modify it." Acheson emphasized that his consultants were "unanimous in their judgment that the second course was the preferable one." Truman, for now, seemed to agree.

Still, this patient approach did nothing to resolve the immediate problem of Ward's captivity. The following day, Hillenkoetter sent

Truman a top-secret C.I.A. memo indicating that the agency believed Ward was being held in a harsh, cold Chinese prison with four other staff members. The report's details were alarming and seemed to indicate that Ward had been beaten. But the intelligence coup itself—an apparent transcript of snippets of Ward's interrogation by Chinese authorities—was remarkable. Although some sections were garbled, the agency's analysts determined that it was probably authentic. Hillenkoetter cautioned that "use of this information in any way that gets wide dissemination will, of course, jeopardize the security of the operation."

Still, even Truman's military advisers, generally more hawkish than the diplomats at State, warned that a rescue operation could backfire. The chairman of the Joint Chiefs of Staff told Johnson on November 18 that any attempt to forcibly extract Ward would require either a sea landing or an air assault; after rescuing Ward, the teams would then need to "fight their way out of Manchuria." In the process, the memo continued, the operation "might well lead to open war with the Chinese Communist government." The J.C.S. chairman emphasized that the Soviets were so committed to defending their interests in the region that any rescue attempt might also draw a response from Moscow. "In view of the foregoing considerations," the memo warned, "there is a likelihood that overt United States military action might lead to global war."

In a limited sense, of course, the United States already was at war, desperately trying to bolster Mao's remaining opponents on the mainland. But by late November, even that last-ditch effort was collapsing. For weeks, Bai had been complaining to his American handlers that he needed more weapons, particularly light machine guns and mortars. Then, on November 22, the P.L.A. finally surged toward Guilin, driving out Bai's resistance fighters. From the cockpit of an airplane, Cox watched the P.L.A. troops advance south across a river in "two almost solid lines of small craft." Bai ordered his forces to regroup at Liuzhou, but Cox recognized the end was swiftly approaching. "We are trying desperately to keep things going, but one by one we are losing our bases," Cox wrote to his wife. "I don't know how much longer we can last." By the last days of November, Cox recognized that his options were narrowing. "The way things are going," he wrote, "almost any day looks like it could mean the end of China as far as the mainland is concerned."

The collapse of Truman's covert aid efforts reinforced his conviction that patience was now the best policy. For the president and his advisers at State, writing off China, at least temporarily, was the only prudent choice. Still, for men like Walter Judd, who had made China their life's work, Mao's conquest represented an ethical and psychological catastrophe. "Tragically," Judd wrote to one correspondent in late November, "it appears likely that the forces against us are about to win." He continued:

If so, it can only bring disaster for all people who believe in genuine freedom, and especially for those who believe there is a God and there are moral laws in this universe. Eventually the latter will triumph. But another generation or even a civilization can go down in destruction because the blind allowed themselves to be led by the blind.

★

"A year ago at this time," the *New York Times* proclaimed on November 27, "the Communist armies of Mao [Zedong] had begun their big drive in the Chinese civil war—the long march of victory south from Manchuria." Now, over the past week, the paper continued, "Mao's armies appeared to be entering the last phase of their conquest of the Chinese mainland."

Three days later, on November 30, Mao's P.L.A. troops punched through to Chongqing, one of the last Nationalist bastions, where Chiang was now staying. The Generalissimo's alarmed security guards woke their boss up, packed him into an escape car, then swept him through the refugee-choked highway leading to the airport. The route was so crowded that Chiang, at one point, was forced to get out and walk. He finally arrived at the airfield at midnight, climbing into the Skymaster on the tarmac. By now, the Generalissimo had come to understand that he was on his own; still, he cursed the Truman Administration for not doing more to come to his rescue. "U.S. China policy," he wrote in his diary on November 30, "is so unwise and so wrong that I worry about the security of the United States."

Publicly, at least, Truman did appear disengaged. As Chiang battled for his political life, Truman flew off for a vacation at his winter White House in Key West. The president, who had not taken a real holiday since March, needed the rest. It had been a stressful year, even by the standards of his demanding office. Now everything seemed to be going wrong. Even Truman's fabled weather-forecasting mojo was failing him. After his plane taxied to a stop at the Florida airfield, he emerged from the aircraft and immediately snapped at the naval base commander: "Tell me what the temperature is right this minute." Truman had bet his daughter, Margaret, a dollar that it would be eighty degrees or above when they landed. This time, though, he was not even close; the naval officer reported that the president had missed the mark by almost ten degrees.

In Florida, Truman tried to relax, barbecuing hot dogs with his family and taking walks to a nearby beach. But he could not really escape the press of events. He scoured the newspapers daily, and aides sent special flights from Washington carrying important documents, which the president scanned after dinner. One memo acknowledged the ongoing rift among the president's cabinet—especially between Acheson and Johnson. Although the two men had made some progress in reconciling their approaches to East Asia, a major gulf remained over Taiwan. Johnson, for his part, refused to give up on the island. Acheson, on the other hand, believed that Chiang's final stronghold was destined to collapse—just like the Generalissimo's other onetime command posts.

And yet, over the course of the preceding year, Acheson's policy had evolved dramatically from the do-nothing approach of his first months in office. Then, East Asia had appeared on his meeting agendas only rarely; he had preferred to concentrate on European affairs. Now, however, China and its neighbors dominated Acheson's strategy sessions. At his morning staff meeting on December 1, the secretary of state agreed to make "the Asia problem" his top foreign policy priority.

Among Acheson's staff, the increasingly savage battles over China policy were beginning to take a physical toll. Stuart, for example, after his return from the mainland in August, had traveled the United States making speeches on China policy. On the surface, at least, the pressure was off: Stuart had done all he could do to prevent this outcome, even if he had ultimately failed. Like Judd, he had dedicated his life to the cause of Chinese-American amity. Mao's victory was more than a political blow; it was an assault on Stuart's entire worldview and vocation. As winter approached, he was on a train returning from an engagement in the Midwest when he stepped into a bathroom—and then collapsed. When the train's crew discovered him, he was slumped on the floor, unconscious. The former diplomat and missionary had suffered a major stroke; he would never fully recover.

Amid the stresses of the approaching winter, there was one sliver of good news. After securing Stalin's invitation to Moscow, Mao had permitted the release of Angus Ward. Although a Chinese court had convicted Ward of assaulting a Chinese employee of the consulate, his sentence was commuted, and the diplomat and his staff were ordered to leave the country. Acheson's staff were relieved at the news, but the secretary of state's political opponents only used it to make hay. Walter Judd protested that the case could have been resolved months earlier, had the Truman Administration taken a harder line. The Minnesota congressmen blustered that Truman should have deployed the Marines, threatening to "quarantine" Mao's forces "like a fresh case of smallpox." Although the point was now moot, with Ward preparing to depart the country, Judd nevertheless used the case to caution against further "appeasement" in East Asia.

Madame Chiang, in Riverdale, had long since lowered her expectations. With the situation increasingly hopeless, she feared that China news would soon fall off American front pages altogether. She half-heartedly tried to stiffen her husband's spine, urging him to make a bold speech to recapture the spotlight. But she knew the end was approaching. Confused, unable to sleep, she found herself praying, although mechanically, by rote. "Then one morning at dawn," she later recalled, "unaware whether I was asleep or awake, I heard a Voice—an ethereal Voice saying distinctly: *'All is right.'*" She walked to her sister's room, explained that she believed God had spoken to her, and said that she was going home—whatever that now meant. On December 5, she cabled her husband and told him to send a plane.

THROUGH A GLASS,
DARKLY

Under the glittering midday sun on December 6, Mao climbed aboard a train in Beijing for the ten-day voyage to Moscow. As the locomotive, freshly painted in green and gold, chugged north toward Manchuria, Mao read, played mah-jongg, and gazed out the windows. Edgy about his safety, his security detail had stationed an armed guard every few hundred feet along the track. From a distance, the procession was a magnificent spectacle; during one leg, the tracks followed the imposing contour of the Great Wall. Inside the carriages, however, the accommodations were austere. The train Mao had chosen had once been used by Chiang Kai-shek to travel back and forth between Nanjing and Shanghai, where the temperatures were higher. Now, as it rolled into frigid Manchuria, Mao huddled around the meager flame of a portable oil burner to stay warm.

In the days before he left, Mao had been anxious about the trip. The enormity of the task ahead weighed on him; he worried that Stalin would renege on his promises of economic aid. Already, friends and former colleagues were besieging him with requests for jobs and other favors. Mao did his best to dispatch these entreaties without giving offense. To one correspondent, who sent letter after letter to Beijing,

Mao replied gently, writing, "It is more appropriate for you, sir, to stay and work in the village; please do not come to the capital." He was less diplomatic with those he knew better. When the brother of one of his former wives asked for a favor, Mao responded, "Do not harbor any unrealistic hopes and do not come to the capital. Whatever job the Hunan Provincial Committee assigns you, do it. Everything should be done in accordance with normal rules. Please don't put the government on the spot."

Physically, Mao was already run-down. His angioneurosis had begun to act up. When the attacks came on, it felt as if the ground were receding beneath his feet: he would start to sweat, his legs would wobble, he would sway and swoon. Now, as he prepared for one of the most important meetings of his life, he felt sick again. The political tension only made things worse. When the train stopped in Shenyang, in Manchuria, Mao discovered that someone had hung large portraits of Stalin throughout the city. But he could not find any of himself. The Chairman, according to one of his traveling companions, was "clearly irritated" by the lack of respect.

Mao did his best to repress these indignities, desperate as he was to secure additional Soviet aid. He knew that the P.L.A.'s next battlefields would be far more formidable than its last ones. Over the course of the year, Mao's troops had fanned out relatively easily across the mainland. But the islands just off the southeastern coast were proving more difficult to conquer. Earlier in the autumn, Mao had ordered a surprise attack on Jinmen, a small island just off the Chinese coast. But the defending Nationalist forces had hidden themselves in the stony cliffs, cutting down the Communist soldiers as they reached the shore. Many of Mao's troops who had grown up in landlocked parts of northern China found themselves seasick and disoriented. The landing, overall, was a disaster: Mao lost three regiments, nine thousand men total. "This is our biggest loss in the war," Mao said, blaming a fatal combination of impatience and overconfidence for the defeat.

Only days later Mao tried again, this time at Dengbu Island, closer to Shanghai. Although the P.L.A. managed to overrun the island,

Nationalist air and naval forces dominated the airspace and sea-lanes; ultimately, they were able to drive back the invaders. Both these setbacks, moreover, took place on small islands just off the coast. Mao recognized that if he could not subdue these relatively minor Nationalist strongholds, he would have no chance of conquering Taiwan, which was far larger and farther from the shore. To do so, Mao understood, he would first need to improve his capabilities to fight in the air and on the high seas. Russian aid and expertise could help him do both.

Even before his trip to Moscow, Mao had begun successfully wringing such concessions from Stalin. Just days before his departure, Soviet experts opened the pilot-training facilities that they had promised to establish the previous summer. Throughout the fall, the Russians had been facilitating the delivery of Yak fighter planes to the Chinese mainland. Dozens of recently arrived Soviet naval advisers were simultaneously working to professionalize Mao's maritime forces. Without a powerful air force and navy to oppose Chiang's own, Mao knew, the Nationalists would continue to harass Shanghai and other key cities with warships and bombers based out of their remaining island bases. Already, as Mao's train streaked across the frozen Russian landscape toward Moscow, Chiang was busily preparing Taiwan for its role in this coming conflict.

★

The Portuguese had referred to Taiwan as Ilha Formosa—Beautiful Island. For months, Chiang had been flooding the enclave with gold and weapons, anticipating his own ultimate retreat. Although he had once hoped to secure an additional base in Yunnan, on the mainland, that prospect had faded after the local governor defected to the Communists. Now Taiwan was Chiang's last remaining refuge. On December 8, the Nationalists announced the establishment of their government on the island. Chiang, depressed and plagued by ulcers, departed for the island two days later. The Generalissimo, in his DC-4, flew across the strait by dead reckoning, touching down in Taipei after a year on the run.

Chiang's arrival in Taiwan presented Truman with several dilemmas. First, the Generalissimo had brought with him enormous quantities of weaponry, most of it American-made. According to the British government, Chiang's stockpiles now included one hundred tanks and eight B-25 bombers. Dozens more bombers were expected to arrive soon. There was nothing overtly untoward about these shipments. The British reported that they had been bought through U.S.-approved private transactions from surplus stockpiles. Still, they did raise the troubling question of what would become of these stores if Mao succeeded in taking the island. The C.I.A. did not believe that Taiwan could last more than a year without outside assistance. With this in mind, the British warned, Chiang's fortification of the island was creating a "dangerous state of affairs." They urged American policy makers to try to stanch the flow of weapons.

Yet before Truman and his advisers could do so, they needed to decide whether the island was strategically crucial. MacArthur, convinced of Taiwan's importance, had pushed hard to include it as part of the American defensive line. Johnson, too, viewed Taiwan both as a defensive bastion and as a potential launching pad for attacks on the mainland. On December 15, he made his case in a memo to Truman, who was still on vacation in Key West. "Generally speaking," Johnson began, "the [military] staffs agree that efforts should be continued and perhaps increased to deny Formosa to the Communists." Johnson acknowledged that "it is not in our interest to become involved to the extent of placing the American flag on Formosa." Still, he urged the president to consider "political and economic aid, and also military advice and assistance short of overt military action."

Acheson, on the other hand, was determined to avoid fortifying the island. The United States, he argued, could defend its interests from a string of offshore bases stretching from Japan to the Philippines. He had never really been able to understand Taiwan's appeal as a strategic strongpoint. "Formosa," he later observed, was "a subject which seems to draw out the boys like a red haired girl on the beach. It appears that what you want most is what you ain't got."

The British did not bother to wait for Truman's inner circle to resolve this debate before finalizing their own approach. Instead, on December 16, they presented Washington with a fait accompli, announcing that they would establish diplomatic ties with Mao's government in the coming weeks. Like Acheson, Bevin believed that it was entirely possible to contain Communism without confronting Mao on the mainland or launching attacks from bases on Taiwan. Although Bevin had not wanted to split with the United States on recognition, he had ultimately determined that Britain's own interests justified the move. Acheson protested, but his advisers understood that the British decision was just the beginning. An internal State Department summary predicted that it would "shortly be followed by recognition by a majority of other governments throughout the world with interests in China."

★

Mao, meanwhile, finally arrived in Moscow around noon on December 16, nervous and ill. During one stop, as he had approached the Soviet capital, he had felt so nauseous that he had stumbled as he stepped out of the train for a breath of fresh air.

Psychologically, too, Mao was ultrasensitive, anxious about his first meeting with Stalin. Now, at the Yaroslavl railroad station, not far from the Kremlin, Mao's entourage had prepared a dinner on board the train for the Russian welcome delegation, which included several top officials—although not Stalin himself. The Russians, however, refused to dine with Mao, citing strict diplomatic protocol. Mao, according to one of his traveling companions, was "visibly chagrined by the coldness of his reception." Nevertheless, Mao dutifully gave a short speech outside the station, cheerfully declaring, "Long live Sino-Soviet friendship and cooperation!" He made a perfunctory inspection of the Moscow garrison's honor guard, then drove off toward the dacha where he would be spending the next nine weeks.

Later the same evening, at six p.m., Mao rode to the Kremlin for his first meeting with Stalin. At Little Corner, the Soviet dictator's large, wood-paneled office suite, Stalin flattered his guest, grasping Mao's hand and exclaiming, "I never quite expected that you would be so young, so healthy and strong!" Short, with amber-colored eyes and tobacco-stained teeth, Stalin himself was none of the above. Nearly seventy years old, he had long since begun to decline, fighting heart trouble and memory loss. He was known to bore guests with lengthy monologues—or frighten them with angry outbursts. ("After the war," Nikita Khrushchev once observed, "he wasn't quite right in the head.") Still, Mao knew that he had no choice but to find a way to work with the aging dictator. The Communist leaders spent the next two hours getting to know each other, testing each other.

Mao explained to Stalin that what he needed most now was calm: three to five years of peace in which to rebuild his ravaged nation. But he also knew that it was not entirely up to him; if war broke out between Washington and Moscow, Mao's new government would inevitably be drawn in. Stalin, however, was reassuring: no nation was in a position to give Mao trouble, he said. Japan was still rebuilding in the aftermath of the American nuclear attacks. Europe had no desire to fight again. "America, though it screams for war, is actually afraid of war more than anything," Stalin added. Unless North Korea's Kim Il-Sung decided to invade China, Stalin joked, Mao should be free to proceed with his reconstruction projects unhindered.

To do that, Mao would need money and supplies, and he told Stalin as much, requesting a $300 million line of credit. "For this trip," Mao explained, "we hope to bring about something that not only looks nice but also tastes delicious." Stalin's aides laughed at the oblique, earthy turn of phrase, but the Soviet leader seems to have grasped Mao's point. He asked Mao for more specifics—exactly what kind of equipment did Mao want? Mao acknowledged that he did not yet have a good grasp even of the basics of China's industrial needs. It would depend, in part, on how quickly he could conclude the war and begin the process of reconstruction. Stalin urged him to focus, for the time being, on developing sources of basic raw materials like petroleum, coal, and metals, which would be useful in both war and peace.

Strategically, Mao's most immediate concern was Taiwan, from which Chiang was continuing to launch attacks against the mainland. Mao told Stalin that a Nationalist "assault landing unit" had switched sides and joined the Communists, but that he still needed additional amphibious forces if he was to mount a successful invasion. Mao asked the Soviet leader if he would loan the People's Republic some Russian pilots, or perhaps some "secret military detachments" to help do the job. Stalin was open to the idea, but cautioned Mao not to provoke the United States with a precipitous assault. "What is most important here," he said, "is not to give Americans a pretext to intervene." Instead, he suggested using subversion to quietly wrest the island from Chiang's control. "One could select a company of landing forces," Stalin said, "train them in propaganda, send them over to Formosa, and through them organize an uprising on the island."

Stalin, however, was far more daring when it came to Southeast Asia. Mao explained that his troops in southern China were nearing the Burmese and Indochinese borders—a development that he knew was causing jitters in London and Washington. Stalin told Mao there would be no harm in keeping the Western powers on edge. "One could create a rumor," he said, "that you are preparing to cross the border and in this way frighten the imperialists a bit." They agreed that there was no point in actively courting the major foreign powers, despite the fact that some countries, like Britain, would offer diplomatic recognition. "We must first bring order to the country, strengthen our position, and then we can talk to foreign imperialists," Mao said.

After so many months of anticipation, the meeting had satisfied Mao's outsize expectations. He later told an aide that he felt that Stalin had been "really sincere" during their encounter. Still, as the days began to pass, with little concrete to show for his efforts, Mao began to worry. Although they shared common interests now, they had not always been easy allies. Stalin had been known to deride Mao as a "margarine Marxist"; Mao, in later years, referred to Stalin as a "hypo-critical foreign devil." Now, as Mao stewed impatiently in his isolated dacha, he groused to one of his traveling companions that he had not come all this way simply to "eat, sleep, and shit."

★

Truman returned to Washington on December 20, after more than three relaxing weeks in Florida. As he descended to the tarmac, tanned and smiling, in his dark overcoat and white fedora, his welcome committee would have provided an unmistakable reminder that it was time to go back to work. Both his warring cabinet officials, Acheson and Johnson, had shown up at the airport to greet him. Johnson, on the ride back to Washington, argued his case for bolstering Taiwan. Acheson, too, briefed the president on his own version of the latest China news, filling him in on the British moves toward recognition and laying out his thinking about a more dovish regional strategy.

While Truman was on vacation, his covert aid program had suffered one setback after another. "Right now, it looks as though it's only a matter of days before the mainland goes," Cox told his wife. "It's awfully discouraging." After Bai's collapse, Cox had begun surveying southern China for anyone else willing to continue the fight. The eastern provinces seemed lost; technically, Chiang still controlled them, but the Generalissimo was pulling out his most critical personnel and equipment to help fortify Taiwan.

In Yunnan, meanwhile, Cox had made a large payment to the local governor—the same man in whom Chiang had placed his hopes. Ultimately, however, the governor and his allies had struck a deal with the Communists as Mao's forces closed in. In this case, Cox felt that the payment was worth it; the governor ultimately helped to ensure the safe evacuation of Americans in the region. Still, these clandestine operations simultaneously risked creating additional hostages, just as Ward was being released. During one flight over Yunnan, an American C-46 pilot, James B. McGovern—nicknamed Earthquake McGoon, for his nearly three-hundred-pound frame—ran out of fuel and was forced to make an emergency landing on a sandbar surrounded by a river. A Communist patrol swiftly captured him.

Truman's operators did their best to accommodate themselves to these bleak new realities. They eventually decided to follow Chiang's lead and establish a base in southern Taiwan. Lines of trucks ferried American equipment back and forth between the port at Kaohsiung and a nearby airfield. Increasingly, however, Acheson's team at State seemed dissatisfied with the results of Wisner's covert project. In late December, Wisner told his staff that a change in strategy was increasingly likely. The administration would probably continue to authorize the dissemination of propaganda, he explained. But most other aid to anti-Communist fighters would have to cease.

Acheson, from his perch in Foggy Bottom, was pushing hard to curtail this harassment along China's periphery. In late December, he sent a cable to the U.S. ambassador in India, informing him that he saw no benefit in encouraging rebels in another sensitive region: Tibet. With its large Buddhist population, Tibet already enjoyed "*de facto* freedom" from Beijing's control, Acheson wrote. Any efforts to formalize this independence would probably only spur Mao to intervene.

Indochina, on the other hand, was slightly more complicated. Acheson genuinely feared that Communist revolutions could spread there and suggested that his staff read an article in *The Economist* titled "China Looks South." Strategically, too, some of Truman's officials saw benefits in operating from the region. Already Wisner's team was quietly flying raw materials—tin ingots, for example—out of Yunnan and storing them for safekeeping in Haiphong, in northern Indochina. But the Americans also recognized that the French authorities were fickle and insecure, and could withdraw permission to use these bases at any time. The need to reassure the French, furthermore, risked opening the door to bureaucratic freelancing. Acheson's staff summary on December 21 reported that Johnson, on a visit to Paris, had taken it upon himself to promise the French that their Vietnamese allies would have access to at least some of the $75 million allocated by the U.S.

Congress for the "general area of China"—an assurance that might have come as news to the secretary of state.

On the morning of December 21, both Acheson and Kennan started their day by traveling across Washington to the National War College, a red brick Beaux Arts–style structure on a peninsula overlooking the Anacostia River. Invited to deliver separate addresses to a group of future military strategists, both men used the opportunity to step back from the flurry of daily diplomacy and consider the broader philosophical lessons of the past year.

Acheson spoke first, delivering a powerful plea for moderation in global affairs. Against the backdrop of 1949, with its increasingly zealous anti-Communism and East Asian adventurism, it was a stunning speech. Acheson blamed the "search for absolutes" for America's failings in the international arena. Rather than reducing the world to simple tropes, he argued, his audience should try to view it in its complexity. He counseled them to think like engineers. "What the engineer has to do," Acheson said, "is to understand the strength of materials at his disposal. He has to understand the limits of cost at his disposal, and he has to understand the limits of his objective. He does not start out to say, 'I will build a bridge which goes around the world.' There is no sense in that."

Kennan, speaking next, went even further than Acheson, poking holes in the most fundamental assumptions of Truman's postwar worldview. Like Acheson, Kennan pleaded with his audience to jettison their universalistic pretensions. "It is simply not given to human beings to know the totality of truth," he said. "Similarly, no one can see in its totality anything so fundamental and so unlimited in all its implications as the development of our people in their relation to their world environment." Kennan warned that even the best strategists only "know in part" and "prophesy in part," referring to Saint Paul's admonition that humans can do no better than to peer through a glass, darkly. With that in mind, Kennan told his audience, they should remain on guard against those who wished to "chart out vast schemes."

A RATHER SPECTACULAR
TRIUMPH

On December 21, the same day that Acheson and Kennan delivered their addresses to the War College, Mao and Stalin stepped onto a balcony at the Bolshoi Theatre in Moscow, for a party to celebrate the Soviet dictator's seventieth birthday. Mao, in a gray tunic, took his seat in the place of honor, to Stalin's right, in a box festooned with crimson banners. Ballerinas flitted around the gold-accented theater; guests collected extravagant gift bags that included gowns, slippers, and shaving kits. But despite the grandeur of the occasion, both men felt terrible. Stalin, the night before, had been so dizzy that he had nearly fallen. Mao, too, was sick enough that he had taken several doses of atropine to try to restore his equilibrium.

Stalin gave Mao the opportunity to make the first speech of the night—a privilege that must have delighted Mao. "Comrade Stalin," he told the theater, "is a teacher and a friend of the people of the world; he is also a teacher and a friend of the Chinese people." Mao wished his host a happy birthday, then proclaimed that he would welcome Stalin's leadership of the global proletariat: "Long live the great Stalin, leader of the working class of the whole world and of the international Communist movement!" Later that evening, close to midnight, Mao drafted a telegram home to Beijing, bragging that his speech "was received with great enthusiasm. Three times everybody stood and applauded for a long time."

Privately, though, Mao was unhappy. He complained about everything. The down pillows in the dacha were too soft. ("How can you sleep on this?" Mao asked. "Your head will disappear!") He was constipated. The staff were serving him frozen fish rather than fresh filets. There was nothing to amuse himself with besides a billiard table on the third floor of the cottage. Personal entertainment, in any case, was not why he had traveled halfway across the world. "I'm not just here for the birthday," he told one of Stalin's liaisons. "I'm here to do business!"

By the day after Stalin's party, Mao was apparently frustrated enough with his hosts to question his past reliance on Soviet goodwill. Now, as he considered China's potential trading partners, he noted that several other nations also wanted "to do business with us." After months of angry rhetoric directed at the United States and other Western powers, Mao's views were softening—or so it seemed. "While we should naturally give top priority to the Soviet Union," Mao wrote in a telegram to his Central Committee on December 22, "we should at the same time prepare to do business with Poland, Czechoslovakia, [East] Germany, Britain, Japan, the United States, and other countries." If Mao was trying to send Stalin a signal, a suggestive telegram might have been a good way to do it. Stalin, eager to gain the upper hand in the negotiations, had bugged Mao's dacha. It seems reasonable to assume that he was monitoring the Chairman's cable traffic as well.

★

While Mao and Stalin courted, and snubbed, each other in Moscow, Truman and his staff worked to complete their new containment strategy. For hawks like Johnson and MacArthur, any such effort had to begin with Taiwan, from which they hoped to start rolling back Mao's conquests. Acheson, on the other hand, believed the United States would have to accept the reality of Mao's victory—including, eventually, on Taiwan—and go from there. "It seems to me inevitable that we are going to live on this globe with a vast number of people who think as oppositely as we do as it is possible for human beings to think," Acheson had explained to his audience at the War College. "We must understand that for a long, long period of time we will both inhabit this spinning ball in the great void of the universe."

Since his meeting with Truman and the East Asia experts in mid-November, Acheson had been making steady progress in winning Truman to his side. Now, on December 22, the president finally confronted Johnson. At their regular Thursday lunch at Blair House, Truman explained that he was leaning toward taking a far more patient approach to Mao's revolution than Johnson had been advocating. The president said that he was not quibbling with the military analysis. Rather, his opposition was purely political; by establishing Taiwan as a base from which to launch U.S. strikes, Truman would be undercutting his larger strategy of attempting to detach Beijing from Moscow's ambit.

Sensing, perhaps, that the battle was approaching its climax, Chiang's friends intensified their efforts to sway the president—or if that failed, to weaken him. Judd wrote to a Connecticut newspaper editor, complaining that Truman's failure to take on Mao now would only lead to a more destructive conflict later. "We apparently are bent on having a second World War in a generation through failure to understand the imperativeness to our own security of having China in the hands of friends instead of enemies," Judd wrote. To another correspondent the Minnesota congressman made darker insinuations, insisting on the "complete removal or transfer of those in our Govt responsible for the policies of the past."

On December 23, both the Chinese Nationalist government and Johnson's advisers at the Defense Department made final, desperate attempts to win support for Taiwan. Chiang's desires, by now, were familiar: he wanted enough equipment to stand up six divisions of troops, American military advisers to guide them, and more than a dozen naval vessels. What troubled Acheson's staff was that the U.S. military's own request appeared almost indistinguishable from that of the Chinese

Nationalists. One of Acheson's assistant secretaries warned his boss that the Joint Chiefs' recommendation "parallels with extraordinary fidelity the request for increased assistance from the Chinese National Government received on the same date." Acheson's team could not help but suspect that the Pentagon had slyly coordinated its push with Chiang and his allies.

★

Truman, despite these machinations, seemed jolly enough as the holidays approached. "The president looked fine, brown, clear-eyed, even plumper than before, and very friendly," one adviser observed in his diary shortly before Christmas. The weather was less than festive: heavy rain poured down on Washington as Truman boarded his plane for a short trip home to Missouri. On the tarmac, as his plane prepared for takeoff, the president gamely jingled a couple of sleigh bells through the window as raindrops accumulated on the glass.

At home, though, there was snow: a thick layer of powder blanketed the Missouri hills. Truman, brandishing his malacca cane, stomped through the fluff, tossing Merry Christmases to his neighbors like candy to children. On Christmas Eve, the president went through the motions of his annual ritual, donning a natty gray suit with peaked lapels, then stepping into the large front parlor of his white Victorian. With a few friends and family members looking on, he took a seat in front of a microphone, near an arrangement of poinsettias and an Audubon bird print. He pressed a finger on a telegraph switch, the signal to light the national tree back in Washington, then began his customary short address.

Truman told his listeners that, this year, he had been "thinking about some families in other once-happy lands. We must not forget that there are thousands and thousands of families homeless, hopeless, destitute, and torn with despair on this Christmas Eve." Truman did not mention China, or any other nation, by name. But his brief speech, amid the turmoil and compromises of 1949, sounded like a forlorn prayer. "In love alone—the love of God and the love of man—will be found the solution of all the ills which afflict the world today," Truman said. "In the spirit of the Christ child—as little children with joy in our hearts and peace in our souls—let us, as a nation, dedicate ourselves anew to the love of our fellow men."

Truman, the following day, celebrated Christmas with his family. But then, almost as soon as he arrived, he returned to Washington. The president had one more critical piece of business to transact before the end of the year. All that autumn his cabinet had been drafting, debating, and revising the set of guidelines that would provide the blueprint for the administration's East Asia strategy going forward. Known as N.S.C.-48, the paper described a plan to extend the doctrine of containment, initially designed for Europe, to the Chinese periphery. The battles over whether to include Taiwan in this perimeter continued through the holidays. But they could not go on forever. Truman's staff scheduled an N.S.C. meeting for December 29 to hash out and approve the final document.

Acheson met that morning with the Joint Chiefs of Staff, forcefully rehearsing his case. In his spacious Foggy Bottom office, the secretary of state began by quizzing the generals about why they thought Taiwan was so important. One officer, General Omar Bradley, responded by saying that Taiwan had always been strategically critical. In the past, however, there had not been any money available to help fortify it. Now, Bradley said, Congress had earmarked funds specifically for the "general area of China." He suggested that the United States should immediately send a "survey team" to the island to get a better sense of what the Nationalist leaders needed. Taiwan, another officer added, also held "diversionary value." If Mao was tied up trying to conquer Taiwan, the officer argued, he would have fewer resources available to interfere in Indochina, Burma, and Siam.

When the generals had finished, Acheson went to work picking apart their arguments. He urged the men to "face the fact" that Mao had won. "We must also face the certainty that throughout Southeast Asia the Communists will seek to extend their domination, probably by subversive methods and not invasion," he said, according to his memorandum of the conversation. "We must do our utmost to strengthen the neighbors of China." To accomplish this, Acheson urged the men to make peace with the forces of nationalism that were reshaping the entire region in the aftermath of the Second World War. The dramas of 1949 had amply demonstrated that the United States could not force its will on the rest of the world. But by bolstering the nations along China's southern border, Acheson suggested, it could at least keep others from doing so.

All this, however, would take time. Acheson urged the generals to adopt "the long view." Mao, he said, considered Stalin's government his "great and only friend." He would not, in a matter of a few months or a year, sever those bonds. Instead, Acheson said, the United States should prepare for a longer struggle, a quiet battle that could last "six or twelve years." Rifts between Beijing and Moscow were "inevitable," Acheson said. But they were not necessarily imminent. With that in mind, he cautioned against doing anything that would drive Mao closer to Stalin. Arming or otherwise assisting the Nationalist forces on Taiwan, he said, would only "excite and bring upon ourselves the united Chinese hatred of foreigners." That might be worth the risk if Taiwan were strategically crucial. Acheson, however, was convinced that it was not.

Later that afternoon, around half past two, Truman and his N.S.C. filtered into the Cabinet Room at the White House, taking their seats around a heavy wooden table. From an oil painting at the front of the room, the face of Woodrow Wilson stared down, judging them. For his entire adult life, Truman had sought to emulate Wilson, to continue the twenty-eighth president's quest to develop a "collective conscience" and a "common will of mankind" that might replace the chaos of conflicting interests that had defined the first half of the twentieth century. Although the China disaster had not ended those hopes, it had pushed them across the horizon, out of sight and out of reach in a terrestrial sphere governed not by the grandiose designs of selfless statesmen but by the clashing forces of competing individual wills.

This particular N.S.C. meeting was notable, partly, for the man who did not attend: Louis Johnson. Understanding that he was about to lose his battle with Acheson, the petulant Johnson had skipped the session, choosing instead to sun himself in Florida. Acheson took advantage of his absence, pushing Truman to clarify the administration's position on Taiwan. Sending additional equipment to the island, Acheson said, would only delay the inevitable. Acheson pressed the president to think harder about whether such shipments were really "worth the price." He argued, as he had been doing all fall, that the United States should "avoid any actions which would deflect Chinese xenophobia from Russia to ourselves." American military aid to Taiwan, he continued, would only "turn Chinese anti-foreign feeling against us and also place us in the position of subsidizing attacks on a government which will soon be generally recognized." Acheson warned that backing a "reactionary" like Chiang would undermine U.S. influence in the wider region.

Truman found Acheson persuasive and told the meeting as much—although he added that he was approving the State Department's approach only "for political reasons." The men agreed to revise their policy paper and submit it to Truman for his signature the following day. The new document concluded that the United States should halt all "military and political support of any non-Communist elements in China," unless such programs were clearly in the national interest. The strategy did, however, permit limited covert operations designed to spread propaganda that might help drive a wedge between Mao and Stalin, so long as policy makers were careful to avoid "the appearance of intervention."

Although the strategy was cautious when it came to the mainland and Taiwan, it advocated more vigorous support for anti-Communists in Southeast Asia. The N.S.C. advised Truman to encourage trade ties among the key regional players, in the hopes that an anti-Communist bloc braced by common economic bonds could more effectively hold its ground. The president's security team also counseled him to bolster the military capabilities of "selected non-Communist nations of Asia," and added that "particular attention" should be paid to achieving a political settlement between the French and Vietnamese in Indochina. Distributing the $75 million authorized by Congress should be considered "a matter of urgency," the N.S.C. concluded. The following day, December 30, Truman signed off on the N.S.C.'s new program—handing Acheson a hard-won victory.

★

Every choice, a British writer once observed, is simultaneously a kind of self-sacrifice, since to choose one path is to pass up all the others. That dynamic had been operating all year to complicate Truman's China policy. By authorizing the N.S.C.'s new paper, the president had made a crucial—and long-overdue—decision. Still, in the process, he had once again undercut his own universalist vision. On the same day that he approved Acheson's strategy, Truman took a phone call from his onetime ally Walter Judd, who wished the president a merry Christmas, then explained that he had read in the newspapers that the president had decided to extend his containment policy to Asia. Despite the warm wishes, the call must have reminded Truman of the consequences of his choice, of goals postponed and old friends now lost.

As Judd talked with Truman, he quickly discovered that a gulf still existed between them. After he said that he thought Truman should "try to save Formosa first," the president snapped, "How many American soldiers do you want to put on Formosa?" Judd explained that he was imagining something small-scale, a program similar to what the United States had done for Greece two years earlier. But Truman did not have the patience for another argument over Taiwan. "It would take ten divisions," Truman said. "I am not willing to do that."

Judd protested that he had no desire to deploy U.S. ground troops. But the conversation was already beginning to infuriate Truman. The president, Judd later recalled, "became intense, angry, [and] explosive about the rottenest government in China that ever existed." Truman retorted that his administration "can't help people who won't even try to help themselves. They surrendered every bit of aid we gave them. They went over to the Communists whole armies at a time." Judd tried to stanch the deluge, arguing that the U.S withdrawal had preceded these desertions—not the other way around. But Truman did not, or would not, hear him. "Why, we had supplied whole Chinese armies," the president raged on.

By this time, it was far too late for Truman to reverse course; his mind was made up. "I know what I'm talking about," he told Judd repeatedly. "No use you arguing with me or me with you." He said he had already exhausted all the options. Now, he grumbled, he had to "get back to work." Judd said he had more ideas, but Truman cut him off. "Write them and send them in," the president said, then hung up the phone.

Word of Truman's decision spread rapidly through the bureaucracy. Kennan cabled Wisner, instructing him to abort the agency's operations on the mainland. According to an internal C.I.A. report, Kennan instructed Wisner that "commitments on the mainland should be withdrawn as rapidly as possible since there was no confidence that any guerrilla operations would produce results commensurate with the risk and political hazards in preparing and following such a course." Wisner also concluded that his operators should stop using northern Indochina as a base, due to the "extremely precarious situation" there. Still, Wisner did not cut all ties with Chinese guerrillas on the mainland, convinced that intelligence gathering should remain a priority, even if more ambitious covert action was not.

On Sunday morning, January 1, 1950, Truman chose to walk the nine blocks from Blair House to the First Baptist Church, for New Year's Day services. From his pew, he listened as the pastor lamented that too few Americans made an effort to participate in the civic life of their country; they were always demanding rights, the preacher complained, but were too often unwilling to fulfill their democratic responsibilities. Truman, as he sat in the church, must have recognized that his own dilemma was different. As president, he was as engaged as a citizen could be, making life-and-death decisions on a daily basis. But those choices had exposed an innate moral paradox, the unavoidable corollary of power. When the service was over, Truman walked back outside, alone again with his determination.

In the days that followed, he and Acheson discussed how to best present their new China strategy to a restive public. Truman himself seems to have leaked the news of his Taiwan decision to a *New York Times* columnist, and the paper printed the scoop on its front page. Still, the capital blame game had begun, with the president's foes spinning their own versions of the drama. Truman and Acheson quickly recognized that they would need to mount a public defense of their policy. On January 4, Acheson stopped by the White House to help Truman draw up a statement, which explained that the president had "no desire to obtain special rights or privileges or to establish military bases on Formosa or to detach Formosa from China."

Johnson and others pushed back, convincing Truman to cut the phrase "or to detach Formosa from China" from his remarks. Privately, however, the president left little doubt about where he really stood; reporters had already seen the original draft of the statement. On the morning of January 5, a White House aide found the president lying naked by the side of his swimming pool, getting a rubdown. Truman, from his prone position, warned the aide that he was going to "pull the rug out" from under his political foes. Although the language he ultimately used in his press conference later that morning was less forceful than the State Department would have liked, the president made clear that he had taken Acheson's side. Three days later, in a column headlined JOHNSON TAKES FORMOSA LICKING, the Alsop brothers proclaimed Truman's new East Asia policy a "rather spectacular triumph" for the secretary of state.

A FORCE SO SWIFT

After weeks of anxiety and frustration, by the New Year, Mao, too, had finally begun to register some of his own triumphs. In the waning days of 1949, India had announced its decision to recognize Mao's new regime, giving the Chinese Communists a jolt of confidence. Then, just after the New Year, Stalin sent two of his top aides, Anastas Mikoyan and Vyacheslav Molotov, to visit Mao at his dacha, where the Chairman had been brooding, staring out the windows at the snow, and once even locking himself in his bedroom to protest Stalin's neglect. Mao told the Russian visitors that he wanted to begin discussions as soon as possible about drafting a new Sino-Soviet treaty. When Molotov agreed, after so many days of stalling, Mao seemed almost surprised. In a cable to his Central Committee in Beijing, he boasted that he had finally "achieved an important breakthrough."

Mao, elated, began furiously making plans, ordering his foreign minister, Zhou Enlai, to come to Moscow to help draw up the accord. At all hours—four a.m., six a.m.—Mao sent telegrams back to Beijing, with thoughts about the details of the preparations. A new treaty, he wrote home to the Central Committee, could help pump Soviet cash into the Chinese economy—but it would also enhance Mao's prestige abroad. An agreement, he wrote, would "press the capitalist countries to come to our terms," while at the same time deterring them "from taking reckless actions." In his notes home, he stressed that his comrades should maintain strict self-control during the talks, avoiding "undisciplined words and actions." After so many years of cultivating the sensitive Stalin, Mao wanted to prevent any careless mistakes.

On January 6, the British government provided Mao with one more reason for optimism, when it officially announced that it would recognize the People's Republic of China. Mao's forces clearly dominated the "greatest part of the territory of China," Bevin's envoy wrote in his statement. "In these circumstances, His Majesty's Government, in response to Chairman Mao [Zedong]'s proclamation of October 1, 1949, is ready to establish diplomatic relations on the basis of equality, mutual benefit and mutual respect." Mao had succeeded in dividing Washington and London; now he continued to press his advantage. On the same day as Bevin's announcement, Mao's forces took the dramatic step of seizing a former American military barracks on the grounds of the U.S. diplomatic compound in Beijing. After a year of fitful gains and vacillation, Mao was finally in control.

★

Two days later, on January 8, at noon, Madame Chiang slipped into a chair in the living room of her sister's Riverdale home, taking her place behind a bulky silver microphone from the National Broadcasting Company. Wearing black and looking drawn, she lifted a thin sheaf of papers, the script of a farewell address. "Friends," she began, "I speak to you today to say goodbye, to thank you for your kind hospitality, and to hope that perhaps my next visit to the United States will be in a happier atmosphere." She acknowledged that she was sad to be leaving "this country to which I come not only as a visitor but also as one who here spent many years of my girlhood, where I received all of my schooling and much of the inspiration for whatever I have been able to do for my people." Nevertheless, she told her audience, in just a few days she would be "returning to China."

By China, of course, she meant Taiwan—one of the few remaining refuges still available to the Chiangs. The island, she said, was "the fortress of our hopes, the citadel of our battle against an alien power which is ravaging our country." With or without American help, she said, she and her husband would fight on: "As long as a breath remains in us, and with faith in the Almighty, we shall continue the struggle." Madame Chiang described the Chinese civil war as a small part of a much larger contest. "China's struggle," she said, "now is the initial phase of a gigantic conflict between good and evil, between liberty and Communism."

Madame Chiang reserved her most biting contempt for the "moral weaklings" who had abandoned the Nationalists. Britain, in particular, she said, had "bartered the soul of a nation for a few pieces of silver. I say 'For shame!' to Britain. One day these pieces of silver will bear interest in British blood, sweat, and tears on the battleground of free-dom. For that which is morally wrong can never be politically right."

If she was resentful toward Truman and Acheson, however, she suppressed her frustration. "The United States and China have a long friendship, as long as the history of the American Republic," she said. "Many of your citizens have lived in our country. Your people have come to our aid and have given us comfort. Yours has been a contribu-tion of affection." Madame Chiang declared that she could "ask the American people for nothing more." Still, her plaintive tone betrayed her disappointment. "It is either in your hearts to love us," she said, "or your hearts have turned from us." At the end of her remarks, she said, simply, "Goodbye, my friends. I thank you."

True to her word, just days after her speech, Madame Chiang flew home. On board the plane, she was overcome with memories of days traveling through China with the Generalissimo. She thought of the tents, mud huts, and trains that she and her husband had occupied as his armies campaigned across the country. "These flashbacks of the past crowded with rapid succession through my mind," she later recalled.

"While the plane was monotonously droning its way to Formosa, I sat looking out of the rectangular window at my side. I watched cottony wool clouds coursing swiftly by." She asked herself where she and her husband had gone wrong and concluded that she had committed sins of pride. "I had been using God," she said, "not letting God use me."

When Madame Chiang landed for a stopover in Manila, large crowds of Chinese expatriates greeted her on the tarmac, waving Nationalist flags. "To them," she recalled, "I was a symbol of their beloved ancestral land. Any sign that Free China would fight on stirred them deeply." Moved by the spectacle, she then climbed back aboard her aircraft for the final leg. Madame Chiang watched out the window as the lush Taiwanese terrain rose to meet her plane. The pilot had arranged to land at a small, out-of-the way airfield, to avoid crowds. But the crowds came anyway. Taken aback by the reception, she offered her husband only a "brief handclasp," one witness observed, before the two of them stepped into a car and sped off toward the Taipei hills.

Americans, as they pondered the news of Madame Chiang's departure, came to mixed conclusions. Some, as she suggested, continued to view her as a moral leader, a symbol of anti-Communist resistance. Others were less kind. James Reston, in the *New York Times*, wrote that Madame Chiang's stay "helped to create in the minds of the American people a most dangerous illusion. This was that China and the United States were not only allies in the same cause, but that they believed in the same things, were fighting loyally together toward roughly the same objectives, and were represented by men of unquestioned honor and probity." Still, even Reston could not bring himself to completely condemn her. "In short," he wrote, "the mission was a failure, but in good times or bad, it would have to be said that she had a certain style."

★

In Washington, even as Madame Chiang was making her way to Taiwan, Acheson was doing his best to puncture any remaining illusions of solidarity with the Chinese Nationalists. On the morning of

January 12, at his house in Georgetown, he reviewed a speech that he was planning to deliver later that day at the National Press Club. Seeking to reiterate the message that the Truman Administration would do nothing to shore up the Generalissimo's defenses, he scribbled in a black loose-leaf binder, revising a speechwriter's "terrible" first draft of the remarks. Later, at the Press Club, he justified his position by explaining to his audience that Chiang Kai-shek's support in China had simply "melted away." The Generalissimo, Acheson declared, was now little more than "a refugee on a small island off the coast of China."

Acheson rehearsed the history of America's relationship with East Asia and insisted that the United States had no intention of withdrawing from the region. "For one hundred years," he said, "some Americans have gone to Asia to bring in what they thought was the most valuable thing they had—their faith. They wanted to tell them what they thought about the nature and relationship of man to God." The United States, he went on, had enduring interests in the Pacific, including trade ties, and was committed to defending a perimeter that ran from the Ryukyu Islands in Japan to the Philippines in the south. But Acheson said nothing about Taiwan—or even Korea. "We can help," he concluded, "only where we are wanted and only where the conditions of help are really sensible and possible."

★

Acheson's speech, along with Truman's press conference the week before, combined to rouse Stalin. Although the Soviet leader had been pledging, all autumn, to help Mao build his naval and air forces, he had been cautious about encouraging Mao to seize Taiwan, determined to avoid provoking the Western powers. Now, after Acheson's address and Britain's decision to recognize the P.R.C., Western intervention seemed far less likely. Stalin authorized Mao to use portions of the hundreds of millions of dollars in Soviet aid to augment the Chinese military, including the purchase of additional naval equipment. Shrewdly, he understood that an attack on the island would likely weaken Truman and Acheson's support at home, emboldening their domestic rivals—even if the invasion failed.

As it was, however, Mao's position was stronger than it had been in years. With Stalin increasingly sympathetic, and Zhou on his way to Moscow for the treaty talks, Mao chose to venture forth from his dacha to do some tourism. He took a train north to Leningrad, where he wandered among the city's riverbanks and gilded, Byzantine-style cathedral domes. He visited the Winter Palace, the majestic former home of the czars. At Kronstadt, a grim, weathered fortress on an island in the Gulf of Finland, winter had bleached the Baltic landscape, and the January chill cloaked the harbor in a sheet of ice. Propelled by a force existing somewhere within himself, Mao stepped toward the shore, then walked out over the water.

EPILOGUE:

THE MILLS OF THE GODS

Six months later, during the last weekend of June 1950, Truman traveled home to Independence, intending to spend a few relaxing days with his family. After supper that Saturday evening, the Trumans retired to the screened-in back porch, where they gossiped "about everything and nothing in particular," Truman's daughter, Margaret, later recalled. When the weather turned cold, they took the party inside, congregating in the library. But only a few minutes later, the phone rang, and Truman withdrew to take the call. When he reappeared, he was wearing "a grim look," Margaret remembered. "That was Dean Acheson," Truman told the group. "The Communists have invaded South Korea."

Truman went to bed, cautioning his guests not to overreact. "Tomorrow," he said, "I want everybody to pretend it's business as usual." But the next morning the news was even worse. After Truman returned from church, just as the family was sitting down to lunch, Acheson called again. "I can remember the pain on Mother's face as Dad went to answer it," Margaret recalled. "This time, Dean Acheson said there was no doubt that it was an all-out invasion." The North Koreans,

Acheson informed the president, had ordered seven tank divisions to cross the border. Truman hung up the phone and stolidly finished his lunch before returning to Washington to huddle with his cabinet and formulate a response.

The Korean War was a civil conflict: a battle, like China's own, between local factions with vastly different philosophies about how to govern. Yet it was also a direct legacy of Mao's victory in 1949—and the resulting superpower maneuvering inspired by it. After Japan's defeat in the Second World War, the United States and the Soviet Union had divided Korea, splitting the peninsula into northern and southern sections at the Thirty-eighth Parallel. American troops had begun arriving in the summer of 1945, filling the vacuum that the defeated Japanese had left. Although the United States had eventually transferred control of South Korea to the U.N., Washington remained deeply involved. A revitalized South Korea, the thinking went, would improve both Japan's security and its economy, offering defense in depth from mainland Asia while simultaneously creating a market for Japanese goods and providing raw materials for its industry. By 1949, however, clashes between the Communist regime led by Kim Il-Sung in the north and the U.S.-backed ultranationalist government in the south threatened to undermine this precarious balance.

Mao's triumph in 1949 finally tipped the scales toward all-out war. Tens of thousands of ethnic Korean soldiers had fought with Mao's armies in the Chinese civil war; by 1949, however, they had begun to return to North Korea, providing Kim with a new infusion of seasoned troops. Even more important, the Communist successes in China had altered the basic power dynamics on the neighboring Korean Peninsula. Before 1949, Kim's North Korean regime had been caught between the U.S. occupation force in the south and Chiang Kai-shek's unfriendly Nationalist regime across the border in China. But now U.S. commanders, downsizing in the aftermath of the Second World War, had finally pulled out the remaining American troops. Mao's victory simultaneously eliminated the threat from Chiang on Kim's northern flank, easing the pressure on the North Korean leader and emboldening him to launch his dramatic assault—an attempt to unite the entire peninsula under his own rule.

The events of 1949 also shaped Stalin's attitude toward Kim's invasion. The North Korean leader had been lobbying Stalin for more than a year to give his blessing to an incursion into the south. But the Soviet dictator had always refused, anxious about inciting a war with the United States in Asia while Europe was still so unsettled. By 1950, however, the prospect of American intervention seemed less likely; the United States had not, after all, made anything other than token efforts in 1949 to prevent Mao's victory. In late January 1950, Stalin had finally indicated his willingness to discuss the issue. When Kim visited Moscow later that spring to press his case, Stalin finally acquiesced. Still, he cautioned Kim that he would need to look to Beijing—not Moscow—if he needed assistance. "If you should get kicked in the teeth, I shall not lift a finger," Stalin told Kim. "You have to ask Mao for all the help." Nevertheless, Stalin ultimately sent Russian weapons and advisers in an attempt to bolster the north on the eve of the war.

Mao, too, had been slightly ambivalent about the prospect of a North Korean invasion. His main priority was to complete his own revolution, consolidating his control over the mainland. Still, successful Chinese leaders—starting with the ancient emperors—also understood that ignoring the territories on China's periphery risked weakening their own regimes at the center. The challenge lay in determining which adjoining regions were most critical, then weighing the trade-offs. A North Korean invasion, for instance, would complicate Mao's attempt to conquer Taiwan if it provoked a military response from Washington. Ultimately, however, Kim kept his own counsel about the wisdom and timing of the assault. Mao, in the end, decided to support his fellow leftist.

Truman's response, like Stalin's and Mao's, was conditioned by the cataclysmic events of 1949. Mao's victory had prompted the American president to globalize his strategy of containment, extending it to Asia. Advisers in Truman's State Department had urged the president to push back against Communist advances at strategic points along China's periphery. Again, however, the difficulty was in the details—in deciding just where to make a stand. Truman and his aides had determined that Southeast Asia was one of those places; by May 1950, the administration had begun shipping weapons to the French to support their war with the Viet Minh. Now, after Kim's invasion, Truman decided that Korea was another such critical spot, vowing to repel the North Korean thrust.

The resulting war was tragic for most of the parties involved—not least the Koreans. Two and a half million people ultimately died in the fighting. For Chiang Kai-shek and his wife, however, now ensconced on Taiwan, the war was a reprieve. For months leading up to the invasion, Mao had been massing his forces in southern China, preparing to invade the last Nationalist stronghold. A rival faction on Taiwan, meanwhile, was planning a coup against Chiang—with the knowledge, if not the full blessing, of U.S. officials. The North Korean incursion, however, changed all that. Truman swiftly ordered the U.S. Navy's Seventh Fleet to steam into the Taiwan Strait, forming a barrier between the island and the Chinese mainland. On the surface, the maneuver was intended as a show of force, designed to hold the line above Taiwan. But it also functioned to keep Chiang's forces from taking advantage of the chaos, using their new island stronghold as a base to assault the mainland. When Chiang offered Truman thirty-three thousand troops to help with the war effort, the U.S. president rejected the overture—affirming once again the difficult decision he had made in the final days of 1949.

Still, the hawks in Truman's cabinet would not let it go. Johnson, in particular, repeatedly urged the president to enlist Chiang's help. Johnson wanted to mine the Taiwan Strait and launch bombing raids against the mainland from the Nationalist-controlled island. After General MacArthur issued a statement that seemed to accuse the president and his State Department of abandoning Taiwan—referring vaguely to "those who advocate appeasement and defeatism in the Pacific"—Truman ordered MacArthur to retract his remarks. The president was so incensed that Acheson could see it on Truman's face, his "lips white and compressed," as Acheson later recalled the scene. Johnson, pushing back, later wondered aloud to Acheson whether Truman would "dare" to contradict his popular commander in the middle of a war.

But Truman held his ground. Increasingly frustrated with his defense secretary, he later recalled that Johnson "began to show an inordinate egotistical desire to run the whole government." For this and other reasons, in September, Truman called Johnson to his office and asked his defense secretary for his resignation. Devastated, Johnson staggered five miles in the middle of the night up Connecticut Avenue, ending up in Chevy Chase. The next day, at another meeting with Truman, Johnson, weeping, begged the president not to fire him. "You are ruining me," Johnson said. But Truman would not change his mind. Firing Johnson, Truman told an aide, was "the toughest job I ever had to do. I [felt] as if I had just whipped my daughter, Margaret."

★

Overall, though, the last weeks of summer had buoyed Truman's spirits, as American-led U.N. forces began to reverse the Communist gains on the Korean Peninsula. After a daring amphibious landing at Inchon, in mid-September, allied troops pushed their way deep into North Korea, occupying Pyongyang and threatening to overwhelm the enemy forces. Mao's envoys frantically conferred with Stalin, who urged the Chinese to intervene. Although Mao was under no formal obligation to do so, he ultimately followed Stalin's advice. He chose to send hundreds of thousands of his troops across the Yalu River to aid the North Koreans. After getting the news, the elderly Stalin was so moved that he exclaimed, with tears in his eyes, "The Chinese comrades are so good!"

Chinese intervention prompted American hawks to push harder to renew old ties with the Chiangs. General MacArthur wanted to enlist the remaining Nationalists on Taiwan to open a second front in the war, harassing Mao on his southern flank. In MacArthur's strategy, Chiang would return to the same policies he had pursued in 1949, including a blockade of the coast and airborne bombing raids. Truman and Acheson, however, remained reluctant to widen the conflict, holding to the more cautious position that they had developed over the course of the previous year. Finally, in April 1951, frustrated by MacArthur's continued insubordination, Truman decided to fire his renegade general. Speaking on television, Truman reiterated the logic that had animated his East Asia policy for the previous two years. "What would suit the ambitions of the Kremlin better," Truman asked, "than for our military forces to be committed to a full-scale war with China?"

Mao, meanwhile, was moving aggressively to secure other stretches of the Chinese periphery. Mao had long feared—with some justification—that U.S. agents were plotting to stir up opposition in Tibet. Acheson, as 1950 unfolded, had privately indicated that he wanted to see Tibet "quietly strengthened," and American operatives in the Tibetan capital of Lhasa had lobbied for military aid. Chinese Communist military commanders had done their best to publicize these plots, citing intelligence collected from White Russian spies who had been working with the Americans. Finally, by October 1950, Mao had had enough. He ordered nine thousand Chinese troops to invade Tibet, where his forces swiftly defeated the local resistance fighters.

Mao viewed the turmoil in Southeast Asia as another opportunity to shore up his borders. In Indochina in particular, French imperial forces continued to struggle to suppress the nationalist revolt led by Ho Chi Minh. A Communist who had spent time in the Soviet Union and spoke Chinese fluently, Ho seemed like a natural ally. After Mao proclaimed the People's Republic, Ho had walked for seventeen days from northern Vietnam into China, to confer with Communist officials there; he later traveled to Moscow to meet with Stalin. By late 1949, Mao was regularly sending shipments of weapons across the southern border, from Guangxi to northern Indochina, to assist Ho's guerrillas.

Truman and his team, meanwhile, had grown so alarmed about the prospect of a Communist revolution in Indochina that they, too, began increasing shipments of military supplies to the region. By the fall of 1950, the Truman Administration had sent dozens of Hellcat and Bearcat fighter planes to Vietnam, along with U.S. advisers, additional loads of bombers, bulldozers, and other heavy equipment. Truman and his top aides now considered the war in Indochina one of their highest priorities; only the troops in Korea received more U.S. military aid.

And eventually, as the Korean War ground on, even Chiang's once-scorned remnant on Taiwan began to play a larger role in the American war plan. By 1951, amid the increasing militarization of the Cold War, the C.I.A. had established a busy station on the Nationalist-controlled island, operating out of a compound just outside Taipei known as Wu Chang Villa. A C.I.A.-run front company, Western Enterprises, created fictitious cover stories for the American officers, who in reality trained guerrilla fighters and spread propaganda on the mainland, using leaflets, radios, and hot-air balloons. In 1954, increasingly concerned about the rising influence of Communism in the region, the United States signed the Southeast Asia Collective Defense Treaty—a milder version of the Pacific Pact that Chiang had advocated in 1949. The same year the United States signed the Sino-American Mutual Defense Treaty, safeguarding Taiwan from invasion.

These measures succeeded in ensuring the survival of Chiang's island stronghold. But the C.I.A.'s efforts to undermine Mao's rule on the mainland proved less auspicious. By the late 1950s, the C.I.A. had parachuted hundreds of agents onto the mainland in an effort to gather intelligence and generally cause trouble. Still, as Acheson had foreseen, none of the missions managed to make much difference. "We'd be in radio contact," one of the C.I.A. station chiefs later recalled, "and then it would just stop."

★

Walter Lippmann, in the months following Mao's victory, had written presciently that the events of 1949 would need "to be understood in a longer perspective than tomorrow's headlines." Lippmann, who considered Acheson's policy basically sound, had particularly admired the secretary of state's "refusal to obscure the conflict [with Russia] by provoking an American conflict with Red China." Still, he pointed out that Acheson's forbearing strategy would likely take years to show results—as indeed it ultimately did. "We must not wait tensely for news that Mao has defied Stalin," he wrote. "For the mills of the gods grind slowly, especially in Asia."

Acheson was patient, but he was not a pacifist. He disliked Johnson not for his militarism but because the defense secretary enabled Truman's most grandiose fantasies—including the notion that the United States could somehow save China from itself. Acheson, a registered Democrat, could be progressive, but he had no tolerance for what one modern writer has called "cheap and cheerful universalism." Acheson believed that Truman's favorite poem, "Locksley Hall," with its prophecies of impending peace, contained a "grand fallacy." Tennyson's optimism, Acheson later explained, overlooked the tragic aspects of human existence, the jealousies and animosities, the patterns of willful conflict that had existed on the earth for millennia.

The strategy that Acheson convinced Truman to adopt in 1949 rested on a dark, but coherent, worldview. Although Acheson, the son of an Episcopal bishop, was not conventionally devout, he had nevertheless absorbed a biblical cosmology—particularly an appreciation for the paradoxical aspects of the human will. On one hand, man was free and potent; on the other, unfettered freedom unfailingly led to war and ruin. Acheson later explained that he believed "force and violence" to be grim but unavoidable realities in the terrestrial sphere. America's enemies—men like Stalin and Mao—were shrewdly crafting their strategies based on a "calculation of forces," Acheson noted. The United States, if it intended to survive in this dangerous world, would need to do the same—but cautiously, prudently.

Acheson's worldview might not have been a sunny one, but neither was it a hopeless one. For Acheson, the first step toward enduring in an unforgiving world was trying to see it as it really was. There was even a kind of comfort in the tragic perspective, a recognition that America's enemies, too, were only human, subject to the same frailties and failings of judgment. Above all, the tragic worldview, with its skepticism about the limits of human reason, left open the prospect of ultimate redemption. As Kennan once put it in his diary, worldviews that "recognize the limits to human wisdom and allow for the existence of genuinely tragic situations" also concede the possibility of "resolutions . . . which are not readily visible to the human eye."

★

Mao, for his part, had little use for metaphysical speculation. He saw no paradox in the exercise of human will—only opportunity. "Some say that we must believe that the moral law comes from the command of God, for only then can it be carried out and not be despised," Mao had scrawled, as a student, in the margin of one of his texts. "This is a slavish mentality. Why should you obey God rather than obey yourself?" In the years following his victories of 1949, Mao seemed to use this sentiment as his template—tolerating an expanding cult of personality and boldly seeking to overturn China's ancient orthodoxies.

Mao's postwar policies included ambitious, but quixotic, attempts at social and economic engineering. During the Great Leap Forward, beginning in the late 1950s, Mao tried to force China into the modern era by radically transforming its economy. Eager to boost China's industrial and agricultural output, he set wildly unrealistic goals for steel and grain production—then demanded that these benchmarks be met through a series of radical reforms. Chinese villages were consolidated into huge communes that Mao hoped would improve efficiency through economies of scale and the division of labor. At the same time, individuals and communities set up makeshift steel furnaces in their backyards—clumsy attempts to increase production. Rural laborers could be heard playing the patriotic song "We will overtake England and catch up to America!"

Mao, however, had little economic expertise, and the Great Leap Forward proved catastrophic. The backyard steel furnaces produced little of use, while diverting labor that could have been employed else-where. The innovations in farm methods—some conceived by Mao himself—spawned absurd excesses: imaginative but impractical novel-ties that supposedly included cross-breeding artichokes with sunflow-ers and pumpkins with papayas. An unfortunate wave of horrendous weather—including typhoons and flooding in some parts of the coun-try, and relentless droughts in others—compounded the suffering. Rural peasants scrounged for leaves, bark, and worms to survive. Be-tween twenty and thirty million people starved to death as a result of the reforms and famine that followed.

Mao's reign, however, survived this insanity, and by the following decade, he had dedicated himself anew to transforming Chinese soci-ety. In the late 1960s, he and his allies launched a movement they called the Great Proletarian Cultural Revolution—an attempt to purify the country by eliminating the last vestiges of bourgeois influence. Mao's acolytes cast this as the logical extension of the revolution of 1949, an effort to continue the metamorphosis that practical considerations had prevented them from completing back then. Now, Mao's loyalists instructed that "everything which does not fit the socialist system and proletarian dictatorship should be attacked." They organized groups of young radicals, known as Red Guards, and deployed them to vandalize old cultural landmarks and assault Chinese intellectuals whom they considered to be atavistic thinkers—or simply political enemies.

Amid this carnage, Mao's personality cult reached its apogee. Pil-grims toting copies of his *Little Red Book* traveled for days to visit the Great Helmsman's old bases, known as the *geming shengdi*—the "sa-cred places." The nationalist devotion frequently took on a hard-edged fervor. Zealous adherents shouted anti-American slogans and panto-mimed thrusts with imaginary bayonets. Eventually, however, this al-ready amorphous movement began to splinter further, unleashing a wave of destructive internecine violence that seriously damaged the Chinese economy and undermined Mao's prestige abroad.

Nevertheless, Mao continued to see himself as a player on the world stage, shipping weapons and personnel to foreign revolutionaries like

Ho's guerrillas in Vietnam. By the late 1960s, the Vietnam War was raging—the "bastard legacy" of 1949. The increasingly deadly, divisive conflict forced Truman and Acheson, now long retired, to reevaluate the consequences of their containment policy in Asia. Lyndon Johnson, understanding that Truman's administration had taken the first steps toward the war now threatening to engulf his presidency, made frequent attempts to gain the ex-president's blessing for his escalations of the conflict—traveling, on several occasions, to Independence to court the aging Truman. In public, at least, Truman remained silent. But Acheson did not hesitate to offer his counsel. "We certainly should not get out of Vietnam," Acheson told Johnson at one White House meeting in 1967, adding that only a demonstration of American resolve would convince Ho to abandon his designs on the south. By the following year, however, after the Tet Offensive and an economic crisis in the United States and Britain, Acheson began to lose faith in the enterprise. He now urged Johnson to disengage from Vietnam, focusing instead on "areas that count"—primarily Europe.

And yet the strategy that Truman and Acheson crafted together in 1949 also pointed the way, two decades later, to the more conciliatory policy toward Beijing adopted by President Nixon. By the 1970s, Nixon, seeking a path out of Vietnam, pushed to reverse the decades-long American program of isolating Mao. For years, the relationship between Moscow and Beijing had been gradually fraying, sped along, in part, by American attempts to incite jealousies between the two Communist powers. Although Nixon's strategy was not identical to Acheson's, the two men did share a big-picture sense that American interests would be best served by trying to encourage such rifts. In February 1972, Nixon became the first U.S. president to travel to China and meet with Mao, now well on his way to becoming the "isolated, obese, mumbling, drooling dictator" of his twilight years. Nearly seven years later Washington finally recognized the People's Republic of China—capping three decades of diplomatic brinksmanship.

★

Acheson, in his old age, found little solace in the growing tensions between Beijing and Moscow. The China issue had tarnished his once-sparkling reputation; he got grief from both the red-baiters on the right and the antiwar protesters on the left. Ultimately the legacy of 1949—in some cases, despite Acheson's best efforts—had included thirty years of nonrecognition of Communist China, a decades-long U.S. commitment to Taiwan, and the wars in Korea and Vietnam. Acheson blamed "holy rollers" whose "blood rushes to their ears" for the intemperance that surrounded the China debate. And yet his own worldview retained a theological tint to the end. At one speech, at an air base in Alabama, Acheson quoted a poem by G. K. Chesterton, a thoughtful student of the human condition. "'I tell you nought for your comfort,'" Acheson read, "'Yea, nought for your desire, / Save that the sky grows darker yet, / And the sea rises higher.'" A little over a year later, at the age of seventy-eight, Acheson died of a stroke at his country house in Maryland.

Truman, too, felt broken and betrayed by the China debacle. In one sense, he never gave up his desire to redeem distant trouble spots. "I have a deep and abiding faith in the destiny of free men," he had said in his farewell address. "With patience and courage, we shall some day move on into a new era—a wonderful golden age—an age when we can use the peaceful tools that science has forged for us to do away with poverty and human misery everywhere on earth." Still, Truman recognized that he had fallen well short of that ideal, especially when it came to China. During one post-presidency shoot for a documentary about his East Asia policies, the film's producer observed that the former president repeatedly slipped into an adjoining room, where there was an open bottle of bourbon. Growing gradually less coherent, Truman began ranting about the "chinks" and the "yellow Chinee." The producer, disgusted, fled the room. A year after Acheson's death—and just months after Nixon's trip to Beijing—Truman, too, fell ill and died.

By the 1970s, Mao's reputation, like Truman's and Acheson's, had become a casualty of his own policies. As with the other victors of 1949, time and fate had not been kind. Although the fervor of Mao worship inside China was reaching its peak, outside the Middle Kingdom, foreign statesmen mocked him for his ineptitude. By the last years of his life, even Mao—once the unapologetic champion of human volition—seemed reflective and subdued. At his house in the Forbidden City, over glasses of *baijiu*, he mused to an American journalist about man's profound need to worship something or somebody. The Chinese leader seemed increasingly conscious of his own mortality. He explained to the journalist that even he would "soon be going to see God." As 1976 unfolded, he suffered repeated heart attacks; in September, Mao died.

Walter Judd lived for almost two decades more—long enough to witness the first twinklings of the P.R.C.'s vertiginous economic ascent. He felt betrayed by Nixon's opening to China, complaining to the president, in a letter, about this "sharp reversal." Even into the 1980s, Judd was still fulminating about the threats posed by the Beijing government. He could not understand how Americans failed to recognize, after decades of evidence, the true character of the regime. In 1982, after an appearance on William F. Buckley's television show, *Firing Line*, Judd received a letter from a viewer, the eighty-five-year-old Madame Chiang, praising him for his continued efforts to publicize the "nature of the beast" and blaming "vengeful, subtly subversive leftist groupies" for their old misguided strategy. He continued, for several more years, to travel and give speeches, as he had for the past five decades. In 1994, at the age of ninety-five, he died.

Madame Chiang, after returning to Taiwan, had set up housekeeping with her husband in a granite villa on a hilltop north of Taipei. In this pleasant spot, adorned with colorful azalea bushes and orchids, she painted, prayed, and plotted. Taiwan, under her husband's rule, could be brutally repressive, clamping down on political dissent. But after Chiang's death in 1975, the island's political climate grew gradually less coercive. Economically, too, it thrived, transforming itself into one of the region's most dynamic territories, an Asian Tiger. As the old animosities faded, Madame Chiang returned to the United States, eventually taking an apartment on the Upper East Side of Manhattan.

From this vantage, she reminisced about the "periods of great tension, days of deep anxieties, of reverses suffered and overcome," scenes that "flashed in kaleidoscopic sequences through my mind." By the time the twentieth century finally turned to the twenty-first, she had long since celebrated her one hundredth birthday. Among the combatants of 1949, she had survived.

★

And yet the mills of the gods grind on. More than a decade after Madame Chiang's death—in 2003, at the age of one hundred and six—East Asia continues to evolve. A person can now fly from New York to Beijing in less than fourteen hours, but there is really no visiting the China of 1949. It is long gone, erased by lengthy stretches of double-digit economic growth, government engineering, and ideological purification. Despite the tributes of modern Chinese statesmen, for the most part, the Middle Kingdom has prospered in spite of—not because of—Mao's influence. The market reforms instituted by Mao's successors have played the more important role in China's twenty-first-century economic ascent. Still, some scholars caution that it would be a mistake to completely dismiss the purgative effect of Mao's revolution. They compare it to a "forest fire" that, however destructive, also prepared the ground for "new growth."

Regardless of the causes, China is once again impossible to ignore. When its stock market plummets, the world takes notice. When its naval forces fortify another island in the South China Sea, superpowers fret. Beijing's political and military leaders agonize about the modern-day prospect of U.S. containment, but really, that battle ended long ago. China, for good or ill, has long since integrated itself into the global economy. A prominent Chinese general recently proclaimed that his nation "can never be contained." Fundamentally, he is right.

Still, echoes of 1949 are everywhere. Americans continue to debate how to best respond to a dynamic China—whether to engage or confront its leaders, and if so, where to draw their red lines. The most volatile territories in 1949 remain some of the most precarious regions today. The future of Taiwan, in particular, seems less assured than it has been in years. The politics of the island—shaped, in part, by the waves of immigration spawned by Mao's victory in 1949—remain fractious. Chiang's Nationalist party, which once ran Taiwan with an iron grip, can no longer dictate events there. In the presidential campaign in 2016, the Taiwanese elected Tsai Ing-wen—only the second president to come from a party other than Chiang's Guomindang. And domestic politics are the least of Taipei's worries. Although President Trump's unpredictable approach to East Asian affairs has encouraged some Taiwanese, others fear that rash provocations will only destabilize the region further.

Beijing's leaders, meanwhile, do not shy from trying to re-create the magic of 1949 when it can be politically useful. This kind of nationalist sleight-of-hand must seem particularly appealing during periods of economic uncertainty, when military assertiveness offers an easy distraction. But even in flush times, historical reminiscence holds a seductive power. Scattered throughout modern China, signposts point the way toward a revolutionary past populated by heroes, villains, and victims. In the museum at Mao's old base camp in Xibaipo, as visitors file out, a quote from Xi Jinping hangs prominently on one wall. "Our tasks are not fulfilled yet," it reads—a well-placed reminder that, in their way, the quarrels of 1949 endure.

NOTES

ABBREVIATIONS

AH	Academia Historica, Taipei, Taiwan
APRF	Arkhiv Prezidenta Rossiskoi Federatsii [Archive of the President of the Russian Federation], Moscow
BLCU	Butler Library, Columbia University, New York, N.Y.
CKS	Chiang Kai-shek
CPR	*Chinese Press Review*, Shanghai edition
CR	*Congressional Record*, Washington, D.C.: Government Printing Office
CWIHP	Cold War International History Project (at WWICS)
FRUS	*Foreign Relations of the United States*, Washington, D.C.: Government Printing Office
HI	Hoover Institution, Stanford, Calif.
HST	Harry S. Truman
JZZD	Jiang Zhongzheng Zongtong Dang'an [President Chiang Kai-shek Collection] (at AH)
LOC	Library of Congress, Washington, D.C.
MCKS	Madame Chiang Kai-shek
MZ	Mao Zedong
NCDN	*North-China Daily News*

NA   U.S. National Archives and Records Administration, College
            Park, Md.
NDE   Shuguang Zhang and Jian Chen, eds., *Chinese Communist For-
            eign Policy and the Cold War in Asia: New Documentary Evidence,*
            1944–50, Chicago: Imprint Publications, 1996
NYT   *New York Times*
OH   Oral history
PSF   President's Secretary's Files (in Truman Papers, TL)
RG   Record Group (at NA)
SMOF   Staff Member and Office Files (in Truman Papers, TL)
SW   *Selected Works of Mao Zedong,* online at Marxists.org
TL   Harry S. Truman Library and Museum, Independence, Mo.
TLP   Truman Library Photographs (at TL)
WCA   Wellesley College Archives, Wellesley, Mass.
WWICS   Woodrow Wilson International Center for Scholars, Washing-
            ton, D.C.

PROLOGUE

xi   **October 1, 1949, Beijing:** *NCDN*, October 3, 1949; William Empson
      notes, reprinted in Empson, "Red on Red," pp. 66–67. See also Quan,
      Mao Zedong, pp. 120–22; and Schell and Delury, *Wealth and Power,*
      p. 229.

xi   **Mao description:** Li Zhisui, *Private Life,* pp. 51, 82, and 108; Snow,
      Red Star, p. 90; Pantsov and Levine, *Real Story,* p. 309; Westad, *De-
      cisive Encounters,* p. 364n48. On Mao's health and appearance during
      this period, see also Pantsov and Levine, *Real Story,* pp. 359 and 363,
      and Kartunova, "Vstrechi v Moskve," p. 126.

xii   **a boy of sixteen:** Chen Yong, interview by author, June 3, 2015, Beijing.

xiv   **"best nutrient":** "Xi Urges China to Keep Red," *Xinhua,* July 12,
      2013.

xiv   **Martyrs' Day:** Ian Johnson, "In Creating 'Martyrs' Day,' China Pro-
      motes a Vision of the Past," *NYT,* September 29, 2014.

xvi   **fault lines in the American character:** Hans Morgenthau, introduc-
      tion to Tsou, *America's Failure,* p. viii. Morgenthau notes the elements
      of myth and sentiment in the traditional, idealistic U.S. approach to
      China, although it should be remembered that Morgenthau's own re-
      alist paradigm is itself a theoretical construct. Morgenthau is right,

however, that writing "history as it actually has been" involves more than "arguing against the myth of our China policy on rational grounds."

xvi **remembering and forgetting:** Anderson, *Imagined Communities*, is excellent on this dynamic. In chap. 11, "Memory and Forgetting," Anderson quotes Ernest Renan: "The essence of a nation is that all the individuals have many things in common, and also that all have forgotten some things."

CHAPTER 1: MISSIMO

3 **Skymaster specs:** "Douglas VC-54C 'Sacred Cow,'" www.national museum.af.mil/Visit/MuseumExhibits/FactSheets/Display/tabid/509/Article/195813/douglas-vc-54c-sacred-cow.aspx (accessed October 5, 2015). See also "The World's Biggest Jig-Saw Puzzle," *Popular Mechanics*, November 1944, pp. 76–79.

3 **MCKS arrival:** *Baltimore Sun*, December 2, 1948; *NCDN*, December 2 and December 11, 1948; *Rochester Times-Union* (N.Y.), December 4, 1948; *New York Herald Tribune*, December 2, 1948; *Evening Star* (Washington), December 1, 1948; *Washington Post*, December 2, 1948; *NYT*, December 2, 1948. See also Koo OH, vol. 6, pt. H, sec. 3, pp. 84–85, Wellington Koo Papers, BLCU; and Li, *Madame Chiang*, p. 295.

4 **secret codes:** Mr. C. S. Li to T. V. Soong, telegram, December 4 to 6, 1948, T. V. Soong Papers, frame 325, reel 23, HI.

4 **description of CKS headquarters:** *NCDN*, December 3, 1948; *Time*, December 6, 1948.

5 **"Can't do":** *Time*, December 6, 1948.

5 **Second World War had left Chiang's armies crippled:** See Mitter, *Forgotten Ally*, passim.

6 **Nationalist losses:** Chassin, *Communist Conquest*, p. 191; Herring, *Colony to Superpower*, p. 632.

6 **horse meat, tree bark:** Mydans and Mydans, *Violent Peace*, p. 53.

6 **description of Xuzhou:** Rowan, *Chasing the Dragon*, loc. 1687; Liu, *Fall and Rise*, pp. 30, 43; Topping, *Journey Between*, pp. 16, 25–26, 28; Topping, *On Front Lines*, pp. 56–57.

7 **fall of Xuzhou:** *NCDN*, November 30, December 2, 4, and 9, 1948, January 6, 1949. See also Westad, *Decisive Encounters*, p. 270, and Liu, *Fall and Rise*, p. 59.

7   **In his private diary:** CKS diary, December 1, 1948, HI.

7   **American ambassador on CKS:** Stuart dispatches, November 10 and December 1, 1948, in Stuart, *Forgotten Ambassador*, pp. 281, 283–84. See also *Time*, December 6, 1948.

7   **CKS telegrams:** CKS to MCKS, December 1, 1948, JZZD, AH (two telegrams). I am indebted to Laura Tyson Li, Ke-wen Wang, Shu-feng Wu, and Lawrence Chiu for helping me track down these telegrams.

8   **no emotions at all:** Acheson, *Present*, p. 213.

8   **MCKS meddlesome and often irritating:** Melby, *Mandate of Heaven*, p. 169.

8   **"get together":** Pakula, *Last Empress*, p. 473.

8   **"spark plug" etc.:** Marshall memorandum, in *FRUS* 1948, vol. VIII, pp. 299–301.

8   **report of Marshall conversations:** MCKS to CKS, December 5, 7, and 9, 1948, JZZD, AH. See also CKS diary, December 2, 1948, HI.

9   **MCKS at Foundry Methodist:** *NCDN*, December 14, 1948.

9   **MCKS early life:** There are two excellent biographies of Madame Chiang: Li, *Madame Chiang*; and Pakula, *Last Empress*. I have drawn extensively on both for my portrait of her. Hahn, *Soong Sisters*, is outdated but still useful. Seagrave, *The Soong Dynasty*, is entertaining but should be used with caution.

10   **"wooden Gods":** Pakula, *Last Empress*, p. 8.

10   **"harum-scarum":** Hahn, *Soong Sisters*, p. 8.

10   **a complex set of demographic, economic, and military factors:** On changes in Chinese society in the eighteenth and nineteenth centuries, see Spence, *Search*, pp. 5, 77–79, 82, 108, 110, 164, 168, 216, and passim; and Schram, *Thought of Mao*, pp. 2–3.

10   **opium trade and extrality:** Taylor, *Generalissimo*, p. 14; Dong, *Shanghai*, pp. 3–4, 7; Cohen, *America's Response*, pp. 5–6.

11   **Herbert Spencer:** Mitter, *Forgotten Ally*, p. 36.

11   **Sun biographical information:** Spence, *Search*, p. 219.

11   **"I do not wish":** *Sunday Telegram* (Worcester, Mass.), March 7, 1943.

12   **"Pardon me":** Hahn, *Soong Sisters*, p. 63.

12   **"a fire about her":** Tuell recollections, box 1, Mayling Soong Chiang Papers, WCA.

12   **lost in Shanghai:** Mayling Soong to Emma Mills, December 7, 1917, Emma DeLong Mills Papers, WCA.

12   **"Don't send":** Hahn, *Soong Sisters*, p. 75; Pakula, *Last Empress*, p. 100.

12   **"I must ask God"**: Basil Mathews, "Soong Family Has U.S. Roots," *Christian Science Monitor*, December 23, 1942, scrapbook in WCA.

12   **"I am *not*"**: Mayling Soong to Emma Mills, July 6, 1921, Emma De-Long Mills Papers, WCA.

13   **"I think if one"**: Mayling Soong to Emma Mills, July 24, 1919, ibid.

13   **"I go to the"**: Mayling Soong to Emma Mills, December 7, 1918, ibid.

13   **"Don't marry that Bluebeard!"**: Dong, *Shanghai*, p. 191.

13   **Mayling persuaded her fiancé**: Hahn, *Soong Sisters*, pp. 138–39.

14   **Mayling's wedding**: *Shanghai Times, China Press*, and *North-China Herald* clips, cited ibid., pp. 139–42.

14   **"Heads rolled"** and **Shanghai massacres**: Dong, *Shanghai*, pp. 183–85.

14   **Mao fled**: Pantsov and Levine, *Real Story*, pp. 187–202.

15   **"to thoroughly militarize"** and **New Life, etc.**: Pakula, *Last Empress*, pp. 215, 232–33.

15   **"There's Methodism"**: Schell and Delury, *Wealth and Power*, p. 192.

15   **Critics accused CKS of fascism**: Taylor, *Generalissimo*, pp. 91, 101.

15   **tents, train cars, mud huts**: Chiang, *Sure Victory*, p. 26.

15   **some scholars have questioned**: Ke-wen Wang to author, November 4, 2016.

15   **"looked embalmed"**: Gellhorn, *Travels with Myself*, p. 57.

15   **"*hao, hao*"**: Audrey Ronning Topping, interview by author, January 6, 2015, Scarsdale, N.Y.

15   **"yelled, threw teacups"**: Schell and Delury, *Wealth and Power*, p. 186.

15   **"A bad temper"**: Li, *Madame Chiang*, p. 71.

16   **Rape of Nanjing, dikes, cannibalism**: Spence, *Search*, pp. 401–2; Mitter, *Forgotten Ally*, pp. 162–64, 268–69. Spence notes that these casualty figures are from "foreign observers living in Nanjing," and adds that "other contemporary estimates made by Chinese observers were as much as ten times higher, and it is difficult to establish exact figures."

16   **"The bombs"**: MCKS to Emma Mills, May 10, 1939, Emma DeLong Mills Papers, WCA.

16   **American commanders disagreed**: See, for instance, Schaller, *U.S. Crusade*, pp. 68-69.

16   **Burma Road**: On the Burma Road, see Spence, *Search*, pp. 409, 419–21.

16   **Stilwell**: The classic biography of Stilwell is Tuchman, *Stilwell*. On Stilwell's strategy see also Spence, *Search*, pp. 419–21, and Mitter, *Forgotten Ally*, pp. 250–51.

17   **"important ally"** and **"Direct, forceful":** Taylor, *Generalissimo*, p. 198.

17   **airfields** and **early-warning system:** Tuchman, *Stilwell*, pp. 192, 217.

17   **launch bombing raids:** Herring, *Colony to Superpower*, pp. 576–77.

17   **"She will always be":** Chennault quoted in Tuchman, *Stilwell*, p. 217.

17   **"mask of makeup . . . use of me":** Alsop, *"I've Seen the Best of It,"* p. 218.

17   **MCKS at Capitol:** Frank McNaughton, "Mme. Chiang in the U.S. Capitol," *Life*, March 8, 1943; Nancy Maclennan, "China's First Lady Captivates Congress with Words and Smile," *Boston Herald–N.Y. Times Dispatch*, February 18, 1943; and "Text of Address by Mme. Chiang," Associated Press, February 18, 1943, clippings in WCA.

17   **"There was something":** Frank McNaughton, "Mme. Chiang in the U.S. Capitol," *Life*, March 8, 1943.

18   **"fighting for the same cause . . . coming home":** Li, *Madame Chiang*, p. 200.

18   **"as fast as":** W. H. Lawrence, "Mme. Chiang Tells Roosevelt Lord Admires Little Self-Help," *Boston Herald/NYT*, February 19, 1943, clipping in WCA.

18   **"vamped":** Pakula, *Last Empress*, p. 417.

18   **"casualness about cruelty":** Roosevelt, *Autobiography of Eleanor*, pp. 249–50.

18   **in need of rescue:** Li, *Madame Chiang*, p. 204; Jespersen, *American Images*, p. 88. Shih, "Eros of International Politics," is excellent on this dynamic, noting that Madame Chiang "easily won compassion from a masculine rescuer, a timely image for America's self-styled leadership during World War II" (p. 92).

18   *Rochester Times-Union:* quoted in Shih, "Eros of International Politics," p. 93.

18   **damsel-in-distress trope:** Jespersen, *American Images*, p. 88; Li, *Madame Chiang*, p. 201.

19   **"She is the only woman":** "Madame Chiang in Hollywood," *Life*, April 19, 1943, p. 36.

19   **"grasping, bigoted":** Herring, *Colony to Superpower*, p. 576.

19   **"milking the United States":** Stilwell quoted in U.S. Department of State, *United States Relations with China*, p. 68.

19   **"decorative object":** CKS quoted in Mitter, *Forgotten Ally*, p. 298.

19 **sent Chiang a personal letter:** U.S. Department of State, *United States Relations with China*, pp. 66–68.

19 **marked a significant deterioration:** Mitter, *Forgotten Ally*, p. 339; Herring, *Colony to Superpower*, p. 577.

19 **leapfrogging from island to island:** Logevall, *Embers of War*, p. 57; Hunt, *Genesis*, p. 199; Herring, *Colony to Superpower*, p. 577.

19 **controlled some eighty percent:** Westad, *Decisive Encounters*, p. 69.

19 **Toll of WWII on China:** Mitter, *Forgotten Ally*, pp. 5, 268, 277, and 378.

20 **Stalin turned over weapons:** Goncharov, Lewis, and Xue, *Uncertain Partners*, pp. 12–14.

CHAPTER 2: THE GREATEST FORCE

21 **"twins":** Schram, *Thought of Mao*, pp. 78–79.

21 **Mao biographical information:** For my portrait of Mao, I have drawn primarily on Snow, *Red Star*; Schram, *Thought of Mao*; Pantsov and Levine, *Real Story*; and Chang and Halliday, *Unknown Story*, which is extensively researched but polemical. For a collection of essays that are critical of Chang and Halliday's book, see Gregor Benton and Lin Chun, *Was Mao Really a Monster?: The Academic Response to Chang and Halliday's* Mao: The Unknown Story (New York, 2010). Other scholars, such as Harvard's Odd Arne Westad, are more complimentary. Although Westad takes issue with some of Chang and Halliday's conclusions, he praises their research and observes that it "should have been followed up much more closely by academic experts on China." (Westad, "Author's Response," *H-Diplo Roundtable Reviews* 15, no. 2 [2013]: 45.)

21 **description of Shaoshan:** Chang and Halliday, *Unknown Story*, p. 3; Snow, *Red Star*, p. 134.

21 **Cixi's death:** Snow, *Red Star*, p. 138; Chang and Halliday, p. 3.

22 **Mao's mother:** Snow, *Red Star*, pp. 132–34.

22 **sold to brothels:** Westad, *Decisive Encounters*, p. 20.

22 **Mao's father:** Snow, *Red Star*, p. 133; Schell and Delury, *Wealth and Power*, p. 200.

22 **"jet-planed":** Chang and Halliday, *Unknown Story*, p. 6.

22 **Mao reading secretly:** Snow, *Red Star*, p. 133; Pantsov and Levine, *Real Story*, p. 21; Chang and Halliday, *Unknown Story*, pp. 4, 6.

22   **Father calls Mao lazy:** Snow, *Red Star*, p. 132.

22   **reading at library:** Ibid., p. 144.

22   **reading tastes:** Ibid., pp. 67, 138, 144.

22   **"family 'scholar'":** Ibid., p. 133.

22   **Liang Qichao:** Schell and Delury, *Wealth and Power*, pp. 91–116.

22   **"In the world":** Liang quoted in Levenson, *Liang Ch'i-ch'ao*, p. 117. See also Schell and Delury, *Wealth and Power*, p. 101.

23   **"worshipped":** Schell and Delury, *Wealth and Power*, p. 116.

23   **"white and slender hands":** Schram, *Mao's Road*, p. 1:116.

23   **"The weak can become":** Ibid., p. 1:119.

23   **"charge on horseback":** Ibid., p. 1:124.

23   **"The greatest force":** Ibid., p. 1:318.

23   **These efforts intensified:** On the Comintern and Mao's early organizing see Spence, *Mao Zedong*, pp. 47, 52, 56–59, 60, 63.

24   **"I believe in Communism":** Schram, *Mao's Road*, p. 2:237.

24   **He retreated more:** Spence, *Mao Zedong*, p. 70.

24   **"The present upsurge":** Schram, *Mao's Road*, p. 2:430.

24   **He acquiesced in the Comintern:** Spence, *Mao Zedong*, pp. 61, 63–67.

24   **Mao was technically a member:** Ibid., pp. 63 and 67.

24   **It was this arrangement:** Ibid., p. 70.

24   **Mao raised troops:** Ibid.

24   **"A revolution":** Schram, *Mao's Road*, p. 2:434.

24   **Mao now applied:** Spence, *Mao Zedong*, p. 98.

25   **description of Jinggang and raids:** Chang and Halliday, *Unknown Story*, pp. 52–56.

25   **Guerrilla tactics:** Schram, *Thought of Mao*, p. 53.

25   **redistributing it to local peasants:** Spence, *Mao Zedong*, p. 78.

25   **"The enemy advances":** MZ quoted in Pantsov and Levine, *Real Story*, p. 222.

25   **Long March:** Chang and Halliday, *Unknown Story*, pp. 128–33. See also Javier C. Hernandez, "With Odes to Military March, China Puts Nationalism into Overdrive," *NYT*, November 14, 2016.

25   **"in the midst of schoolboys":** Snow, *Red Star*, p. 125.

25   **Mao's sophomoric antics:** Ibid., pp. 92, 96.

25   **"a gaunt, rather Lincolnesque":** Ibid., p. 90.

26   **proximity to the Soviet Union:** Chang and Halliday, *Unknown Story*, p. 127.

26   **Stalin repeatedly urged Mao:** Goncharov, Lewis, and Xue, *Uncertain Partners*, p. 8.

26   **"We are certainly not":** Mao quoted in Schram, *Thought of Mao*, p. 68.

26   **a committed Marxist:** Sheng, *Battling Western Imperialism*, pp. 6, 9–10.

26   **domestic politics:** Schram, *Thought of Mao*, p. 84.

26   **"sinification"** and **purges:** Ibid., p. 85.

26   **cult of personality:** Ibid. See also Leese, *Mao Cult*, p. 8.

26   **supporter of Open Door:** Snow, *Red Star*, p. 154.

26   **Theodore Roosevelt:** Schram, *Mao's Road*, p. 1:108.

26   **F.D.R. antifascism:** Snow, *Red Star*, p. 94. See also Cohen, *America's Response*, p. 161.

27   **Strong interview:** "Talk with the American Correspondent Anna Louise Strong," August 6, 1946, WWICS, History and Public Policy Program Digital Archive, *Mao Zedong xuanji* [Selected Works of Mao Zedong] (Beijing: Renmin chubanshe, 1996), pp. 4:1191–92. Translation from the Ministry of Foreign Affairs of the People's Republic of China and the Party Literature Research Center under the Central Committee of the Communist Party of China, eds., *Mao Zedong on Diplomacy* (Beijing: Foreign Languages Press, 1998), 45–48, http://digitalarchive.wilsoncenter.org/document/121327 (accessed October 27, 2015). See also Sheng, *Battling Western Imperialism*, p. 151.

27   **"Long live Generalissimo Chiang!":** Chang and Halliday, *Unknown Story*, p. 286.

27   **"It was the first time":** MZ quoted in Gaddis, *We Now Know*, p. 63.

27   **"sand in a rat hole":** Connelly notes, March 7, 1947, box 1, Matthew Connelly Papers, TL.

28   **"That is the":** Melby, *Mandate of Heaven*, p. 228.

28   **and winked:** Li, *Madame Chiang*, p. 282.

28   **Chiang . . . cautioned his wife:** CKS to MCKS, December 6 and 7, 1948; MCKS to CKS, December 9, 1948; all in JZZD, AH.

28   **MCKS at Blair House:** *NYT*, December 11, 1948; *NCDN*, December 12, 1948; *Baltimore Sun*, December 11, 1948; *Evening Star* (Washington, D.C.), December 11, 1948.

29   **"grim smile":** Koo OH, vol. 6, pt. H, sec. 3, p. 99, Wellington Koo Papers, BLCU.

29   **"behaved beautifully":** Reuters report in *NCDN*, December 17, 1948.

29   **Bergdorf Goodman:** *NYT,* December 9, 1948.

29   WAITING FOR SANTA: *Pittsburgh Post-Gazette* cartoon in *NYT,* December 12, 1948.

29   **Phone call:** *Heping ribao* newspaper (Shanghai), December 27, 1948, *CPR.*

29   **made . . . fateful choice:** CKS diary, December 24, 1948, HI.

29   **Song of Victory service:** Topping, *Journey Between,* p. 49.

CHAPTER 3: THE OLD DEVILS

30   **Christmas Eve ceremony:** *NYT,* December 25, 1948; *New York Herald Tribune,* December 25, 1948; TLP, accession numbers 66-2870 and 66-3096.

31   **Christmas morning:** *NYT,* December 26, 1948; *Chicago Tribune,* December 26, 1948; *New York Herald Tribune,* December 26, 1948; *Washington Post,* December 26, 1948.

31   **lightning** and **"Harry will get along":** Hamby, *Man of People,* pp. 293, 297.

31   **cocksure** and **poll numbers:** Ibid., pp. 486–87, 506.

32   **"completely wiped out":** *NYT,* December 25, 1948.

32   **"war criminals"** and **"just penalty":** Ibid., December 26, 1948.

32   **Qingdao decision:** Rearden, *History of Office,* pp. 221–25.

32   **Marshall speculation:** *NYT,* December 26, 1948.

33   **Forrestal troubles:** Rearden, *History of Office,* p. 225; Hoopes and Brinkley, *Driven Patriot,* pp. 437, 440.

33   **return to DC** and **"No, oh, my, no":** *NYT,* December 30, 1948; TLP, accession numbers 77-831 and 77-832.

33   **stomach troubles:** Ayers diary, entry for December 13–18, 1948, box 20, Eben A. Ayers Papers, TL.

34   **"I want to"** and **"a stunner":** *Newsweek,* January 17, 1949.

34   **comparison of Acheson and Truman:** Beisner, *Dean Acheson,* pp. 107–8.

34   *ahfter* and *pabst: Fort Wayne Journal-Gazette,* June 28, 1949.

34   **Forrestal scratching head:** Forrestal, *Diaries,* p. 547.

35   **"son of a bitch":** Pearson diary, entry for January 13, 1949, in Pearson, *Diaries,* p. 9.

35   **"Yes, I am":** Forrestal, *Diaries,* p. 544.

35   **Louis Johnson:** McFarland and Roll, *Louis Johnson,* is the best biography of Johnson.

35   **"I just want to tell you"**: Pearson diary, entry for January 13, 1949, in Pearson, *Diaries*, p. 9.

35   **"vultures"**: Lilienthal diary, entry for April 13, 1949, in Lilienthal, *Journals*, p. 2:508.

35   **"like the introduction"**: Alsop, "Matter of Fact," *Washington Post*, January 10, 1949.

36   **"For the first time"**: *Washington Star*, January 10, 1949.

36   **Truman's sense:** For Truman's early life, I have drawn primarily on McCullough, *Truman*, and Hamby, *Man of People*.

36   *chink*: McCullough, *Truman*, p. 83.

36   **"I think one man"**: HST to Bess Wallace, June 22, 1911, Family, Business, and Personal Affairs Papers, Harry S. Truman Papers, TL.

36   **"Let your light"**: McCullough, *Truman*, p. 55.

36   **"I felt that"**: HST note, ca. May 1931, PSF, Harry S. Truman Papers, TL. See also Hamby, *Man of People*, p. 57.

36   **Lafayette's:** Hamby, *Man of People*, p. 57.

36   **"I wouldn't be"**: McCullough, *Truman*, p. 106.

37   **Truman's First World War service:** McCullough, *Truman*, pp. 117–35; Hamby, *Man of People*, pp. 62–78; Donald, *Citizen Soldier*, pp. 48–56.

37   **"Most of us"**: McCullough, *Truman*, p. 138.

37   **"she'd have to"**: HST, longhand note, PSF, Harry S. Truman Papers, TL. See also Miscamble, "Evolution of Internationalist," p. 269. Miscamble's article is the best discussion of Truman's pre-presidential development as a foreign policy thinker.

37   *"Vive Président Wilson!"*: Hamby, *Man of People*, p. 78.

37   **"a single vicinage"**: Ninkovich, *Modernity*, p. 39.

37   **no real foreign policy experience:** Miscamble, "Evolution of Internationalist," p. 268.

38   **"My friends"**: Ibid., p. 270.

38   **Truman's visibility:** Dallek, *Truman*, pp. 12–14.

38   **Truman replaces Wallace:** McCullough, *Truman*, pp. 294–95, 299, 314, 320; Dallek, *Truman*, pp. 14–15.

38   **"international cartels"**: Wallace quoted in Ross, "Uncommon Man," *New Yorker*, October 14, 2013.

38   **"Oh, shit!"**: McCullough, *Truman*, p. 314.

38   **"I think Almighty God"**: Miscamble, "Evolution of Internationalist," p. 281.

39 **"Isolationism is dead":** Offner, *Another Such Victory*, p. 18; Miscamble, "Evolution of Internationalist," p. 282.

39 **ailing president met privately:** Dallek, *Truman*, pp. 16–17.

39 **"In the long cabinet room":** Hamby, *Man of People*, p. 293.

39 **Nearly two weeks elapsed:** Dallek, *Truman*, p. 23; McCullough, *Truman*, pp. 376–77.

39 **"new machine of peace":** Hamby, *Man of People*, p. 268; Miscamble, "Evolution of Internationalist," p. 280.

39 **vowed to go ahead:** Dallek, *Truman*, p. 19.

39 **"Let us not fail":** HST, "Truman Address in San Francisco at the Closing Session of the United Nations Conference," June 26, 1945, in *Public Papers of the Presidents: Harry S. Truman*, 1945, p. 144. See also Hamby, *Man of People*, p. 321.

40 **"the fire destruction":** Ibid., p. 332.

40 **only nation to emerge . . . stronger:** Herring, *Colony to Superpower*, p. 594.

40 **"at the summit":** Herring, *Colony to Superpower*, p. 594.

40 ***U.S.S. Rocky Mount:*** Dong, *Shanghai*, pp. 280–81.

41 **"go to the movies":** Harriman quoted in Rosenthal, *Righteous Realists*, p. 39.

41 **products of European backgrounds:** See Isaacson and Thomas, *Wise Men*, passim.

41 **fair recompense:** Gaddis, *Cold War*, p. 11.

41 **"declaration of World War Three":** Offner, *Another Such Victory*, p. 128.

41 **Canadian authorities arrested:** Offner, *Another Such Victory*, p. 126; Dallek, *Truman*, p. 42.

42 **1946 elections:** Dallek, *Truman*, p. 53.

42 **two young Republican firebrands:** Ibid., p. 49.

42 **rapidly liquidating:** Isaacson and Thomas, *Wise Men*, pp. 386–87.

42 **"a charnel house":** Patterson, p. 130.

43 **Progressive Party** and **Dixiecrats:** Dallek, *Truman*, pp. 79, 81.

43 **"gone goose":** Hamby, *Man of People*, p. 439; McCullough, *Truman*, p. 629; Dallek, *Truman*, p. 78.

43 **half-dozen speeches:** Hamby, *Man of People*, p. 457.

43 **shot of bourbon:** Ibid.

43 **Dewey, did his best:** Goodno, "Walter H. Judd," p. 271.

44 **Some government documents:** Li, *Madame Chiang*, p. 294.

44   WELCOME HOME: McCullough, *Truman*, p. 718.

44   **Mayflower breakfast:** *NYT*, January 21, 1949.

44   **On Truman's weight gain:** See, for example, Lilienthal diary, entry for February 9, 1949, in Lilienthal, *Journals*, pp. 2:463–64.

44   **Truman's inaugural:** *NYT*, January 21, 1949; *NCDN*, January 22, 1949; McCullough, *Truman*, pp. 723–25, 727–33.

45   **burn bare skin:** Lilienthal diary, entry for January 21, 1949, in Lilienthal, *Journals*, p. 2:448.

46   **"rumble from the raw lumber":** *NYT*, January 21, 1949.

47   **"a guy with spectacles":** Hamby, *Man of People*, p. 33.

47   **"Never . . . have I seen":** Pearson diary, entry for January 20, 1949, in Pearson, *Diaries*, p. 13.

47   **"Never before":** Walter Lippmann, "Today and Tomorrow," January 24, 1949, copy in box 110, George M. Elsey Papers, TL.

47   **The C.I.A. had been warning:** R. H. Hillenkoetter memo, December 16, 1948, box 2, CIA File, NSC File, SMOF, Harry S. Truman Papers, TL; R. H. Hillenkoetter memo, December 28, 1948, ibid.; R. H. Hillenkoetter memo, December 15, 1948, CIA 23006, box 152, PSF, Harry S. Truman Papers, TL.

47   **U.S. embassy . . . reported:** Stuart dispatches, January 8 and 15, 1949, in Stuart, *Forgotten Ambassador*, pp. 297–300.

48   **"all walks of life"** and **"critical moment":** MCKS to CKS, January 19, 1949, JZZD, AH. See also MCKS to CKS, January 21, 1949, JZZD, AH.

48   **"getting nowhere"** and **"shake up":** CKS diary, entries for December 31, 1948, and January 4, 1949, cited in Taylor, *Generalissimo*, pp. 397–98.

48   **"express any definite view":** *Qianxian ribao*, January 19, 1949, *CPR*.

48   **CKS morning meeting:** Westad, *Decisive Encounters*, p. 219.

48   *yintui:* Koo OH, vol. 6, pt. I, p. 6, Wellington Koo Papers, BLCU; Tucker, *Patterns in Dust*, p. 240n11.

48   **CKS departure:** *NYT*, January 22, 1949; *NCDN*, January 22, 1949.

CHAPTER 4: BEDBUGS

50   **Mikoyan's arrival at Xibaipo:** Ledovsky, "Mikoyan's Secret Mission," p. 84; Shi, "With Mao and Stalin," p. 37; Quan, *Mao Zedong*, p. 109; Montefiore, *Stalin*, p. 590. For a vivid description of Xibaipo, see Rittenberg and Bennett, *Man Who Stayed*, locs. 2198, 2296. Mikoyan's

memoranda to Stalin (hereafter "Mikoyan memorandum"), January 30, 1949, to February 6, 1949, which are housed at APRF, are available in English translation online from WWICS's History and Public Policy Program Digital Archive, at http://digitalarchive.wilsoncenter.org/collection/172/conversations-with-mao-zedong (accessed October 27, 2015). See also "Anastas Mikoyan's Recollections of His Trip to China," September 4, 1958, History and Public Policy Program Digital Archive, Provided to the National Security Archive/Svetlana Savranskaya by Sergo Mikoyan. With permission of the National Security Archive. Translated by Sergey Radchenko. http://digitalarchive.wilsoncenter.org/document/121774 (accessed March 4, 2017).

51   **Mikoyan's background:** Montefiore, *Stalin*, pp. 48, 50, 68, 515, 520.

51   **Stalin canceled Mao's trip:** Stalin to Mao, January 14, 1949, WWICS, History and Public Policy Program Digital Archive, APRF, f. 45, op. 1, d. 330, pp. 110–13, http://digitalarchive.wilsoncenter.org/document/116969 (accessed October 27, 2015). See also Westad, *Decisive Encounters*, pp. 217, 232.

51   **first Mao-Mikoyan meetings:** Mikoyan memorandum, January 30 and 31, 1949, APRF, WWICS.

52   **siege of Beijing:** Bodde, *Peking Diary*, pp. xvii, 7, 90.

52   **"deeply depressed":** CKS diary, entry for December 12, 1948, quoted in Chang and Halliday, *Unknown Story*, pp. 309.

52   **Fu slapping face:** Chang and Halliday, *Unknown Story*, p. 308.

52   **Fu's daughter:** Titov, "Looking Back," pp. 84–87.

52   **Fu surrenders:** Westad, *Decisive Encounters*, p. 226.

52   **"almost ecstatic ritual":** Ibid., p. 203.

52   **Mao listening to operas:** Quan, *Mao Zedong*, pp. 44, 136.

53   **"short breather"** and **"expecting the worst":** Mikoyan memorandum, January 30, 1949, APRF, WWICS.

53   **P.L.A. enters Beijing:** Bodde diary, entry for January 31, 1949, *Peking Diary*, p. 100.

53   **Xibaipo recreation:** Shi, "With Mao and Stalin," p. 45.

53   **"as if it were water":** Quan, *Mao Zedong*, p. 109.

53   **Mao's fears:** MZ, "Resolution, CCP Central Committee Politburo, 'The Current Situation and the Party's Tasks in 1949,'" January 8, 1949, in *NDE*, pp. 93–94.

53   **"caught unprepared":** Ibid., p. 93.

54   **"sabotage the revolution":** Ibid., p. 94.

54   **Mao on treatment of foreign diplomats:** Mikoyan memorandum to Stalin, January 31, 1949, APRF, WWICS.

54   **"tramped through":** Shi, "With Mao and Stalin," p. 40.

54   **Mao on Xinjiang:** Mikoyan memorandum, February 4, 1949, APRF, WWICS; Ledovsky, "Mikoyan's Secret Mission," pp. 87–88.

54   **thoroughly anti-imperialist:** Mikoyan memorandum, February 4, 1949, APRF, WWICS.

54   **China's farms:** The economic statistics are in Chen, *China's Road*, p. 11.

54   **asked Mikoyan for a loan:** Mikoyan memorandum, February 6, 1949, APRF, WWICS.

55   **Chiang had attempted a currency reform:** On the gold yuan reforms, see Eastman, *Seeds of Destruction*, pp. 172–202; Dong, *Shanghai*, pp. 287–89.

55   **"wet firewood":** Townsend, *China Phoenix*, pp. 36–37.

55   **Chiang's son had:** Westad, *Decisive Encounters*, p. 185.

55   **"We do not have":** Mikoyan memorandum, February 4, 1949, APRF, WWICS.

55   TOP SECRET: State Department Daily Staff Summary, January 31, 1949, box 7, entry 396I, RG 59, NA.

CHAPTER 5: THE DEAN

56   **"chewing gum factory":** Isaacson and Thomas, *Wise Men*, p. 387.

56   **Acheson's office:** Hamburger, "Mr. Secretary," pt. 1, pp. 42–44.

57   **David Acheson descriptions:** Acheson, *Acheson Country*, pp. 25–26, 108, 110–13, 151–52, 211.

57   **"triumph of policy planning":** James Reston quoted in Gaddis, *George F. Kennan*, p. 339.

57   CHIANG RELINQUISHES POST: *NYT*, January 22, 1949.

57   **"Chiang was in the last stages":** Acheson, *Present*, p. 257.

58   **"Let there be light":** Stuart, *Fifty Years*, p. 175.

58   *ren* and **Mencius:** Shaw, *American Missionary*, pp. 146–47. See also Osnos, *Age of Ambition*, p. 298.

58   **"reinforce the teachings":** Stuart to Acheson, February 5, 1949, in Stuart, *Forgotten Ambassador*, pp. 302–5.

58   **"There is an immense . . . present administration":** Ibid.

58   **Wednesday drop-ins, Acheson kicking door:** Beisner, *Dean Acheson*, p. 112.

58   **PPS room:** Philip Harkins, "Mysterious Mr. X," *This Week*, January 4, 1948.

59   **"Avoid trivia":** Kennan, *Memoirs*, p. 1:326.

59   **"vast poor house . . . power to control," etc.:** Policy Planning Staff Paper (PPS) 39, September 7, 1948, *FRUS* 1948, vol. VIII, pp. 146–55; Chang, *Friends and Enemies*, p. 14.

59   **U.S. assets in China:** Chang, *Friends and Enemies*, p. 14.

60   **Acheson on Sundays:** Acheson, *Acheson Country*, pp. 63, 130, 213.

60   **"baffled by the mysticism":** Acheson, *Present*, p. 68.

60   **"Atlantic man":** Schoenbaum, *Waging Peace*, p. 193.

60   **Chinese voices:** Acheson, *Acheson Country*, pp. 89–90.

60   **"wild Ulster streak":** Chace, *Acheson*, p. 19.

60   **"I believe":** Beisner, *Dean Acheson*, p. 8.

60   **"force of nature":** Chace, *Acheson*, p. 19.

60   **"The penalty":** Acheson, *Morning and Noon*, p. 23.

61   **"exclude light":** Ibid., p. 7.

61   **"spiritual wound":** Ibid., p. 23.

61   **"could not be affected":** Ibid., p. 18.

61   **Middletown background:** Acheson, *Morning and Noon*, pp. 1–2; Chace, *Acheson*, pp. 15–16.

61   **"I imagined myself plowing":** Hamburger, "Mr. Secretary," pt. 2, p. 40.

61   **"pumping":** Chace, *Acheson*, p. 23.

62   **did not rank high:** Ibid., p. 24.

62   **"He was the typical":** Ibid., p. 32.

62   **"love portion":** Acheson, *Present*, p. 8.

62   **"We made pets":** Acheson quoted in Chace, *Acheson*, p. 211.

62   **"this wonderful mechanism":** Hamburger, "Mr. Secretary," pt. 1, p. 39.

62   **"wolves tore":** Acheson, *Morning and Noon*, p. 40.

62   **"like Lucifer":** Ibid.

63   **"chins":** Ibid., p. 63.

63   **"His presence":** Ibid., p. 62.

63   **"At the outset":** Ibid., p. 63.

63   **"continually made aware":** Chace, *Acheson*, p. 58.

64   **"I think it is clear":** Ibid., p. 78. See also Acheson, *Present*, pp. 19–20, 22–27.

64   **"stood breathless and bewildered":** Acheson, *Present*, p. 39.

64   **"a throat-slitter":** Beisner, *Dean Acheson*, p. 17.

64   **Wolsey:** Acheson, *Fragments of Fleece*, p. 153.

64   **"proper request":** Beisner, *Dean Acheson*, p. 79.

64   **the Dean:** Malcolm Muggeridge, "Mr. Acheson Brings a New Touch to an Unchanged Policy," *London Telegraph and Morning Post*, January 10, 1949.

64   **"the city had vanished":** Acheson, *Present*, p. 103.

64   **F.D.R.'s style of leadership:** Acheson, *Morning and Noon*, p. 165.

65   **"straight-forward":** Acheson, *Present*, p. 104.

65   **"striped-pants boys":** Hamby, *Man of People*, p. 314.

65   **United Nations:** Acheson, *Fragments of Fleece*, p. 23.

65   **"superseded by reason"** and **"force and violence":** Acheson, *Present*, p. 112.

65   **"mutually exclusive":** Ibid., p. 135.

65   **highball for breakfast:** Isaacson and Thomas, *Wise Men*, p. 462.

65   **Blair House meeting:** Acheson, *Present*, p. 249.

66   **"You know":** Isaacson and Thomas, *Wise Men*, p. 464.

66   **"the exercise of vital powers,"** etc.: Acheson, *Present*, p. 239.

66   **"developing all the human bodily":** Schram, *Mao's Road*, p. 1:434.

66   **February 3, 1949, celebration:** Bodde diary, entry for February 3, 1949, *Peking Diary*, pp. 102–4.

66   **"carnival air":** *NYT*, February 8, 1949.

67   **N.S.C. meeting:** "Memorandum for the President," February 4, 1949, box 188, PSF, Harry S. Truman Papers, TL.

68   **cabinet meeting:** Connelly notes, February 4, 1949, box 2, Matthew Connelly Papers, TL; "Memorandum of Conversation with the Cabinet," February 4, 1949, Dean Acheson Papers, TL.

68   **Saturday morning meeting:** "Memorandum of Off-the-Record Meeting with Congressional Leaders, the President, and the Vice President," February 7, 1949, Dean Acheson Papers, TL; "Memorandum of Conversation with the President," February 7, 1949, Dean Acheson Papers, TL.

69   **J.F.K. speech:** "An Address by John F. Kennedy, at Salem, Mass.," January 30, 1949, reprinted in Keeley, *China Lobby Man*, pp. 406–10.

CHAPTER 6: ALL THE ACES

70   **"extraordinarily courageous,"** etc.: Judd to Gideon Seymour, January 31, 1949, folder A, box 159, Walter H. Judd Papers, HI.

71   **At the podium:** Edwards, *Missionary for Freedom*, p. xi.

71   **Hebrew prophet:** Stuart, *Fifty Years*, p. 135.

71   **Judd circulated:** Blum, *Drawing the Line*, p. 39. For the text of the document, see "Letter from 51 congressmen to President Truman," February 7, 1949, folder 7, box 37, Walter H. Judd Papers, HI.

71   **"deeply disturbed":** Letter to HST, February 7, 1949, ibid.

71   **Lilienthal meeting:** Lilienthal diary, entry for February 14, 1949, in Lilienthal, *Journals*, pp. 2:470–75.

71   **"We are not yet":** George F. Kennan, "Basic Factors in American Foreign Policy," lecture at Dartmouth College, February 14, 1949, p. 10, folder 23, box 299, George F. Kennan Papers, Public Policy Papers, Department of Rare Books and Special Collections, Princeton University Library. See also Rosenthal, *Righteous Realists*, p. 152.

72   **"non-committal reply," etc.:** "Memorandum of Conversation with the President," February 15, 1949, Dean Acheson Papers, TL.

72   **Portrait of Judd's background:** I have drawn primarily on Edwards, *Missionary for Freedom*; Goodno, "Walter H. Judd"; and "GOP Keynoter Judd an Expert on Asian Policy," *Congressional Quarterly Weekly Report* 18 (July 15, 1960).

72   **"deportment":** Edwards, *Missionary for Freedom*, p. 8.

72   **constantly in motion:** Ibid.

72   **Livingstone:** Ibid., p. 9.

72   **"The first journey":** Ibid.

73   **"make the world see":** Ibid., p. 17.

73   **Shaowu description:** Ibid., pp. 26–27.

73   **Judd's capture:** "GOP Keynoter Judd an Expert on Asian Policy," *Congressional Quarterly Weekly Report* 18 (July 15, 1960), p. 1266.

73   **other evidence:** Goodno, "Walter H. Judd," p. 9.

73   **Judd says he's not an imperialist:** Ibid.

73   **"you capitalists":** Edwards, *Missionary for Freedom*, pp. 35.

73   **"a giant . . . of a people":** Ibid., p. 34.

74   **Treating victims of Japanese:** Ibid., pp. 57–62.

74   **It incensed him:** Ibid., p. 57.

74   **Uses savings for tour:** Goodno, "Walter H. Judd," p. 14.

74   **"I have been bombed":** Ibid., p. 39.

74   **Japan might soon launch:** Ibid., p. 62.

74   **Judd drafted to run:** Ibid., p. 63.

75   **Judd and Truman tour:** Judd OH, interview by Jerry N. Hess,

April 13, 1970, pp. 2–10, TL, www.trumanlibrary.org/oralhist/judd
.htm (accessed March 26, 2016).

75   **"wasn't very much of a speaker"**: Ibid., p. 5.

75   **"keep China in the ring"**: Judd, "Which Direction?" p. 13.

75   **"we will lose ultimately"**: Judd, "Control of Asia," p. 19.

75   **"If China is taken"**: Goodno, "Walter H. Judd," p. 236.

75   **"Christian democracy"**: *CR*, March 1, 1949, p. 1678, in folder 5, box 37, Walter H. Judd Papers, HI.

76   **"all the aces"**: Goodno, "Walter H. Judd," p. 258.

76   **Judd blames racism**: Ibid., p. 226.

76   **"You know far better"**: Ibid., p. 214.

76   **"hidden sinister forces"**: Judd to Father Thomas Cushen, August 26, 1949, folder C, box 159, Walter H. Judd Papers, HI.

76   **never volunteer**: Acheson OH, Princeton Seminars, July 22, 1953, p. 15, reel 2, box 79, Dean Acheson Papers, TL.

76   **"virus x"**: Acheson press conference, February 25, 1949, box 72, Dean Acheson Papers, TL.

77   **eerily motionless**: *Life*, February 21, 1949.

77   **"solemn, slow"**: Lilienthal diary, entry for May 4, 1949, in Lilienthal, *Journals*, p. 2:520.

77   **"If you prick"**: Judd OH, interview by Jerry N. Hess, April 13, 1970, p. 117, TL, www.trumanlibrary.org/oralhist/judd.htm (accessed March 26, 2016).

77   **Acheson notes**: "Secretary Dean Acheson's Handwritten Notes for Meeting with Republican Congressmen," February 24, 1949, Dean Acheson Papers, TL.

78   **"U.S. policy could almost"**: Judd quoted in Blum, *Drawing the Line*, p. 41.

78   **face turned red**: Koo OH, vol. 6, pt. I, p. 69, Wellington Koo Papers, BLCU. See also *NYT*, February 25, 1949.

78   **"We are not getting"**: Acheson quoted in Blum, *Drawing the Line*, p. 41.

78   **"wait until the dust settles"**: Acheson, *Present*, p. 306.

78   **"Don't just do something"**: Beisner, *Dean Acheson*, p. 101.

78   **"Any stick"**: Acheson, *Present*, p. 306.

78   **Mitchum and Leeds**: *NCDN*, February 17, 1949.

78   **"space-ship"**: *NYT*, February 17, 1949.

78   **new technology of television**: *NYT*, May 22, 1949; May 23, 1949.

79   **"the pest of the peace":** Herring, *Colony to Superpower*, p. 3.

79   **Gallup poll:** Tucker, *Patterns in Dust*, p. 157.

80   **beside the Hudson:** Li, *Madame Chiang*, pp. 258, 302.

CHAPTER 7: RIVERDALE

81   **Snow fell:** *NYT*, March 1, 1949.

81   **Riverdale:** Tucker, *Patterns in Dust*, p. 76.

81   **Madame Chiang did her best to organize:** Horton, "China Lobby," pt. 2, p. 5; Li, *Madame Chiang*, p. 302.

82   **"combination of Christian fortitude":** Roy Howard notes, "Strictly Confidential Memorandum," January 14, 1949, Roy Howard Private Papers, courtesy of Pamela Howard. I am indebted to Laura Tyson Li for helping me track down a copy of this document.

82   **"vivid expressions," etc.:** CKS to MCKS, January 8, 1949; MCKS to CKS, January 8, 1949, both in JZZD, AH.

82   **Riverdale sessions focused:** Horton, "China Lobby," pt. 2, p. 6.

82   **public relations organization:** MCKS to CKS, January 9, 1949, JZZD, AH.

82   **Metropolitan Club:** Koo OH, vol. 6, pt. I, p. 32, Wellington Koo Papers, BLCU.

82   **Yu Pin, etc.:** MCKS to CKS, January 27, 1949; CKS to MCKS, January 14, 1949, and February 1, 1949; all in JZZD, AH.

83   **"very good friend":** MCKS to CKS, March 6, 1949, JZZD, AH.

83   **needed to rest:** CKS to MCKS, February 1, 1949, JZZD, AH.

83   **"transitional period . . . to be built":** CKS quoted in Taylor, *Generalissimo*, p. 400.

83   **pleaded with his wife:** CKS to MCKS, February 11 and 16, 1949, JZZD, AH.

83   **resisted his pleas:** MCKS to CKS, February 15, 1949, and March 6, 1949, JZZD, AH. See also MCKS to CKS, January 22, 1949, JZZD, AH.

83   **"a lot of feigning":** Pakula, *Last Empress*, p. 573.

83   **H. H. Kung background:** Wertenbaker, "China Lobby," p. 4; Pakula, *Last Empress*, p. 337; Stueck, *Road to Confrontation*, p. 12; Morgenthau Diary (China), vol. 2 (Washington, 1965), pp. 1486–88; Schaller, *U.S. Crusade*, p. 98.

84   **"large, smooth, fat":** Alsop, *"I've Seen the Best of It,"* p. 162.

84   **box of chocolates:** Gellhorn, *Travels with Myself*, p. 56.

84   **"stout rich vulgar," etc.:** Ibid.

84   **"plainer but tougher-looking":** Alsop, *"I've Seen the Best of It,"* p. 220.

84   **"the Generalissimo would have been dead":** Ibid., p. 227.

84   **Louis Kung:** Wertenbaker, "China Lobby," pp. 22–24.

84   **"secretly"** and **"urgently":** MCKS to CKS, January 27, 1949, JZZD, AH.

85   **"I wish I were":** Kung to Judd, September 9, 1948, folder 2, box 165, Walter H. Judd Papers, HI.

85   **"sudden visit":** Koo OH, vol. 6, part I, p. 84, Wellington Koo Papers, BLCU.

85   **"Preponderant power"** and **"shattered":** NSC 34/2, *FRUS* 1949, vol. IX, p. 492.

86   **"We are most anxious":** "Statement by the Secretary of State at the Thirty-Fifth Meeting of the National Security Council on the Formosan Problem," March 3, 1949, *FRUS* 1949, vol. IX, p. 295.

86   **a clever bureaucratic tactic:** Beisner, *Dean Acheson*, p. 180.

86   **sought to use American trade:** NSC 41, *FRUS* 1949, vol. IX, pp. 826–34.

87   **In the mid-1880s:** Logevall, *Embers of War*, p. 5.

87   **reengineered the local economy:** FitzGerald, *Fire*, pp. 53–56; Logevall, *Embers of War*, p. 8.

87   **Espousing ideas about self-determination:** Logevall, *Embers of War*, pp. 9, 49, 97; Herring, *America's Longest War*, p. 3.

87   **Ho viewed the chaos:** Herring, *America's Longest War*, pp. 5–6; Logevall, *Embers of War*, pp. 19, 67–71.

87   **elevating anti-French local figures:** Logevall, *Embers of War*, p. 72.

87   **demonstrated to the Vietnamese:** Herring, *America's Longest War*, p. 6; Logevall, *Embers of War*, pp. 71–72.

87   **on September 2, 1945:** Herring, *America's Longest War*, p. 3.

87   **launching attacks on cafés:** Ibid., pp. 22–23; Logevall, *Embers of War*, p. 175.

88   **a good working relationship with French leaders:** Logevall, *Embers of War*, p. 99.

88   **grenade:** *NCDN*, March 5, 1949.

CHAPTER 8: WAIT, LOOK, SEE

91   **Naval gun wakes Truman:** *NYT*, March 8, 1949. For Truman's bedroom, see also TLP, accession number 66-996.

92   **March 8 meeting:** "Summary of Daily Meeting with the Secretary," March 8, 1949, folder 2, box 1, entry 393, RG 59, NA. See also Beisner, *Dean Acheson*, pp. 51 and 112; and Acheson, *Present*, p. 237.

93   **"frustrated schoolteacher":** Acheson, *Present*, p. 302.

93   **"Almost for one hundred":** U.S. Senate, *Economic Assistance*, p. 35.

93   **the Taiping Rebellion:** Platt, *Autumn*, and Spence, *God's Chinese Son*. Platt notes that while many Chinese historians consider the Taiping to have been "proto-Communist peasant rebels," he adds that it is "an exaggeration to claim they were building some kind of peasant utopia" (p. xxviii).

94   **"That new revolutionary party":** U.S. Senate, *Economic Assistance*, p. 35.

94   **"colossal job":** Ibid., p. 24.

94   **"They had to be":** Ibid.

94   **"extreme elements"** and **"solution by force":** Ibid., p. 26.

94   **"General Marshall, month after month":** Ibid., pp. 26–27.

95   **"These operations":** Ibid., p. 27.

95   **"Some of those supplies," etc.:** Ibid., p. 28.

95   **"lifeless shell":** CKS quoted in Eastman, *Seeds of Destruction*, p. 208.

95   **Never viewed China as critical:** Mitter, *Forgotten Ally*, pp. 343–44.

96   **the Generalissimo wept:** Ibid., pp. 338–39.

96   **"I do not want":** U.S. Senate, *Economic Assistance*, p. 30.

96   **"My own personal belief":** Ibid., p. 34.

97   **"strategic morass":** Ibid, p. 30.

97   **"Mr. Secretary . . . I am willing":** Ibid., pp. 38–39.

CHAPTER 9: A NEW WORLD

98   **Mao leaves Xibaipo:** Salisbury, *New Emperors*, p. 8.

98   **"examinations":** Pang, *Mao Zedong Nianpu*, entry for March 23, 1949, vol. 3.

98   **"First the rural areas":** MZ, "Turn the Army into a Working Force," February 8, 1949, *SW*, vol. 4, www.marxists.org/reference/archive/mao/selected-works/volume-4/mswv4_54.htm (accessed December 8, 2015).

99   **"We are not only":** MZ, "Report to the Second Plenary Session of

the Seventh Central Committee of the Communist Party of China,"
March 5, 1949, *SW*, vol. 4, www.marxists.org/reference/archive/mao/
selected-works/volume-4/mswv4_58.htm (accessed December 8, 2015).

99   **Mao boards train:** Salisbury, *New Emperors*, p. 10.

99   **Beijing devastation:** Bodde diary, entry for March 4, 1949, in *Peking Diary*, p. 114.

99   **Xiyuan ceremony:** *Renmin ribao*, March 26, 1949, cited in Salisbury, *New Emperors*, p. 11.

99   TODAY IS THE HAPPIEST: Xinhua, March 25, 1949, clipping displayed at Xibaipo Memorial Hall, Xibaipo, China.

99   **"Labor University":** Li Zhisui, *Private Life*, p. 45.

100 **Jiang Qing description:** Kartunova, "Vstrechi v Moskve," p. 122.

100 **"I have never met":** Nixon quoted in Li, *Madame Chiang*, p. 411.

100 **"A week after I die":** Mao quoted in Salisbury, *New Emperors*, p. 64.

100 **Jiang Qing on stretcher:** Kartunova, "Vstrechi v Moskve," p. 121.

100 **"stupid" and "bourgeois egotism":** Salisbury, *New Emperors*, p. 64.

100 **touching feet at mah-jongg:** Li Zhisui, *Private Life*, p. 83.

100 **Li Min:** Li Min, *Wo de fuqin*, pp. 29–35.

101 **Li Zongren wants troops at Qingdao:** State Department Daily Staff Summary, February 15, 1949, box 7, entry 396I, RG 59, NA.

101 **secret American plan:** Goncharov, "Stalin-Mao Dialogue," pt. 1, pp. 106–8. See also Goncharov, Lewis, and Xue, *Uncertain Partners*, p. 58–59.

101 **It remains unclear:** Goncharov, Lewis, and Xue, *Uncertain Partners*, p. 59.

101 **Stalin's response:** Goncharov, "The Stalin-Mao Dialogue," pt. 1, p. 107.

101 **"the possibility that the imperialists":** MZ, "Instruction, CCP Central Military Commission, 'Take Precautions against the Enemy's Harassment of Our Rear Areas,'" February 28, 1949, in *NDE*, p. 104.

102 **"After the enemies":** MZ, "Report to the Second Plenary Session of the Seventh Central Committee of the Communist Party of China," March 5, 1949, *SW*, vol. 4, www.marxists.org/reference/archive/mao/selected-works/volume-4/mswv4_58.htm (accessed December 8, 2015).

102 **"The army is not only":** MZ, "Turn the Army into a Working Force," February 8, 1949, *SW*, vol. 4, www.marxists.org/reference/archive/mao/selected-works/volume-4/mswv4_54.htm (accessed December 8, 2015).

102 **"gigantic school"**: MZ, "Report to the Second Plenary Session of the Seventh Central Committee of the Communist Party of China," March 5, 1949, *SW*, vol. 4, www.marxists.org/reference/archive/mao/selected-works/volume-4/mswv4_58.htm (accessed December 8, 2015).

102 **"ancient times"**: Ibid.

102 **"imperialists and their lackeys"**: Ibid.

102 **Tensions**: Chen, *China's Road*, p. 43.

102 **$840 million**: Chang, *Friends and Enemies*, pp. 14–15.

102 **British and Hong Kong**: Ovendale, "Britain, United States," pp. 144, 150.

102 **"Hong Kong will be eliminated"**: Churchill quoted in Tucker, *Patterns in Dust*, p. 20.

103 **stopped in at Blair House**: HST diary, entry for March 24, 1949, PSF, Harry S. Truman Papers, TL.

103 **Luce-Churchill dinner**: Churchill speech and photographs, OV1 and OV2 boxes, Clare Booth Luce Papers, LOC.

104 **Bevin's arrival**: *NYT*, March 31, 1949.

104 **"His gait"**: Acheson, *Sketches from Life*, p. 2; see also pp. 22–23, 27.

105 **Truman dislikes Bevin**: Ayers diary, entry for March 21, 1949, box 20, Eben A. Ayers Papers, TL.

105 **"He could easily"**: Acheson, *Sketches from Life*, p. 1.

105 **"tough, and often stubborn"**: Ibid., p. 29.

105 **"defenseless against"**: Ibid., p. 3.

105 **Me Lad**: Ibid., p. 5.

105 **April 2 Bevin meeting**: *FRUS* 49, vol. VII, pt. 2, pp. 1138–41.

105 **"One step at a time"**: *NCDN*, April 3, 1949.

105 **NATO ceremony**: Ceremony program, box 154, Dean Acheson Papers, TL; *NCDN*, April 5, 1949; *New York Herald Tribune*, April 5, 1949; *NYT*, April 5, 1949; *Washington Times-Herald*, April 6, 1949.

106 **Judd-Marcantonio debate**: See also undated clipping, *Pathfinder*, folder 4, box 37, Walter H. Judd Papers, HI.

106 **"world domination"**: *CR*, April 4, 1949, p. 3828.

106 **"With empire comes disaster"**: Ibid.

106 **"purpose in China . . . at this moment"**: *CR*, April 4, 1949, pp. 3827–28.

107 **Judd depressed**: Judd to Jean S. Gates, April 12, 1949, "Correspondence, general, 1949 (C)" folder, box 159, Walter H. Judd Papers, HI.

107 **"march forward"**: *NCDN*, April 4, 1949.

107 **"sinister":** Bodde diary, entry for April 1, 1949, in *Peking Diary*, p. 144.

107 **Xinhua article:** *NCDN*, March 24, 1949.

107 **NATO empowers Mao:** Goncharov, Lewis, and Xue, *Uncertain Partners*, p. 51.

107 **"considerable difficulty":** C.I.A. report, "Prospects for Soviet Control of a Communist China," in Hutchings, *Tracking the Dragon*, p. 35.

107 **"identifies itself":** Ibid., p. 34.

107 **"the enormous territory":** Ibid.

107 **"Spring":** Judd remarks, *CR*, April 4, 1949, p. 3827.

CHAPTER 10: HEAVEN AND HELL

108 **"a sense of impending crisis":** Stuart, *Fifty Years*, p. 230.

108 **meteor:** *NYT*, April 12, 1949.

108 **"black eclipse":** *NYT*, April 13, 1949.

108 **earthquake:** *NYT*, April 14, 1949.

108 **two hundred and fifty atomic bombs:** *NYT*, April 15, 1949.

109 **"one of nature's mysteries":** Ibid.

109 **Episcopal church membership:** *NYT*, December 27, 1948. See also Patterson, *Grand Expectations*, p. 17; the Association of Religion Data Archives, "Episcopal Church," http://www.thearda.com/ Denoms/D_849.asp (accessed Dec. 12, 2016).

109 **Garden of the Gods:** *NYT*, April 16, 1949.

109 **British consulate service:** *NCDN*, April 13, 1949.

109 **Campbell review:** *NYT*, June 26, 1949.

110 **"You are God":** Schram, *Mao's Road*, p. 1:273. Stuart Schram, the editor of Mao's writings, notes that Mao's handwritten annotation actually reads, "Is there any God other than God?" But based on the context of the passage, both Chinese and U.S. scholars have concluded that Mao clearly intended to write "self" instead of the second "God." See also Schram, *Mao's Road*, p. 1:312n30.

110 **Truman on Easter:** *NYT*, April 18, 1949.

111 **troops massed in Beijing:** Bodde diary, entry for April 18, 1949, in *Peking Diary*, p. 152.

111 **population center:** Taylor, *Generalissimo*, p. 90.

111 **carving broad avenues:** Ibid., pp. 90–91.

111 **"ships caught by low tide":** Townsend, *China Phoenix*, p. 35.

111 **"a third-rate village":** Ezpeleta, *Red Shadows*, p. 5.

112   **Nanjing climate:** Topping, *Journey Between*, p. 15.

112   **air reeked:** Pakula, *Last Empress*, p. 205.

112   **refugees:** Townsend, *China Phoenix*, p. 35.

112   **eating grass:** Seymour Topping and Audrey Ronning Topping, interview by author, January 6, 2015. See also Topping, *China Mission*, p. 316.

112   **canvas blankets:** Seymour Topping and Audrey Ronning Topping, interview by author, January 6, 2015.

112   **"in entirely innocent":** Stuart, *Fifty Years*, p. 208.

112   **"The diplomats were":** Audrey Ronning Topping, interview by author, January 6, 2015.

112   **Nationalists preparing for siege:** Topping, *Journey Between*, pp. 16–17.

112   **pillboxes:** Barber, *Fall of Shanghai*, p. 96.

112   **two million P.L.A. troops:** Westad, *Decisive Encounters*, p. 241.

112   **Wedemeyer broomsticks comment:** Tsou, *America's Failure*, p. 495.

112   **"wild yet systematic":** Ronning diary, entry for April 25, 1949, in Ronning, *Memoir of China*, p. 136.

112   **march toward Yangtze:** Barber, *Fall of Shanghai*, pp. 81–82; *Dagong bao*, June 5, 1949, *CPR*.

113   **practiced for the crossing:** *Dagong bao*, June 5, 1949, *CPR*.

113   **arches, posters, etc.:** Barber, *Fall of Shanghai*, p. 84.

113   **C.I.A. warned President Truman:** C.I.A. memorandum, April 19, 1949, box 2, CIA File, NSC File, SMOF, Harry S. Truman Papers, TL.

113   *Amethyst* **attack:** *NCDN*, April 21, 1949; Barber, *Fall of Shanghai*, pp. 85–86.

114   UNDER HEAVY FIRE: Barber, *Fall of Shanghai*, p. 86.

114   *Consort* **attack:** *NCDN*, April 22, 1949; Barber, *Fall of Shanghai*, p. 88.

114   **"They were throwing off":** *NCDN*, April 22, 1949.

114   **fifty sailors died:** Westad, *Decisive Encounters*, p. 245.

114   **Mao initially approved:** MZ, "CCP Central Military Commission to Su Yu and Zhang Zhen," April 21, 1949, in *NDE*, p. 105.

114   **revised his original assessment:** MZ, "CCP Central Military Commission to CCP General Front-line Committee," April 22, 1949, in *NDE*, pp. 105–6.

114   **Yangtze crossing, mosquitoes, etc:** Townsend, *China Phoenix*, pp. 48–50; Barber, *Fall of Shanghai*, p. 82.

115   **green flares:** Barber, *Fall of Shanghai*, p. 95.

115   **"opened up with":** Ronning diary, entry for April 21, 1949, in Ronning, *Memoir of China*, p. 135.

115   **P.L.A. troops finally pushed:** Topping dispatch, *NCDN*, April 25, 1949; Topping, *Journey Between*, pp. 16, 72–73.

115   **"stripped residences":** Topping, *Journey Between*, p. 76.

115   **Deng Xiaoping:** Westad, *Decisive Encounters*, p. 244.

116   **"Get a small bag . . . Taiwan or Tokyo?":** Dora Fugh Lee, interview by author, February 12, 2016.

116   **Stuart's bedroom invaded:** Stuart to Acheson, April 25, 1949, *FRUS 1949*, vol. VIII, p. 723.

116   **"The Ambassador was not":** Ibid.

116   **"violation of discipline":** MZ, "Instruction, CCP Central Military Commission, 'Report and Ask for Instructions before Doing Anything in Diplomatic Affairs,'" April 26, 1949, in *NDE*, pp. 107–8.

117   **"capriciousness . . . ignorance":** Stuart to Acheson, April 29, 1949, Stuart, *Forgotten Ambassador*, p. 321; Stuart diary, entry for May 7, 1949, box 1, John Leighton Stuart Papers, HI.

117   **Li Zongren rivalry:** Lin, *Accidental State*, pp. 6–7, 74, and passim. See also Westad, *Decisive Encounters*, p. 182.

117   **Acheson's office received a tip:** State Department Daily Staff Summary, April 26, 1949, box 7, entry 396I, RG 59, NA.

118   **"strategic triangle":** Lin, *Accidental State*, pp. 84–85, 89.

118   **had built an airfield and a harbor:** Ibid., p. 86.

118   **hundreds of millions of dollars:** Ibid., pp. 82–83.

118   **managed to siphon off:** Ibid., p. 83.

118   **"we will defend Shanghai":** CKS to MCKS, April 23, 1949, JZZD, AH.

118   **Chiang leaves Xikou:** Taylor, *Generalissimo*, p. 407; Chiang, *Calm*, p. 208.

118   **"open split":** R. H. Hillenkoetter memo, April 28, 1949, box 2, CIA File, NSC File, SMOF, Harry S. Truman Papers, TL.

118   **"Regardless of real":** R. H. Hillenkoetter memo, April 26, 1949, ibid.

CHAPTER 11:
A VAST AND DELICATE ENTERPRISE

119   **"impromptu victory parades":** Bodde diary, entry for April 24, 1949, in *Peking Diary*, p. 164.

119   **Mao and Liu Yazi:** Pang, *Mao Zedong Nianpu*, entry for May 1, 1949, pp. 3:495–96.

119   **"We won":** Ibid.

119 **Mao instructed his military commanders:** MZ, "Instruction, CCP Central Military Commission, 'On Preparations for Taking Over Shanghai,'" April 27, 1949, in *NDE*, pp. 108–9.

120 **Mao believed . . . business class:** Ibid, p. 109.

120 **"other foreign capitalists":** Stalin to Kovalev, April 26, 1949, WWICS, History and Public Policy Program Digital Archive, APRF: f. 45, op. 1, d. 3331 [sic, probably 331], l. 3. Reprinted in Andrei Ledovskii, Raisa Mirovitskaia, and Vladimir Miasnikov, *Sovetsko-Kitaiskie Otnosheniia*, vol. 5, bk. 2, 1946–*February* 1950 (Moscow: Pamiatniki Istoricheskoi Mysli, 2005), p. 126. Translated for CWIHP by Sergey Radchenko, http://digitalarchive.wilsoncenter.org/document/113357 (accessed December 23, 2015).

120 **"eager to do business":** MZ, "Instruction, Central Military Commission, 'Our Policy Toward British and American Citizens and Diplomats,'" April 28, 1949, in *NDE*, p. 110.

120 **Even the United States:** Ibid., pp. 110–11.

120 **"we shld strongly oppose":** Acheson to Stuart, May 13, 1949, *FRUS* 1949, vol. IX, pp. 21–23.

120 **"common front":** Ibid.

120 **Mao also seemed to misunderstand:** See, for example, Gaddis, *We Now Know*, p. 64.

121 **Public opinion . . . two to one:** Hamby, *Man of People*, p. 520.

121 **"indigenous Chinese elements":** Redacted paragraph 18, NSC 34/2, cited in the C.I.A.'s recently declassified internal history describing U.S. operations on the Chinese mainland in 1949: Cox, "Civil Air Transport," p. 12.

121 **"Because we bear":** Ibid.

121 **Wisner's background:** See Thomas, *Very Best Men*, pp. 17–31.

122 **Wisner sent a memo:** "Memo from ADPC [Wisner] to State/PP (Joyce), 'Subject: Policy Direction in China, Implementation of NSC 32/4,'" March 8, 1949, cited in Cox, "Civil Air Transport," p. 12.

122 **the secretary of state's advisers told Wisner:** "Memo from State/PP (George H. Butler), 'Subject: Interpretation of NSC 34/2,'" March 23, 1949, cited ibid., pp. 12–13.

122 **"large scale clandestine":** Ibid., p. 13.

122 **"Both the situation":** Ibid.

122 **Hotel Washington meeting:** "Memo of Conversation with Major

General C. L. Chennault, USA (ret.), unsigned," May 10, 1949, cited ibid., p. 15.

122 **"The United States is losing":** Claire Chennault, *Way of a Fighter* [reprint pamphlet], folder 5, box 198, Walter H. Judd Papers, HI.

122 **Walter Judd had loved the book:** *CR*, February 3, 1949, p. 812, clipping in folder 5, box 37, ibid.

122 **"chain reaction":** Claire Chennault, "Summary of Present Communist Crisis in Asia," May 10, 1949, pp. 3 and 6, box 11, "History—Civil War" folder, Claire Chennault Papers, HI. The C.I.A.'s memo of conversation of the Wisner meeting remains classified, but this document, dated one day after the Hotel Washington meeting, outlines the basic elements of Chennault's plan.

122 **"belt of resistance":** Ibid., p. 8.

123 **"cordon sanitaire":** Ibid., p. 10.

123 **"hardy mountaineers":** Ibid., p. 7.

123 **He estimated . . . fund the entire operation:** Ibid., p. 9.

123 **"There is only one man":** Chennault testimony, "Stenographic Transcript of Hearings Before the Joint Committee on Foreign Economic Cooperation," May 3, 1949, p. 18, box 12, "Declassified Records—Misc—2011 July Release" folder, Claire Chennault Papers, HI.

123 **Wisner liked Chennault's plan:** Leary, *Perilous Missions*, p. 72.

123 **"greatly relaxed":** State Department Daily Staff Summary, May 3, 1949, box 7, entry 396I, RG 59, NA.

124 **"better mutual understanding":** Stuart to Acheson, March 10, 1949, in Stuart, *Forgotten Ambassador*, p. 309.

124 **"I should like to":** Ibid., p. 310.

124 **Clever and affable:** Topping, *Journey Between*, p. 82.

124 **"thoroughly communized":** Stuart, *Fifty Years*, p. 247.

124 **brick building:** Topping, *Journey Between*, p. 81.

124 **"inconvenient":** Stuart to Acheson, May 11, 1949, in Stuart, *Forgotten Ambassador*, pp. 322–23.

124 **"old college president":** Ibid.

124 **"distressed":** Ibid.

124 **"most friendly":** Ibid.

124 **Huang had walked Fugh:** Ibid.

125 **briefed Soviet diplomats:** Shen and Xia, *Mao and Sino-Soviet*, p. 33.

125 **Mao instructed Huang:** MZ, "Telegram, CCP Central Committee

to CCP Nanjing Municipal Committee," May 10, 1949, in *NDE*, pp. 111–12.

125 **"listen more"**: Ibid., p. 112.

125 **"If Stuart's attitude"**: Ibid.

125 **"should not reject"**: Ibid.

125 **"friendly and informal"**: Stuart to Acheson, May 14, 1949, in Stuart, *Forgotten Ambassador*, pp. 324–26.

125 **"much, but not all"**: Ibid.

125 **"promised to do"**: Ibid.

126 **"obviously impressed"**: Ibid.

126 **"could do nothing"**: Ibid.

126 **"Nothing can be done"**: Lilienthal diary, entry for May 11, 1949, in Lilienthal, *Journals*, p. 2:525.

126 **"I had a couple"**: Ibid.

126 **"so-called Communists"**: Ibid.

126 **"Joe Stalin says"**: Ibid.

127 **"grafters and crooks"**: Ibid.

127 **"I'll bet you"**: Ibid.

127 **Truman orders investigation**: Li, *Madame Chiang*, p. 310; Pakula, *Last Empress*, p. 600.

127 **Johnson was asking**: MCKS to CKS, May 9, 1949, JZZD, AH.

127 **As May unfolded**: MCKS to CKS, May 18, 1949, JZZD, AH.

127 **Bank of China's assets**: MCKS to CKS, April 27, 1949, JZZD, AH.

127 **"safe withdrawal . . . early stage"**: MCKS to CKS, May 9, 1949, JZZD, AH.

127 **food shortages, weapons**: Ibid.

128 **"secret negotiations"**: Ibid.

128 **"The situation is"**: Ibid.

128 **"Reliable sources"**: MCKS to CKS, May 6, 1949, JZZD, AH.

128 **"national propaganda institution"**: Ibid.

128 **Zhoushan Islands incident**: CKS diary, entry for May 12, 1949, cited in Lin, *Accidental State*, p. 91.

128 **code book**: MCKS to CKS, May 16, 1949, JZZD, AH.

128 **"On the issue of"**: CKS to MCKS, May 21, 1949, JZZD, AH.

129 **Barkley . . . asked**: Connelly notes, May 13, 1949, box 1, Matthew Connelly Papers, TL.

129 **"misguided"**: Ibid.

129 **"a better soldier"**: Ibid.

129 **"reigning families"**: Ibid.

129 **"a great turning point"**: Alsop, "Better Late Than Never," *New York Herald Tribune*, May 23, 1949, p. 21.

129 **"For four long"**: Ibid.

129 **"positive definition"**: Ibid.

129 **"a line will be drawn"**: Ibid.

CHAPTER 12: NEVERLAND

130 **Acheson's departure**: *Washington Post*, May 21, 1949. See also TLP, accession nos. 66-2331-33.

130 **"Goodbye, Dean"**: *Washington Post*, May 21, 1949.

131 **China . . . not expected to be**: "Memorandum of Conversation with V. K. Wellington Koo," May 11, 1949, Acheson papers, TL. See also Koo OH, vol. 6, pt. I, p. 129, Wellington Koo Papers, BLCU.

131 **"It's all in the lap"**: *Washington Post*, May 21, 1949.

131 **"confusion and bewilderment"**: George F. Kennan, PPS 45, in *FRUS* 1948, vol. VIII, p. 214.

131 **"It is now less important"**: Ibid.

132 **Wedemeyer report debate**: "Summar[ies] of Daily Meeting with the Secretary," May 9–11, 1949, folder 2, box 1, entry 393, RG 59, NA; "Meeting with the President," May 12, 1949, Dean Acheson Papers, TL; Ayers diary, entries for May 13 and 17, 1949, box 20, Eben A. Ayers Papers, TL.

132 **"the rug out from under"**: Ayers diary, entries for May 13 and 17, 1949, box 20, Eben A. Ayers Papers, TL.

132 **"quite unsound"**: Acheson OH, Princeton Seminars, July 22, 1953, pp. 19–20, reel 2, box 79, Dean Acheson Papers, TL.

132 **"solid foundation"**: Acheson press conference, May 18, 1949, box 72, Dean Acheson Papers, TL.

132 **"internal conflicts"**: Ibid.

132 **Palais Rose**: *NYT*, May 15 and 24, 1949.

133 **"the color of an acute sunburn"**: *NYT*, May 24, 1949.

133 **frescoes of satyrs**: Acheson, *Sketches from Life*, p. 8.

133 **Vishinsky . . . brought up Asia**: *NYT*, May 24, 1949.

133 **"The Far Eastern problem"**: *NYT*, May 22, 1949.

133 **Forrestal . . . suicide**: Hoopes and Brinkley, *Driven Patriot*, pp. 464–65.

133 **"shocked and grieved"**: *NYT*, May 23, 1949.

133 **Shells fell . . . along the waterfront**: *NYT*, May 19 and 20, 1949.

133   the Communists still seemed hesitant: *NYT*, May 23, 1949.

133   RED TROOPS ENTER SHANGHAI: *NYT*, May 26, 1949.

134   "above the sea": Dong, *Shanghai*, p. 2.

134   building boom: Ezpeleta, *Red Shadows*, pp. 7–8.

134   British merchants hired coolies: Dong, *Shanghai*, p. 10.

134   "their own little never-never land": Snow, *Red Star*, p. 40.

134   "big managers": Dong, *Shanghai*, p. 15.

134   pink gins: Barber, *Fall of Shanghai*, p. 24; Rowan, *Chasing the Dragon*, loc. 40.

134   lawn bowls: *NCDN*, May 17, 1949.

134   White Russian refugees: Dong, *Shanghai*, pp. 130–34.

134   taxi dancers: Ibid., pp. 139–44.

134   "probably the most un-Christian": Ezpeleta, *Red Shadows*, p. 9.

134   Troops in steel helmets, etc.: *NCDN*, May 14 and 16, 1949; Ezpeleta, *Red Shadows*, pp. 107, 108, 180; Forman, *Blunder in Asia*, p. 51.

135   rifle range: Crozier, *Man Who Lost*, p. 336.

135   B-24 and B-25: Forman, *Blunder in Asia*, p. 57.

135   curfew: *NCDN*, May 21, 1949.

135   executions: Ezpeleta, *Red Shadows*, pp. 146–48; Forman, *Blunder in Asia*, pp. 52–53; Dong, *Shanghai*, p. 292.

135   "Roman arena": Ezpeleta, *Red Shadows*, p. 146.

135   "victory parades": Forman, *Blunder in Asia*, p. 66; Ezpeleta, *Red Shadows*, pp. 111, 160.

135   Flying Fortresses and leaflets, etc.: *NCDN*, May 12, 1949.

135   "Marching Through Georgia": Forman, *Blunder in Asia*, p. 66.

135   "looked as though a tornado": *NCDN*, May 23, 1949.

135   light show: Ezpeleta, *Red Shadows*, pp. 176–77; *NCDN*, May 25, 1949; Forman, *Blunder in Asia*, pp. 62–65; *NYT*, May 24, 1949.

135   "The whole sky . . . fireworks": Forman, *Blunder in Asia*, pp. 62–65.

136   "They proceeded on foot": *NCDN*, May 25, 1949.

136   sank four tankers, etc.: Ibid.

136   FOR EVERY HOUSE THAT HIDES: Ibid.

136   Around sunset: Ezpeleta, *Red Shadows*, p. 181.

136   the skies cleared: Forman, *Blunder in Asia*, p. 67.

137   "plainly tired": *NCDN*, May 26, 1949.

137   marching on the sidewalks: *NYT*, May 25, 1949.

137   scrubbed the walls: Ibid.

137   White flags: *NCDN*, May 26, 1949; *Dagong bao*, June 9, 1949, *CPR*.

137   "teenagers in the first blush . . . almost obsequiously": Ezpeleta, *Red Shadows*, pp. 185–86.

137   watched through binoculars: Forman, *Blunder in Asia*, pp. 72–74.

137   "Come out . . . all around": Ibid., p. 72.

138   "Bullets cracked past": Ibid.

138   ticket booth and band stand: Ibid.

138   mortars and flamethrowers: Cabot reminiscence in Barber, *Fall of Shanghai*, p. 153.

138   "The whole sky lit up": Forman, *Blunder in Asia*, p. 75.

138   "Firing starts": Cabot diary, entry for May 26, 1949, quoted in Barber, *Fall of Shanghai*, p. 153.

138   By the morning: Forman, *Blunder in Asia*, p. 78.

138   Soong residence: *NCDN*, May 28, 1949.

139   Money changers: *NCDN*, May 26, 1949.

139   "canned goods": Ibid.

139   New China Bookstore: *Shanghai renmin*, May 27, 1949, *CPR*.

139   "semi-colonial and feudalistic": *China Daily Tribune*, June 2, 1949, *CPR*.

139   Cabot announced: *NCDN*, May 28, 1949.

139   Withdrawal from Qingdao: State Department Daily Staff Summaries (May 10, May 16, and May 27, 1949), box 7, entry 396I, RG 59, NA.

139   "some signs recently": MZ, "Instruction, CCP Central Military Commission, 'Policies Concerning the Prevention of Imperialist Intervention against the Chinese Revolution,' May 28, 1949, in *NDE*, p. 114.

CHAPTER 13: HEAT

141   steamed down the Potomac: Ayers diary, entries for May 28–30, 1949, box 20, Eben A. Ayers Papers, TL.

141   *Williamsburg* descriptions: MacDonald, "President Truman's Yacht," pp. 48–49.

141   "all kinds of whisky": Ibid.

141   griping to his aides: Ayers diary, entry for May 28, 1949, box 20, Eben A. Ayers Papers, TL.

142   "a perfect day": Ibid., May 29, 1949.

142   "disagreements of [a] serious nature": *FRUS* 1949, vol. VIII, p. 358.

142   "*de facto* working relations": Ibid.

142   "complete economic and physical": Ibid., p. 359.

142 **"nervous and worried"**: Ibid., p. 360.

142 **"extremely hopeful line of effort"**: Stuart diary, entry for June 3, 1949, John Leighton Stuart Papers, HI.

142 **Chinese officials later insisted**: Cohen, "Conversations with Chinese Friends," p. 88.

142 **Scholars have never been able**: Chen, *China's Road*, pp. 241–42n82.

143 **out of character**: Chang, *Friends and Enemies*, p. 304n60.

143 **"nonsense"**: Ibid. See also Cohen, "Conversations," pp. 287–88.

143 **F.B.I. investigation**: N.S.C. memo, May 27, 1949, box 2, CIA File, NSC File, SMOF, Harry S. Truman Papers, TL.

143 **"Soong-Kung group"**: Ibid.

144 **Judd openly touted**: See, for example, *Cedar Rapids Gazette*, May 8, 1949, folder 7, box 37, Walter H. Judd Papers, HI.

144 **"some real signs"**: Acheson OH, Princeton Seminars, July 22, 1953, p. 21, reel 2, box 79, Dean Acheson Papers, TL.

144 **Foley Square protests**: *NYT*, June 7, 1949.

144 **"the 'spy' theme"**: *NYT*, June 12, 1949.

144 **issued an executive order**: Dallek, *Truman*, p. 54.

145 **"wild and false . . . innocent men"**: Tanenhaus, *Whittaker Chambers*, p. 283.

145 **"sat quietly against"**: Ibid., June 7, 1949.

145 **worked together** and **neighbors**: Beisner, *Dean Acheson*, pp. 283, 289.

145 **Madame Chiang mentioned**: MCKS to CKS, January 8, 1949, JZZD, AH.

145 **Alger's brother, Donald**: Beisner, *Dean Acheson*, pp. 289–90.

145 **"my friendship is not"**: Ibid.

146 **"If we can't sell"**: McCrum, "Masterpiece That Killed Orwell."

146 **Generalissimo had brokered**: Pantsov and Levine, *Real Story*, p. 346.

147 **Koo visits Riverdale**: Koo OH, vol. 6, pt. I, pp. 173–74, Wellington Koo Papers, BLCU.

147 **bad-mouthing MCKS**: Hillenkoetter/C.I.A. memo, December 10, 1948, no. 27065-A, box 152, PSF, Harry S. Truman Papers, TL.

147 **"an incessant supply . . . or abroad"**: Koo OH, vol. 6, pt. I, pp. 173–74, Wellington Koo Papers, BLCU.

147 **Chiang told his wife**: CKS to MCKS, May 20, 1949, JZZD, AH.

148 **hinted to friends:** Koo OH, vol. 6, pt. I, p. 152, Wellington Koo Papers, BLCU.

148 **She told her husband . . . arranged for a journalist:** MCKS to CKS, June 13, 1949, JZZD, AH (two telegrams, same date).

148 **The Generalissimo . . . protested:** CKS to MCKS, June 15, 1949, JZZD, AH.

148 **She forwarded him a draft:** MCKS to CKS, June 15, 1949, JZZD, AH.

148 **sabotage Mao's efforts:** Ibid. See also MCKS to CKS, June 2, 1949, JZZD, AH.

148 **Koo meeting with Johnson:** Koo memo, June 15, 1949, box 130, folder 3, Wellington Koo Papers, BLCU. See also Koo OH, vol. 6, pt. I, p. 174, ibid.

149 **"appeared to be interested . . . not lost interest":** Koo memo, June 15, 1949, box 130, folder 3, Wellington Koo Papers, BLCU.

149 **"constant menace":** Acheson, *Present*, p. 192.

149 **Truman news conference:** *NYT*, June 19, 1949.

149 **"Mr. President . . . to now":** Ibid.

150 **"the U.S. cannot . . . leading officials":** C.I.A. report, "Probable Developments in China," June 16, 1949, in Hutchings, *Tracking the Dragon*, pp. 39–60.

150 **"to be most careful":** *FRUS* 1949, vol. VIII, p. 388.

150 **"maintain friendly . . . into deeds":** Ibid., p. 384.

150 **June 19 broadside:** Xinhua, June 19, 1949, *CPR*. See also *FRUS* 1949, vol. VIII, pp. 965–67.

151 **"six American-made . . . revolutionary enterprise":** *FRUS* 1949, vol. VIII, pp. 965.

151 **almost certainly some truth:** Westad, *Decisive Encounters*, p. 307.

151 **Recently declassified intelligence reports:** See, for example, Cox, "Civil Air Transport."

151 **hacking a shortwave radio:** Roy Rowan, interview by author, February 3, 2015. See also Rowan, *Chasing the Dragon*, loc. 1275.

151 **Chinese scholarship has suggested:** Chen, *China's Road*, p. 56. See also Westad, *Decisive Encounters*, p. 307.

152 **"By midnight":** Acheson, *Sketches from Life*, p. 16.

152 **Vishinsky** and **Japanese peace treaty:** *NYT*, June 22, 1949.

152 **"Acheson went to Paris . . . about China":** Ibid.

152 **ordered a blockade:** *NYT,* June 21, 1949.

152 **impossible to enforce . . . mines:** Ibid.

152 **Nationalist bombing raids:** *Jiefang ribao,* June 21, 1949, *CPR; NCDN,* June 22–23, 1949. See also *NCDN,* June 30, 1949.

153 **Acheson . . . did not want to get in the middle:** "Summary of Daily Meeting with the Secretary," June 22, 1949, folder 2, box 1, entry 393, RG 59, NA.

153 **"season of the Great Heat":** *NCDN,* June 23, 1949.

CHAPTER 14: KILLING THE TIGER

154 **June 22 Koo-Truman meeting:** Koo memorandum of conversation with Truman, June 22, 1949, box 130, folder 3, Wellington Koo Papers, BLCU.

154 **"always cherished . . . from Missouri":** Ibid.

155 **Acheson press conference:** Press conference, June 23, 1949, box 72, Dean Acheson Papers, TL.

155 **"Mr. Secretary . . . that connection":** Ibid.

156 **"field day":** "Summary of Daily Meeting with the Secretary," June 13, 1949, folder 2, box 1, entry 393, RG 59, NA.

156 **"I am not in":** Acheson quoted in Leary and Stueck, "Chennault Plan," p. 353.

156 **"hostile attack":** MCKS to CKS, June 24, 1949, JZZD, AH.

156 **Taiwan background:** For an interesting discussion of Taiwan's demographic history, see Austin Ramzy, "Taiwan's President Apologizes to Aborigines for Centuries of Injustice," *NYT,* August 1, 2016.

157 **strategic base area:** Lin, *Accidental State,* p. 85. Lin is excellent on the maneuverings of Chiang and his rivals for influence on Taiwan. See pp. 6, 77–79, 92, 95.

157 **"Am I safe here?":** Ibid., p. 96.

157 **Chiang to Grass Mountain:** Taylor, *Generalissimo,* p. 411.

157 **Chiang would do the interviews:** CKS to MCKS, June 25, 1949, JZZD, AH.

158 **"legal status . . . from within":** MZ, "Telegram, CCP Central Military Commission to Shanghai Municipal Committee," June 23, 1949, in *NDE,* p. 117.

158 **Chinese emperors had long:** Hunt, *Genesis,* pp. 221–24; Schell and Delury, *Wealth and Power,* pp. 68–69.

158 **Experience had shown:** Hunt, *Genesis,* p. 16.

158   **"pay attention . . . severely threatened":** MZ, "Telegram, CCP Central Military Commission to Su Yu and others," June 14, 1949, in *NDE*, p. 117.

158   **Bao Dai:** See Herring, *America's Longest War*, pp. 21–23; and Logevall, *Embers of War*, pp. 210–12.

159   **"a dissolute playboy":** Schaller, *American Occupation*, pp. 152–53.

159   **Yet Mao . . . Ho and his rebels:** Chen, *China's Road*, p. 26; Chen, *Mao's China*, p. 122.

159   **"pay serious attention . . . not that strong":** "Cable, Filippov [Stalin] to Mao Zedong [via Kovalev]," June 18, 1949, WWICS, History and Public Policy Program Digital Archive, APRF: f. 45, op. 1, d. 331, Ll. 119. Reprinted in Andrei Ledovskii, Raisa Mirovitskaia, and Vladimir Miasnikov, *Sovetsko-Kitaiskie Otnosheniia*, vol. 5, bk. 2, 1946–*February* 1950 (Moscow: Pamiatniki Istoricheskoi Mysli, 2005), p. 148. Translated for CWIHP by Sergey Radchenko. http://digital archive.wilsoncenter.org/document/113379 (accessed January 23, 2016). See also Mao to Stalin, June 14, 1949, ibid., pp. 141–46.

159   **Liu Shaoqi trip:** Shi, "With Mao and Stalin," pt. 2, p. 69. Shi's account, written long after the fact, gets the date of this trip wrong by one week. For the accurate timetable, based on recently declassified documents, see Westad, *Decisive Encounters*, p. 266.

159   **Stalin-Liu meeting:** "Memorandum of Conversation Between Stalin and CCP Delegation," June 27, 1949, WWICS, History and Public Policy Program Digital Archive, APRF: f. 45, op. 1, d. 329, Ll. 1–7. Reprinted in Andrei Ledovskii, Raisa Mirovitskaia, and Vladimir Miasnikov, *Sovetsko-Kitaiskie Otnosheniia*, vol. 5, bk. 2, 1946–*February* 1950 (Moscow: Pamiatniki Istoricheskoi Mysli, 2005), pp. 148–51. Translated for CWIHP from Russian by Sergey Radchenko. Published in *CWIHP Bulletin*, no. 16. http://digitalarchive.wilsoncenter.org /document/113380 (accessed January 23, 2016).

160   **"Well, if you insist . . . against the Communists":** Ibid.

161   **"visit [Yanjing] University . . . their motives":** Stuart to Acheson, June 30, 1949, in *FRUS* 1949, vol. VIII, p. 766–67.

161   **"All Chinese . . . running dogs":** MZ, "On the People's Democratic Dictatorship: In Commemoration of the Twenty-eighth Anniversary of the Communist Party of China," June 30, 1949, WWICS, History and Public Policy Program Digital Archive, Translation from *Selected Works of Mao Tse-tung* (Peking: Foreign Languages Press, 1961),

pp. 4:411–23, http://digitalarchive.wilsoncenter.org/document/119300 (accessed January 23, 2016).

161   **"You have to choose":** *NYT,* July 1, 1949.

161   MAO EXPECTS NO HELP: *NYT,* July 1, 1949. See also Blum, *Drawing the Line,* p. 63.

161   **"You are instructed":** Acheson cable quoted in Blum, *Drawing the Line,* p. 64. Blum points out that the *FRUS* version of this document includes a slight inaccuracy.

162   **"vote of thanks . . . sharp lines":** Stuart to Acheson, July 6, 1949, in Stuart, *Forgotten Ambassador,* p. 335.

162   **Stuart reading Apocalypse:** Stuart diary, entry for July 10, 1949, John Leighton Stuart Papers, HI.

CHAPTER 15: THE GREAT CRESCENT

163   **July 4 in Tokyo:** *NYT,* July 5, 1949.

163   **Julius Caesar:** Kennan memorandum of conversation with MacArthur, March 1, 1948, *FRUS* 1948, vol. VI, p. 697.

163   **"great events":** Ibid., p. 698.

164   **"plant the seeds":** Ibid.

164   **cache of documents:** *NYT,* February 23, 1949.

164   **"sex tactics":** Ibid.

164   **radicals persisted:** *NYT,* May 22, 1949.

164   **Acheson forwarded a paper:** Schaller, *American Occupation,* p. 163.

164   **"great crescent":** Policy Planning Staff Paper on United States Policy Toward Southeast Asia (PPS 51), March 29, 1949, *FRUS* 1949, vol. VII, pt. 2, p. 1129.

164   **Japanese emperors . . . risked war:** Schaller, *American Occupation,* p. 205. See also Kagan, *World America Made,* p. 42.

165   **"imperialist intervention . . . friendly guidance":** Policy Planning Staff Paper on United States Policy Toward Southeast Asia (PPS 51), March 29, 1949, *FRUS* 1949, vol. VII, pt. 2, pp. 1128–33.

165   **Another official:** *FRUS* 1949, vol. VII, pt. 2, p. 1149.

165   **"shaken by events . . . in making":** Judd to Henry Luce, July 7, 1949, folder 11, box 31, Walter H. Judd Papers, HI.

166   **The secretary of state refused . . . border regions:** Cox, "Civil Air Transport," pp. 16–17.

166   **Rosholt:** Ibid., pp. 17–20.

166   **"all the blame":** MCKS to CKS, July 5, 1949, JZZD, AH.

166 **"reached an agreement"**: MCKS to CKS, July 7, 1949, JZZD, AH.

166 **"very difficult"**: MCKS to CKS, July 6, 1949, JZZD, AH.

167 **After carefully studying**: CKS to MCKS, July 4, 1949, JZZD, AH.

167 **"revolutionary leadership . . . inevitable"**: *NYT*, July 6, 1949.

167 **Baguio talks**: CKS diary, entries for July 10 and July 12, 1949, HI; Chiang, *Calm*, pp. 242–44.

167 **storing his vast gold stocks**: State Department Daily Staff Summary, July 14, 1949, box 7, entry 396I, RG 59, NA.

167 **"Quirino-Chiang get-together"**: "Summary of Daily Meeting with the Secretary," July 14, 1949, folder 1, box 1, entry 393, ibid.

167 **meeting with Truman**: "Memorandum of Conversation with the President," July 14, 1949, Dean Acheson Papers, TL.

168 **"considerable resentment"**: State Department Daily Staff Summary, July 15, 1949, box 7, entry 396I, RG 59, NA.

168 **"small stooge" . . . "puppets"**: *Dagong bao*, July 18, 1949, *CPR*.

168 **"General, you're a liar"**: Johnson quoted in Borklund, *Men of Pentagon*, p. 68.

168 **"Big Boy"** and **"Man of Heroic Mould"**: Lilienthal diary, entry for December 25, 1949, in Lilienthal, *Journals*, p. 2:614.

168 **mentally ill**: Acheson, *Present*, p. 374.

168 **"nuttier than a fruitcake"**: Acheson quoted in McFarland and Roll, *Louis Johnson*, p. 320.

169 **"I'll keep asking"**: Johnson quoted ibid., p. 255.

169 **liaison in India**: Ibid., pp. 116–26.

169 **"favorable reference"**: Pearson diary, entry for April 15, 1952, in Pearson, *Diaries*, p. 209.

169 **"tired owl"**: Lilienthal diary, entry for July 19, 1949, in Lilienthal, *Journals*, p. 2:547.

169 **Truman had ordered Acheson**: "Memorandum of Conversation with the President," July 14, 1949, Dean Acheson Papers, TL.

169 **A Chinese journalist**: Koo OH, vol. 6, pt. I, sec. 5, pp. 245–46, Wellington Koo Papers, BLCU.

169 **"very cool and serene"**: Lilienthal diary, entry for July 14, 1949, in Lilienthal, *Journals*, p. 2:543.

169 **failed to resolve most divisive issues**: Koo OH, vol. 6, pt. I, sec. 5, pp. 245–46, Wellington Koo Papers, BLCU.

169 **editing the draft**: Melby OH, p. 173, John F. Melby Papers, TL.

170 **Acheson called Johnson**: "Memorandum of Telephone Conversation

with Secretary of Defense Louis Johnson," July 15, 1949, Dean Acheson Papers, TL.

170 **"watered down":** "Memorandum of Conversation with the President," July 18, 1949, ibid.

170 **wider regional strategy:** Ibid.

170 **"You will please . . . in Asia":** Acheson memo (top secret), July 18, 1949, quoted in Jessup, *Birth of Nations*, p. 29.

171 **"You and the president":** Johnson to Acheson, July 21, 1949, quoted in McFarland and Roll, *Louis Johnson*, pp. 256–57.

171 **Bohemian Grove:** Koo OH, vol. 6, pt. I, sec. 5, pp. 248–49, Wellington Koo Papers, BLCU; McFarland and Roll, *Louis Johnson*, p. 257.

171 **"proceed with the publication":** "Memorandum of Conversation with the President," July 21, 1949, Dean Acheson Papers, TL.

171 **Griffith briefed Koo:** Koo OH, vol. 6, pt. I, sec. 5, p. 248, Wellington Koo Papers, BLCU.

171 **Koo traveled to Riverdale:** Ibid., p. 255.

171 **"harried and drawn":** Lilienthal diary, entry for July 28, 1949, in Lilienthal, *Journals*, p. 2:557.

172 **"an early invasion . . . imminent":** State Department Daily Staff Summary, July 28, 1949, box 7, entry 396I, RG 59, NA.

172 **the temperature in Washington soared:** *NYT*, July 30, 1949.

172 **Acheson met with Truman:** "Memorandum of Conversation with the President," July 29, 1949, Dean Acheson Papers, TL.

172 **Truman . . . drove himself:** *NYT*, July 30, 1949.

172 **"serious mistake . . . as at present":** Judd to CKS, July 30, 1949, folder 17, box 163, Walter H. Judd Papers, HI.

173 **On Sunday morning:** *NYT*, August 1, 1949.

173 **Truman met with Acheson on Monday:** "Memorandum of Conversation with the President," August 1, 1949, Dean Acheson Papers, TL.

173 U.S. PUTS SOLE BLAME: *NYT*, August 6, 1949.

CHAPTER 16: FIRECRACKER

177 **"interior force":** Tuell recollections, box 1, Papers of Mayling Soong Chiang, WCA.

178 **"To kill the rider":** Audrey Ronning Topping, interview by author, January 6, 2015, Scarsdale, N.Y. See also Topping, *China Mission*, p. 306.

178 **Madame Chiang worried:** MCKS to CKS, June 9, 1949; CKS to MCKS, June 10, 1949, both in JZZD, AH.

178 **"Chinese politics is impossible":** Mayling Soong to Emma Mills, December 7, 1917, Emma DeLong Mills Papers, WCA.

178 **She would call friends:** Mills diary, entry for March 13, 1949, vol. 17, Emma DeLong Mills Papers, WCA.

178 **"coarse and brutal face":** Oursler, *Behold*, pp. 349–53.

179 **Madame Chiang fled:** Mills diary, entry for August 15, 1949, vol. 17, Emma DeLong Mills Papers, WCA. See also DeLong, *Madame Chiang*, pp. 201–2.

179 **Stuart . . . felt useless:** Stuart to Acheson, July 11, 1949, in Stuart, *Forgotten Ambassador*, p. 337.

179 **He arranged his departure:** Stuart, *Fifty Years*, pp. 260–69.

179 **The ambassador could not believe:** Ibid.

179 **Stuart was particularly dismayed:** Ibid., pp. 267, 269.

179 **"leaders had proved . . . but could not":** U.S. Department of State, *United States Relations with China*, p. xiv.

180 **"giant firecracker":** Acheson OH, Princeton Seminars, July 16, 1953, p. 18, reel 5, box 79, Dean Acheson Papers, TL.

180 **"not as bad . . . without remedy":** *CR*, August 5, 1949, p. 10875, copy in folder 5, box 37, Walter H. Judd Papers, HI.

181 **Judd and Chennault traded ideas:** Judd to Chennault, August 1949; and Chennault to Judd, August 9, 1949, both in folder 15, box 163, Walter H. Judd Papers, HI.

181 **"A comparatively small":** Acheson testimony, August 8, 1949, quoted in Blum, *Drawing the Line*, p. 131.

181 **Truman had been pressing:** Ayers diary, entry for August 8, 1949, box 20, Eben A. Ayers Papers, TL.

181 **Quirino's arrival:** TLP, accession nos. 66-2393 and 66-2391; *NYT*, August 9, 1949.

182 **Truman hosted Quirino:** "Dinner at the Carlton Hotel," May 21, 1949 to January 19, 1950, Files of the White House Social Office, Social Function File, box 59, Harry S. Truman Papers, TL.

182 **"advancing tide . . . living standards":** Quirino remarks to the U.S. Senate, reprinted in *NYT*, August 10, 1949.

182 **"vague and haphazard . . . right in the end":** "Memorandum of Conversation with the President of the Philippines Elpidio Quirino," August 9, 1949, Acheson papers, TL.

183   **Koo meeting with Quirino:** Koo memorandum of conversation with Quirino, August 10, 1949, box 130, folder 3, Wellington Koo Papers, BLCU.

183   **"statesmanlike . . . much about it":** Ibid.

183   **Judd protested that:** Koo OH, vol. 6, pt. I, sec. 5, pp. 257–58, Wellington Koo Papers, BLCU.

183   **"If we cannot lead":** *CR*, August 9, 1949, p. 11140, copy in folder 5, box 37, Walter H. Judd Papers, HI.

183   **anodyne joint statement:** *NYT*, August 12, 1949.

183   **Fifty-six motorcycles . . . from the windows:** Ibid.

184   **"tie of our . . . Christianity and democracy":** *NCDN*, August 14, 1949.

184   **"nation on fire . . . firewall":** *NYT*, August 15, 1949.

184   **"plans for world . . . behind every move":** *Wenhui bao*, August 10, 1949, *CPR*.

184   **"stark and merciless whipping":** *Jiefang ribao*, August 13, 1949, *CPR*.

184   **"example . . . work harder":** *Wenhui bao*, August 12, 1949, *CPR*.

184   **"insignificant":** Ibid., August 10, 1949, *CPR*.

184   **"slave of the slaves":** *Dagong bao*, August 13, 1949, *CPR*.

185   **Rumor of Mao death:** C.I.A. memo, July 14, 1949, box 2, CIA File, NSC File, SMOF, Harry S. Truman Papers, TL.

185   **gravely ill:** *NYT*, August 14, 1949.

185   **lumbago and sleeplessness:** Pantsov and Levine, *Real Story*, p. 363.

185   **"democratic individualism":** U.S. Department of State, *United States Relations with China*, p. xvi. See also Hunt, *Genesis*, p. 196, and McLean, "American Nationalism," p. 25.

185   **"troublemaking . . . honeyed words":** Mao, "Cast Away Illusions, Prepare for Struggle," August 14, 1949, *SW*, vol. 4, www.marxists .org/reference/archive/mao/selected-works/volume-4/mswv4_66.htm (accessed February 6, 2016).

185   **Mao had been pushing . . . on Taiwan:** He Di, "Last Campaign," pp. 3–4.

186   **Yak fighter jets . . . seventeen hundred pilots:** "Telegram, CCP Central Committee to Liu Shaoqi, July 26, 1949 (extract)," in *NDE*, p. 123.

186   **Stalin countered:** Chen, *China's Road*, p. 76.

186   **Liu finally returned:** Ibid., pp. 76–77.

CHAPTER 17: NO DEVIL SHALL ESCAPE

187 **August 17 . . . weather maps:** Ayers diary, entry for August 17, 1949, box 20, Eben A. Ayers Papers, TL.

187 **Truman's weather hobby:** *NYT*, October 8, 1949.

188 **"in the hands . . . the same time":** *CR*, August 17, 1949, p. 11676, in folder 5, box 37, Walter H. Judd Papers, HI.

188 **"from appease to oppose":** Ibid., p. 11678.

188 **Judd wanted:** Blum, *Drawing the Line*, p. 132.

188 **"all-out intervention . . . American officers":** *CR*, August 18, 1949, p. 11788, in folder 5, box 37, Walter H. Judd Papers, HI.

188 **August 18 staff meeting:** "Summary of Daily Meeting with the Secretary," August 18, 1949, folder 1, box 1, entry 393, RG 59, NA.

189 **the president told Acheson:** "Memorandum of Conversation with the President," August 18, 1949, Dean Acheson Papers, TL.

189 **the Burmese foreign minister:** "Memorandum of Conversation with the Minister of Foreign Affairs of Burma and Others," August 15, 1949, ibid.

189 **"propaganda, intrigue":** *CR*, August 18, 1949, p. 11787, in folder 5, box 37, Walter H. Judd Papers, HI.

189 **"like letting . . . hub is gone?":** *CR*, August 17, 1949, p. 11677, Walter H. Judd Papers, HI.

189 **"throw off the foreign yoke":** *CR*, August 18, 1949, p. 11787, Walter H. Judd Papers, HI.

190 **House of Representatives defeated it:** Blum, *Drawing the Line*, p. 133.

190 **"intends to rest on":** *CR*, August 19, 1949, p. 11882, in folder 5, box 37, Walter H. Judd Papers, HI.

190 **"then we have a right . . . pro-Communist":** Ibid.

190 **a summary of a secret military report:** *NYT*, August 21, 1949.

190 **"a person of outstanding integrity":** *NYT*, August 22, 1949.

191 **Lippmann column:** *New York Herald Tribune*, September 6, 1949.

191 **Acheson's morning meetings / "properly briefed":** "Summar[ies] of Daily Meeting with the Secretary," August 22 and 23, 1949, folder 1, box 1, entry 393, RG 59, NA.

191 **"a very tired man":** Kennan diary, entry for August 23, 1949, in Kennan, *Diaries*, p. 221.

191 **"trying to view . . . consequences of others":** Acheson press conference transcript, August 24, 1949, in box 72, Dean Acheson Papers, TL.

192 **"a completely honest . . . they can have it"**: Acheson off-the-record press conference transcript, August 26, 1949, ibid.

192 **"immediately instructed"**: Merchant to Sprouse, *FRUS* 1949, vol. IX, p. 871.

192 **Chennault pushing aid to Bai Chongxi**: Chennault, "Last Call for China," *Life*, undated clipping, box 11, Claire Chennault Papers, HI.

192 **Chennault . . . continued to quietly discuss**: Leary and Stueck, "Chennault Plan," p. 355.

193 **"an unpublic, realistic . . . inevitable"**: Alsop, "Asia—Summing Up: II," *New York Herald Tribune*, August 24, 1949.

193 **"whether such assistance . . . from their control"**: State Department Daily Staff Summary, August 25, 1949, box 8, entry 3961, RG 59, NA.

193 **Stuart meets C.I.A.**: Stuart diary, entry for August 25, 1949, John Leighton Stuart Papers, HI.

193 **Rosholt . . . returned to Washington**: Cox, "Civil Air Transport," p. 20.

193 **Rosholt on Ma Hongkui**: Ibid.

193 **Wisner meetings with Acheson, Kennan, etc.**: Ibid.

194 **"he could not understand"**: Ibid., p. 21.

194 **"Acheson is a good teacher"**: MZ, "Farewell, Leighton Stuart!" August 18, 1949, in *SW*, vol. 4, www.marxists.org/reference/archive/mao/selected-works/volume-4/mswv4_67.htm (accessed February 15, 2016).

194 **"getting hopelessly bogged . . . bellyache"**: Ibid.

195 **"drunken American telephone operator"**: *Shen bao*, February 14, 1949, *CPR*.

195 **"'overlording' attitude . . . an imperialist"**: *Jiefang ribao*, July 10, 1949, *CPR*.

195 **American officials complained**: Cabot to Acheson, July 9, 1949, *FRUS* 1949, vol. VIII, pp. 1220–22.

195 **"sabotage . . . to the end!"**: *Dagong bao*, August 20, 1949, *CPR*.

CHAPTER 18: DIG UP THE DIRT

196 ***Journal-American* interview**: David Sentner, "Mme. Chiang Plans Return to Stand by Generalissimo," *New York Journal-American*, September 7, 1949; Sentner, "Chiang Convinced MacArthur Could Turn Back Red Tide," *New York Journal-American*, September 8, 1949.

196 **her friends warned her:** Chiang, *Sure Victory*, pp. 22–23; Li, *Madame Chiang*, p. 316.

197 **the approach to Wedemeyer:** Wedemeyer, "Memorandum for Record [Reynolds visit]," September 13, 1949, folder 20, box 165, Walter H. Judd Papers, HI.

197 **"any amount . . . commitments whatsoever":** Ibid.

198 **Stuart . . . dined with Madame Chiang:** Stuart diary, entry for September 8, 1949, John Leighton Stuart Papers, HI. Stuart's diary also indicates that he went to church with the Reynolds family on September 4, and his entry for that date includes the phrase "Invitation to Wedemeyer." But Wedemeyer's own notes indicate that he was not approached by Reynolds, at least in person, until September 9.

198 **"several people . . . the 'W' proposal":** Stuart diary, entry for September 11, 1949, John Leighton Stuart Papers, HI.

198 **"agreed to accept . . . individual Chinese":** Wedemeyer, "Memorandum for Record [Stuart visit]," September 13, 1949, folder 20, box 165, Walter H. Judd Papers, HI.

198 **"speedily":** CKS to MCKS, September 10, 1949, JZZD, AH.

198 **"arranged":** CKS to MCKS, September 11, 1949, JZZD, AH.

198 **had been arranged:** MCKS to CKS, September 13, 1949, JZZD, AH.

198 **"a matter of great":** Johnson memo, September 9, 1949, box 9, NSC File, SMOF, Harry S. Truman Papers, TL.

199 **the "general area of China":** *NYT*, September 13, 1949. See also *NYT*, September 11, 1949.

199 **"crucify":** Mills diary, entry for September 14, 1949, Emma DeLong Mills Papers, WCA. This entry describes a meeting that took place with Judd on September 12.

199 **"dig up all":** Ibid.

199 ***South Pacific:*** Acheson, *Sketches from Life*, pp. 19–20; Behrman, *Most Noble Adventure*, p. 258. For the plot of *South Pacific*, see Klein, "Family Ties," pp. 50–64.

200 **"an international community":** Klein, "Family Ties," p. 59.

200 **he collapsed in the aisle:** Acheson, *Sketches from Life*, pp. 19–20.

200 **"I need a drink":** Ibid.

201 **"The over-all British attitude":** Yost, "Discussion of Far Eastern Affairs in Preparation for Conversations with Mr. Bevin," September 16, 1949 [meeting held September 13, 1949], *FRUS 1949*, vol. VII, pt. 2, p. 1205.

201 **"here to stay":** Jones to Acheson, September 3, 1949, *FRUS* 1949, vol. VIII, p. 519. At the September 13 meeting (see previous note), the staff largely agreed on the analysis in this Jones dispatch, no. 1994.

201 **short-sighted greed:** Yost, "Discussion of Far Eastern Affairs in Preparation for Conversations with Mr. Bevin," September 16, 1949 [meeting held September 13, 1949], *FRUS* 1949, vol. VII, pt. 2, p. 1205.

201 **Stuart argued:** Ibid.

201 **avoid rash provocations:** Jones to Acheson, September 3, 1949, *FRUS* 1949, vol. VIII, p. 520.

201 **"the hard way":** Ibid. But see also Acheson's questions about the contradictions inherent in this policy in Yost, "Discussion of Far Eastern Affairs in Preparation for Conversations with Mr. Bevin," September 16, 1949 [meeting held September 13, 1949], *FRUS* 1949, vol. VII, pt. 2, p. 1206.

201 **"go slow":** Yost, "Discussion of Far Eastern Affairs in Preparation for Conversations with Mr. Bevin," September 16, 1949 [meeting held September 13, 1949], *FRUS* 1949, vol. VII, pt. 2, p. 1206.

201 **Bao Dai:** Ibid., p. 1207.

201 **development aid:** Butterworth, "Memorandum of Conversation," September 12, 1949, *FRUS* 1949, vol. VII, pt. 2, p. 1198.

202 **"pull the strings . . . limelight":** Ibid., p. 1199.

202 **Acheson and Bevin met:** Acheson, "Memorandum of Conversation," September 13, 1949, *FRUS* 1949, vol. IX, p. 81.

202 **"hasty":** Ibid.

202 **"depressed":** Ibid., p. 82.

202 **"big commercial interests":** Ibid.

202 **"bolted for . . . foreseeable future":** Ibid., p. 83.

202 **massive propaganda campaign:** Ibid., p. 85.

203 **"The Communists . . . drive a wedge":** Ibid., p. 84.

203 **some scholars have raised:** Gaddis, *We Now Know*, p. 72; Zubok, " 'To Hell with Yalta!' " p. 25.

203 **Venona:** On the Venona project, see Haynes and Klehr, *Venona*.

203 **assigned to the Far East department:** Ovendale, "Britain, United States," p. 140; Holzman, *Guy Burgess*, locs. 4635–46.

203 **Burgess background:** Holzman, *Guy Burgess*, locs. 392, 481, 613.

203 **"menacingly healthy . . . go overboard":** Burn, "The Burgess," *Times* (London), May 9, 2003, cited in Holzman, *Guy Burgess*, loc. 860.

204 **boisterous parties:** John S. Mather, ed., "The Great Spy Scandal,"

U.S. News & World Report, February 17, 1956, pp. 121–29, clipping in "Burgess and Maclean file," box 21, Alfred Kohlberg Papers, HI.

204 **"Whenever I saw him":** Ibid.

204 **"anything that came . . . was brilliant":** Nicolson quoted ibid.

204 **orthodox Communists:** Ovendale, "Britain, United States," p. 140.

204 **Burgess urged his government:** Ibid., p. 145.

204 **"muddled thinking":** Ibid., p. 147.

CHAPTER 19: FIRST LIGHTNING

205 **Soviet nuclear test:** Holloway, *Stalin*, pp. 213–16. See also "First Soviet Test," *American Experience*, PBS, www.pbs.org/wgbh/amex/bomb/peopleevents/pandeAMEX53.html (accessed February 26, 2016).

205 **"For a moment . . . into a funnel":** Komel'kov quoted Holloway, *Stalin*, p. 217.

206 **"It works! It works!":** Kurchatov quoted in "First Soviet Test," *American Experience*, PBS.

206 **B-29 weather plane:** Isaacson and Thomas, *Wise Men*, p. 480.

206 **"It changed everything":** Acheson quoted in Ninkovich, *Modernity*, p. 183.

206 **"quiet and composed. . . Really?":** Lilienthal diary, entry for September 21, 1949, in Lilienthal, *Journals*, pp. 2:570–71.

207 **"We have . . . by us":** *NYT*, September 24, 1949.

207 SOVIET ACHIEVEMENT: Ibid.

207 **"people took it calmly":** Kennan diary, entry for September 24, 1949, in Kennan, *Diaries*, p. 226.

207 **"The American public . . . atomic energy":** Pearson diary, entry for September 23, 1949, in Pearson, *Diaries*, p. 75.

207 **ten million people:** Halberstam, *Summer of '49*, p. 287.

207 **Ted Williams's nickname:** Ibid., p. 18.

207 **"Conscious of the great":** Ibid., p. 229.

208 **"stay-behind networks," etc.:** Cox, "Civil Air Transport," p. 22.

209 **Mackiernan departs Urumqi:** Gup, *Book of Honor*, loc. 399; Laird, *Into Tibet*, p. 111. See also Frank Bessac, "This Was the Perilous Trek to Tragedy," *Life*, November 13, 1950. On Mackiernan, see also "Remembering CIA's Heroes: Douglas S. Mackiernan," C.I.A., www.cia.gov/news-information/featured-story-archive/2010-featured-story-archive/douglas-s.-mackiernan.html (accessed February 26, 2016).

209   **guns, ammunition . . . "one-time pads":** Gup, *Book of Honor*, loc. 399; Laird, *Into Tibet*, p. 111.

209   **fifteen hundred miles:** Frank Bessac, "This Was the Perilous Trek to Tragedy," *Life*, November 13, 1950.

209   **long stretches on horseback:** Halper and Halper, *Tibet*, p. 81.

210   **Canadian backcountry:** "State Department Daily Staff Summary," September 16 and 27, 1949, folder 1, box 1, entry 393, RG 59, NA.

210   **"a major shift in U.S. foreign policy":** "State Department Daily Staff Summary," September 30, 1949, ibid.

210   **Communists intensified . . . covert operations:** Westad, *Decisive Encounters*, p. 270.

210   **Mao . . . wanted to wait:** Goncharov, Lewis, and Xue, *Uncertain Partners*, p. 74.

210   **the Chairman overslept:** Quan, *Mao Zedong*, pp. 119–20. This account, based on the recollection of Mao's bodyguard Li Yinqiao, conflicts with some other accounts, such as that of Mao's personal physician, Li Zhisui, who recalled that Mao appeared at ten a.m. Contemporary newspaper accounts, however, report that Mao appeared at three p.m., as Quan writes.

210   **"vast totalitarian space":** Becker, *City*, p. 15.

211   **a majestic footpath:** Schell and Delury, *Wealth and Power*, p. 229.

211   **red pompons:** Empson, "Red on Red," p. 67.

211   **"leave my country":** Soong Chingling quoted in Li, *Madame Chiang*, p. 315.

211   **national amnesia:** In later years, Rana Mitter observes, the CCP also employed "memories of the war against Japan" in an effort to "heal scars" left by the civil war. See Mitter, *Forgotten Ally*, p. 9.

211   **"Our People's . . . and sovereignty":** MZ, "Proclamation of the Central People's Government of the PRC," October 1, 1949, WWICS, History and Public Policy Program Digital Archive, *Renmin ribao* [People's Daily], October 2, 1949. English translation from Kau and Leung, *Writings of Mao*, pp. 1:10–11, http://digitalarchive.wilsoncenter.org/document/121557 (accessed February 26, 2016).

212   **torrential rains:** *Jiefang ribao*, September 30 and October 5, 1949, both in *CPR*. See also *NCDN*, October 3 and 5, 1949.

212   **"water carnival"** and **Shanghai march:** *Xinwen ribao*, October 9, 1949; *Jiefang ribao*, October 9, 1949; both in *CPR*. See also *NCDN*, October 9–12.

212   "the battered . . . 'Japanese warlord' ": *NCDN*, October 9, 1949.

212   "The dark and muddy": *NCDN*, October 11, 1949.

213   "In about six . . . Ho Chi Minh": CIA Intelligence Memorandum no. 231, October 7, 1949, box 213, PSF, Harry S. Truman Papers, TL.

214   Nehru . . . wary . . . of shipping arms: Halper and Halper, *Tibet*, p. 71.

214   Nehru liked to emphasize: Acheson, "Memorandum of Conversation with Jawaharlal Nehru, Prime Minister of India," October 12, 1949, Dean Acheson Papers, TL; Acheson, *Present*, p. 335.

214   Nehru arrived: *NYT*, October 12, 1949.

214   "a motion picture star": Ayers diary, entry for October 13, 1949, box 20, Eben A. Ayers Papers, TL.

214   "way of holding . . . weapon of persuasion": Stewart Alsop, "Nehru," *New York Herald Tribune*, August 5, 1949.

214   "a vain, sensitive": Henderson quoted in Halper and Halper, *Tibet*, p. 56.

214   "a prickly mood": Acheson, *Present*, p. 334.

214   inviting Nehru back: Acheson, "Memorandum of Conversation with Jawaharlal Nehru, Prime Minister of India," October 12, 1949, Dean Acheson Papers, TL.

214   Acheson's red brick Georgetown lair: Hamburger, "Mr. Secretary," pt. 1, p. 41; Hamburger, "Mr. Secretary," pt. 2, pp. 60–61.

214   "the greatest freedom": Acheson, "Memorandum of Conversation with Jawaharlal Nehru, Prime Minister of India," October 12, 1949, Dean Acheson Papers, TL.

214   "would not relax": Acheson, *Present*, p. 335.

214   "a public meeting": Ibid.

215   Nehru . . . leaning toward recognizing: Acheson, "Memorandum of Conversation with Jawaharlal Nehru, Prime Minister of India," October 12, 1949, Dean Acheson Papers, TL.

215   "His general attitude . . . adjourn the discussion": Ibid.

215   virtues of bourbon whisky: Halper and Halper, *Tibet*, p. 273n97.

215   "India's proximity . . . concert their action": Acheson, "Memorandum of Conversation with the President and Jawaharlal Nehru," October 13, 1949, Dean Acheson Papers, TL.

215   "wasn't very consulting": Acheson OH, Princeton Seminars, July 23, 1953, p. 9, reel 3, box 79, ibid.

215   Greenbrier Hotel: Halper and Halper, *Tibet*, p. 61.

215   **"an ecstatic account"**: Pearson diary, entry for October 31, 1949, in Pearson, *Diaries*, p. 88.

215   **gaudy costumes:** Halper and Halper, *Tibet*, p. 61.

216   **"long and exotic":** Ibid.

216   **"dead tired":** Pearson diary, entry for October 31, 1949, in Pearson, *Diaries*, p. 88.

216   **"could not have . . . upset him":** Halper and Halper, *Tibet*, p. 61.

216   **"grave doubts . . . and charity":** Judd to Rev. E. Ezra Ellis, October 19, 1949, folder 5, box 143, Walter H. Judd Papers, HI.

CHAPTER 20: RISKY BUSINESS

217   **Truman Administration finally approved:** Wisner approval, October 12, 1949, TS-31918, cited in Cox, "Civil Air Transport," pp. 26, 132.

217   **Wisner arranged for Chennault's airline:** Cox, "Civil Air Transport," p. 24.

217   **"adequate standby facilities":** Ibid., p. 27.

217   **"The Commies . . . risky business":** Alfred T. Cox to Dorothy and Steve Cox, October 14, 1949, Alfred T. Cox Private Papers, courtesy of Steven Cox.

218   **Cox and Chennault meeting with CKS:** Cox, "Civil Air Transport," pp. 28–29.

218   **"beautiful limousine":** Alfred T. Cox to Dorothy and Steve Cox, October 19, 1949, Alfred T. Cox Private Papers, courtesy of Steven Cox.

218   **Chennault briefed Chiang:** "Resumé of Conversation between Generalissimo Chiang Kai-shek and General C. L. Chennault regarding private aid for resistance to Communism in China; conversation occurred 16 October 1949 by Chennault, undated, pouched to Headquarters from Hong Kong, passed [redacted] to OPC 30 November 1949," cited in Cox, "Civil Air Transport," pp. 29.

218   **All summer:** Chennault, "Last Call for China," *Life*, undated clipping, box 11, Claire Chennault Papers, HI.

219   **Chiang's Yunnan gambit:** Lin, *Accidental State*, pp. 109–11.

219   **one million silver dollars:** Ibid., p. 111.

219   **strengthening Guilin:** Cox, "Civil Air Transport," pp. 30–32.

219   **"raw and cold . . . thin covering":** Alfred T. Cox to Dorothy and Steve Cox, October 19, 1949, Alfred T. Cox Private Papers, courtesy of Steven Cox.

219   **To avoid a money trail:** Cox, "Civil Air Transport," pp. 32–33.

219   **two large wicker baskets:** Ibid., p. 34.

219   **"dilapidated but still operable":** Ibid.

220   **"You can imagine":** Ibid.

220   **wrote out a receipt:** Ibid., p. 35.

220   **"pretty badly cut up":** "Progress Report Number 1, to O.P.C. from Alfred T. Cox, 26 October 1949, TS-35270," cited in Cox, "Civil Air Transport," pp. 36–37, 133.

220   **"Things are certainly . . . running out":** Alfred T. Cox to Dorothy and Steve Cox, October 19, 1949, Alfred T. Cox Private Papers, courtesy of Steven Cox.

220   **held a ceremony:** "From the Diary of N.V. Roshchin: Memorandum of Conversation with Chairman Mao Zedong on 16 October 1949," December 1, 1949, WWICS, History and Public Policy Program Digital Archive, AVPRF, f. 0100, op. 42, por. 19, pap. 288, ll. 28–31. Translated for CWIHP by David Wolff. http://digitalarchive.wilson center.org/document/117863 (accessed March 4, 2016).

220   *esteemed*: MZ, "Mao Speech After Receiving the Credentials of Soviet Ambassador to China N. V. Roshchin, October 16, 1949," *Jianguo Yilai Mao Zedong Wengao Diyi Ce* (1949.9–1950.12) [Mao Zedong's Manuscripts Since the Founding of the Republic, vol. 1, September 1949–December 1950], p. 71, translated and reprinted in Goncharov, Lewis, and Xue, *Uncertain Partners*, p. 235.

221   **"extremely upset":** "From the Diary of N.V. Roshchin: Memorandum of Conversation with Chairman Mao Zedong on 16 October 1949," December 1, 1949, WWICS, History and Public Policy Program Digital Archive, AVPRF, f. 0100, op. 42, por. 19, pap. 288, ll. 28–31. Translated for CWIHP by David Wolff. http://digitalarchive .wilsoncenter.org/document/117863 (accessed March 4, 2016).

221   **"wait-and-see . . . early time":** "Instruction, New China News Agency, 'On the Propaganda Concerning Establishing Diplomatic Relations with Britain and the United States,'" October 16, 1949, in *NDE*, pp. 125–26.

221   **"a strong step . . . the Communists":** State Department Daily Staff Summary, October 17, 1949, box 8, entry 396I, RG 59, NA.

221   **"the British had not":** Acheson, "Memorandum of Conversation with the President," October 17, 1949, Dean Acheson Papers, TL.

221   **Bevin attempted to salve the wound:** State Department Daily Staff Summary, October 19, 1949, box 8, entry 396I, RG 59, NA.

222 **"The Department . . . Communist control":** Johnson to N.S.C., October 18, 1949, box 213, PSF, Harry S. Truman Papers, TL.

222 **"too vague":** Ibid.

222 **Johnson dinner with MCKS:** Koo OH, v. 6, pt. J, sec. 2, p. 111, Wellington Koo Papers, BLCU; McFarland and Roll, *Louis Johnson*, p. 258.

222 **"promise":** Koo memorandum of conversation, June 30, 1950, box 180, folder 1, Wellington Koo Papers, BLCU.

223 **"unrealistic, impractical":** Schaller, *American Occupation*, p. 206.

223 **"We can . . . of chaos":** *NYT*, October 21, 1949.

223 **cornerstone ceremony:** *NYT*, October 25, 1949. See also TLP, accession nos. 92-193 and 92-196.

223 **"saris, chipaos":** *NYT*, October 25 and 26, 1949.

224 **"must be . . . act of faith":** *NYT*, October 25, 1949.

224 **"I sincerely . . . the world":** Ibid.

224 **miserable conditions:** Elden B. Erickson OH, Association for Diplomatic Studies and Training, Foreign Affairs Oral History Project, June 25, 1992, interviewed by Charles Stuart Kennedy, www.adst.org/OH%20TOCs/Erickson,%20Eldon%20B.toc.pdf (accessed March 4, 2015).

224 **"We would . . . sides off":** Ibid.

225 **"area from Japan . . . be realistic":** Acheson held meetings with the East Asia consultants on October 26 and 27. See Ogburn, Jr., memorandum, "Decisions Reached by Consensus at the Meetings with the Secretary and the Consultants on the Far East," *FRUS* 1949, vol. IX, pp. 160–62.

225 **"different now . . . months ago":** Acheson press conference transcript, October 26, 1949, box 72, Dean Acheson Papers, TL.

225 **"the strongest . . . be effective":** James E. Webb, "Meeting with the President" [top secret], October 31, 1949, box 1, entry 394, RG 59, NA.

226 **"Had dinner . . . a life!":** HST diary, entry for November 1, 1949, PSF, Harry S. Truman Papers, TL; McCullough, *Truman*, p. 751.

CHAPTER 21: THE VOICE

227 **Truman's appearance:** TLP, accession nos. 92-202, 92-204. See also Lilienthal diary, entry for November 7, 1949, in Lilienthal, *Journals*, pp. 2:591–92.

227   **"full control"**: Hillenkoetter memo, November 1, 1949, box 2, CIA File, NSC File, SMOF, Harry S. Truman Papers, TL.

227   **"magnificent accomplishments"**: Alfred T. Cox to Dorothy Cox, October 30, 1949, Alfred T. Cox Private Papers, courtesy of Steven Cox.

227   **authorized $500,000**: Leary and Stueck, "Chennault Plan," pp. 357–58.

228   **"The joker throughout"**: Hillenkoetter memo, November 1, 1949, box 2, CIA File, NSC File, SMOF, Harry S. Truman Papers, TL.

228   **"worse than Mao"**: Hillenkoetter memo, October 25, 1949, ibid.

228   **wondered whether Mao was retaliating**: "Summary of Daily Meeting with the Acting Secretary," November 15, 1949, folder 1, box 1, entry 393, RG 59, NA.

228   **Mao reached out to Stalin**: "PRC Central Committee Cable to Ambassador Wang Jiaxiang re Mao Zedong's Departure for Moscow," November 9, 1949, and "Mao Cable to Stalin re I. V. Kovalev Accompanying Him," November 12, 1949, both reprinted in Goncharov, Lewis, and Xue, *Uncertain Partners*, p. 236. See also *NDE*, pp. 127–28.

228   **Scholars now suggest**: See, for example, Chen, "Ward Case," p. 165.

228   **"that we meant . . . heed our warning"**: Webb memo, November 14, 1949, *FRUS* 1949, vol. VIII, p. 1008.

229   *Flying Cloud* **incident**: *NCDN*, November 12, 17, 19, and 20, 1949; *NYT*, November 16, 1949.

229   **"radical suggestions"**: Stuart diary, entry for November 17, 1949, box 1, John Leighton Stuart Papers, HI.

229   **"quick panaceas . . . Soviet imperialism"**: "Outline of Far Eastern and Asian Policy for Review with the President," November 14, 1949, *FRUS* 1949, vol. VII, pt. 2, pp. 1210–14.

230   **"tremendously helpful . . . preferable one"**: Acheson memorandum of conversation with HST, November 17, 1949, Dean Acheson Papers, TL.

231   **top-secret C.I.A. memo**: Hillenkoetter memo, November 18, 1949, box 2, CIA File, NSC File, SMOF, Harry S. Truman Papers, TL.

231   **"use of . . . the operation"**: Ibid.

231   **"fight their . . . global war"**: Bradley to Johnson, November 18, 1949, *FRUS* 1949, vol. VIII, p. 1011.

231   **Bai had been complaining**: Bai to Chennault, November 13, 1949, "China.President" folder, box 10, Claire Chennault Papers, HI.

231   **P.L.A. . . . surged toward Guilin:** Leary and Stueck, "Chennault Plan," p. 358.

231   **"two almost solid lines":** Cox, "Civil Air Transport," p. 38.

231   **"We are trying desperately":** Alfred T. Cox to Dorothy Cox, November 1949, Alfred T. Cox Private Papers, courtesy of Steven Cox.

232   **"The way things . . . is concerned":** Alfred T. Cox to Dorothy Cox, November 29, 1949, ibid.

232   **"Tragically . . . by the blind":** Judd to Hannon, November 18, 1949, "Correspondence General, 1949 (A)" folder, box 159, Walter H. Judd Papers, HI.

232   **"A year ago . . . Chinese mainland":** *NYT*, November 27, 1949.

232   **woken by his security guards:** Westad, *Decisive Encounters*, p. 288.

233   **forced to . . . walk:** *NYT*, December 3, 1949.

233   **"U.S. China policy . . . United States":** CKS diary, entry for November 30, 1949, quoted in Taylor, *Generalissimo*, p. 419.

233   **"Tell me what the temperature":** *NYT*, November 29, 1949.

233   **Truman tried to relax:** *NYT*, December 4, 1949.

233   **scoured the newspapers . . . special flights:** Ibid.

233   **One memo acknowledged:** Souers memo, December 1, 1949, box 2, CIA File, NSC File, SMOF, Harry S. Truman Papers, TL.

234   **"the Asia problem":** "Summary of Daily Meeting with the Secretary," December 1, 1949, folder 1, box 1, entry 393, RG 59, NA.

234   **Stuart's stroke:** Stuart, *Fifty Years*, p. 285. See also Shaw, *American Missionary*, pp. 265, 274.

234   **release of Angus Ward:** *NYT*, November 24, 1949.

234   **"quarantine . . . appeasement":** Judd, "Rep. Judd Clarifies Stand on Ward Incident," *Minneapolis Tribune*, December 5, 1949.

235   **tried to stiffen her husband's spine:** MCKS to CKS, December 5, 1949, JZZD, AH.

235   **found herself praying:** Chiang, *Sure Victory*, p. 23.

235   **"Then one morning":** Ibid.

235   **she cabled her husband:** MCKS to CKS, December 5, 1949, JZZD, AH.

CHAPTER 22: THROUGH A GLASS, DARKLY

236   **Mao leaves Beijing:** Shi, "'I Accompanied Chairman Mao,'" pp. 128–29; Goncharov, "Stalin's Dialogue with Mao," pp. 57, 70–71;

Goncharov, Lewis, and Xue, *Uncertain Partners*, p. 84; Pantsov and Levine, *Real Story*, p. 368; Salisbury, *New Emperors*, pp. 92–93.

237 **"It is more appropriate"**: MZ to Mao Xusheng, November 15, 1949, in Kau and Leung, *Writings of Mao*, p. 35.

237 **"Do not harbor any unrealistic"**: MZ to Yang Kaizhi, October 9, 1949, ibid., p. 14.

237 **angioneurosis**: Russian medical report, December 10, 1949, cited in Pantsov and Levine, *Real Story*, p. 363. See also p. 370.

237 **receding beneath his feet**: Kartunova, "Vstrechi v Moskve," p. 126. See also Pantsov and Levine, *Real Story*, p. 363.

237 **large portraits of Stalin**: Goncharov, "Stalin's Dialogue with Mao," p. 57.

237 **"clearly irritated"**: Ibid.

237 **Jinmen**: Taylor, *Generalissimo*, p. 416; Westad, *Decisive Encounters*, p. 299.

237 **three regiments**: He Di, "Last Campaign," p. 6.

237 **"This is our biggest loss"**: MZ quoted in Westad, *Decisive Encounters*, pp. 299–301.

237 **Dengbu Island**: Chen, *China's Road*, pp. 99, 101.

238 **pilot-training facilities**: Ibid., p. 77.

238 **delivery of Yak fighter planes**: Ibid.

238 **Soviet naval advisers**: Ibid.

238 **Ilha Formosa**: Pakula, *Last Empress*, p. 587.

238 **defected to the Communists**: Lin, *Accidental State*, p. 119.

238 **depressed and plagued by ulcers**: Westad, *Decisive Encounters*, p. 290.

238 **dead reckoning**: Taylor, *Generalissimo*, p. 419.

239 **According to the British government**: "Memorandum Regarding Formosa," December 6, 1949, Dean Acheson Papers, TL.

239 **The C.I.A. did not believe**: Cohen, *America's Response*, p. 186.

239 **"dangerous state of affairs"**: "Memorandum Regarding Formosa," December 6, 1949, Dean Acheson Papers, TL.

239 **potential launching pad**: Schaller, *American Occupation*, pp. 195, 203.

239 **"Generally speaking . . . military action"**: Johnson memo, December 15, 1949, quoted in Rearden, *History of Office*, p. 236.

239 **from a string of offshore bases**: Schaller, *American Occupation*, pp. 195, 203.

239   **"Formosa . . . ain't got":** Acheson quoted in Beisner, *Dean Acheson*, p. 200.

239   **British recognition:** Ovendale, "Britain, United States," p. 148; Schaller, *American Occupation*, p. 215.

240   **"shortly be . . . in China":** State Department Daily Staff Summary, December 19, 1949, box 8, entry 3961, RG 59, NA.

240   **felt so nauseous:** Shi, "'I Accompanied Chairman Mao,'" pp. 128–29; Short, *Mao*, p. 422.

240   **Psychologically, too:** Goncharov, "Stalin's Dialogue with Mao," p. 70.

240   **not far from the Kremlin:** Short, *Mao*, p. 422.

240   **Mao's entourage had prepared a dinner:** Goncharov, "Stalin's Dialogue with Mao," p. 71.

240   **"visibly chagrined":** Ibid.

240   **"Long live Sino-Soviet":** MZ speech, December 16, 1949, in Goncharov, Lewis, and Xue, *Uncertain Partners*, pp. 237–38.

240   **perfunctory inspection:** *NYT*, December 17, 1949.

241   **first meeting with Stalin:** Montefiore, *Stalin*, pp. 603–4.

241   **wood-paneled office suite:** Ibid., pp. 115, 436–37.

241   **"I never quite expected":** Stalin quoted in Chang, *Friends and Enemies*, p. 64.

241   **Short, with amber-colored eyes:** Montefiore, *Stalin*, pp. 4–5, 466.

241   **heart trouble and memory loss:** Ibid., pp. 513, 525.

241   **lengthy monologues . . . angry outbursts:** Ibid., p. 525.

241   **"After the war . . . in the head":** Khrushchev quoted ibid., p. 514.

241   **"America, though it screams":** "Conversation Between Stalin and Mao, Moscow, 16 December 1949," *CWIHP Bulletin*, nos. 6/7, pp. 5–7.

241   **"For this trip . . . tastes delicious":** MZ quoted in Chen, *China's Road*, p. 80.

242   **petroleum, coal, metals:** "Conversation Between Stalin and Mao, Moscow, 16 December 1949," *CWIHP Bulletin*, nos. 6/7, pp. 5–7.

242   **"assault landing unit . . . on the island":** Ibid.

242   **"One could . . . foreign imperialists":** Ibid.

242   **"really sincere":** MZ to Liu Shaoqi, December 18, 1949, reprinted in *CWIHP Bulletin*, nos. 8/9, p. 226.

243   **"margarine Marxist":** Montefiore, *Stalin*, p. 590.

243   **"hypocritical foreign devil":** MZ quoted in Pantsov and Levine, *Real Story*, pp. 346–47.

243 **"eat, sleep, and shit"**: MZ quoted in Westad, *Decisive Encounters*, p. 312.

243 **Truman returned to Washington**: TLP, accession no. 92-215; *NCDN*, December 21, 1949; Ayers diary, entry for December 20, 1949, box 20, Eben A. Ayers Papers, TL.

243 **Johnson . . . argued his case**: McFarland and Roll, *Louis Johnson*, p. 260.

243 **Acheson, too, briefed the president**: Acheson, memorandum of conversation with Truman, December 20, 1949, Dean Acheson Papers, TL.

243 **"Right now . . . awfully discouraging"**: Alfred T. Cox to Dorothy Cox, 1949, Alfred T. Cox Private Papers, courtesy of Steven Cox. See also Leary and Stueck, "Chennault Plan," p. 358.

243 **The eastern provinces seemed lost**: Cox, "Civil Air Transport," p. 40.

243 **Cox had made a large payment**: Ibid., pp. 42–44.

243 **Earthquake McGoon**: Ibid., p. 48.

244 **Lines of trucks ferried**: Ibid., p. 47.

244 **Wisner told his staff**: Wisner to Frank, Lindsay, and Offie, "Policy Guidance on OPC Operations in China," December 19, 1949, TS-35688, cited in Cox, "Civil Air Transport," p. 53.

244 **"*de facto* freedom"**: Acheson to Henderson, *FRUS* 1949, vol. IX, pp. 1096–97.

244 **"China Looks South"**: "Summary of Daily Meeting with the Secretary," December 14, 1949, folder 1, box 1, entry 393, RG 59, NA.

244 **Wisner's team was quietly flying**: Cox, "Civil Air Transport," pp. 47–49, 52.

244 **Acheson's staff summary**: State Department Daily Staff Summary, December 21, 1949, box 8, entry 396I, RG 59, NA.

245 **"search for absolutes . . . sense in that"**: Acheson, "Remarks at the National War College," December 21, 1949, box 20, James E. Webb Papers, TL.

245 **"It is simply not"**: Kennan, "Where Do We Stand?" December 21, 1949, folder 32, box 299, Kennan Papers, Public Policy Papers, Department of Rare Books and Special Collections, Princeton University Library.

245 **"know in part"**: Ibid.

245 **"chart out vast schemes"**: Ibid.

CHAPTER 23:
A RATHER SPECTACULAR TRIUMPH

246 **Bolshoi party:** Montefiore, *Stalin*, pp. 604–6; Salisbury, *New Emperors*, p. 96.

246 **both men felt terrible:** Montefiore, *Stalin*, p. 605; Pantsov and Levine, *Real Story*, p. 369.

246 **"Comrade Stalin . . . Communist movement!":** MZ, "Mao Congratulatory Speech at the Ceremony in Honor of Stalin's Seventieth Birthday in Moscow," December 21, 1949, in Goncharov, Lewis, and Xue, *Uncertain Partners*, pp. 239–40.

247 **"was received . . . long time":** MZ cable, December 21, 1949, in Goncharov, Lewis, and Xue, *Uncertain Partners*, p. 239.

247 **"How can you":** Chang and Halliday, *Unknown Story*, p. 352.

247 **constipated:** Ibid.

247 **frozen fish:** Ibid.

247 **billiard table:** Wang Dongxing, *Riji*, entry for December 16, 1949.

247 **"I'm not just . . . do business":** Chang and Halliday, *Unknown Story*, pp. 351–52. See also Westad, *Decisive Encounters*, p. 312.

247 **"to do business . . . other countries":** MZ, "Telegram, Mao Zedong to CCP Central Committee," December 22, 1949, in *NDE*, p. 129. See also the analysis of Mao's motivations in Chang and Halliday, p. 352. See also Goncharov, Lewis, and Xue, *Uncertain Partners*, p. 91.

247 **bugged Mao's dacha:** Chang and Halliday, *Unknown Story*, pp. 351–52.

247 **new containment strategy:** Schaller, *American Occupation*, p. 203.

248 **"It seems . . . of the universe":** Acheson, "Remarks at the National War College," December 21, 1949, box 20, James E. Webb Papers, TL.

248 **Truman finally confronted:** *Military Situation in the Far East*, pt. 4, p. 2578. See also McFarland and Roll, *Louis Johnson*, pp. 250, 260–61.

248 **"We apparently are bent":** Judd to Hemenway, December 22, 1949, "Correspondence General, 1949 (B)" folder, box 159, Walter H. Judd Papers, HI.

248 **"complete removal or transfer":** Judd to Kopf, December 23, 1949, ibid.

248 **Chiang's desires:** Koo memorandum, December 23, 1949, *FRUS 1949*, vol. IX, pp. 457–60.

249 **"parallels with extraordinary":** Butterworth to Acheson, December 28, 1949, *FRUS 1949*, vol. IX, pp. 461–62; Schaller, *American Occupation*, p. 209.

249   **"The president looked fine"**: Lilienthal diary, entry for December 24, 1949 (describing December 21 meeting), in Lilienthal, *Journals*, p. 2:611.

249   **heavy rain:** *NYT*, December 24, 1949.

249   **jingled . . . sleigh bells:** TLP, accession no. 77-1108.

249   **Truman in Independence:** *NYT*, December 24–26, 1949.

249   **"thinking about . . . fellow men":** *NYT*, December 25, 1949.

250   **Acheson met that morning:** Acheson memorandum, December 29, 1949, FRUS 1949, vol. IX, pp. 463–67.

251   **keep others from doing so:** John Gaddis explains this characteristic of the State Department's containment strategy in *Strategies of Containment*, p. 55.

251   **Later that afternoon:** Souers memorandum, December 28, 1949, box 9, NSC File, SMOF, Harry S. Truman Papers, TL.

251   **Wilson stared down:** TLP, accession no. 73-2976. See also McCullough, *Truman*, p. 751.

251   **"collective conscience"** and **"common will of mankind":** Wilson quoted in Ninkovich, *Modernity*, pp. 57, 59.

252   **"worth the price . . . political reasons":** Memorandum for the President (Top Secret), December 30, 1949, box 188, PSF, Harry S. Truman Papers, TL. See also Minutes of the 50th Meeting of the NSC, December 29, 1949, box 180, ibid.

252   **The new document:** NSC 48/2, *FRUS* 1949, vol. VII, pt. 2, pp. 1215–20.

252   **"military and political . . . matter of urgency":** Ibid.

253   **Truman signed off:** Souers memo, December 30, 1949, box 180, PSF, Harry S. Truman Papers, TL. In his approval of the strategy, Truman added the caveat: "A program will be all right, but whether we implement it depends on circumstances."

253   **Every choice, a British writer once observed:** G. K. Chesterton, *Orthodoxy* (New York: Knopf, 2011), p. 292.

253   **Judd phone call:** Judd handwritten notes of call with HST, December 30, 1949, folder 9, box 79, Walter H. Judd Papers, HI; Judd OH, interview by Jerry N. Hess, April 13, 1970, TL, www.trumanlibrary.org/oralhist/judd.htm (accessed March 26, 2016).

254   **Kennan cabled Wisner:** Kennan to Wisner, "Subject: Covert Operations in China" [December 30, 1949], TS-35850, cited in Cox, "Civil Air Transport," pp. 53–54.

254   **"commitments on the mainland":** Cox, "Civil Air Transport," p. 53.

254 **"extremely precarious situation":** Ibid., p. 54.

254 **January 1, 1950, church service:** *NYT*, January 2, 1950.

255 **innate moral paradox:** For an insightful discussion of realist ethics, see Rosenthal, *Righteous Realists*, pp. 45, 62–64.

255 **Truman himself seems:** Blum, *Drawing the Line*, p. 178.

255 **Acheson stopped by:** Acheson OH, Princeton Seminars, July 23, 1953, p. 5, reel 1, Dean Acheson Papers, TL.

255 **"no desire to obtain":** Beisner, *Dean Acheson*, pp. 200–1.

255 **pushed back:** Ibid.

255 **president lying naked:** Ayers diary, entry for January 5, 1950, box 20, Eben A. Ayers Papers, TL.

255 **"pull the rug out":** Ibid.

255 JOHNSON TAKES FORMOSA LICKING: *Washington Post*, January 8, 1950.

255 **"rather spectacular triumph":** Ibid.

CHAPTER 24: A FORCE SO SWIFT

256 **Mikoyan and Molotov visit:** MZ to CCP Central Committee, January 2, 1950, in *NDE*, p. 131.

256 **staring out the windows:** Chang and Halliday, *Unknown Story*, p. 351.

256 **locking himself in his bedroom:** Pantsov and Levine, *Real Story*, p. 371.

256 **"achieved an important breakthrough":** MZ to CCP Central Committee, January 2, 1950, in *NDE*, p. 131.

256 **At all hours:** MZ to CCP Central Committee, January 3 and 5, 1950, both in *NDE*, pp. 132–33.

257 **"press the capitalist countries":** Ibid., p. 133.

257 **"undisciplined words":** MZ to CCP Central Committee, January 5, 1950, in *NDE*, p. 134.

257 **"greatest part . . . mutual respect":** *NYT*, January 7, 1950.

257 **Madame Chiang slipped:** *NYT*, January 9, 1950.

257 **"Friends . . . thank you":** Ibid.

258 **overcome with memories:** Chiang, *Sure Victory*, pp. 26–27.

258 **"These flashbacks . . . swiftly by":** Ibid., p. 27.

259 **"I had been using God":** Ibid.

259 **large crowds:** Ibid., p. 28.

259 **"To them . . . them deeply":** Ibid.

259 **Madame Chiang watched:** Ibid.

259   **The pilot had arranged:** Ibid.

259   **"brief handclasp":** *NYT*, January 13, 1950.

259   **"helped to create . . . certain style":** James Reston, "Mme. Chiang Won Triumph in US, But Mission Failed," *NYT*, January 11, 1950.

260   **Acheson reviewed a speech:** Acheson OH, Princeton Seminars, July 23, 1953, p. 11, reel 2, Dean Acheson Papers, TL.

260   **"terrible":** Ibid, p. 10.

260   **"melted away . . . sensible and possible":** Acheson, "Crisis in Asia: An Examination of U.S. Policy," *Department of State Bulletin*, January 23, 1950.

260   **combined to rouse Stalin:** Goncharov, Lewis, and Xue, *Uncertain Partners*, pp. 99–102.

261   **emboldening their domestic rivals:** Ibid., p. 100.

261   **Leningrad trip:** Shi, "I Accompanied Chairman Mao," p. 130; Salisbury, *New Emperors*, p. 98.

EPILOGUE: THE MILLS OF THE GODS

262   **"about everything":** Truman, *Bess Truman*, p. 355.

262   **"a grim look":** Ibid.

262   **"That was Dean":** Ibid.

262   **"Tomorrow . . . business as usual":** Ibid.

262   **"I can remember the pain":** Ibid.

263   **a civil conflict:** Cumings, *Origins*, p. 598.

263   **Washington remained deeply involved:** Ibid., pp. 35, 189, 232, 283–84.

263   **A revitalized South Korea:** Ibid., p. 50.

263   **they had begun to return:** Ibid., pp. 364, 451, 617; Chen, *China's Road*, p. 110; Goncharov, Lewis, and Xue, *Uncertain Partners*, p. 140.

263   **had been caught:** Cumings observes that, prior to 1949, Kim's government faced "a tiger at the front door and a wolf at the back. Chiang and Rhee would unquestionably seek to squeeze North Korea like an irritating pimple." In 1949, however, "Mao's victory dramatically changed North Korea's situation." Cumings, *Origins*, p. 327. See also Chen, *China's Road*, p. 119.

263   **U.S. commanders . . . finally pulled out:** Chen, *China's Road*, p. 119; Cumings, *Origins*, pp. 53, 66.

264   **Soviet dictator had always refused:** Chen, *China's Road*, pp. 86–87; Goncharov, Lewis, and Xue, *Uncertain Partners*, p. 139.

264 **In late January 1950:** Stalin had first indicated his willingness to discuss an invasion on Jan. 30, 1950, when he cabled Terenti Shtykov: ". . . tell [Kim] that I am ready to help him in this matter." See Stalin to Shtykov, Jan. 30, 1959, WWICS, http://digitalarchive.wilsoncenter.org/document/112136 (accessed Jan. 22, 2017).

264 **When Kim visited Moscow:** Goncharov, Lewis, and Xue, *Uncertain Partners*, p. 145; Chen, *China's Road*, p. 90.

264 **"If you should get kicked":** Goncharov, Lewis, and Xue, *Uncertain Partners*, p. 145.

264 **Stalin ultimately sent:** Ibid., pp. 147, 149; Chen, *China's Road*, p. 125.

264 **slightly ambivalent:** Chen Jian notes that "Mao Zedong supported his North Korean comrades' intention to unify their country through a revolutionary war," but adds that the two men "did not trust each other." Chen, *China's Road*, p. x.

264 **successful Chinese leaders:** Hunt, *Genesis*, pp. 16, 221–24; Chen, *China's Road*, pp. 25, 104.

264 **would complicate Mao's attempt:** Goncharov, Lewis, and Xue, *Uncertain Partners*, pp. 139–40; Chen, *China's Road*, p. x.

264 **Kim kept his own counsel:** Goncharov, Lewis, and Xue, *Uncertain Partners*, pp. 153–54; Chang and Halliday, *Unknown Story*, pp. 360–61.

265 **the administration had begun shipping:** Chen, *China's Road*, p. 115; Cumings, *Origins*, p. 438.

265 **the war was a reprieve:** Cumings, *Origins*, p. 601.

265 **Mao had been massing his forces:** Goncharov, Lewis, and Xue, *Uncertain Partners*, p. 149; Taylor, *Generalissimo*, p. 430; Cumings, *Origins*, p. 526.

265 **A rival faction . . . planning a coup:** Cumings, *Origins*, p. 543; Taylor, *Generalissimo*, pp. 432–35.

265 **But it also functioned:** Schaller, *American Occupation*, p. 282; Gaddis, *We Now Know*, p. 77; McFarland and Roll, *Louis Johnson*, pp. 323–24; Hamby, *Man of People*, pp. 535–36.

265 **When Chiang offered Truman:** Schoenbaum, *Waging Peace*, p. 213.

265 **Johnson wanted to mine the Taiwan Strait:** McFarland and Roll, *Louis Johnson*, p. 324.

265 **"those who advocate appeasement":** MacArthur quoted in Glain, *State vs. Defense*, pp. 104–5.

266 **"lips white and compressed":** Hamby, *Man of People*, p. 543.

266 **"dare":** Glain, *State vs. Defense*, pp. 104–5.

266 "began to show an inordinate": Ferrell, *Off the Record*, p. 192.

266 Truman called Johnson to his office: McFarland and Roll, *Louis Johnson*, p. 343.

266 Devastated, Johnson staggered: Ibid., p. 344.

266 Johnson, weeping: Ibid., p. 345.

266 "You are ruining me": Ibid.

266 "the toughest job": Ibid., p. 343.

266 "The Chinese comrades are so good!": MZ quoted in Pantsov and Levine, *Real Story*, p. 374.

266 MacArthur's strategy: Hamby, *Man of People*, pp. 536–60.

267 "What would suit": Ibid., p. 560.

267 "quietly strengthened": Halper and Halper, *Tibet*, p. 92.

267 American operatives . . . had lobbied: Ibid., p. 85.

267 to publicize these plots: Ibid., pp. 83, 281n36.

267 He ordered nine thousand Chinese troops: Ibid., p. 97.

267 spoke Chinese fluently: Chen, *China's Road*, p. 102.

267 walked for seventeen days: *NDE*, p. 141; Goncharov, Lewis, and Xue, *Uncertain Partners*, p. 107.

267 later traveled to Moscow: Chang and Halliday, *Unknown Story*, pp. 356–57.

267 Mao was regularly sending shipments: Westad, *Decisive Encounters*, pp. 316–17.

268 dozens of Hellcat and Bearcat: Logevall, *Embers of War*, pp. 257–58.

268 only the troops in Korea: Ibid.

268 Wu Chang Villa: Leary, *Perilous Missions*, p. 133.

268 Western Enterprises: Ibid.

268 using leaflets, radios, and hot-air balloons: Leary, *Perilous Missions*, p. 133.

268 Southeast Asia Collective Defense Treaty: Taylor, *Generalissimo*, p. 415.

268 "We'd be in radio contact": Halper and Halper, *Tibet*, p. 135.

268 "to be understood . . . especially in Asia": Walter Lippmann, "Today and Tomorrow," January 15, 1950, copy in box 59, George M. Elsey Papers, TL.

269 "cheap and cheerful": N. T. Wright, *Surprised by Hope* (New York: HarperCollins, 2008), p. 180.

269 "grand fallacy": Acheson, *Present*, p. 112.

269 absorbed a biblical cosmology: Beisner, *Dean Acheson*, p. 101.

269   **"force and violence"**: Acheson, *Present*, p. 112.

269   **"calculation of forces"**: Ibid., p. 275.

269   **America's enemies, too:** Herodotus, *Histories*, p. 438.

270   **"recognize the limits . . . human eye"**: Kennan diary, entry for June 18, 1986, Kennan, *Diaries*, p. 570.

270   **"Some say . . . obey yourself?"**: MZ, in Schram, *Mao's Road*, p. 1:273.

270   **Great Leap Forward:** Pantsov and Levine, *Real Story*, pp. 449–70.

270   **"We will overtake England"**: Ibid., p. 457.

271   **artichokes with sunflowers:** Becker, *Hungry Ghosts*, p. 70; Buruma, "Divine Killer," p. 23.

271   **leaves, bark, and worms:** Pantsov and Levine, *Real Story*, p. 470.

271   **"everything which does not fit"**: Spence, *Search*, p. 546.

271   *geming shengdi* . . . **imaginary bayonets:** Leese, *Mao Cult*, pp. 139, 202–3.

271   **shipping weapons:** Chen, "China's Involvement," p. 371.

272   **"bastard legacy"**: Isaacson and Thomas, *Wise Men*, p. 30.

272   **Johnson . . . made frequent attempts:** McCullough, *Truman*, p. 985.

272   **"We certainly should not"**: Isaacson and Thomas, *Wise Men*, p. 679.

272   **"areas that count"**: Ibid., p. 684. See also Herring, *America's Longest War*, pp. 246–47.

272   **Nixon's strategy was not identical:** For a nuanced discussion of the similarities and differences in these strategies, see Chang, *Friends and Enemies*, pp. 3, 291–92.

272   **"isolated, obese"**: Schell and Delury, *Wealth and Power*, p. 252.

273   **he got grief from both:** Isaacson and Thomas, *Wise Men*, pp. 26–27.

273   **"holy rollers . . . to their ears"**: Acheson quoted in Beisner, *Dean Acheson*, p. 204.

273   **" 'I tell you nought . . . sea rises higher' "**: Acheson, *Fragments of Fleece*, p. 197.

273   **died of a stroke:** Chace, *Acheson*, p. 437.

273   **"I have a deep . . . everywhere on earth"**: HST, "The President's Farewell Address to the American People," January 15, 1953, in *Public Papers of the Presidents: Harry S. Truman*, 1952–53, p. 1201.

273   **During one post-presidency shoot:** Aurthur, "Wit and Sass," p. 64.

273   **"chinks . . . yellow Chinese"**: Ibid.

273   **Truman . . . fell ill:** McCullough, *Truman*, pp. 987–88.

274   **he mused to an American journalist:** Snow, "Conversation with Mao."

274   **"soon be going":** Ibid.

274   **"sharp reversal":** Judd to Nixon, September 15, 1971, quoted in Chang, *Friends and Enemies*, p. 289.

274   **"nature of the beast . . . leftist groupies":** MCKS to Judd, March 6, 1982, folder 17, box 163, Walter H. Judd Papers, HI.

274   **He continued . . . to travel:** *NYT*, February 15, 1994.

274   **granite villa . . . azalea bushes and orchids:** *NYT*, February 12, 1950.

274   **painted, prayed, and plotted:** Li, *Madame Chiang*, pp. 285, 339–41.

274   **brutally repressive:** He Di, "Last Campaign," p. 12; Li, *Madame Chiang*, p. 347.

274   **taking an apartment:** Li, *Madame Chiang*, pp. 424, 462.

275   **"periods of great . . . my mind":** MCKS, "Sursum Corda by Madame Chiang Kai-shek," *China Post*, December 6, 1986; Li, *Madame Chiang*, p. 433.

275   **"forest fire":** Schell and Delury, *Wealth and Power*, p. 9.

275   **"can never be contained":** Chang Wanquan quoted in Gopal Ratnam, "Hagel to Meet Xi as China Vows No Compromising on Sea Disputes," *Bloomberg*, April 9, 2014.

SELECTED BIBLIOGRAPHY

MANUSCRIPT COLLECTIONS

ACADEMIA HISTORICA, TAIPEI, TAIWAN
Jiang Zhongzheng Zongtong Dang'an [President Chiang Kai-shek Collection]

COLUMBIA UNIVERSITY, NEW YORK, N.Y.
Wellington Koo Papers

HOOVER INSTITUTION, STANFORD, CALIF.
Claire Chennault Papers
Chiang Kai-shek Diary
Walter H. Judd Papers
Alfred Kohlberg Papers
T.V. Soong Papers
John Leighton Stuart Papers

LIBRARY OF CONGRESS, WASHINGTON, D.C.
Clare Booth Luce Papers

NATIONAL ARCHIVES, COLLEGE PARK, MD.
General Records of the Department of State

PRINCETON UNIVERSITY LIBRARY, PRINCETON, N.J.
George F. Kennan Papers

PRIVATE COLLECTIONS
Alfred T. Cox Private Papers. Courtesy of Steven Cox.
Roy Howard Private Papers. Courtesy of Pamela Howard.

HARRY S. TRUMAN PRESIDENTIAL LIBRARY AND MUSEUM,
    INDEPENDENCE, MO.
Dean Acheson Papers
Eben A. Ayers Papers
Matthew Connelly Papers
George M. Elsey Papers
John F. Melby Papers
Harry S. Truman Papers
James E. Webb Papers

UNIVERSITY OF TEXAS AT DALLAS, RICHARDSON, TEX.
William M. Leary Papers

WELLESLEY COLLEGE ARCHIVE, WELLESLEY, MASS.
Mayling Soong Chiang Papers
Emma DeLong Mills Papers

ORAL HISTORIES

Dean G. Acheson
Elden B. Erickson
Walter H. Judd
V. K. Wellington Koo
John F. Melby
Edward H. Pruden
Louis H. Renfrow
William N. Stokes

BOOKS AND ARTICLES

Acheson, David C. *Acheson Country: A Memoir.* New York: Norton, 1993.
Acheson, Dean. *Fragments of My Fleece.* New York: Norton, 1971.
———. *Morning and Noon.* Boston: Houghton Mifflin, 1965.

———. *Present at the Creation: My Years in the State Department*. New York: Norton, 1969.

———. *Sketches from Life of Men I Have Known*. New York: Harper & Bros., 1959.

Adams, Helen Lee, and Dora Fugh Lee, eds. *The Collected Letters: Philip Jingpo Fugh (1900–1988)*. Claremont, Calif.: Claremont Graduate University, 2012.

Alsop, Joseph W., with Adam Platt. *"I've Seen the Best of It": Memoirs*. New York: Norton, 1992.

Anderson, Benedict. *Imagined Communities: Reflections on the Origin and Spread of Nationalism*. 1983; reprint London: Verso, 2006.

Anderson, Jack, with James Boyd. *Confessions of a Muckraker: The Inside Story of Life in Washington During the Truman, Eisenhower, Kennedy, and Johnson Years*. New York: Random House, 1979.

Aurthur, Robert Alan. "The Wit and Sass of Harry S. Truman." *Esquire* (August 1971): 62–67, 115–18.

Barber, Noel. *The Fall of Shanghai*. New York: Coward, McCann and Geoghegan, 1979.

Barnett, A. Doak. *China on the Eve of Communist Takeover*. New York: Praeger, 1961.

Becker, Jasper. *City of Heavenly Tranquility: Beijing in the History of China*. Oxford: Oxford University Press, 2008.

———. *Hungry Ghosts: Mao's Secret Famine*. New York: Free Press, 1996.

Behrman, Greg. *The Most Noble Adventure: The Marshall Plan and the Time When America Helped Save Europe*. New York: Free Press, 2007.

Beisner, Robert L. *Dean Acheson: A Life in the Cold War*. Oxford: Oxford University Press, 2006.

Beisner, Robert L., ed. *American Foreign Relations Since 1600: A Guide to the Literature*, 2nd ed. Santa Barbara, Calif.: ABC-CLIO, 2003.

Belden, Jack. *China Shakes the World*. New York: Harper & Bros., 1949.

Bernstein, Richard. *China 1945: Mao's Revolution and America's Fateful Choice*. New York: Knopf, 2014.

Blum, Robert M. *Drawing the Line: The Origin of American Containment Policy in East Asia*. New York: Norton, 1982.

Bodde, Derk. *Peking Diary: A Year of Revolution*. New York: Henry Schuman, 1950.

Borg, Dorothy, and Waldo Heinrichs, eds. *Uncertain Years: Chinese-American Relations, 1947–1950*. New York: Columbia University Press, 1980.

Borklund, C. W. *Men of the Pentagon: From Forrestal to McNamara.* New York: Praeger, 1966.

Brinkley, Alan. *The Publisher: Henry Luce and His American Century.* New York: Knopf, 2010.

Buruma, Ian. "Divine Killer." *New York Review of Books,* February 24, 2000, pp. 20–25.

Chace, James. *Acheson: The Secretary of State Who Created the American World.* New York: Simon & Schuster, 1998.

Chang, Gordon H. *Friends and Enemies: The United States, China, and the Soviet Union, 1948–1972.* Stanford, Calif.: Stanford University Press, 1990.

Chang, Jung, and Jon Halliday. *Mao: The Unknown Story.* New York: Knopf, 2005.

Chassin, Lionel Max. *The Communist Conquest of China: A History of the Civil War, 1945–1949.* Translated by Timothy Osato and Louis Gelas. Cambridge, Mass.: Harvard University Press, 1965.

Chen Jian. "China's Involvement in the Vietnam War, 1964–69." *China Quarterly,* no. 142 (June 1995): 356–87.

———. *China's Road to the Korean War: The Making of the Sino-American Confrontation.* New York: Columbia University Press, 1994.

———. *Mao's China and the Cold War.* Chapel Hill: University of North Carolina Press, 2001.

———. "The Myth of America's 'Lost Chance' in China: A Chinese Perspective in Light of New Evidence." *Diplomatic History* 21, no. 1 (Winter 1997): 77–86.

———. "The Ward Case and the Emergence of Sino-American Confrontation, 1948–50." *Australian Journal of Chinese Affairs* 30 (July 1993): 149–70.

Chiang, Ching-kuo. *Calm in the Eye of a Storm.* Taipei: Li Ming Cultural Enterprise Co., 1978.

Chiang, Soong Mayling. *The Sure Victory.* Westwood, N.J.: Fleming H. Revell, 1955.

Christensen, Thomas J. *The China Challenge: Shaping the Choices of a Rising Power.* New York: Norton, 2015.

Cohen, Warren I. "Acheson, His Advisers, and China, 1949–50," in Dorothy Borg and Waldo Heinrichs, eds., *Uncertain Years: Chinese-American Relations, 1947–1950.* New York: Columbia University Press, 1980.

———. *America's Response to China: A History of Sino-American Relations,* 5th ed. New York: Columbia University Press, 2010.

———. "Conversations with Chinese Friends: Zhou Enlai's Associates Reflect on Chinese-American Relations in the 1940s and the Korean War." *Diplomatic History* 11 (1987): 283–89.

Corson, William R. *The Armies of Ignorance: The Rise of the American Intelligence Empire.* New York: Dial Press, 1977.

Cox, Alfred T. "Civil Air Transport (CAT): A Proprietary Airline, 1946–55," April 1967, Clandestine Services Historical Paper no. 87, vol. 1. Washington, D.C.: Central Intelligence Agency, 1969. Declassified in 2011.

Crozier, Brian. *The Man Who Lost China: The First Full Biography of Chiang Kai-shek.* New York: Scribner's, 1976.

Cumings, Bruce. *The Origins of the Korean War.* Vol. 2, *The Roaring of the Cataract, 1947–50.* Princeton, N.J.: Princeton University Press, 1990.

Dallek, Robert. *Harry S. Truman.* New York: Henry Holt, 2008.

DeLong, Thomas A. *Madame Chiang Kai-shek and Miss Emma Mills: China's First Lady and Her American Friend.* Jefferson, N.C.: McFarland, 2007.

Donald, Aida D. *Citizen Soldier: A Life of Harry S. Truman.* New York: Basic Books, 2012.

Dong, Stella. *Shanghai, 1842–1949: The Rise and Fall of a Decadent City.* New York: Morrow, 2000.

Eastman, Lloyd E. *Seeds of Destruction: Nationalist China in War and Revolution, 1937–1949.* Stanford, Calif.: Stanford University Press, 1984.

Edwards, Lee. *Missionary for Freedom: The Life and Times of Walter Judd.* St. Paul, Minn.: Paragon House, 1990.

Empson, William. "Red on Red: William Empson Witnesses the Inauguration of the People's Republic of China." *London Review of Books* 21, no. 19 (September 30, 1999): 66–67.

Ezpeleta, Mariano. *Red Shadows Over Shanghai.* Quezon City, Philippines: Zita, 1972.

Fairbank, John King, ed. *The Missionary Enterprise in China and America.* Cambridge, Mass.: Harvard University Press, 1974.

Fedorenko, N. "The Stalin-Mao Summit in Moscow." *Far Eastern Affairs* 2 (1989): 134–48.

Ferrell, Robert H., ed. *Off the Record: The Private Papers of Harry S. Truman.* Columbia: University of Missouri Press, 1980.

FitzGerald, Frances. *Fire in the Lake: The Vietnamese and the Americans in Vietnam.* 1972; reprint New York: Back Bay, 2002.

Forman, Harrison. *Blunder in Asia.* New York: Didier, 1950.

Forrestal, James. *The Forrestal Diaries*. Edited by Walter Millis. New York: Viking Press, 1951.

Gaddis, John Lewis. *The Cold War: A New History*. New York: Penguin Press, 2005.

———. *George F. Kennan: An American Life*. New York: Penguin Press, 2011.

———. "Harry S. Truman and the Origins of Containment," in Frank J. Merli and Theodore A. Wilson, eds., *Makers of American Diplomacy: From Benjamin Franklin to Henry Kissinger*. New York: Scribner's, 1974.

———. *Strategies of Containment: A Critical Appraisal of American National Security Policy During the Cold War*. 1982; reprint Oxford: Oxford University Press, 2005.

———. *We Now Know: Rethinking Cold War History*. Oxford: Clarendon Press, 1997.

Gellhorn, Martha. *Travels with Myself and Another*. New York: Dodd, Mead, 1978.

Glain, Stephen. *State vs. Defense: The Battle to Define America's Empire*. New York: Crown, 2011.

Goldstein, Lyle J. *Meeting China Halfway: How to Defuse the Emerging U.S.-China Rivalry*. Washington, D.C.: Georgetown University Press, 2015.

Goncharov, Sergei. "The Stalin-Mao Dialogue [Interview with Ivan Kovalev]." Pts. 1 and 2. *Far Eastern Affairs* 1 (1992): 100–16; 2 (1992): 94–111.

———. "Stalin's Dialogue with Mao Zedong." *Journal of Northeast Asian Studies* 10, no. 4 (Winter 1991): 45–76.

Goncharov, Sergei N., John W. Lewis, and Xue Litai. *Uncertain Partners: Stalin, Mao, and the Korean War*. Stanford, Calif.: Stanford University Press, 1993.

Goodno, Floyd Russel. "Walter H. Judd: Spokesman for China in the United States House of Representatives." Ph.D. diss., Oklahoma State University, 1970.

"GOP Keynoter Judd an Expert on Asian Policy." *Congressional Quarterly Weekly Report* 18 (July 15, 1960): 1266–67.

Gup, Ted. *The Book of Honor: The Secret Lives and Deaths of CIA Operatives*. New York: Anchor Books, 2007.

Hahn, Emily. *The Soong Sisters*. Garden City: Doubleday, Doran, 1941.

Halberstam, David. *Summer of '49: The Classic Chronicle of Baseball's Most Magnificent Season as Seen Through the Yankees–Red Sox Rivalry*. New York: HarperPerennial, 1989.

Halper, Lezlee Brown, and Stefan Halper. *Tibet: An Unfinished Story*. Oxford: Oxford University Press, 2014.

Hamburger, Philip. "Mr. Secretary." Pts. 1 and 2. *New Yorker*, November 12 and 19, 1949.

Hamby, Alonzo L. *Man of the People: A Life of Harry S. Truman*. New York: Oxford University Press, 1995.

Haynes, John Earl, and Harvey Klehr. *Venona: Decoding Soviet Espionage in America*. New Haven, Conn.: Yale University Press, 1999.

He Di. "'The Last Campaign to Unify China: The CCP's Unmaterialized Plan to Liberate Taiwan, 1949–1950." *Chinese Historians* 5, no. 1 (Spring 1992): 1–16.

Herodotus. *The Histories*. London: Penguin, 1996.

Herring, George C. *America's Longest War: The United States and Vietnam, 1950–75*, 4th ed. Boston: McGraw-Hill, 2002.

———. *From Colony to Superpower: U.S. Foreign Relations Since 1776*. New York: Oxford University Press, 2008.

Herzstein, Robert Edwin. *Henry R. Luce, Time, and the American Crusade in Asia*. Cambridge, U.K.: Cambridge University Press, 2005.

Holloway, David. *Stalin and the Bomb: The Soviet Union and Atomic Energy, 1939–1956*. New Haven, Conn.: Yale University Press, 1994.

Holzman, Michael. *Guy Burgess: Revolutionary in an Old School Tie*. Briarcliff Manor, N.Y.: Chelmsford Press, 2013.

Hoopes, Townsend, and Douglas Brinkley. *Driven Patriot: The Life and Times of James Forrestal*. New York: Knopf, 1992.

Hooten, E. R. *The Greatest Tumult: The Chinese Civil War 1936–49*. London: Brassey's, 1991.

Horton, Philip. "The China Lobby—Part II." *Reporter*, April 29, 1952, pp. 5–10.

Hunt, Michael H. *The Genesis of Chinese Communist Foreign Policy*. New York: Columbia University Press, 1996.

Hutchings, Robert L., ed. *Tracking the Dragon: National Intelligence Estimates on China During the Era of Mao, 1948–1976*. Pittsburgh: Government Printing Office, 2004.

Isaacson, Walter, and Evan Thomas. *The Wise Men: Six Friends and the World They Made*. New York: Simon & Schuster, 1986.

Jespersen, T. Christopher. *American Images of China, 1931–49*. Stanford, Calif.: Stanford University Press, 1996.

Jessup, Philip C. *The Birth of Nations*. New York: Columbia University Press, 1974.

Judd, Walter H. "Control of Asia Is Crucial Question." *Midland Schools* 63 (May 1948): 18–19.

———. "Which Direction in Foreign Policy?" *Midland Schools* (December 1948): 12–13.

Kagan, Robert. *The World America Made*. New York: Knopf, 2012.

Kaplan, Robert. "The Geography of Chinese Power: How Far Can Beijing Reach on Land and at Sea?" *Foreign Affairs*. May–June 2010: 22–41.

Kartunova, A.I. "Vstrechi v Moskve s Tszian Tsin, Zhenoi Mao Tszeduna [Meetings in Moscow with Jiang Qing, the Wife of Mao Zedong]." *Kentavr* 1–2 (1992): 121–27.

Kau, Michael Y. M., and John K. Leung. *The Writings of Mao Zedong, 1949–1976*. Armonk, N.Y.: M. E. Sharpe, 1986.

Kazuko, Ono, and Joshua Fogel, eds. *Chinese Women in a Century of Revolution, 1850–1950*. Stanford, Calif.: Stanford University Press, 1988.

Keeley, Joseph. *The China Lobby Man: The Story of Alfred Kohlberg*. New Rochelle, N.Y.: Arlington House, 1969.

Kennan, George F. *American Diplomacy*. 1951; reprint Chicago: University of Chicago Press, 2012.

———. *The Kennan Diaries*. Edited by Frank Costigliola. New York: Norton, 2014.

———. *Memoirs: 1925–1950*. Boston: Little, Brown, 1967.

Kissinger, Henry. *On China*. New York: Penguin Press, 2011.

Klein, Christina. "Family Ties and Political Obligation: The Discourse of Adoption and the Cold War Commitment to Asia." In Christian G. Appy, ed., *Cold War Constructions: The Political Culture of United States Imperialism, 1945–1966*. Amherst: University of Massachusetts Press, 2000.

Laird, Thomas. *Into Tibet: The CIA's First Atomic Spy and His Secret Expedition to Lhasa*. New York: Grove Press, 2002.

Lapwood, Ralph, and Nancy Lapwood. *Through the Chinese Revolution*. 1954; reprint Westport, Conn.: Hyperion Press, 1973.

Leary, William M. *Perilous Missions: Civil Air Transport and CIA Covert Operations in Asia*. University: University of Alabama Press, 1984.

Leary, William M., and William Stueck. "The Chennault Plan to Save China: U.S. Containment in Asia and the Origins of the CIA's Aerial Empire, 1949–50." *Diplomatic History* 8, no. 4 (Fall 1984): 349–64.

Ledovsky, Andrei. "Mikoyan's Secret Mission to China in January and February 1949." *Far Eastern Affairs* 2 (1995): 72–94.

———. "The Moscow Visit of a Delegation of the Communist Party of China in June and August 1949." *Far Eastern Affairs* 4 (1996): 64–86.

Leese, Daniel. *Mao Cult: Rhetoric and Ritual in China's Cultural Revolution.* Cambridge, U.K.: Cambridge University Press, 2011.

Levenson, Joseph R. *Liang Ch'i-ch'ao and the Mind of Modern China.* Berkeley: University of California Press, 1967.

Li, Laura Tyson. *Madame Chiang Kai-shek: China's Eternal First Lady.* New York: Atlantic Monthly Press, 2006.

Li Min. *Wo de fuqin Mao Zedong* [My Father Mao Zedong]. Beijing: Renmin chubanshe, 2009.

Li Zhisui. *The Private Life of Chairman Mao: The Memoirs of Mao's Personal Physician, Dr. Li Zhisui.* New York: Random House, 1994.

Lilienthal, David E. *The Journals of David E. Lilienthal.* Vol. 2, *The Atomic Energy Years, 1945–1950.* New York: Harper & Row, 1964.

Liu, Hsiang-Wang. *The Fall and Rise of the Nationalist Chinese: The Chinese Civil War from Huaihai to the Taiwan Strait, 1948–50.* Ph.D. thesis., Pennsylvania State University, 1997.

Lin, Hsiao-ting. *Accidental State: Chiang Kai-shek, the United States, and the Making of Taiwan.* Cambridge, Mass.: Harvard University Press, 2016.

Logevall, Fredrik. *Embers of War: The Fall of an Empire and the Making of America's Vietnam.* New York: Random House, 2012.

Mabon, David W. "Elusive Agreements: The Pacific Pact Proposals of 1949–51." *Pacific Historical Review* 57, no. 2 (May 1988): 147–77.

MacDonald, Donald J. "President Truman's Yacht." *Naval History* 4, no. 1 (Winter 1990): 48–49.

Mao Zedong. *The Poems of Mao Tse-tung.* Translated by Hua-ling Nieh Engle and Paul Engle. New York: Simon & Schuster, 1972.

McCrum, Robert. "The Masterpiece That Killed George Orwell." *Observer.* May 9, 2009.

McCullough, David. *Truman.* New York: Simon & Schuster, 1992.

McFarland, Keith D., and David L. Roll. *Louis Johnson and the Arming of America: The Roosevelt and Truman Years.* Bloomington: Indiana University Press, 2005.

McGlothlen, Ronald L. *Controlling the Waves: Dean Acheson and U.S. Foreign Policy in Asia.* New York: Norton, 1993.

McLean, David. "American Nationalism, the China Myth, and the Truman

Doctrine: The Question of Accommodation with Peking, 1949–50." *Diplomatic History* 10 (Winter 1986): 25–42.

Mearsheimer, John. "The Gathering Storm: China's Challenge to U.S. Power in Asia." *Chinese Journal of International Politics* 3 (2010): 381–96.

Melby, John F. *The Mandate of Heaven: Record of a Civil War, China 1945–49.* Toronto: University of Toronto Press, 1968.

Miscamble, Wilson D. "The Evolution of an Internationalist: Harry S. Truman and American Foreign Policy." *Australian Journal of Politics and History* 23, no. 2 (August 1977): 268–83.

Mitter, Rana. *Forgotten Ally: China's World War II, 1937–1945.* Boston: Houghton Mifflin Harcourt, 2013.

Montefiore, Simon Sebag. *Stalin: The Court of the Red Tsar.* New York: Knopf, 2004.

Morris, Sylvia Jukes. *Price of Fame: The Honorable Clare Boothe Luce.* New York: Random House, 2014.

Mydans, Carl, and Shelley Mydans. *The Violent Peace.* New York: Atheneum, 1968.

Ninkovich, Frank. *Modernity and Power: A History of the Domino Theory in the Twentieth Century.* Chicago: University of Chicago Press, 1994.

Offner, Arnold A. *Another Such Victory: President Truman and the Cold War, 1945–1953.* Stanford, Calif.: Stanford University Press, 2002.

Osnos, Evan. *Age of Ambition: Chasing Fortune, Truth, and Faith in the New China.* New York: Farrar, Straus and Giroux, 2014.

———. "Born Red." *New Yorker,* April 6, 2015.

Oursler, Fulton. *Behold This Dreamer!* Boston: Little, Brown, 1964.

Ovendale, R. "Britain, the United States, and the Recognition of Communist China." *Historical Journal* 26, no. 1 (March 1983): 139–58.

Pakula, Hannah. *The Last Empress: Madame Chiang Kai-shek and the Birth of Modern China.* New York: Simon & Schuster, 2009.

Pang Xianzhi, ed. *Mao Zedong Nianpu* [Chronology of Mao Zedong]. Beijing: Zhongyang Wenxian Chubanshe, 2013.

Pantsov, Alexander V., with Steven I. Levine. *Mao: The Real Story.* New York: Simon & Schuster, 2012.

Patterson, James T. *Grand Expectations: The United States, 1945–1974.* New York: Oxford University Press, 1996.

Pearson, Drew. *Diaries, 1949–1959.* Edited by Tyler Abell. New York: Holt, Rinehart and Winston, 1974.

Pepper, Suzanne. *Civil War in China: The Political Struggle, 1945–1949*. Lanham, Md.: Rowman and Littlefield, 1999.

Platt, Stephen R. *Autumn in the Heavenly Kingdom: China, the West, and the Epic Story of the Taiping Civil War*. New York: Knopf, 2012.

Pomeranz, Kenneth. "Musings on a Museum: A Trip to Xibaipo." *China Beat*. July 22, 2010, www.thechinabeat.org/?p=2384 (accessed August 11, 2015).

Pomfret, John. *The Beautiful Country and the Middle Kingdom: America and China, 1776 to the Present*. New York: Henry Holt, 2016.

Public Papers of the Presidents of the United States: Harry S. Truman, 1945. Washington, D.C.: Government Printing Office, 1961.

Public Papers of the Presidents of the United States: Harry S. Truman, 1952–53. Washington, D.C.: Government Printing Office, 1966.

Qing, Simei. *From Allies to Enemies: Visions of Modernity, Identity, and U.S.-China Diplomacy, 1945–1960*. Cambridge, Mass.: Harvard University Press, 2007.

Quan, Yanchi. *Mao Zedong: Man, Not God*. Beijing: Foreign Languages Press, 1992.

Ramzy, Austin. "Taiwan's President Apologizes to Aborigines for Centuries of Injustice." *New York Times*, August 1, 2016.

Rearden, Steven L. *History of the Office of the Secretary of Defense*. Vol. 1, *The Formative Years, 1947–1950*. Washington, D.C.: Office of the Secretary of Defense, 1984.

Rittenberg, Sidney, Sr., and Amanda Bennett. *The Man Who Stayed Behind*. Durham, N.C.: Duke University Press, 2001.

Robbins, Christopher. *Air America*. New York: G. P. Putnam's Sons, 1979.

Ronning, Chester. *A Memoir of China in Revolution: From the Boxer Rebellion to the People's Republic*. New York: Pantheon, 1974.

Roosevelt, Eleanor. *The Autobiography of Eleanor Roosevelt*. 1961; reprint New York: Harper Perennial, 2014.

Rosenthal, Joel H. *Righteous Realists: Political Realism, Responsible Power, and American Culture in the Nuclear Age*. Baton Rouge: Louisiana State University Press, 1991.

Ross, Alex. "Uncommon Man: The Strange Life of Henry Wallace, the New Deal Visionary." *New Yorker*, October 14, 2013.

Rowan, Roy. *Chasing the Dragon: A Veteran Journalist's Firsthand Account of the 1949 Chinese Revolution*. Guilford, Conn.: Lyons Press, 2004.

Salisbury, Harrison E. *The New Emperors: China in the Era of Mao and Deng.* Boston: Little, Brown, 1992.

Schaller, Michael. *The American Occupation of Japan: The Origins of the Cold War in Asia.* New York: Oxford University Press, 1985.

———. *The United States and China: Into the Twenty-first Century.* Fourth ed. New York: Oxford University Press, 2015.

———. *The U.S. Crusade in China,* 1938–1945. New York: Columbia University Press, 1979.

Schell, Orville, and John Delury. *Wealth and Power: China's Long March to the Twenty-first Century.* New York: Random House, 2013.

Schoenbaum, Thomas J. *Waging Peace and War: Dean Rusk in the Truman, Kennedy and Johnson Years.* New York: Simon & Schuster, 1988.

Schram, Stuart R., ed. *Mao's Road to Power: Revolutionary Writings, 1912–1949.* Vols. 1 and 2. Armonk, N.Y.: M.E. Sharpe, 1992, 1994.

———. *The Thought of Mao Tse-Tung.* Cambridge, U.K.: Cambridge University Press, 1989.

Seagrave, Sterling. *The Soong Dynasty.* New York: Harper & Row, 1985.

Shambaugh, David. *China Goes Global: The Partial Power.* Oxford: Oxford University Press, 2013.

Shaw, Yu-ming. *An American Missionary in China: John Leighton Stuart and Chinese-American Relations.* Cambridge, Mass.: Harvard University Press, 1992.

Shen Zhihua. *Mao, Stalin and the Korean War: Trilateral Communist Relations in the 1950s.* Translated by Neil Silver. New York: Routledge, 2012.

Shen Zhihua and Yafeng Xia. *Mao and the Sino-Soviet Partnership, 1945–1959: A New History.* Lanham, Md.: Lexington Books, 2015.

Sheng, Michael M. *Battling Western Imperialism: Mao, Stalin, and the United States.* Princeton, N.J.: Princeton University Press, 1997.

Shi Zhe. "'I Accompanied Chairman Mao.'" *Far Eastern Affairs* 2 (1989): 125–33.

———. "With Mao and Stalin: The Reminiscences of a Chinese Interpreter." Translated by Chen Jian. Pts. 1 and 2. *Chinese Historians* 5, no. 1 (Spring 1992): 35–46; 6 (Spring 1993): 67–90.

Shih, Chih-yu. "The Eros of International Politics: Madame Chiang Kaishek and the Question of the State in China." *Comparative Civilizations Review* 46 (2002): 91–119.

Short, Philip. *Mao: A Life.* New York: Henry Holt, 1999.

Shuguang Zhang and Jian Chen, eds. *Chinese Communist Foreign Policy and the Cold War in Asia: New Documentary Evidence, 1944–1950.* Chicago: Imprint, 1996.

Snow, Edgar. "A Conversation with Mao Tse-Tung." *Life*, April 30, 1971.

———. *Red Star Over China.* 1938; reprint New York: Grove Press, 1968.

Spence, Jonathan D. *God's Chinese Son: The Taiping Heavenly Kingdom of Hong Xiuquan.* New York: Norton, 1996.

———. *Mao Zedong.* New York: Viking, 1999.

———. *The Search for Modern China.* 3rd ed. New York: Norton, 2013.

———. *To Change China: Western Advisers in China.* 1969; reprint New York: Penguin Books, 1980.

Stilwell, Joseph W. *The Stilwell Papers.* Edited by Theodore H. White. 1948; reprint New York: Da Capo Press, 1991.

Stokes, William N. "The Future Between America and China." *Foreign Service Journal* 45, no. 1 (January 1968): 14–16.

Stuart, John Leighton. *Fifty Years in China: The Memoirs of John Leighton Stuart, Missionary and Ambassador.* New York: Random House, 1954.

———. *The Forgotten Ambassador: The Reports of John Leighton Stuart, 1946–1949.* Edited by Kenneth W. Rea and John C. Brewer. Boulder, Colo.: Westview Press, 1981.

Stueck, William Whitney, Jr. *The Road to Confrontation: American Policy Toward China and Korea, 1947–1950.* Chapel Hill: University of North Carolina Press, 1981.

Sulzberger, C. L. *A Long Row of Candles: Memoirs and Diaries, 1934–1954.* Toronto: Macmillan, 1969.

Sutherland, Ian. "The OSS Operational Groups: Origin of Army Special Forces." *Special Warfare* 15, no. 2 (June 2002): 2–13.

Tanenhaus, Sam. *Whittaker Chambers: A Biography.* New York: Random House, 1997.

Taylor, Jay. *The Generalissimo: Chiang Kai-shek and the Struggle for Modern China.* Cambridge, Mass.: Belknap Press, 2009.

Thomas, Evan. *The Very Best Men: Four Who Dared: The Early Years of the CIA.* New York: Simon & Schuster, 1995.

Titov, Alexander. "Looking Back on My Work in China in 1948–1950." *Far Eastern Affairs* 5 (1995): 82–93.

Tong, Hollington K. *Chiang Kai-shek.* Taipei: China Publishing Co., 1953.

Topping, Audrey Ronning. *China Mission: A Personal History from the Last Imperial Dynasty to the People's Republic.* Baton Rouge: Louisiana State University Press, 2013.

Topping, Seymour. *Journey Between Two Chinas*. New York: Harper & Row, 1972.

———. *On the Front Lines of the Cold War: An American Correspondent's Journal from the Chinese Civil War to the Cuban Missile Crisis and Vietnam*. Baton Rouge: Louisiana State University Press, 2010.

Townsend, Peter. *China Phoenix: The Revolution in China*. London: Jonathan Cape, 1955.

Truman, Margaret. *Bess W. Truman*. New York: Macmillan, 1986.

Tsou, Tang. *America's Failure in China, 1941–50*. Chicago: University of Chicago Press, 1963.

Tuchman, Barbara W. *Stilwell and the American Experience in China, 1911–45*. New York: Grove Press, 1970.

Tucker, Nancy Bernkopf. *Patterns in the Dust: Chinese-American Relations and the Recognition Controversy, 1949–1950*. New York: Columbia University Press, 1983.

Tucker, Nancy Bernkopf, ed. *China Confidential: American Diplomats and Sino-American Relations, 1945–1996*. New York: Columbia University Press, 2001.

Ullman, Richard. "The U.S. and the World: An Interview with George Kennan." *New York Review of Books*, August 12, 1999.

U.S. Department of State. *United States Relations with China, with Special Reference to the Period 1944–1949*. Washington, D.C.: Government Printing Office, 1949.

U.S. Senate. *Economic Assistance to China and Korea, 1949–50: Hearings Held in Executive Session Before the Committee on Foreign Relations*. Eighty-first Congress. Washington, D.C.: Government Printing Office, 1974.

———. *Military Situation in the Far East: Hearings Before the Committee on Armed Services and the Committee on Foreign Relations*. Eighty-second Congress. Part 4. June 14, 15, 18, 19, 20, 21, 22, 25, and 27, 1951. Washington, D.C.: Government Printing Office, 1951.

———. *Nomination of Dean G. Acheson: Hearing Before the Committee on Foreign Relations*. Eighty-first Congress. January 13, 1949. Washington, D.C.: Government Printing Office, 1949.

Wang Dongxing. *Wang Dongxing Riji* [Wang Dongxing Diary]. Beijing: Dangdai Zhongguo Chubanshe, 2012.

Ward, Angus. "The Mukden Affair." *American Foreign Service Journal* (February 1950): 14–17, 40–44.

Weiner, Tim. *Legacy of Ashes: The History of the CIA*. New York: Doubleday, 2007.

Wertenbaker, Charles. "The China Lobby." *Reporter.* April 15, 1952, pp. 4–24.

Westad, Odd Arne. *Decisive Encounters: The Chinese Civil War, 1946–1950*. Stanford, Calif.: Stanford University Press, 2003.

———. "Fighting for Friendship: Mao, Stalin, and the Sino-Soviet Treaty of 1950." *Cold War International History Project Bulletin* 8–9 (Winter 1996–97): 224–36.

Witke, Roxane. *Comrade Chiang Ch'ing*. Boston: Little, Brown, 1977.

Xiao Qian. *Traveller Without a Map*. Translated by Jeffrey C. Kinkley. Stanford, Calif.: Stanford University Press, 1994.

Zubok, Vladislav. "'To Hell with Yalta!': Stalin Opts for a New Status Quo," *CWIHP Bulletin*, nos. 6–7 (Winter 1995–96): 24–27.

ACKNOWLEDGMENTS

In writing this book I relied on the kindness and good judgment of a number of scholars and friends, who read early versions of the manuscript and shared their impressions and expertise. Ke-wen Wang, a wise and gracious historian of modern China, combed through an initial draft and offered many helpful suggestions. Ke-wen and Laura Tyson Li, who wrote the best biography of Madame Chiang Kai-shek, helped me track down the dozens of revealing telegrams between Chiang Kai-shek and Madame Chiang Kai-shek that are housed in an archive in Taipei. George Herring, the distinguished historian of the Vietnam War and U.S. foreign policy, once again agreed to subject one of my manuscripts to his discerning eye. My old friend Evan Osnos offered source suggestions and reporting advice. Melinda Liu kindly put me in touch with colleagues in Beijing. Warren I. Cohen read the manuscript and raised several smart points. David Abrahamson, one of my favorite professors at Northwestern, read the draft with his usual fastidiousness. Evan Thomas, who has written his own classic books on Dean Acheson, Frank Wisner, and the early Cold War, encouraged me to pursue this project from the beginning. Seymour and Audrey Topping welcomed me into their home, shared their recollections of the Chinese civil war, and put me in touch with other eyewitnesses. Ying Ying Li kindly read the book and made several helpful suggestions. Charles Kraus at the Woodrow Wilson International Center for Scholars' History and Public Policy Program steered me in the direction of useful documents in the center's digital archive. Steven Cox shared revealing letters that his father sent home from China. Pamela Howard passed along an elusive memorandum. Nisid Hajari, author of a fine book on the partition of India, scanned my sections on Nehru. Finally, I benefited from discussions of East Asia and U.S. foreign policy with Gordon H. Chang, Elizabeth Economy, Frances FitzGerald, John Lewis Gaddis, Dora Fugh Lee, John Pomfret, Roy Rowan, Schuyler Schouten, and Odd Arne Westad, among others.

I feel fortunate, as always, to have Binky Urban in my corner. She is a shrewd agent and strategist, a perceptive reader, and a loyal friend. My editor at Crown, Roger Scholl, helped to shape this book early on over lunches in New York—and then again during the editing phase. Roger's intelligence, keen sense of structure, and good-natured queries made this a far better book. The wonderful Vanessa Mobley, my previous editor at Crown, also supported the project at an early stage and helped to refine the idea. I am grateful, too, to Sean Desmond, a terrific editor, for bringing me to Crown nearly seven years ago. Thanks, finally, to Molly Stern, Annsley Rosner, Christopher Brand, Julia Elliott, and the rest of the team at Crown for skillfully guiding this manuscript through the publishing process.

I was aided in the research at various stages by several talented colleagues. The indefatigable Chad Frazier, a gifted doctoral student in history at Georgetown, plumbed the depths of the National Archives. Wang Zhenru helped with Chinese sources, gathering hard-to-locate secondary literature and translating difficult primary documents. In China, James Yin was a superb guide and fun traveling companion. Lawrence Chiu spent his precious lunch breaks copying down telegrams. I am indebted, also, to Shu-feng Wu, at the Academia Historica in Taipei, for her guidance. Natalia Alexandrova and Tenei Naka hara tracked down and translated sources. My thanks also to Anna Nemtsova for connecting me with Natalia.

I drove good people in various libraries nearly insane with my research requests. Everett Perdue adroitly wrangled all kinds of books, articles, doctoral dissertations, and committee transcripts—fortified by his good humor (and a little Scotch whisky). Tina Bothe helped me track down dozens of books in far-flung libraries, cheerfully and skillfully fielding my queries. At the U.S. Senate and House historical offices, Kate Scott, Farar Elliott, and Matthew Wasniewski helped locate some elusive photographs.

I am lucky to have been born into a family of fine editors. My father, Sam Peraino, read the draft with care and caught several errors that everyone else missed. My mother, Donna Peraino, offered helpful input as we considered the title and cover. My brother, Jim Peraino, went through the manuscript with a sharp eye for clichés and overheated prose. My sister, Joanna Musumeci, and brother-in-law Joe Musumeci made valuable suggestions at various stages. My in-laws, Mathew and Molly Ninan, kindly provided sustenance (and babysitting) during my travels. Tony and Seena Ninan endured my going on about Chinese history for years. My kids, Jack and Kate, poked their heads into my office fifty times a day, swiping supplies and making their old dad laugh. My wife, Reena, once again patiently tolerated her husband spending countless hours with dead people, as she likes to put it. I could not have written it without her love and support; this book is dedicated to her.

PHOTO INSERT CREDITS

INDEX

ABOUT THE AUTHOR

KEVIN PERAINO is a veteran foreign correspondent who has reported from around the world. A writer and bureau chief at *Newsweek* for a decade, he was a finalist for the Livingston Award for foreign reporting and was part of a team that won a National Magazine Award in 2004. He has also written for the *Wall Street Journal, Foreign Policy,* and other publications. He is the author of *Lincoln in the World: The Making of a Statesman and the Dawn of American Power.*